GOVERNANCE, SECURITY AND DEVELOPMENT

By the same author
Whither Governance: Reflections of an Assam Civilian

ABOUT THE AUTHOR

K. Sreedhar Rao was in the IAS having passed out of the Loyola College Chennai with a Masters degree in Economics in 1962. He comes from a family of intellectuals; his grandfather was the first Indian Principal of the Central College Bangalore and had made original contributions in Zoology. The well-known management Guru C.K. Prahalad is his uncle. His wife's grandfather V.V. Giri was the President of India

Shri Rao served in Assam under some of the most trying circumstances, dealing *inter alia* with emergencies such as the Indo-Pak War 1971, refugee influx, the "Foreigners' agitation" riots, insurgency, etc. He served in the centre in several ministries and rose to the rank of Secretary to the GoI. He retired as the Chief Secretary of Sikkim.

After retirement, he served as member NSAB, adviser in the UPSC, and was Chairman of the State Knowledge Commission with rank of a Cabinet Minister in the State of Sikkim. He was also the first VC of the Sikkim Manipal University.

He has contributed articles in IDSA's strategic journal, on National security issues.

His son, Vivek works in the ADB, Manila and his Daughter-in-law in the World Bank.

He lives with his wife in Bengaluro. His e-mail ID is shreedharkrao@yahoo.co.in

GOVERNANCE, SECURITY AND DEVELOPMENT

Hope for Tomorrow

K. Sreedhar Rao
IAS (R)

Jointly Published

SOUTH ASIA FOUNDATION
and
CONCEPT PUBLISHING COMPANY PVT. LTD.,
NEW DELHI-110059

ISBN-13: 978-81-8069-927-6

First Published 2013

Published and Printed by

Concept
Since 1974

Concept Publishing Company Pvt. Ltd.
A/15-16, Commercial Block, Mohan Garden
New Delhi-110059 (India)
T: 25351460, 25351794, *F*: 091-11-25357109
E: publishing@conceptpub.com, W: www.conceptpub.com
Editorial Office: H-13, Bali Nagar, New Delhi-110 015, India.

Cataloging in Publication Data--*Courtesy:* D.K. Agencies (P) Ltd. <docinfo@dkagencies.com>

Sreedhar Rao, K.
Governance, security and development : hope for tomorrow / K. Sreedhar Rao.
p. cm.
Includes bibliographical references (p.) and index.
ISBN 9788180699276

1. India—Politics and government. 2. India—Foreign relations. 3. Security, International—India. 4. Internal security—India. 5. Economic development—India. I. Title.

DDC 320.954 23

To my mother,
Smt. Sita Bai who was an embodiment
of all that is called
Dharma

PREFACE

Jawaharlal Nehru at the midnight hour of India's independence spoke of "the soul of a nation long suppressed finding utterance" and described this as a moment that comes but rarely in the history of a nation. His speech remembered to this day, evoking patriotism in every heart, carries extraordinary meaning and significance for every Indian, as it encapsulated in ringing words, our long history of subjugation and subservience. External invasions and internal dissensions came very near crushing our ancient civilization many times in our history. The Greek and the Scythian, the Persian and the Mogul, the French and the English have by turn attempted to suppress it and yet, it has survived, possibly because it has the ability to continuously reinvent itself and go through a process of self-renewal. Perhaps this is unique in the annals of human history as we know that many an ancient civilization, elsewhere in the world, were simply obliterated from the face of the earth by foreign occupiers.

For the first time after nearly a thousand years, we regained control over our lives and our destiny and acquired the ability to determine our future in a manner which served our national purpose. We have been given one more opportunity by history, to preserve the great heritage, culture and character of our unique civilization which is the oldest living in the world and restore these to their rightful place in the comity of nations. We have now the power in our own hands to refashion our nation and enable our people to get rid of poverty and ignorance, by taking the best from modern thought processes and scientific and technological progress, as well as our own ancient wisdom, while ensuring that the best of our own traditions is preserved and fostered.

This book has been born out of the anguish experienced in the latter part of my service life, when after the initial years of idealism and national spirit combined with a high degree of patriotism, I, along with all those who have the welfare and progress of this country at heart, witnessed a precipitous decline in the quality of leadership, which has not been able to appreciate the historic opportunity that has been given to us by destiny, to do the right thing for our people, wipe out poverty, ignorance and illiteracy once and for all, as well as all the societal ills that have afflicted the nation for so long. The grand vision for the future of a strong, united, vibrant and prosperous India that we dreamed of during our struggle for independence has all but disappeared and on the contrary, there has occurred a systematic erosion of all values, devaluation of all institutions and exacerbation of internal dissensions as well as divisive and sectarian strife. Low and declining standards of governance have by now made many parts of the country ungoverned and ungovernable. High standards of governance, is a *sine qua non* for both peace and prosperity. A comprehensive discussion on this issue, in the context of the situation that prevails in this country where because of declining standards of governance, we have not been able to provide either peace or prosperity to our people, is the main purpose of writing this book and constitutes its main theme.

At the moment at least the prospects for the future of the country are in no way bright, beset as we are with innumerable internal and external threats and challenges. The fear that we may once again fail to learn from our history, fail in our promises and fail to recapture our past glory cannot be altogether dismissed.

The factors which compel one to be so pessimistic are what the book is all about. These are, to my mind, the extremely flawed system of selection of the leadership at all levels to govern this country. Fitness and ability to perform the complex tasks of a leader are not the consideration for selection of leaders at any level. Our freedom struggle attracted some of the best brains of the country who were prepared to sacrifice everything for the sake of the nation's freedom. Gokhale, Tilak, Gandhi, Rajaji, Subhas Chandra Bose, Lala Lajpat Rai, Madanmohan Malviya, Patel and a host of intellectuals and patriots joined the struggle and quite a few of them administered the country during the first two decades of independence. At every level there were stalwarts, intellectual giants—Bidhan Roy, Sachidananda Sinha, G.B. Pant, C. Rajagopalachari, etc., whose commitment to the nation, to the welfare and progress of all people and to the highest standards of integrity, helped the nation to organize itself for the stupendous task of nation building. The faith of the people in the leadership was high as noone doubted their patriotism, integrity or commitment to the welfare of everyone in this country. Nehru's cabinet had some of the finest minds of independent India. This happened because as Gandhiji stressed, fitness to hold the particular office and not non-merit considerations were the deciding factor in all the appointments, especially at these critical levels of decision making. This is no more the case and today; caste and community considerations and loyalty to a particular family determine who gets what. It is unfortunate that in India of today, democracy is being misinterpreted as disbelief in great men which has meant devaluation of the importance of the quality of leadership. It has been forgotten that great men are path makers who blaze the trail for other men to follow. They are, in the words of Jesus Christ, the 'salt', the 'leaven' and the 'light' for human communities. When they proclaim the splendour of this light, others recognize this and many become followers.

The Bhagwat Gita states: *"Yad yad acarati sreshtas, tad tad eva taro janah, sa yat pramanam kurute lokas tad anuvartate"*.

(Whatsoever a great man does, the same is done by others as well. Whatever standards he sets others follow.)

This clearly should be the fundamental guiding principle for all those who claim to be leaders in this country and who get elected to be leaders. The standards they set become the norm for all others and hence, it is of overwhelming importance that the leaders do set up immaculate standards for themselves and their conduct is unimpeachable at all times. If for example, the Home Minister or a Chief Minster is corrupt and if legislators indulge in fisticuffs inside the legislatures, how can we prevent the constable or a sub-inspector from accepting bribes or indulge in brutal conduct?

Secondly, performance as the primary consideration for re-election has become practically nonexistent. There is no accountability at any level and those who have repeatedly failed to discharge their responsibilities with any degree of competence, are permitted to occupy offices indefinitely. Thirdly, as a nation we have devalued merit and achievement not merely in the selection of our leaders but in all walks of life. Mediocrity is promoted and championed in every field without regard to the fact that a nation can ill afford to de-motivate those who excel and remove all incentives for better and still better performance. No country anywhere in the world has thrived by ensuring that merit and achievement have no value in the life of the nation. It is a sad fact of our national life that even though throughout our history and in our great traditions, knowledge was respected and those with knowledge were worshipped, today there is so little regard for knowledge and knowledge is looked down upon as elitist and those who have the knowledge and expertise are not allowed to enter the corridors of power. Those who occupy positions of authority due to non-merit considerations are wary of interacting with those with knowledge and expertise, as they apprehend that their true worth will be exposed, if such an exercise does take place. In the highly competitive international environment that prevails today, we will be the losers if the best talent is not allowed to enter the decision making processes.

Fourthly, we have been made to feel quite ashamed of our ancient past and our heritage and the great achievements of our civilization in so many fields. This is a contribution of particularly those who have been educated in leftist-oriented ideologies and are persuaded to believe that Marxian thought alone is the ultimate solution for all of our problems and this implies that other belief systems should be removed from the conscience of the nation. Marx and Marxism are both dead long ago but there are still in this country who cling on to this belief and have made a whole generation look down upon our ancient and extraordinarily rich civilization. A nation which is not proud of its past glory and its contribution to human thought and endeavour can lose all pride in itself, its self-esteem and its self confidence. It can be made to submit to others' will much more easily. A country that fails to learn from its past history is condemned to repeat its past, said the sage Santayana. In our case, I feel that such a mindset has undermined the moral underpinnings of our society and polity and the nation has lost its moral bearings.

There is so much in our past that we can be truly proud of and which can contribute so much for a better India and a better world. India has the world's largest treasure trove of 'Moral Wealth' with her unique contribution of the concept of DHARMA as a guide, for worldly conduct and redemption. The Mahabharata and the Upanishads state that Dharma encompasses justice, what is right in a given circumstance, moral values in life, pious obligations of individuals, righteous conduct in every activity as well as the merits of being of help to other living beings, giving charity to the needy and the deserving, performance of one's duty to the society and family and compliance with law. The Mahabharata also asserts that Dharma maintains social order, it ensures the well- being and progress of humanity and Dharma is all that fulfils these objectives. Madhvacharya sums up, "Dharma is that which sustains and ensures progress and welfare of all in this world and in the other world." By failing to learn this great wisdom which has been available to us for ages and failing to inculcate these values into the present generation and in the children, we have done incalculable damage to the moral fibre of the nation.

It may be added that our very existence as a nation can be threatened by the continuous weakening of the authority of the Central Government. The hold of the national parties over the political system is declining while regional satraps are becoming more assertive and powerful. They seem to have started exercising a veto power even on subjects which are the exclusive concern of the Centre (e.g., foreign policy). The fear that regionalism and narrow considerations may pose a threat to the unity and integrity of India is the reason why our Constitution had been given a unitary bias, though essentially of a federal character.

Today, India is regarded in spite of the current slowdown, as an emerging economy and our GDP is set to become the third largest in the world-ahead of Japan—in 2011-12 with a GDP (PPP) of US$ 4.47 trillion. There are great challenges but also great opportunities coming our way. For the first time in our independent history, we are regarded as a desirable bride by many suitors—the US, Russia, the EU, countries of South-East Asia and Australia. India is definitely in the eyes of many, the countervailing power against the rise of China. Our main adversary which has done so much damage to India and still retains a great deal of potential for harming India further, namely Pakistan is in grave disarray and may possibly disintegrate. It has a President who has had psychological problems, had been charged with money laundering, etc., and is now afflicted with undisclosed cardiac problems. The dysfunctional executive is at loggerheads with the proactive judiciary and the all-powerful army establishment is only interested in further weakening the executive. Each of the players seems to be warring with each other and bleeding its rivals casting the interests of the nation and the people to wild winds. China, though growing at a fast pace, can face both internal and external problems including the possibility of a 'Chinese spring' erupting, as the more affluent seek real freedoms. China is also regarded as a threat by many a nation in the region.

How do we take advantage of the positives in our favour and negate the negatives that may stifle our progress? To my mind, everything depends upon the degree to which we succeed in improving the quality of leadership that we have and the quality of governance.

India has an obsessively hostile neighbour in its northwest in cohorts with China, a four decades long Maoist insurgency, a corrupt and ineffective system of governance, and over 445 million people still poor. On the other hand, our economy and markets are growing despite political misgovernance. The entrepreneurial energy unleashed by the reforms of 1991 can take the country fast forward and we should not allow timid and ineffective responses to stand in the way of utilizing the advantages that the new world order offers. For this, India needs to think and act like a major player, fix bad governance and inequality at home, build a strategic foreign policy to leverage its assets such as a large market, a growing economy and pluralistic democracy. In the new order the Indo-US partnership can prove to be as pivotal as the Anglo-US axis of the last century.

This book explores all these themes in considerable detail and attempts to offer comprehensive solutions for enabling the country to overcome its problems and achieve a higher trajectory of progress while once and for all, we succeed in abolishing poverty, ignorance and all the social ills that have plagued this country for ages.

The primary focus of the book is on the intimate relationship between the standards and quality of governance and both security and development, a theme which has not received adequate attention from scholars so far. The traditional wisdom has been that economic and social development is the function of accumulation of physical capital and the efficiency with which this is utilized, expressed by the concept of capital: output ratio and total factor productivity (TFR). Physical capital is getting increasingly supplemented and even supplanted by human intellectual capital, as evidenced by resource-poor countries (Holland, Japan, Singapore, etc.,) attaining higher standards of living and superior quality of life than resource-rich countries (in the Arab world, many in Africa). A common element in all countries which have attained high levels of progress is the quality of governance. The burden of the song in this book is that without good governance, there can be no peace and without peace and order, there can be no prosperity. All three are interlinked and empirical evidence presented in this book suggests strongly that there is a positive correlation between levels of governance and levels of living. High levels of governance create all the essential preconditions of sustained economic performance, which in turn ensures peace and orderly conduct of affairs in a society. On the other hand, absence of good governance leads to immiserisation of the people, dissatisfaction, disillusionment, disorder and armed insurrection, which in turn destroy all prospects of orderly progress. This is the story of many countries which are caught in a vicious cycle of poor governance, low levels of development, high unemployment, dissatisfaction and armed conflict, insurgency and civil wars. These warnings from history can be ignored only at our own peril. Equally importantly, the book argues that there can be no improvement in standards of governance if we do not take urgent measures to improve the quality of our rulers and this will not happen if we do not change the system of selecting our leaders. The country's future can be dreary if these objectives are not achieved.

This book is an expression of hope in the future as I believe that given a determined effort to get our basics right, we can transform India from a third to a first world country within the foreseeable future, primarily because we still have the structures and institutions for good governance and if only these can be fostered and allowed to perform, our future can be assured.

The cover design of this book—a tree withered at first look, but has one lone leaf freshly sprouted in the same tree—illustrates this hope for a better tomorrow. The design incorporates the painting of the tree and the lone leaf called 'Hope' by my friend in Manila, Swati Pandey.

Bangalore

K. Sreedhar Rao

ACKNOWLEDGEMENTS

More than anyone else, my wife Saraswati Rao encouraged me to get down to write all that I keep talking and complaining about. She kept repeating that there is no use of merely complaining, unless you can do something about correcting all the ills that afflict the country. The mistakes that are being made will make the future generations pay a heavy price, she argued. Since I had no weapon in my hands other than my pen and my computer, she stressed that these be used to suggest solutions, in the hope that these will be acted upon by someone, someday. Her words made me sit down and work on this book and if the words I have written find resonance, it is because she shared my anxiety for the future of our country.

Our son and daughter-in-law, Vivek and Vandana, helped me by providing a collegial atmosphere in their Manila home and placing their large collection of books at my disposal. I could spend hours writing parts of this book there, free from noise and atmospheric pollution which has become such a nuisance in Bangalore. My sincere gratitude goes to all these members of my family.

This book could not have been written without the assistance of my former secretary, Reena Kakade who with her competence in handling all secretarial tasks, voluntarily typed out large parts of this book, made all the corrections, arranged and rearranged the paragraphs to achieve a high degree of consistency and continuity of thought, as well as proper sequencing of the various ideas. I owe a deep debt of gratitude to her.

My long-standing friend and Secretary General of the South Asia Foundation, Rahul Barua whose altruism knows no bounds, deserves my sincere thanks for taking on the responsibility of publishing this book, as was the case with my last book. He who is most of the time travelling to some exotic place or the other somehow finds time to so many things so unhesitatingly and so well. He seems to be the ultimate master of multi-tasking. I express my deep gratitude to him and his organization.

It is he who got the book edited by Ms. Sharmila Chandra. Ms. Chandra who succeeded in record time, in refining the text and transforming it into a work which is eminently readable. She ensured that there is a high degree of consistency in the language and all the ideas are cogently and elegantly articulated. She was meticulous in taking care that every sentence and every paragraph is polished, making every chapter worthy of the time spent in reading it. I admire her immense patience in reading through nearly four hundred and fifty pages with great care and suggesting changes all of which relevant for improving the language and conveying the right meaning. I owe a deep debt of gratitude to her for all the efforts she has put in. I feel lucky to have got such a conscientious and devoted editor.

I also owe a great deal to my friend, A.D. Mishra and his wife Anu who taught me the art of perseverance, forbearance and fortitude in the face of great odds.

My debt is also due, to Swati Pandey, a great friend of our son and daughter-in-law in Manila, for so graciously permitting me to use on the cover of the book, her painting called 'Hope' a tree withered but with one fresh leaf, illustrating beautifully and eloquently that there can be hope for the future despite all the withering that is so apparent. The actual design is that of our daughter-in-law, Vandana.

CONTENTS

1
INTRODUCTION

A nation that has completed over 65 years of independent existence, and has if at all, only partially succeeded in redeeming the pledges that were taken when it made its "tryst with destiny", is entitled to ask itself and more importantly its rulers, as to why do we find ourselves in what undoubtedly is a highly unsatisfactory situation, both with respect to security and development. The question assumes great importance when we find that a host of countries who became independent from colonial rule along with or soon after us and who possibly took similar pledges, have overtaken us by several leaps, giving their citizens all-round prosperity and much greater peace and security, than what we have been able to provide to our people. No doubt, there are others in our own immediate neighbourhood and in the continent of Africa, whose failures are far more glaring than ours and whose rulers have managed to destroy potentially very rich countries with enviable stocks of natural resources, condemning their citizens to such levels of impoverishment, misery, disease, deprivation and ruin unknown even in the worst of colonial times. While with some variations, this was also true of several countries in Latin America for decades; but more recently, these countries have managed to improve living standards and human development indices to a remarkable extent, and today many have per capita incomes far above India.

The debate on this score has mainly centred around the economic and social policies that have been followed by the countries in question, making it appear that systems which allow individual initiative and market-driven policies to play a predominant role, have inherent advantages and have indeed been far more successful in bringing about substantive improvements in the quality of life of the citizen. International experience, however, does indicate that this is only part of the story and what is equally, if not more, important is the quality of governance provided in any system. The recent waywardness in the behaviour of the market-oriented systems, recession, burgeoning debt burdens, increasing rates of unemployment and slowdown of western economies, underline the need for high standards of governance and regulation at appropriate levels for the smooth functioning of the system. It is, to my mind, incorrect to draw the conclusion that the system itself is a failure and has outlived its usefulness. It is my belief that while a right policy mix is important, the quality of governance provided does make a critical and qualitative difference to the success of the policies formulated and implemented and vastly improves the prospects for both security and development.

Some left-leaning intellectuals have, in the context of the recent focus on the essentiality of probity in public life, suggested that corruption is an inevitable concomitant of capitalism arguing that 'all capitalism is crony capitalism'. They have argued that in India, the scale of corruption has vastly increased after the reforms of 1991, which dismantled the 'licence permit raj' and has resulted in greater freedom of enterprise, accompanied by an unprecedented acceleration in growth rates. It is, to my mind, an entirely wrong reading of the situation and is reflective of the ideological predilections of these intellectuals. The scope for corruption indeed decreases when the citizens' overdependence on the government and state monopolies is decreased and he is enabled to exercise choice through a multiplicity of players. The competition to get the consumer to accept the greater variety on offer and continuously upgrade quality has the potential to bring down prices. One cannot ignore the enormous benefits that have accrued to the nation because of the liberalization of the economy and loosening of the stranglehold of the government. As Gurucharan Das points out "India grows at night when the Government sleeps' Corruption has increased, not because of the much needed and overdue shift from the leftist-oriented economic and social policies, but due to the greed of those who come to power, their anxiety to retain power, use money as an instrument for gaining and retaining power and the absence of effective systems to check corruption. Institutions created to check corruption and bring the guilty to book have been sabotaged, robbed of their independence and misused to target the opposition.

It needs to be underlined that all Communist regimes the worldover are now known to have misused their unbridled power, benefiting a very limited number of party apparatchiks—the *'nomenklatura'*, while unleashing reigns of terror with impunity. The much touted Mao's great leap forward, was nothing but a great leap backward, a massive failure, resulting in great famine. There was mass starvation both in Stalin's Russia and Mao's China while the leaders themselves lived lives of luxury. In Mao's China, some 60 million died but Mao lived like an Emperor in the exclusive Zongananhai, happy to read and write poetry and coining slogans such as, 'serve the people' and unleashing the violent Cultural Revolution on the hapless population. China's growth story post-Deng Xiao Ping is an eloquent affirmation of the values of freedom of enterprise. Communism has altogether disappeared in the ex-Soviet Union and Eastern Europe and even in China; capitalist-oriented policies—euphemistically called Socialism with Chinese characteristics—are the order of the day. These developments are an eloquent testimony which supports the view that the communist model of economic management is outdated and has failed to provide enduring benefits to the people. It survives in an anaemic form in Cuba and Venezuela where considerable damage to the lives of citizens and prospects for the economy continues to be done. Changes are already taking place even in Cuba. North Korea where it is practiced with some vigour is known to be unable to meet even the most basic needs of its people and depends upon food aid from many countries even while it wastes its precious resources on its nuclear and missile programmes. Even in India, in the two major states where Communism had endured for quite long, causing a great deal of damage to the growth prospects of these states, the electorate has voted them out. It may be recalled that the most stinging criticism of Marx and communism came from Marx's own wife who after his death commented that she would have been happier if he had left behind some capital, instead of simply writing volumes about it.

It needs, however, to be stated that so far, the focus of those fighting against corruption has been on corruption in the government and its organs, the politicians, the bureaucrats and the police. Corruption in India takes many forms. The poor have to pay for obtaining what they are entitled as per law, while the rich are willing to pay to obtain what they are not entitled to obtain or to get away even after violating the law. Corruption within the corporate sector, compromising on standards of corporate governance, failure to pay taxes, tax evasion, failure to comply with accountancy norms, under invoicing and over invoicing, all need to be addressed. The taxes due, from even the leaders of India's corporate elite and the non-performing assets of banks, due to failure to repay loans by the corporate sector, amount to hundreds of thousands of crores. There has been no hesitation in taking advantage of every loop-hole in the law and using lobbyists to derive undue advantage. This again underlines the importance of high standards of governance, high standards of probity and adequate regulation.

It is the purpose of this book to explore the theme of the critical importance of highest standards of governance-more than natural endowments—for social and economic development and for winning the battle against poverty and deprivation in some detail. In every part of the world, there is increasing evidence that good governance, strong and effective leadership, institutions of public governance imbued with a spirit of service and a value system that attaches importance to the principles of rule of law, non-discriminatory application of law, speedy and impartial systems for dispensation of justice and redressal of grievances, participative character of the polity and zero tolerance of corruption are all of crucial importance in enhancing the performance of the economy. These are also essential elements in providing high degree of security for all its citizens; so do procedures and practices which while being transparent ensure that the highest standards of probity are observed in the conduct of all public servants.

Within our country, while our founding fathers attached great importance to the building of strong institutions based on sound principles of rule of law and participative democracy unfortunately over the years the quality of all the institutions of governance has shown progressive and sustained decline and devaluation. More recently, the standards of probity have declined to such an extent that India has now the dubious distinction of being among the most corrupt countries in the world. Every pillar of the State is now tarnished and battered. Corruption and mendacity are now regarded as ways of life. What was conceived and erected as the architecture for good-governance has been effectively transformed into an architecture of misgovernance. We have been witnessing the strange and horrifying spectacle of quite a few of our elected representatives, instead of enthusiastically supporting civil society activists in their campaign against corruption which is supported by large segments of the society, attacking and denigrating the activists in vile and intemperate language. Every single step forward in the battle to combat corruption had to be extracted from a reluctant Government which had to be literally dragged by the hair, kicking and screaming, to accept what were so patently the very first essential steps for starting the long war against corruption and the corrupt. The final outcome of the exercises underway—whether we will indeed have an effective, independent and strong ombudsman, is still uncertain. It is increasingly clear that the Government is in the hands of those who have a vested interest in ensuring that corruption continues unabated, those who are corrupt are protected and institutions that exist to fight corruption are sabotaged while any new initiative is hijacked to ensure that the ultimate result is nothing more than creation of one more toothless body. A quite determined effort was made to pit the civil society against the Parliament, uncharitably characterizing the movement as undemocratic and a conspiracy to undermine democracy and the Constitution. Dark hints of a foreign hand with efforts to destabilize the elected Government were made and the urgent need to take effective measures to control corruption were sought to be sidelined. For over 40 years, the Parliament of India has failed to enact an effective legislation to create an ombudsman even though India is a signatory to the UN convention on control of corruption and there are fine examples of what can indeed be achieved through such a mechanism in places such as Hong Kong. On the contrary, even existing institutions for controlling corruption—the CBI and the CVC, have been robbed of their independence and are politicized, while independent authorities like the C&AG are routinely ignored. That such a movement had to be initiated only because the institutions created by the Constitution failed to respond to the needs of the hour, has been deliberately kept out of the debate.

Gandhiji bemoaned the creeping menace of corruption when his party came to power in 1937 and appealed, "Corruption and hypocrisy ought not to be the inevitable byproducts of democracy as they are undoubtedly today". In May 1939, Gandhi declared "I would go to the length of giving the whole Congress a decent burial rather than put up with the corruption that is rampant."

The Rigveda states "Corruption destroys all noble attributes of human beings in pursuit of the material, bereft of spiritual and divine knowledge and this is true ignorance." No one today cares for such noble thoughts.

The all-round lack of probity in public life has inhibited growth of the economy and disabled the country from realizing its full potential as a world power, in accord with the size of its population and its physical and intellectual capital. It is estimated that the country can improve its rate of growth by 2 per cent if it can control corruption and improve the standards of governance.

There has been abject failure to provide basic services to the people while the nation's internal and external security has been gravely undermined. The progressive decline in the effectiveness of our institutions combined with corruption has resulted in abject and repeated failure on the part of the system in providing even minimum security to its citizens and effectively dealing with the growing number of internal and external threats to India's security. "India insecure" has now replaced "India Shining". Institutions created specifically for combating terror are rendered toothless in no time due to meddling by politicians who are more concerned about not offending the minorities. They mistakenly apprehend that taking effective measures against terrorists will offend the minorities and will be harmful to their political prospects. The police are cautioned to be careful of the sensitivities of minorities and treat suspects with kid gloves. Naturally, the police would much rather not act at all, than annoy their political masters. It is strange that in secular society, a terrorist is given a communal colour, whereas in the eyes of law, he is nothing but a criminal, intent upon killing innocent people.

The point that requires strong emphasis is that while on the one hand, the magnitude of the development and security problems that the nation needs to tackle and overcome has been progressively increasing; the efficiency, effectiveness and responsiveness of the mechanisms that the nation has created for tackling the problems have been continuously declining. At the same time, there is the pronounced tendency to impose ever-increasing burdens on the system, by statutorily granting one right after another—to education, to employment, to food at subsidized rates, special dispensation for minorities, subsidized electricity, water, etc. even if such actions have the potential to bankrupt the State. We practice what has been termed 'helicopter socialism', where our *netas* periodically descend from the sky and make a number of announcements and promises and then disappear. This happens especially when elections are at hand and so far, our leaders have been able to garner votes by such dramatics. The fact that if the very same resources had been used for building the much needed high quality infrastructure it would have brought about much better, more enduring and sustained all-round growth, is repeatedly brought out by all concerned and yet, it is repeatedly ignored. Winning elections through promises and announcement of one *yojana* after another and touting even further reservations for one category or the other, is considered the *mantra* for success. This growing asymmetry between the increasing magnitude of the challenges to be faced, and ever-increasing burden on the system on the one hand and the continuous decline in its efficiency and effectiveness, will have grave implications for the long-term stability of the nation and our society, while endangering the sovereignty and territorial integrity of the country.

The view that India is fast becoming a violent country and parts of the country are ungoverned and becoming increasingly ungovernable while indigence and deprivation continue to haunt large segments of the population, may not altogether be misconceived. Relatively higher growth rates cannot conceal such ugly facts. In 2010 alone, an estimated 1,902 citizens of this country lost their lives in terrorist or insurgency related violence. Of these, Maoist violence claimed 1,180 victims; Pakistan supported militancy 375 lives, insurgency in the North East 322 lives and Pakistan-backed terrorism outside J&K another 25 lives. 223 districts are affected by Maoist violence, 20 districts of J&K by Pakistan-backed terrorism and another 67 districts in the six states of the North East by separatist insurgencies. Lives are also being lost in the agitation for the creation of a separate Telengana state and with respect to acquisition of land for various development projects.

No institution has escaped this decline in performance standards, be it the legislature, the judiciary or the executive. Even the armed forces of this country have not been immune to catching this virus of decline in standards and corruption. Consequently, there is considerable disillusionment with all institutions and in some parts of the country at least, organized systems of governance as mandated by the Constitution and the laws of the land have ceased to operate and the people have been left with no option but to seek alternative systems. Conditions of anarchy are already a fact of life in parts of India and unfortunately, such ungoverned and ungovernable areas are expanding. Admittedly, the decline in the efficacy of institutions has not been, shall we say fortunately, uniform. This, to my mind however, is a mixed blessing for such variations in the rate, degree and depth of decline, have already manifested themselves in the fairly sharp variations in the rate of economic growth recorded by different states, the performance levels in the social sectors–health, education, reduction of poverty, etc.—the success of population stabilization policies, the ability to attract investment of any kind, infrastructure development and indeed enhancement of the overall quality of life. The state of Gujarat, for example, has been growing at around 15 per cent per annum and its per capita income is now 300 per cent more than that of UP. It has been able to achieve nearly 10 per cent growth in agriculture even as in the rest of the country, the growth has stagnated at around 2 per cent. This also applies to the degree with which the State can be counted upon to provide security of life and property to the residents. The long-term consequences of such unbalanced development across regions, in terms of social unrest and reinforcement of divisive tendencies need to be taken seriously. No segment of governmental effort, be it security management, financial management, infrastructure development, poverty alleviation, or rural development, health or education has remained untouched by the inefficiency and corruption in the systems of administration and delivery of services.

In my last book, "Whither Governance" I had drawn pointed attention to the impact of the decline in standards governance on the peace and security of the nation and the individual citizen, arguing that this has emboldened the forces inimical to our nation's interests to undermine the nation's unity, sovereignty and integrity, while encouraging divisive and sectarian tendencies to gain ascendancy. It would be my endeavour to analyze in greater detail the impact of poor and declining standards of governance upon all aspects of internal and external security and development in this study.

It is my conviction that it is of paramount importance to study closely the causes and consequences of this all pervasive decline in the efficacy of our institutions and initiate remedial action. The nation can afford to ignore the warnings emanating from every corner of the country and every segment of our society, only at its peril. This book is an effort to draw the attention of the decision makers to the urgency of addressing the need for improving the standards of governance in each and every department of life in this country in the most comprehensive and holistic manner.

2

THE STATE WE ARE IN

When elections are called every five years for the Parliament and the state assemblies, one is justified in wondering what difference is this lengthy and expensive exercise going to make for the common man and in particular for the poor, the jobless and the disadvantaged.

Nothing that we have for the past several decades heard or seen inspires us to believe that there is going to be a measurable change in the way the country is being run. The old slogans and promises are repeated at every election and commitments to fight this or the other problem—poverty, terrorism, etc.—are made by every candidate in one form or the other. No one has the courage to state clearly what happened to the last set of promises. Yes, when we consider the enormity of the problems faced by the country and decline in the quality of the leadership, it would be a delusion to believe that any dramatic improvement can be brought about within a short time, but can we hope for some fundamental change in direction, some clear set of initiatives or systemic improvements including improvement in the quality and calibre of leadership, fulfillment of promises and reforms so that there is enlarged space for the citizens, with the economy enabled to grow at a faster pace and there is all-round progress on a self-sustaining basis? Can we indeed hope to altogether wipe out poverty and illiteracy within the foreseeable future? I am of the view that it is indeed possible for this country to wipe out poverty and illiteracy and this is based on the conviction that in India today, there is a new culture of entrepreneurship which given greater economic freedom and an enabling regulatory environment, can achieve world beating performance. What are required are better standards of governance which can unleash the potential of individual initiative in this country. One must note that everyday we hear of some new idea or innovation notched up by Indian scientists in several countries, Indian talent being cited increasingly as having turned around this company or the other, or an Indian company taking over some well-known entity or the other and turning it around successfully. We even have a Lord Kumar Bhattacharya chairman of the Warwick Manufacturing Group of the Warwick University, whose views on the revolution underway—called the third industrial revolution—involving digitalization of manufacturing which will change processes out of all recognition,— is quoted extensively by the *'Economist'*, 21-27th April, 2012.

However, as pointed out in the recent (13th March, 2012) Global Entrepreneurship Congress in Liverpool, UK, entrepreneurship is a fragile plant that needs careful nurturing by an enabling environment. The entrepreneurial flame is easier to put out than to light or relight. Policy makers and politicians are often focused on short-time election cycles and tend to junk their predecessor's policies even if these are eminently justified and indeed beneficial for the country. Take the case of the disinvestment programme which had achieved so much during the Vajpayee regime but was downgraded by the succeeding government.

It is my conviction that the quality of governance is of fundamental importance in dealing with the humongous problems that the country is faced with, on the clear understanding that the governing system has the bounden duty to provide peace, security and prosperity to all citizens. In spite of the recent history (post 1991), of a significant acceleration of economic growth, I feel that the problems to be tackled by the nation are growing in magnitude and possibly becoming more intractable.

Briefly the list is as follows:

a. The recent global meltdown has serious implications for India and we cannot afford to be in a state of denial. While the Government spokesmen continue to project growth rates above 7 per cent for 2011-12, independent analysts project much less. Unlike China, which has more than 3 trillion US dollar of reserves, our reserves have been eroded reducing our headroom to undertake massive investments in infrastructure which continues to be the nation's 'Achilles heel' and has the potential to provide the strongest possible stimulus for growth. In the next 10-year period, if we take the estimates of the Union Government, to achieve the 9 per cent growth target, India needs US $1 trillion (from 2007-2017 spread over the 11th and 12th Plan periods) for building new roads, ports, airports, power plants, sewage treatment and related urban infrastructure. We need $ 500 billion over the next five years itself (more than 50 per cent of India's GDP) to create new infrastructure to meet the 9 per cent growth target. Infrastructure investment as a percentage of GDP has however dropped from a high of about 6 per cent (1991) to a 33-year low of 3.3 per cent (2003). The year 2008-09 would close at about 4 per cent. That is way below the 8 per cent target which India has set for itself.

In 2012-13 alone, it is estimated that to deal with the crisis in all its dimensions, Government may have to borrow Rs. 5,000 billion and this can only mean that fiscal deficit will rise, private investment will be starved of funds and inflationary pressures will intensify. In a word if we regard infrastructure not only as the key to accelerated growth but as the salvation mantra for the downturn, the prospects are bleak. As of the end of the year 2011, the nation's economy seems to be heading towards a substantial slowdown if not an actual recession, with inflation around 10 per cent, uncontrolled fiscal and revenue deficit, burgeoining subsidy bill, continuous fall in the external value of the rupee and negative growth of industrial production. The continuing crisis in the Euro zone and slowdown of the US economy can only worsen the situation. There is policy paralysis and a deep disconnect between the fiscal and monetary policies. The Government, due to lack of political will and conflicts within the ruling coalition and a non-cooperative opposition, is unable to move forward on any front and deal with the emerging crisis with the required imagination and determination. The RBI at the moment is left alone to fight the battle for salvaging the economy on four different fronts, namely falling growth, plummeting rupee, high inflation and receding capital inflows. Electoral considerations being paramount, new schemes are being taken up to add to the already unbearable subsidy burden, while borrowing keeps increasing. All this can only add to inflationary pressures. A small silver lining is the slight fall in food inflation but further increases in fuel prices may reverse the trend. The outlook for 2012 is quite gloomy and the budget for the year 2012-13 promises no new initiatives that may accelerate growth and control inflation. There is a meek effort to control the fiscal deficit (from an all time high of 5.6 per cent of the GDP to 5.1 per cent). The imposition of a variety of new indirect taxes and enlargement of the ambit of service taxes will surely exacerbate inflationary pressures. The expectation that the Government will deal with the problem of burgeoning subsidies has been belied. The next budget can be even more populist and the growth story of India can be seriously undermined. It needs to be pointed out that the huge deficit could have been contained if only the Government had shown the courage to do away with a whole variety of tax exemptions and tax breaks as the tax foregone as a result of these exemptions is estimated to be Rs. 5.22 lakh crore. Also, if the recovery of all the unpaid taxes—both disputed and undisputed—, is effected with the required rigour, we can have a surplus budget. While there is a statement of intention to bring down fiscal deficit from the present 5.6 per cent of the GDP to 5.1 per cent; there is no credible road map to achieve this objective. Fiscal deficit can be brought down if the Government can reduce wasteful expenditure such as huge subsidies, prune the innumerable populist programmes and cut down its borrowing. Some twenty-nine such populist schemes are being implemented and many of them are overlapping. The expenditure on these schemes will go up to Rs. 3.25 lakh crore in 2012-13. All such expenditure is mainly financed by borrowing. In the year 2011, the Government borrowed Rs. 1397 crore everyday and this will go up to

Rs. 1560 crore. Interest payments alone will shoot up from Rs. 2.75 lakh crore to Rs. 3.19 lakh crore. Our subsidy burden has been going up uncontrollably from Rs. 70,000 crore (US $ 15 billion) in 2007-08 to Rs. 2,16,000 crore (US $ 45 billion) in 2011-12, a threefold increase in five years. This is slated to go up further in 2012-13. The much talked about fiscal consolidation and greater fiscal responsibility has been forgotten and without such consolidation, inflation cannot be controlled. The *'aam aadmi'* who is supposed to be the main focus of Government's every policy will have to suffer even more, with a heavier burden caused by Government's own profligacy. Also, when Government borrows so heavily, other borrowers are crowded out and the cost of borrowing—a key determinant of investment and growth—can keep rising. The economic management of the country has reached new lows and unless definitive steps are taken to improve fiscal management, effect structural reforms and cut subsidies as well as wasteful expenditure, one cannot hope to achieve a higher growth trajectory without which the nation's basic problems of poverty and squalor cannot be effectively tackled. Every percentage decline in growth rate, translates itself into a reduction in the quantum of jobs created and as is well known there is no better way to eliminate poverty than giving everyone a productive job. Loss of jobs or failure to get jobs hit the common man the hardest. If our growth rate is only 7 per cent the present GDP of $ 4,47 trillion dollars can go up to $ 6.30 trillion by 2017; but if we succeed in achieving a 9 per cent growth the GDP will go up to $ 6.80 trillion. As per NSSO estimates the number of poor will decrease by 50 million if the growth rate is only 7 per cent but the nation will be able to reduce the number of poor by an additional 25 million if the growth rate is accelerated to 9 per cent. The per capita income (PPP) will also go up to just below $6000. India can reach the threshold of a middle income country. All this is eminently achievable if only the government can get out of the present policy paralysis. Substantial increase in investment, upgradation of infrastructure, freeing farm prices, reduction of fiscal deficit while loosening the monetary policy will all be essential.

b. In spite of two decades of high growth, there are still 300 million people (almost equal to the population at the dawn of independence) below the Poverty Line, i.e., people who do not earn one dollar per capita per day. There are 500 million who live without sanitation and some 300 million without any water supply. Clean drinking water is not available even in urban areas. Yes, all this in spite of the fact that long years ago, we resolved to redeem a whole lot of pledges and vowed repeatedly to wipe out poverty. In parts of India, people still experience what Jeffrey Sachs calls, "Gut wrenching, soul destroying and life threatening" poverty and squalor. A whole lot of people were rescued out of the poverty trap because of accelerated growth, but the global meltdown may have grave impact on those who have just managed to get out of the poverty trap. The World Bank estimates that those who escaped the poverty trap are in the range of per capita daily income of 2 dollars to 13 US dollars, but in this bracket those below $9 are around 75 per cent and they are mainly in India and Africa, and can easily slide back into the poverty trap again. In a recent study by the International Food Policy Research Institute, it was highlighted that India's food security is under threat and is fragile and may worsen in the coming years given the poor performance of our agriculture and growth of population. In 2011, India ranked 67th in a list of 81 countries worst-affected by lack of adequate food and afflicted by hunger. In the Global Hunger Index evolved by this institute, India has consistently been below Pakistan from 1990 onwards. China has brought down its index dramatically from 11.7 in 1990 to just 5.5 in 2011, whereas India has during the same period, managed to improve the index from 30.4 to 23.7, a record worse than Nepal, war-torn Rwanda and Sudan. Iran and Brazil have achieved improvements similar to China.

c. Our agriculture is in poor shape with dwindling per capita land availability, increasing soil salinity, neglect of agricultural research, collapse of the extension machinery which had engineered the green revolution, poor spread of irrigation and ill-conceived and badly administered subsidy, marketing and storage strategies. The latest UN data on agricultural productivity (Editorial of *Indian Express* dated 30th March, 2012) shows that productivity of major food crops such as wheat, maize, rice and pulses in India is almost half of China. The yield of staple grains is less than that in Pakistan, Bangladesh and Myanmar. Growth of this sector, the investment it receives and capital formation, have all been declining since the 1980s. The post-harvest losses in India are estimated to be no less than Rs. 58,000 crore and poor rural connectivity still prevails in large parts of the country. Food grains and vegetables are allowed to rot, even while several million live on starvation diets and none is held accountable. This is happening at a time when the earlier solutions of more fertilizer, more pesticides and more water are becoming less and less effective due to soil salinity and exhaustion. The environmental damage caused by these practices has also emerged as increasing concerns. Also, dramatic improvements in yield through development of new varieties of crops are also becoming less possible. Maybe, we should first delink cricket from agriculture.

d. Global warming and climate change can have grave impact on our agriculture, considering that India utilizes its water resources in the most inefficient manner. Global warming can dry up the Himalayas. The water table in many states has seen precipitous decline and soil salinity is increasing at an alarming rate. Grave doubts are being expressed about India's ability to feed itself in the near future even while economists are warning that if the world's population exceeds 8 billion, we may witness not only ecological disasters but that the Malthusian positive checks of war, social upheavals and famine are bound to occur. It needs to be underlined that India is already regarded as highly water-stressed, dependent as it is upon the vagaries of the monsoon. The per capita availability of water in both urban and rural areas has been going down and western part of the country is highly drought-prone. Due to deforestation, soil run-off is increasing. Our rivers and water bodies are highly polluted, making availability of safe drinking water an increasingly difficult problem. It is known that even today, nearly 60 per cent of the population is dependent upon agriculture but this sector contributes a mere 18 per cent to the GDP. Agriculture needs irrigation and technology but the Government offers loan waiver. Rural unemployment and deteriorating land-man ratio require shifting of labour from farms to factories through creation of skills, accelerated industrial progress and generation of adequate electricity but the Government is happy to offer a rural employment dole. Even the 2012-13 budget has failed to pay adequate attention to vital issues such as improvement in productivity, access to markets, finance, energy availability, supply chain management and infrastructure. Food inflation, which has spiraled by 97 per cent in seven years is sought to be combated by food security. Garnering of votes through temporary sops is all that is being done and each one of the measures instead of dealing with the fundamental problems plaguing the economy only adds to inflationary pressures.

e. Our health and educational standards continue to be those of the third world. Except some islands of excellence, which are themselves under threat, the general educational standards at all levels are poor and substandard. No more than 15 per cent of the youth in age group of 18 to 24 years has access to higher education in India and female enrollment is just about 6 per cent compared to 90 per cent in Canada, 81 per cent in the US. Our Research and Development output is woefully inadequate and our scientific manpower is 3.5 per thousand population, compared to 110 per thousand in Japan, 86 of Germany, 55 of the USA, 76 of Israel, 29.5 of Brazil, 46 of South Korea and 9 of China. One cannot over-emphasize the importance of higher education and R&D in building the nation's intellectual capital which is of vital importance in today's world whereas Alvin Toffler averred 'Knowledge is Power'. It may be noted in this context that today, when we talk of Comprehensive

National Power (CNP) (a concept developed by the Chinese Military Academy), this includes not only military strength, but the nation's achievements in terms of technological sophistication, scientific manpower, research and development capabilities, energy adequacy and of course, the quality and personality of its leaders in all fields. Winston Churchill long ago stated that, "the Empires of the future will be Empires of the mind". The 'third industrial revolution' involving digitalization of all manufacturing processes will demand even greater skills and higher standards of education. Labour productivity rather than labour costs will increasingly determine location of industries and India needs to gear itself up to meet the challenges of this revolution.

f. The incidence of infant and maternal mortality in India is among the highest in the world. Some 8 million children die of malnutrition every year and some 60 million adults are victims. Malnutrition wrecks both the body and the mind. For a population of 1.2 billion, India has no more than 700,000 doctors with one doctor for 1,700 souls, compared to 400 in US and 220 in Israel.

g. The country's energy scenario is truly dismal. For the country to achieve a higher growth path on an enduring basis, sustained efforts are required to create adequate energy in all forms to fuel the economy. In every plan we have failed to achieve the targets. The present electricity generation is around 160 Gega watts and if the economy has to grow at 9 to 10 per cent per year by 2030, we need 800 Gega watts. China is already producing 800 Gega watts and adds 50 Gega watts every five years. It must be emphasized that India's energy consumption is one of the lowest in the world, just 325 Kg compared to nearly 8,000 in US. (Only Pakistan has a lower figure of 310 in Asia). Over 500 million Indians do not have access to electricity while 30 per cent of energy is still obtained from cow dung, agricultural waste and firewood. Coal shortages have become a continuous problem and India, which has over 200 billion tons of coal, has become dependent upon imports to feed existing thermal power plants. Coal fired Power plants are operating at 50 per cent of their rated capacity. Power shortages occur regularly all over the country. The year 2011 has been particularly bad due to coal shortages caused by the agitation for Telengana and flooding of coal mines in Bihar. Industrial growth has been hit by all-round power shortages. The year 2012 promises to be even worse with coal fired power plants reporting critical shortages due the inability of Coal India to ensure even the promised supplies. Importing coal is not an option as it is much costlier to do so. The power deficit with respect to urban areas throughout the country has ballooned to over 21000 MWs. There is great reluctance to adjust power tariff to match actual costs even by independent tariff regulatory authorities due to political pressure and consequently, power producers who have borrowed heavily to produce power are likely to default. As of now, up to Rs. 135 lakh crore of bank loans are at risk. Even Delhi which had privatized power distribution has not seen any revision in tariff for the past ten years. Nothing is more important than fundamental reforms in the power sector to accelerate growth and eliminate poverty. We should pay much greater attention to energy conservation and R&D relating to renewable energy, i.e., fuels from heaven (solar, wind and hydro) than increasing our dependence on fuels from hell (coal, oil and gas). Scandinavia where the Sun shines but intermittently is far ahead of us in these areas. In 2011 India invested just 10 billion US$ in solar energy whereas the US spent 50 billion, China 45 billion, Germany and Italy around 30 billion. Japan, Spain, Britain and Brazil all invested some 10 billion each.

h. One must also focus on the growing inequality in the realm of economic and social development among the states. This has serious disruptive implications. There seems to be a North, South and East, West divide in the making. Unfortunately, those states which are performing poorly are also states which have high rates of population growth, complicating the situation in a major way. UP is a prime example of this. It's distressing economic performance and failure to control the runaway growth in population can prove to be a drag on the rest of the country. The finances of several states are in a mess and they keep demanding loan waivers from the Centre. The Centre would be quite justified in invoking the provisions under Article 360 of the Constitution to declare a financial emergency in some of the extreme cases where the financial stability of the state is threatened but has somehow has never had the courage to do so.

i. I am also deeply perturbed by the total amnesia that the leadership has been displaying with respect to the population dynamics in India. The so called "population dividend" has to my mind induced unwarranted complacency and silence on this score. Both Jeffrey Sachs and Thomas Friedman warn that the ghost of Rev Robert Malthus can visit us in a more virulent form triggering what Malthus called positive checks (war, disease, civil strife and famine).

The facts speak for themselves. Today, the world is already overcrowded with 7 billion people (October 2011) and without any change in Total fertility rate (TFR), it will rise to a startling and catastrophic 11.7 billion by 2050. Almost all the increase will be from the developing world and India will overtake China as the world's most crowded nation. We are thrusting over 20 million every year into our limited geographical space, while importing large numbers from Bangladesh. That the bulk of our population is young, over 500 million and counting but unemployed and unemployable, can mean that they can be easy prey to unrest and insurgency, as has happened and will happen on an ever-increasing scale in Pakistan. The UN estimates that the world can be saved only if population can be stabilized around 8 billion. Beyond this, Malthus will be back in force. Witness Darfur-war, disease, famine—the positive checks are there already.

Every problem that we face, decline in per capita land availability [down from 5.8 (1947) to 1.8 (2007)], loss of habitat and species, overcrowding everywhere, unemployment, poverty, squalor, competition for resources, cut-throat competition in politics, the vicious cycle of lack of development leading to dissatisfaction, disillusionment, unrest, insurgency and violence are all ultimately traceable to the high and unaffordable rates of growth in population. In India, in my view, Malthus's positive checks are already being witnessed in pockets. Imagine farmers being driven to suicide and parents killing their children, in this day and age. The country's wildlife and rich biodiversity is under serious threat and our forest cover is dwindling. Trees and wild animals do not have votes and our politicians show no understanding about the issues involved and little interest or inclination to initiate effective measures to stabilize the population or conserve our ecology and environment.

The 'demographic dividend' can be a reality if the population is enabled to acquire all the required skills through education and training and more importantly, if the growth in employment roughly matches the accretions to the labour force. The 'demographic dividend' can become a 'demographic nightmare' if the bulge in the younger age groups does not get absorbed by the market. We will then have the unemployed taking to the streets and creating mayhem. This is what is happening all over the Arab world where population control is frowned upon, Malthus never heard of and the young unemployed are in the frontline of unrest and are also a fertile source of recruitment for terrorist outfits.

j. We are also facing an ecological disaster. As Jeffrey Sachs argues there is a huge human impact on the environment. The impact (I) increases exponentially if increase in numbers (P) is combined with increase in income (A) and the present environmentally unfriendly use of technology (T) remains unchanged. Sachs terms this as the, I = P × A × T (The Eye Pat) equation.

The world's population on a business-as-usual track can rise by roughly 40 per cent by 2050, and the world's income per person on a business-as-usual track can also rise perhaps fourfold. Thus, P × A, or total world income, is on track to rise roughly six-fold. The human impact on the environment, I, with an unchanged set of technologies would, therefore, be six-fold. Since the human impact on the environment today is already unsustainable, a six-fold increase in impact would be devastating and would almost surely feedback, to block the rise in world income. In other words, we would never achieve the targeted economic growth because it would be frustrated by environmental catastrophes, unless there are massive improvements in technology. Man is emerging as a threat to not merely all other species on Earth as also to himself. Surely, the most dangerous animal on Earth is man. With the population growth in India still at an unaffordable rate, population stabilization a very distant goal and the target date being periodically revised we will be victims of devastating catastrophes that Sachs refers to.

In India, I feel we are now seeing a phenomenon called "demographic fatigue", i.e. the sheer increase in the size of the problems to be tackled because of the population explosion, making it increasingly impossible for the response mechanisms to handle these effectively and this is happening at a time when there is a sustained decline in the efficiency of the response mechanism. The existing asymmetry between the size and complexity of the problems to be tackled and the ability and efficiency of the response mechanism, is set to increase in the coming years with frightening consequences.

k. We are also witnessing a definite slow down in the rate of economic growth in the foreseeable future. Foreign investment has dried up due to political uncertainties and failure of the governing system to take proactive measures. There has been no improvement in the ease of doing business in India. The Planning Commission has now settled for a growth rate of 9 per cent for the twelfth plan, a comedown from the earlier 10 per cent target but even this will require a big increase in capital formation and the efficiency with which the nation utilizes its resources. The record of 2011 is anything but encouraging, as the growth rate in the manufacturing sector has declined drastically to 3 per cent and the growth rate in the services sector has become stagnant. Key growth sectors such as construction and mining have witnessed serious slowdowns, and the power sector is being constrained by coal shortages. Industrial growth in the first two quarters of 2011 has touched its lowest in the 24 months, while inflation has crossed 10 per cent and food inflation which hits the poor the hardest, despite a fairly good monsoon is now over 9.4 per cent. Among all the BRIC countries, India has now the highest inflation and interest rates. The value of the Rupee has slid to an all-time low making imports more costly while Government expenditure has exceeded budget and business confidence is at a new low. Investment decisions are getting postponed as the cost of capital has gone up due to the RBI's hike in key interest rates. There is serious disconnect between the country's fiscal and monetary policy, as the RBI rate hikes are aimed at controlling inflation whereas it is the Government's profligacy that is the main cause for inflation. The interest rates have been hiked 13 times without any tangible effect on inflation while affecting the prospects of growth. In spite of the FRBM Act, the Government has not been serious about control of fiscal deficit and programmes which are designed to garner votes and untargeted subsidies are being provided larger outlays all the while. The loan waiver of Rs. 130,000 crore was followed by increases of budget allocation for all the 'dole'programmes which generate a huge imbalance between demand and supply reinforcing inflationary pressures. There is inadequate liquidity in the market and Government borrowings which have been going up, makes it difficult for the other players to access funds for investment. All these add to inflationary pressures. Out of the Rs. 11 lakh crore the Government spends, some Rs. 4 lakh crore is funded by borrowing and this keeps on increasing. Of the Rs. 1,142 crore that it borrows every-day, no less than Rs. 400 crore goes to pay interest costs. That the economy is so poorly managed even when we have such brilliant economists at the helm can be surprising but has to weighed against the fact that Government's policies are today not determined by the Government but by extra-Constitutional entities, who are not answerable either to the Parliament or to the people and seem to be determined by electoral calculus alone. If the dire predictions regarding the future of the

Euro, collapse of the Euro Zone and depression in the Western world including the US come true there can be severe impact on the prospects for growth and it may become impossible to keep up the rates of growth that the country had achieved in the recent past and has been aiming at for the Twelfth Plan.

It is strange that while advanced economies are today paying the price for excessive welfarism we continue to enthusiastically and prematurely embrace welfarism. Advanced economies transformed themselves into welfare economies and welfare societies at a gradual pace and only after they had passed the "take off" stage of economic development and were becoming mature by the year. Our economy is nowhere at or near these stages of development and can ill-afford the kind of largesse that is given away every year. In advance economies the expenditure on welfare projects, were met, until recent times through taxation and since the economies had matured, and growth was self-sustaining, tax revenues were also growing and adequate to meet the expenditure on welfare schemes. We are on the other hand financing all welfare projects, designed to garner votes, through borrowing and deficit financing both of which fuel inflation. Everyone gets punished by inflation while some segments may be benefiting, by the largesse of government. Brazil it may be recalled went into hyperinflation primarily because of the profligacy of the Government and uncontrolled borrowing. What an achievement for the government to have managed to bring down the growth rate from 9 per cent to 6 or 7 per cent? And now the rating agency Standard and Poor has downgraded the country's economic outlook from stable-BBB—to negative BBB minus—the lowest investment grade—one more feather in the cap of our government of economists. The reasons given by S&P are as expected the uncontrolled deficit, policy paralysis, unwillingness or inability to go through even the most essential economic reforms and enact the required legislations. Moodys another rating firm characterises the government as the "single biggest drag on business activity". Moodys also suggest that "the government has lost all momentum and progress is unlikely on the legislative front even on vital issues such as land reforms, labour reforms and FDI." It has termed the Prime Minster as "ageing technocrat who now appears tired of the rough and tumble of Indian politics." Gloomy prognosis indeed.

l. India will also have to be prepared to meet the emerging global challenges which can be expected to intensify in the coming years such as resource scarcities caused by population increases, climate change and continuous rise in the prices of fossil fuels. In particular, the possibility of armed confrontation between Iran and Israel with indirect involvement of the US can induce not only sharp escalation in crude oil prices but also disrupt flow of oil from the entire Middle East. Demand for strategic resources such as energy, food and water is already outstripping supplies. The subcontinent is particularly vulnerable to water scarcity and this can cause regional and interstate conflicts. All these may engender severe shocks and crises of large proportions.

m. On top of this, the serious issues relating to land acquisition, abnormal delays in according various clearances, power shortages, failure to come out with a new industrial policy and our consistent failure to improve the ease of doing business index, have all compounded the problem. It may be noted that even today, two-thirds of the population live off less than one-third of the national income even as we claim to be working for the '*aam admi*' all the while. In a word, the serious all-round governance deficit is bound to adversely affect the development prospects of the nation. The dream of wiping out poverty from this country is evaporating.

Turning to the security scenario in the country, it is no exaggeration to state that this presents an extraordinarily difficult set of challenges demanding intelligent cohesive, well-planned and well-executed strategies and actions.

Briefly Speaking

a. The entire North-East continues to be in turmoil. The ULFA has no doubt lost much of its appeal and the ongoing peace talks may yet restore normalcy. The hill districts of Assam have however seen the emergence of new outfits which indulge in periodic violence such as the Karbi Longri liberation army and Dimasa Halong Daga, etc. They all have armed wings which are uncompromising in their demand for separate states. States like Manipur and Nagaland are only cartographically part of India. The writ of the Constitution does not run beyond the Rajbhawans in Kohima or Imphal. There are no less than 27 separate insurgency groups which indulge in widespread extortion and violence. The links between politicians and insurgents are well documented. In Manipur for example, insurgents allegedly double up as ministers during the day. The creation of, the new state of Meghalaya by the State's Reorganization Act of 1972, to satisfy the political and economic aspirations of the hill tribes of the composite state of Assam, has now unfortunately led to a further reinforcement of narrow chauvinism, tribal loyalties and inter-tribal conflicts between the Khasis and Garos and the Garos and the Rabhas. No less than 50,000 Rabhas were kicked out of the Garo hills and are languishing in refugee camps in the Gaolpara district of western Assam. Each of these tribes has now created its own armed insurgency outfit, all indulging in extortion and black mail. The North Eastern Hill University is hostage to the Khasi Students Union, a narrow minded and chauvinistic body, which is determined to see that non-Khasis have no place in that institution and it frequently indulges in violence to ensure this. This body has also succeeded so far in ensuring that uranium reserves in Meghalaya are not mined. The Government, both at the Centre and the State level, has no nerve to stand up to this sort of blackmail and central investments meant for building fine institutions of higher learning have not been allowed to achieve the desired results.

b. Unchecked illegal immigration from Bangladesh has altered the demographic composition in the bordering districts of West Bengal and Assam. The loyalty of these new entrants is at best untested and they are easy prey to influences inimical to India's security interests. Bodies such as HUJI, LET and the ISI have already established their presence in the area. The Siliguri corridor, rightly called the "Chicken's neck", a vital link in the country's security grid, is becoming increasingly violent and unstable with several competing interests—Gorkhaland, Kamtapur, Amra Bangali, etc. and can be exploited by all elements inimical to India's security. It is wedged precariously between Bhutan and Bangladesh and can be cut off by any adversary and the defence of the entire North-East can be easily jeopardized. If the loyalty of the population in this critical corridor cannot be taken for granted, then the situation may become very difficult indeed.

c. The low intensity conflict in Jammu and Kashmir continues to simmer, supported by Jihadi elements that in turn are supported by financiers from the Middle East. The Jihadis are openly supported, trained, armed and motivated by Pakistan keeping a large part of our armed forces almost indefinitely on what are basically internal security duties.

d. The Naxalities have been able to carve out territories where the Government writ does not run in the states of Maharashtra, Orissa, Jharkhand, Chhattisgarh, Madhya Pradesh and Andhra Pradesh and even in Karnataka. Some 223 districts of the country are said to be part of the red corridor. This can have grave security and development implications as the Naxalites are violently against investment in the exploitation of much-needed natural resources. Naxalites are now believed to be building strategic links with the insurgents of the North-East and J&K.

e. Religious extremism and terrorism inspired and supported by external agencies have periodically struck metropolitan areas with impunity and what is of grave concern is their successful effort to enlist the support of minorities of the country. India is one of the worst victims of international terrorism inspired by radical Islam and more than 4,000 people have been killed in terrorist attacks since 2001. Only Iraq has a higher figure.

It must be understood that this new threat to the existing international order (to my mind the true dimensions of the threat is indeed of this nature) arises from a combination of circumstances, namely the reiteration of the concept of Islamic Umma, accumulation of grievances against the West and other civilizations, an extreme and radicalized interpretation of Islam bent on spreading its particular version backed by almost unlimited flow of funds from West Asia, in particular Saudi Arabia and Iran, and endless supply of foot soldiers from countries like Pakistan. While other countries have no doubt experienced violence perpetrated by this combination, India is a particular target and has suffered grievously.

f. Divisive tendencies, aggravated by casteism, communalism, linguistic and regional chauvinism are on the rise, with sporadic outbreaks of violence.

g. To further complicate the security nightmare we have the problem of ineffective policing of our borders, and our long coastline (the BSF is called the Border Security Farce). The nation has to battle fake currency inflows and generation of black money, links between the underworld and terrorists, Bollywood and even some politicians. The NN Vohra (former Union Home Secretary) Committee, clearly brought out the nexus among politicians, police personnel and terrorists in engineering the Mumbai carnage of 1993 but nothing has been done about its recommendations for the past 18 years. Measures to remedy the failures which led to the carnage in Mumbai on 26th November, 2008 have not been taken either. Our coastal defences continue to be weak with poor coordination among all the agencies involved. The criminalization of politics in the country which has been going on for some time, has reached new heights with a large number in both the Parliament and the legislatures facing criminal proceedings in one court or the other.

Many are also under investigation by the Central and State investigating agencies.

h. The ever-widening and deepening corruption, along with large amounts of money slashed away illegally, allegedly in other countries and tax havens (no less than US $1.5 trillion) undermines both security and development. Corruption is taken advantage by terrorists while money slashed away reduces the quantum of capital available for investment. In the recent past, we have witnessed the sorry spectacle of the political class in general and the Government in particular going to any lengths to thwart civil society initiatives to bring about the enactment of strong and effective legislation for the creation of a properly empowered and independent ombudsman in accord with the UN convention and in line with what countries such as the UK, Singapore as well as Hong Kong have established. The most worrying aspect of corruption is the impact this has had on our defence preparedness. Indira Gandhi was the first to see the potential for tapping defence deals for party funds, when she banned contributions by corporate entities. This hit the opposition while the Government was able to get what it wanted from defence contracts. Scrious questions have been raised about the big submarine deal during her regime and in any case, after the Bofors scam with everybody becoming more cautious and less willing to take final decisions, a near paralysis situation has resulted with respect to defence procurement and no wonder, even our service chiefs have had reason to openly complain that faced with determined and well-equipped adversaries, our ability to defend ourselves is now extremely unsatisfactory.

As if the list of woes that I have referred to above is not enough, India also faces a series of foreign policy challenges with a fast-changing international security environment. The world is facing a transformation in terms of a shift in the centre of gravity from the West to the East, religious extremism challenging long-accepted notions of sovereignty and civilization and the inadequacy of the UN system to cope with the growing security and economic challenges being faced by the world. The UN still reflects the world as it was at the end of the Second World War.

Our most serious foreign policy challenges no doubt, come from our extremely turbulent neighborhood. Pakistan faces the danger of internal collapse and spread of an increasingly assertive Taliban right into its heart. The Al Qaeda is now in close collaboration with the Taliban with common objectives and access to funds from the Arab world and opium and now emeralds from Afghanistan. These developments have grave consequences for our own internal stability. The problem really is that even today, the Pakistani establishment, particularly the military and the ISI, are unwilling and indeed refusing to accept that their real enemy is within and not India. All the training, weaponry, indoctrination, motivation and strategic planning of the Pakistan Army and its security apparatus are against India and there is continued belief that Pakistan must acquire so called strategic depth, i.e. a subservient Afghanistan and India not permitted to having any presence in Afghanistan. Pakistan has been under military rule for decades directly as well as indirectly. Yes, the only country conquered by the army of Pakistan is, hold your breath—Pakistan. Indeed, it must be stressed that the very rationale for the existence of the army is hostility to India. The army exaggerates the threat from India to justify all the budgetary allocations that it demands and the extraordinary perks it enjoys and the clout it has with respect to both the country's foreign and nuclear postures. The Taliban and the various militant outfits promoted by the army are essential elements in its offensive and defensive capabilities.

To be sure, the Taliban is a monster created to a large extent, by the Americans who foolishly used religion to fight the ideology of communism and today, this monster is threatening the stability of not only the region but several parts of the world. In 1992, the *Washington Post* had revealed how the CIA had actively assisted the Mujahideen by supplying plastic explosives to make bombs, satellite intelligence on Soviet military movements and gave some $ 2 billion to the Mujahideen. It also highlighted how the supply of Stinger antiaircraft missiles was a decisive force multiplier in the defeat of the Soviets. It is the CIA which again sent thousands of Korans to the Soviet Union's southern republics. The Americans also flooded the area with weapons of all types, much of which was appropriated by the Pakistan Army but a large part was distributed to various militant groups and carefully preserved by them and now being used against the very agencies which supplied these.

It is possible that the situation in Afghanistan would have been far different if the Soviets had not been defeated through US machinations and use of religion for this purpose. It is the CIA which supported the Pakistan Atomic Energy Commission and turned a blind eye to all that A.Q. Khan was doing. America has itself to blame for the situation today both in Afghanistan and Pakistan. Many a revolution has swallowed its children but this has the potential of devouring the father.

As of today, Pakistan is at war with itself with sectarian, religious, regional, communal, ideological and ethnic fault lines and conflicts enveloping every part of the country. It may well implode and get fragmented. Baluchistan is in turmoil, Karachi is ungovernable and insurgency of every type has engulfed the entire area all along the Durand Line. Baluchistan has a population of 9 million out of Pakistan's 193 million but covers some 44 per cent of its geographical area. It has valuable deposits of gas, copper iron ore and oil. Pakistan has followed a deliberate policy of changing the demographic composition of Baluchistan by settling a large numbers of Punjabis in this province. There are at least three insurgent outfits operating in Baluchistan, namely the Baluchistan Liberation Army, the Baluch Republican Army and the Baluchistan Liberation Front. All of them are fighting for independence from Pakistan and are subjected to brutal suppression by the Pakistan Army. The Frontier Corps numbering some 50,000 is mainly responsible for controlling this region and known for its extreme brutality with no accountability to anyone. No one speaks of the massive human rights violations and virtual genocide in Baluchistan and India never raises this in any forum. Only recently, the US has taken note of this but has not gone beyond expression of concern over what really constitutes inhuman atrocities on a people who have been in continuous rebellion against the Pakistani State from 1948 onwards and who have been dealt with unmatched cruelty and repression. Reports speak of the fact that the National Anthem of Pakistan is not sung in Baluch schools and even the national flag is not hoisted. However, while officially the US Government has been somewhat subdued in its comments and reactions, the US Congress has openly come out in support of what has been termed as the struggle for Baluch self-determination, much to the embarrassment of Pakistan. Certain think tanks in the US are veering round to the view that the separation of Baluchistan from Pakistan may be in keeping with US's long-term security interests in the region. A separate and friendly Baluchistan will help the US to deal with Afghanistan without the present dependence on Pakistan, which periodically disrupts all supplies to the NATO forces and actively assists elements which kill US soldiers. The Gwadar port will be good enough substitute for Karachi and the US can use this port as a base for its carrier-borne fleet. Further, a Baluchistan friendly to the US can be of considerable value in combating China's influence in the area and in fact, thwart China's ambitions to gain free access to the Arabian Sea and the Indian Ocean. The road built by China with the clear intent of gaining direct access to the Arabian Sea via the Karakorum highway will cease to serve this particular strategic objective. No doubt, there are many imponderables in this scenario but what is very interesting is the fact that while the US was openly hostile to the struggle for independence by the then East Pakistan (now Bangladesh), with respect to Baluchistan the US appears to have quite substantially changed its attitude. The US is also unhappy with the growing economic cooperation between Iran and Pakistan and the proposed gas pipeline from Iran to Pakistan is a particular irritant. An independent Baluchistan can be a useful buffer between Pakistan and Iran as well as Pakistan and Afghanistan.

The Shia-Sunni conflict is now endemic in Pakistan and though an Islamic country, there has been no hesitation to indulge in bombings and carnage even during the holy month of Ramadan and statistics have shown that Friday, the day of Prayer has in the past year, seen more violence and death than any other day of the week. Karachi has been on the boil for decades and every year thousands get killed in internecine warfare between the Mohajirs and Sindhis and between the Mohajirs and the Pashtuns. In all parts of Pakistan, the Shias are under continuous threat and are regularly attacked while the police machinery does nothing.

The Gilgit Baltistan area which was part of the kingdom of the Maharaja of Jammu and Kashmir—a princely state of British controlled India is now virtually a battle ground for the Sunni-Shia conflict. The area was inhabited by Shias and Pakistan has followed a deliberate policy of drastically altering the demography by suppressing the Shias, while encouraging Sunnis from Pakistan to settle there. In the period from 1998 to 2011, whereas the population of POK increased by 1.54 per cent, that of Gilgit and Baltistan shot up by 63 per cent; the result of the deliberate policy of the Government of Pakistan to wipe out the Shias from this area. This area is declared as Northern Territories separate from POK and is directly controlled by the Federal Government. Nothing called representative government has ever been introduced and the Shias are seething with dissatisfaction. Many wonder as to why India which keeps asserting that the whole of the erstwhile kingdom of J&K (including Gilgit and Baltistan) is an integral part of India, never raises this issue of suppression of people there and denial of basic human rights in international forums. We have not even bothered to fill up the seats kept vacant in the J&K assembly for the representatives of Gilgit and Baltistan. The defensiveness of India in all her dealings with Pakistan is indeed mystifying. It is perhaps reflective of the bankruptcy of our foreign policy and failure of all aspects of governance.

The Pakistan economy is not growing even at a rate equal to the very high rate of growth of population. Though during the Musharraf regime, it managed to grow at a fairly fast clip varying between 6 to 9 per cent, but has since declined to barely 3 per cent and the actual growth rate of 2010 is estimated to be a mere 2.4 per cent, while the population grows at over 2.8 per cent. Pakistan's population which was 34 million in 1951 has now crossed 190 million and may go up to over 300 million by the year 2025. Inflation is at an all-time high and no one, no institution whether the army or the civilian government has shown the ability or willingness to tackle any of the problems. After the unsuccessful attempts by General Ayub, no Government in Pakistan has even dared to talk about population stabilization.

The World Bank has drawn attention to the acute shortage of water in several parts of Pakistan and the tensions that this has started creating between the states, especially the Punjab and Sindh. The Woodrow Wilson Centre has predicted that given the rate of growth of population, the annual water demand in Pakistan will rise to around 338 billion cubic metres by 2020 whereas the supply, unless drastic remedies are found, may not exceed 236 billion. While Pakistan may not as yet qualify as a failed State on the lines of Congo or Sudan, but the State has surely become irrelevant to the people whose lives are increasingly controlled by non-state and violent actors. The massive floods of 2010 showed how ineffective the Government was in providing basic relief and rehabilitation to the people and after one full year, some ten million people still live in tents. It is the charities, such as the Edhi foundation, that were far more effective and contributed a great deal in reducing actual casualties. Floods during 2011 have already claimed hundreds of lives even while the victims of last year's floods continue to live in temporary shelters. If climate change does bring about the much-feared consequences, parts of Pakistan may be turned into a desert. The country will not be able to support the rapidly growing population and calamities of unprecedented dimensions may follow.

The problem for India is that Pakistan has the tendency to blame India for all her ills as also the US and Israel and it has been determining its identity in purely anti-India terms. Perpetual enmity is the only reason, it maintains a huge army and spends a disproportionate share of its budget and its GDP on its armed forces. The army justifies its existence and all the privileges and funds it receives on the ground, that it is the only saviour of Pakistan and must be ready to combat India at all times. "No Army No Pakistan" is what the officer corps believes. Since it cannot afford a direct armed struggle with India, it has found a low-cost and effective weapon in exporting terror, to destabilize India and to grab Kashmir.

With China as well we have unresolved problems, and its growing influence in the world can reduce the space for us in all fields. China is today economically and militarily a challenge even to the US and it is working assiduously to ensure that India is contained and constrained and kept nervous. We also have the problem of cyber attacks originating from China.

Nepal, Sri Lanka and Bangladesh pose serious problems because of their own internal problems and undercurrents of hostility towards India. Bangladesh is a safe haven for insurgent groups of the North-East but has recently shown a remarkable and commendable sense of accommodation and willingness to cooperate with India. One hopes that such a change will be enduring and not subject to the vicissitudes of regime change in that country.

If this, by no means complete list of woes has to be addressed and overcome and if the fundamental desires of the society, to have peaceful existence, conflict-free atmosphere and orderly progress have to be fulfilled the machinery of the State should indeed be fighting fit. The fundamental issue to my mind is whether the government and its entire machinery is capable of delivering high standards of governance, which alone can effectively tackle the problems I have enumerated.

I must also refer to the tendency on the part of our leaders to shy away from telling the truth to the people and prepare the people to cooperate to solve the problems. Winston Churchill promised nothing but "blood and toil, tears and sweat "and prepared Britain to face all the privations of the war. At the height of the blitzkrieg, he anxiously enquired if the courts were functioning well; such was the importance attached to the rule of law. He also said a few nasty things about our leaders. Many are straining every nerve to prove him right. What we need if the nation is to overcome all the myriad challenges, therefore the highest standards of governance in all its dimensions and in all institutions of governance.

The economist, Robert Barro of the Harvard University propounded a thesis (quoted by the *Economist* dated December 2011) that is so relevant to the situation in which we find ourselves. He states emphatically that poor countries can grow at a faster rate than rich counties and improve the prospects of catching up, as they start from a lower base and can imitate techniques already in practice rather than having to invent them. But this is possible only if rule of law in all its dimensions prevailed, the terms of trade remains favourable, inflation and government profligacy remains in check, and families are sufficiently small, healthy and educated. I am afraid that even after 65 years of independent existence, when no one but us, have been responsible for our affairs, we have failed to create these fundamental enabling conditions for sustained acceleration of growth and for all-round progress and cannot be confident of wiping out poverty from this country.

Each of the themes covered in this chapter will be examined in greater detail in the following chapters.

3
INTERNATIONAL SECURITY ENVIRONMENT

It would be appropriate to present a brief overview of the International Security Environment and use this as the backdrop for an analysis of the threats to India's security, in particular external threats. An attempt will also be made to spell out policy options that are available to the country. The purpose of this effort is to emphasize that in this area as well, the quality and standards of governance are of critical importance as today conflicts between nations or group of nations are fought and won not in the field of battle, but across conference tables and in international forums.

If one looks at the global scenario, a number of "hot spots" can be identified which have the potential of threatening the security and stability of countries and regions and pose serious challenges to the system of international security management.

In the Western Hemisphere, the US despite still being the sole superpower, has become vulnerable to international terrorism, motivated by radical Islam, which articulates grievances allegedly emanating from the US's own "follies" such as aggressive foreign policy postures, backed by ill advised armed interventions in Iraq and Afghanistan and its unqualified support for Israel. The US's policies have of late been interpreted as "Anti-Islam" leading to characterization of these policies in civilizational terms, with shades of the Huntington thesis of "Clash of Civilizations". Apart from this today, the US seems to be on the decline with her economy floundering, unemployment rising, its huge deficits, low or negative growth rates and unmanageable trade imbalances. Its sole super power status is coming under threat. However, there are already signs that the economy is on the path of revival and job creation is improvirg.

In a new book titled *"Eclipse: Living in the Shadow of China's Economic Dominance"*, Arvind Subramaniam argues that US economic dominance has been eroding for some time now. Its past resilience seems to be a thing of the past. The Chinese economy is larger than that of the US as of 2010, with a GDP of $14.8 trillion compared to US$14.6 trillion of the US. China's per capita GDP is much lower but what matters more is the total economic strength. Subramaniam has suggested an innovative Economic Dominance Index based on three parametres, namely, GDP, trade and external financial strength. These three helped Britain to be dominant in the 19th Century and the US in the 20th. Already in 2010, China was just ahead of the US with respect to these parameters and by 2020, it can be well ahead of every country. Such a rise will be driven by demography and consistently higher economic and trade performance by China compared to the US and the West. China can hope to grow at around 7 per cent whereas the US may just about achieve 2.5 per cent growth. Such a rise will inevitably lead to accretion of military strength and political clout. China may overtake the US as the world's largest economy by the year 2018.

In the 19th and the 20th centuries, America's development trajectory was based on a balanced growth of all sectors, fuelled by wars and arms manufacture but in the last part of the 20th and in the new millennium, manufacturing migrated to China and Information Technology to India. America then specialized in making money out of money—financial services—through inventing newer and more sophisticated financial instruments which provided high rewards for select few but created very little new employment. It also widened disparities. This is what the 'Occupy Wall Street' protests are all about. Economists have been warning for a long time that the West's habit of borrowing more and consuming more, while the East saved more and invested more is fundamentally an unstable economic arrangement.

Some American strategic thinkers such as Jimmy Carter's national security adviser, Zbigniew Brezezinski and Charles Kupchan, a security analyst, have in their recent books reviewed by the *Economist* (24 March, 2012) argued that it is premature to consider that the US will lose its preeminence in world affairs. In their view, world stability requires a strong US, as they feel that the world is more stable when one nation dominates "especially if it is a nation like America". This is a questionable thesis, given the US's role in actively supporting dictators when it suited its interests, tolerating nuclear proliferation by the likes of Pakistan when it was convenient, involving religion in Afghanistan as a strategy to kick out the Soviets, invading Iraq most unwarrantedly and leaving a mess wherever it has intervened. These authors also feel that the alternative to a world dominated by the US is "No One's World"—again a very questionable proposition as it declares no confidence in international institutions such as the UN, the International Court of Justice etc. as conflict resolution mechanisms. These authors consider that right now there is no power good enough and benign enough to supplant the US and if the US is disabled to play this kind of a role, "for the first time in history the world will have no global guardian". These views may not find wide acceptance but surely several Americans still think on these lines.

In the backyard of the US, there seems to be a resurgence of "anti-capitalism" with significant socialistic overtones caused primarily by growing inequalities of income and opportunities in several Latin American countries. This is a discomfiting development from the US's point of view, leading to the possibility of an invitation to China, for carving out a new area of influence in an arena which the US has always considered its pocket borough. Cuba it must be noted is however at last taking the first steps to get out of the rigidities of the Castro brand of Communism. Chile has for some time now been regarded as a country set to become the first developed country of Latin America. Its income per head has tripled since 1990 and is now around US $ 16000. Its success was based on the formula of; a free market economy, backed by rule of law and a fiscally responsible state. For the past year however this model has been under attack with student demonstrations demanding free education, greater state intervention and a definite shift towards welfarism.

In Western Europe, except Germany all others are facing serious economic down turn. 'Welfarism' gone mad, has landed many countries in grave debt crises needing bailouts at humiliating terms. Efforts to cut back on Governments handouts and profligacy have met with serious civil unrest. The Euro is under threat as the Euro Zone countries had surrendered their autonomy with respect to their monetary policies to the EU bureaucracy. Countries which did not have the economic strength of the original members of the Euro Zone joined the EU with misguided enthusiasm and are unable to withstand the strains of common economic policies.

It needs to be however reaffirmed that the grand idea of European integration was without doubt an antidote to the madness that had almost destroyed the Western civilization. It was inspired by statecraft regarded by some as undemocratic and too bureaucratic but answered the deep anxieties of Europeans who after the Second World War feared the ghastly cycle of economic depression, instability and wars that had plagued Europe for more than a century and a half. They were caught between the horror of German revanchist tendencies and the nightmare of a Communist takeover. The architects of the European idea opted for a basically bureaucratic structure instead of a more popular oriented system, as in the past such popular enthusiasm had given rise to both Fascism and Communism. It cannot be denied that this mechanism had indeed given Europe what can justifiably be called the longest uninterrupted period of peace and prosperity after all the ravages of wars right from the time of the French Revolution. Grave doubts are being expressed in the face of the crisis that has spread from Greece to Italy to Spain and Portugal, the Euro can survive. These doubts have not been fully dispelled as yet. Even if the leadership, particularly of Germany and France as well as the European Central Bank, is able to muster the will to take hard decisions, risk to the Euro and the EU can be eliminated only if Europe finds answers to some of the fundamental questions which it has run away from for many years. Europe and for that matter the US have now to devise ways of responding to the new world rapidly changing around them. Globalization has already stripped the West of its monopoly over technologies that had made them rich. Europe has an ageing population and its governments have spent so much of their energy, time and resources to build model welfare societies without matching efforts on the part of its citizenry that these governments may be hard put to keep the present levels of welfarism. It is possible that Europe will have to settle for a further decline in growth rates, lowering of living standards, doses of austerity and unemployment. The divergence in the levels of development between northern and southern Europe can also cause problems. Basically, the tendency to borrow and spend instead of saving and investing and over-dependence on government will have to change.

Western Europe is also facing, threats similar to the US with restive ethnic minorities, growing influence of radical Islam and changing demographic profiles. Foreign policy postures which are interpreted as aligned to US interests and supportive of Israel appear to invite angry reactions, providing fertile soil for promoting radical religious-oriented agendas. Actions by NATO and the US in Afghanistan and Iraq are adding to Muslim anger and are radicalizing Muslim youth to seek retribution. This has at the same time, resulted in growing anti Muslim sentiments in many European countries and in the US leaving many to wonder if the "Clash of Civilizations" between the Islamic and Christian world is slowly but surely underway.

Eastern Europe has had to deal with the problems of transition from Communism to democratic forms of governance, whilst established institutional frameworks have collapsed, causing a great deal of misery to the people, long used an intrusive but protective system, which had ensured satisfaction of basic minimum needs. The population of some of these countries is ageing and declining. Ukraine has been showing the steepest decline in numbers. At the same time the vast untapped natural resources particularly energy, have attracted large investments which while improving prospects of growth, have widened disparities and disturbed the sedate and even pace of life under Communism. A new oligarchy that is corrupt to the core has replaced the old. No doubt some countries such as Poland and Ukraine have started to succeed and have made visible progress. China, Russia and Japan and a host of western companies are competing for a share of the energy output of this region.

It would appear that the economic, technological and political dominance of Europe for some 300 years and the US for the past century is slowly but surely coming to a close. The pendulum is swinging eastward and China is surely attempting to become the dominant power in the 21st century. It may not altogether succeed as it has a host of unresolved internal and external issues and in terms of both economic and technological strengths it is still far behind the West. It is catching up, however, in many ways under a determined leadership. Its rise makes a whole lot of players nervous and a world dominated by China may not be altogether stable.

On the other hand India is seen as a less aggressive and accommodating player by the West and many in South-East Asia. India needs to take full account of these developments and play its cards with finesse, to emerge as a power which can balance China and be a factor in world stability. We ought to prepare ourselves for a multi-polar world with power centres in US, Latin America, Europe, China, Russia and Indonesia—all competing for influence through a variety of means. New alliance, new regional groupings and new methods of international cooperation may have to be evolved. The existing institutions for economic and security management of the world will have to undergo substantial changes. The US in this context taking note of the anxiety of Asia-Pacific nations with respect to the new assertiveness of China has started signaling that its presence in the region will continue and may in fact be strengthened. The decision of the US President to attend the East-Asia Summit a grouping of Asia-Pacific nations including India and Myanmar (November 2011) in Bali, Indonesia and its decision to enter into an enhanced military and strategic relationship with Australia signal clearly that the US does not plan to yield ground to China in the foreseeable future and will maintain its deterrent in the area. The stationing of marines in Darwin-North Australia though at the moment a small 2,500 but to be increased over time and the joint visit of Julia Gillard, the Australian PM and Barack Obama to that northern tip of Australia which occupies a commanding position in both the Indian and pacific Oceans underline this commitment drawing icy comments from China as a manifestation of US intentions of encircling China. As an answer to the aggressiveness of China in the region the South East Asian nations are also furiously acquiring a whole lot of weaponry and strengthening their armed forces particularly their navies.

One must however take a balanced view of all these important developments. While undeniably China is rapidly increasing its military and economic might and becoming more aggressive in its international postures it is a country that is, in my view both feared and hated in equal measure. The negatives that must be entered into the equation are that China is still far behind the US in both technological and military strength. Its per capita GDP is nowhere near even middle income countries. There are vast income disparities and in fact China's 'gini coefficient' is a shade worse than that of India. The gini coefficient of China has been worsening from the 1990s. It is presided over by a discredited and failed political system that carries out large scale of human rights abuses and has a nervous regime fearful of its own people. It brutally suppresses the people of Tibet and Xinxiang and is nervous of the possibility of Inner Mongolia breaking away. More than anything else China's moral standing in the eyes of the world, what can be termed as the 'moral wealth' is relatively low. The US, despite its own poor record in the past and open interference in the internal affairs of many a country still is the repository of the great ideas of liberty, equality, democracy, individual initiative, freedom of thought and expression and human rights. Its constitution was inspired by some of the greatest thinkers the world has ever produced. It is still perceived, except by those, who are blinded by religious fanaticism, as a force for good and has learnt its lessons from past experience.

Nevertheless it would appear that a new chapter in geopolitics is being played out in the Asia-Pacific region. The United States is looking to the Asia-Pacific countries to help it to regain its economic momentum. On the other hand the countries of this region while recognizing the intensification of the US-China rivalry, would like to benefit economically from China's growth while ensuring that their security is assured by the US. Each of them is undertaking a delicate balancing act.

Russia is also struggling to manage the transformation from Communism into a form of capitalism. Blessed with vast natural resources, the country is anxious to retain its influence in world affairs, but is plagued by corruption assuming endemic proportions, growing disparities in incomes and levels of living, declining population and failure of the new system to provide even a modicum of security and basic services to a population long used to the stability and security of the "*ancien régime*". It has also to deal with the ongoing conflict in Chechnya where militant Islam has played a role. Its recent economic upsurge has been highly uneven and has created tensions and fissures in the society. Recent events indicate that the country's "managed democracy" with the media muzzled and only tame opposition permitted is under threat. While the elections had greatly reduced the share of votes for Putin's United Russia what is important that there have been widespread demonstrations against this victory. Putin who was personally popular and who could keep the populace well looked after cashing in on the high oil prices may find that both these advantages may not continue for too long. Repression which has worked so far may also become counterproductive and today with the internet, twitters, blogs etc. discontent can spread much faster than ever before. The real solutions to contain the rising discontent, namely opening the economy, curbing corruption and reforming institutions especially the judicial system and getting rid of cronyism so far have not found a place in Putin's arsenal. The Russians still long for a strong leader and Putin can provide the much-needed stability and remove the rigidities in the system. He cannot afford to think that time is on his side.

Japan which had been an economic power house for long is now entering a difficult phase. China is all set to overtake it as far as economic and military strength is concerned. China will be overtaking Japan in terms of GDP as well. The Japanese population is ageing and shrinking. The economy is sluggish and consumption growth too is sluggish. Japanese firms find it impossible to expand domestically. The yen has been getting stronger making exports all the more difficult. Its big companies are now busy expanding abroad and acquiring stakes in many overseas companies.

Japan is also plagued by scandals and far too frequent political changes and its international profile can undergo changes. It is therefore anxious to strengthen its ties with the US, the West and India mainly to safeguard its long-term security interests.

The Middle East is easily the most volatile region of the world with violence being taken for granted as an integral part of daily life. The Israel-Arab conflict is getting more complicated by the day. The signs of flexibility that had emerged in the last part of the 20th century have all but disappeared. New factors and players have entered the fray, with Iran emerging as an important regional power with its own radical agenda. Apart from the rhetoric of wiping out Israel from the world Map, the entry of Shia Iran with substantive influence and hold in Lebanon and Iraq and a collaborative relationship with Syria has the potential of multiplying the complexity of the situation manifold. The invasion of Iraq and the regime change there has also transformed the historic Arab-Persian rivalries into a broader Shia-Sunni divide. To find a common ground between the Arabs and Iran, between the Shias and the Sunnis, or the way forward to deal with the Israel-Palestinian question is, itself fraught with grave difficulties and even if such a common ground can be found, to get Israel to come to terms with such a stance seems to be a hopeless dream at least at the moment. There is a new mood of defiance in the Middle East caused by the stalemate in the Israeli-Hezbollah War, with Hezbollah claiming victory over Israel leading to the possibly ill-founded belief that a Muslim army can take on Israel and defeat it. It would appear that when it comes to confronting Israel the age old Shia-Sunni antagonism can be temporarily set aside. In the entire region, there is a continuous rise in the hostility towards US, attributed to the American intervention in Iraq, its policies towards Iran, its support for autocratic regimes while talking of democracy, and unqualified support for Israel, all seen and interpreted as anti-Islam.

The possible emergence of Iran as a nuclear power within the foreseeable future has already sent shivers down the spines of quite a few Western powers and in the neighbourhood as well. Israel is greatly and justifiably alarmed, and if the United Nations' initiatives to contain Iran's nuclear ambitions do not work, Israel may take unilateral action, raising the level of tension in the area and laying the seeds for a new round of conflict. Iran is a self proclaimed regional power and its defiant posture while earning the grudging admiration of others, is discomfiting to the Sunni States in the region who already face internal threats from radical elements. Iran has threatened to shut down the gulf of Hormuz—a vital channel for international trade, if oil embargo is enforced fully and such a provocation may compel the international community to take active steps to keep the channel open if necessary with armed intervention. Iran is playing a clever 'cat and mouse' game offering to resume dialogue when under pressure and withdrawing from the dialogue process when it finds it convenient. While repeatedly claiming that its nuclear programmes are only for peaceful energy generation it continues to fortify some of the nuclear facilities in order to withstand any attack. It is in these fortified facilities that it is suspected that enrichment of uranium does take place of bomb to grade levels.

Iran has never explained as to why it needs a nuclear energy programme at all, and is spending billions of dollars to build one facility after another, when it has the world's second biggest oil reserves. Iran is a signatory of the nuclear non proliferation treaty and had concealed its nuclear programme from the IAEA for years. It is only when some of the dissident groups revealed the existence of such a clandestine programme that the world and the IAEA woke up to this reality. An Israeli attack whether supported by the US or not can have unpredictable consequences. The chances of totally destroying Iran's weapons programme seem to be remote given the operational difficulties of targeting the underground and heavily guarded facilities. The Muslim world may unite against the West and Israel and give a huge fillip to international terrorism. To my mind as an alternative to armed intervention, if the US and the West can take concerted action-reduce consumption, release the substantial strategic oil reserves held by the US etc. promote alternative energies—to bring down the price of oil to say $80 or less the Iranian regime will collapse. It is the high oil prices which has enabled Iran and other autocratic regimes in the Middle-East to keep themselves in power. A combination of suppression and distribution of largesse is what keeps these regimes afloat. There may be no need to launch an attack on Iran, if the people rise against the regime and this can happen when Iran's economy already under severe strain because of the ongoing sanctions, is unable to afford the huge subsidies being provided to the people.

The current developments in Syria where a virtual civil war is being waged to unseat Bashir Al Assad are turning into one more contest between Iran and the Arabs and a new manifestation of the Shia-Sunni conflict. It may be recalled that till Hafiz Assad the father of the present ruler took over Syria was a weak and unstable state and many international rivalries were played out. While the present struggle is primarily between the regime and its people it is also a war by proxy for regional powers, primarily between Iran and the Arab countries. It is also a contest of will between the West on the one hand and Russia and China on the other. The UN conflict resolution mechanisms are being out to a severe test as evidenced by the Kofi Annan mission which has managed to broker a tenuous cease fire after a protracted effort. This ceasefire has already broken down and the pile-up of bodies continues. Having built an axis consisting of itself as the major player with Hezbollah in Lebanon, Hamas in Gaza, Syria and the regime in Iraq its clout was seen as increasing with its nuclear and missile programme. A collapse of Bashir Assad, if it does take place will deal a heavy blow to this axis. In counter moves against the growing strength of Iran, Turkey which had maintained friendly relations with Syria has turned hostile mainly because of the repercussions on its Kurdish minority. The Arab league dominated by Saudi Arabia sees the unrest in Syria as a chance to end the dominance of the minority Alawite sect while combating Iran's regional ambitions. Israel which was friendly with Syria is unhappy after the discovery of the secret relations that Syria had built with North Korea and would be inclined to support any move to reduce Iran's regional hegemony.

In the meanwhile the Syrian regime has unleashed unprecedented violence against its own people inviting international condemnation. Some ten thousand people have been killed and thousands have sought refuge across the border in Syria. Only Russia and China are as yet unprepared to write off Assad. The Russians are worried about the fate of their naval base in Syria. Sectarian conflict between Alawites and Sunnis, with widespread cases of murder and kidnapping has occurred in cities such as Horns and Hama and even in Aleppo. The Christians are under threat as well and many would prefer to migrate than get killed in the sectarian conflict. The Alawites and Christians account for just about 20 per cent of the population. That most Syrians have had some basic military training and weapons are widely available makes the mixture all the more lethal. The problem confronted by all of Syria's neighbours and indeed the entire region is that a collapse of the Assad regime will have serious repercussions for many countries as there are restive populations in each of them—Kurds in Turkey and Iraq, Sunnis in Iraq, Shias in Bahrain, Muslims and Christians in Lebanon and Egypt—increasing the potential for instability and violence. The war weary West-US, NATO—whose interventions at huge cost in Iraq and Afghanistan have yielded none of the results expected—is reluctant to get into Syria.

This entire area is it appears condemned to remain prone to confrontation conflict and violence in the foreseeable future. That this area is the repository of an overwhelming proportion of the world's fossil fuels, on which the world will continue to depend for the next few decades, means that the world's vital economic interests are hostage to any instability and conflict in this area. The oil importing countries such as ours are bound to be affected by the increases in oil prices which happen whenever tension escalates in this region.

The Middle East security scenario has assumed even greater volatility due to the basically uncalled for US intervention in Iraq. While regime change was achieved none of the other declared US aims have fructified. Iraq has been sucked into a quagmire of sectarian conflict, opening the door for radical Islamic elements to enter the arena, increasing the hostility towards the US and the West to new levels. Here again, the conflict is being interpreted in civilizational terms—Islam *vs* the West, the US being the main adversary. As of now daily bloodletting on an unprecedented scale is occurring in large parts of Iraq particularly in Baghdad, with civil war raging, except that no one is as yet ready to apply this appellation. The exit of US forces has opened the doors for elements such as Al Qaeda to enlarge their presence and one witnesses daily carnages caused by the intensification of the Shia-Sunni conflict. The Sunnis who were dominant under Saddam Hussein and routinely oppressed the Shia majority are unhappy that their dominance has come to an end and use every possible opportunity to express their anger by targeted killing of Shias, particularly in public gatherings and pilgrim centres. The Shia's holiest site—Karbala has witnessed the most ghastly massacres in recent times. Iran it appears is emerging as a key player and its influence is increasing in the Shia-dominated Government. Many analysts have been expressing the fear that what is happening in Iraq, consequent upon the exit of US forces can happen on a much larger scale in post 2014 Afghanistan, where the number of mutually hostile elements are if any larger, much better equipped and motivated and infected with a strong religious zeal. Some are the proteges of Pakistan. Afghanistan seems to be all set for a new round of bloodletting.

The past year has seen what is characterized as the "Arab Spring", a revolution to throw out dictators across the Saharan belt. Long standing, despotic, and oppressive but basically secular and pro-Western regimes have seen their end in Tunisia and Egypt. In Libya the Gaddafi regime has let loose a civil war, which has caused grave damage to the economy and considerable loss of life. Gaddafi has been eliminated brutally and the country has now to go through the painful process of transition and reconstruction. In Syria there is prolonged unrest. The revolt in Bahrain has been suppressed violently with Saudi armed intervention, while that in Yemen is getting more and more violent. Bahrain has again erupted with violence and the Shia majority is keen to get rid of the Sunni dominated governing system. It may be noted that the uprisings have taken place mainly in the less endowed nations, who do not have the ability to distribute infinite amounts of largesse. Saudi Arabia has so far managed to ensure that its regime, even if oppressive and obscurantist in character, remains fully in control and has even intervened in Bahrain to suppress the Shia majority.

The question remains as to what will be the character of the regimes that will replace the fallen dictators. In the absence of viable institutional systems to replace the dictators except the army, the possibility of extremist elements such as the Muslim brotherhood, taking control can be a worrying prospect for the West and Israel and indeed the rest of the world. In Tunisia, in the just completed elections in October 2011—the Islamist party Ennahda (renaissance) banned earlier as a terrorist group, has won 41 per cent of the seats, namely 89 out of 217 members in the constituent assembly. Its support mainly comes from the more conservative rural areas. Will they increase their share when under the new constitution, they may reverse progressive legislations such right to abortion, prohibition of polygamy, etc. In Egypt as well, the Islamic parties have won a large number of seats. Will the Arab spring become a nightmare for the rest of the world? The Muslim brotherhood has won some 46 per cent of the seats and what is more frightening is the fact that the Salafists who espouse an extreme form of Islam have won 21 per cent of the seats. The Salafists desire to emulate the ideal that prevailed at the time of the Prophet and his companions and decry all Western ways of living. They want to ban interest in banks, want women to fully covered, want them confined to the home and are severely antagonistic to all other belief systems including other sects of Islam. What will be the fate of Christian, Jews and minorities of Egypt and women if the two parties come together and what will be the policy towards Israel and the West?

While in the Parliamentary elections which ended in January 2012 the Muslim brotherhood won some 47 per cent seats a sizeable number went to the Salafists. In the Presidential elections due on 23rd May, 2012 the most popular among all the contenders, attracting huge crowds, is an arch Salafist Abu Ismail who wants to liberate Egypt from subservience to Israel. His domestic agenda may scare all tourists and deal a severe blow to possibly the biggest single foreign exchange earner of Egypt. He wants to lower the age of marriage. Abu Ismail a lawyer-cum-sermonizer promises to take Egypt back to the days of the Prophet in the seventh century CE. No doubt there are quite a few other contenders including the former intelligence chief of Hosni Mubarak but with the Parliament already under the control of the Muslim brotherhood, if a Salafist does indeed become the next Pharaoh of Egypt the Middle East would have taken one more step towards becoming a wholly radicalized region. Fortunately the Election Commission has disqualified Abu Ismail along with nine others.

Even in Morocco, Islamists of similar inclinations have won handsomely while in Gaza, Hamas which is close to the Muslim brotherhood is well entrenched. In Iran and Algeria, revolutionary movements have not led to more inclusive polity or greater gender equality and in fact, the reverse has happened. While the Arabs are turning to Islamist parties and Saudi Arabia has resisted all efforts to reform and remains as obscurantist as ever with an intolerant clerical establishment, two other great peoples of the region, the Persians and the Turks are both under the sway of governments with an Islamic label though with wildly different hues. Indeed, political Islam has today much more clout in the entire region than at any time since the end of the Ottoman Empire. All these are of serious concern to the liberals and secularists in these countries, women's groups, human rights campaigners and no doubt, foreign policy mandarins the worldover. Increasing radicalism can enable forces such as Al Qaeda to acquire wider influence though so far in the Arab spring, the part played by Al Qaeda has not been significant. It is possible that the entire arc of countries from Algeria to Pakistan may get more radicalized. There seems to be some evidence of this happening as seen by the way the minorities—Coptic Christians—are being targeted in Egypt and the fact that the Israeli embassy in Cairo was attacked.

The minorities have suffered immensely in Somalia and in Sudan as also in Nigeria. An organization called 'Boko Haram' which rejects everything that is regarded as Western has regularly targeted Christians with great violence. Women who had advanced rapidly in countries such as Tunisia and Egypt may see a definite setback with respect to their rights and freedom.

The developments in recent weeks indicate that in all the countries where regime changes have taken place, the status of both women and minorities has declined and all the liberal measures taken by the earlier regimes, to remove the more oppressive aspects of treatment meted out to women and minorities have been dismantled progressively and the application of what is termed as Sharia Law has been stepped up.

The 'Arab Spring' has also opened the door for intensification of Shia-Sunni rivalries and competition between the Saudis and the Iranians to expand their areas of influence. Shia Iran supports Syria while Saudi Arabia supports the opposition. The mainly Shia uprising in Bahrain was aided by Iran but suppressed through armed intervention by the Saudis. In Yemen as well, this rivalry is being played out. Iran has created a host of Shiite militias in the area the chief of which is Hezbollah who can stir up trouble. The Saudis are particularly wary of Iran's mischief in the eastern provinces of Saudi Arabia which has a sizeable Shia population. The Americans with their traditional hostility to Iran are doing their best to counter Iran but considering their own problems, their ability to influence events is declining. The Arab spring is already turning into an Islamic winter and may even become a nightmare. Will this compel the world's economies to reduce their dependence on fossil fuels at a faster pace? To my mind, this more than anything else, will reduce the potential of radical Islam to be a grave threat to the rest of the world.

One year after the uprisings collectively called the Arab Spring, there are extremely troubling signs that the promise of true democracy is nowhere in sight and on the other hand, along with creeping Islamization, there is sharp increase in the level of polarization and sectarianism in the entire region. Political parties closely aligned with specific sects—Sunnis and Shias—have been steadily gaining ground. There is also the increasing intolerance displayed by both the sects towards each other and this easily translates into mindless violence and loss of innocent lives, given the easy availability of lethal weaponry all over and the virtual collapse of systems of governance. It appears that even if elections are held in all these countries, either the Shias or the Sunnis will be in power depending upon who is in a majority and since all the states have Shias and Sunnis conflicts, often violent are bound to be endemic. The Al-Qaeda, mainly Sunni, can have a field day in such as situation. A Sunni Islamist television channel recently called for Jihad against all Shias throughout the region while radical Shias prophesize that they will inherit all Muslim lands including those held by Sunnis with the much anticipated arrival of the hidden Imam. In Iraq the Shia-Sunni divide is getting worse by the day. Both Sunni and Shia parts of the country are pressing for more regional autonomy suggesting that political boundaries may soon cement sectarian divisions. Institutions such as universities, decimated by years of brain drain, limp along divided into sectarian fiefs, faculty by faculty. The unrest in the region has reinforced the divisions, with the Shia led government vocally supporting Shia protesters in Bahrain while Sunni activists stage rallies in solidarity with the mostly Sunni rebels of Syria. The Iraqi Parliament barely functions divided as it is on sectarian lines and deep seated animosities.

Will democracy and pluralism triumph in the Arab world? The Tunisians have held elections, while the Egyptians and Moroccans have also had free elections, at a time when the world over, democracy itself is losing some of its appeal as the most preferred political system. Politicians in many countries are plagued by scandals of one type or the other. Stagnant living standards, high inflation, poor economic management, social inequality and corruption have no doubt eroded faith in democracy. What need to be achieved are better standards of governance and superior economic management and to my mind, democracy in spite of its limitations remains the best of possible alternatives which promise the dreaded Gulag Archipelago and suppression.

It needs to be stressed that all the Arab countries confront humongous economic problems caused by huge and sustained increases in population. Those with huge oil revenues, keep the growing population quiet by enlarging freebies and subsidizing everything. They also consume more and more of their oil resources to provide water for their people and for keeping their citizens in air-conditioned comfort. The ever increasing expenditure bill has been met only because of increase in crude prices and if the crude prices dip below say US $100, the regimes cannot sustain such profligacy. All Arab countries whether with oil or without oil, face acute shortages of water, have to purify sea water at great cost and have to import almost all their food. With food prices shooting up all over the world, import bills are shooting up. In 2007-08, some staple items doubled in prices and in Egypt, food prices rose by 37 per cent in 2008-10. Such developments have increased the level of dissatisfaction across the countries in the Middle East. The stability of this sensitive region is under serious threat and one wonders how democracy or indeed any of the present systems of governance, can rise to the occasion and make effective attempts to solve the region's problems.

Closer home, the conflict in Afghanistan continues practically unabated with the US and NATO achieving only limited successes, casting a deep shadow on the entire border between Afghanistan and Pakistan. The Hamid Karzai regime is seen to be ineffective and corrupt and its writ runs only in limited areas. Recent operations, particularly in southern Afghanistan and drone attacks by the US into Pakistan, can possibly reduce the areas controlled by the Taliban, but so long as the source of the problem, namely the almost limitless supply of foot soldiers for Islam fully indoctrinated by a militant ideology, backed by abundant availability of weapons and support by elements within the Government of Pakistan, is not effectively dealt with, the Afghanistan situation cannot be resolved and will continue to boil. The planned and well executed attack on the heavily fortified diplomatic enclave in Kabul on the 15th of April, 2012 combined with the attack on the Prison at Bannu in Pakistan resulting in the release of nearly 400 Taliban fighters clearly signal that the Taliban retains its lethal ability to strike at will. The prospects for peace in Afghanistan is today perhaps more fragile than a year back and the international community will have to ponder deeply, as to in what way it can insulate Afghanistan from the possible take-over by Taliban and descent into chaos and civil war. The US and NATO should not ignore ground realities and exit from Afghanistan without making alternative arrangements to ensure peace and stability in that country. One possible option is for the UN to take over from the ISAF with a clear mandate to help the Afghan Government to get rid of the likes of Taliban.

Afghanistan has alleged that it is the Haqqani network that carried the attack on the diplomatic enclave in Kabul. The attack seems to have all the standard features of a Haqqani carnage. This once again emphatically brings out that the problems of Afghanistan originate in Pakistan and no solution can be found so long as Pakistan continues to harbour a variety of militant outfits and they are permitted to roam around, collect funds, train fighters and arm them and are able to cross the border to create mayhem and get back to the safety of Pakistan. The solution to the Afghan problem lies in Pakistan and the international community has so far shown no inclination to punish Pakistan for such open support to terrorism. Pakistan for all intents and purposes is a terrorist state, should be declared to be so and dealt with accordingly.

It seems that the American establishment has started recognizing that the strategic interests of the US and Pakistan are in conflict and not harmony and will remain so as long as Pakistan harbours regional ambitions and continues its policy of challenging India in every possible way. The Americans may have to consider a policy of containment of Pakistan which can be done if military aid is cut off, while encouraging trade and economic ties. The much exaggerated threat from India needs to be shown as what it really is, namely an excuse for the army to retain its control over Pakistan.

It is very interesting in this context, to note the blunt views of author, journalist and thinker Christopher Hitchens who died in December 2011, who provides an account of the stupidity of US policy of molly-coddling Pakistan. While characterizing Pakistan as a venal and shameless artificial state, he maintains that 'the two main symbols of Pakistan's pride—its army and its nuclear programme—are wholly parasitic on American indulgence and patronage.' In a July 2011 essay in 'Vanity Fair', he berates the "big rich and dumb Americans" for not understanding that the army and the nukes from that degraded country are intended for one purpose only, namely war against the neighbouring democracy. He is of the view that proliferation activities are a threat to US's interests. He stated that the US belief that if it stops swallowing its pride, the Pakistani oligarchy will behave even more abysmally than what it already does and the situation will get worse, is fatally flawed as the awful historical fact is that each time the Pakistani leadership behaved badly or worsened its behaviour, it was handsomely rewarded by the United States. He goes on to scold the US by stating "we have been the enablers of every stage of that wretched state's counter revolution, to the point where it is a serious regional menace, an undisguised ally of our worst enemies, and a sworn enemy of some of our best allies." It may be added that Hitchens was an unabashed admirer of India's multicultural polity and a great defender of freedom of expression. He was one of the first to spring to the defence of Salman Rushdie after the Iranian Fatwa against Rushdie and was a relentless campaigner against all forms of tyranny courageously accusing Henry Kissinger of war crimes and crimes against humanity.

The projected withdrawal of the US and NATO forces in 2014, while creating whole lot of uncertainties has catalyzed players in Pakistan to try and capture the power structure that may emerge, and make it serve their interests alone. Pakistan retains its influence through the Afghan Taliban and terrorist outfits such as the Haqquani network and the vacuum that may develop when the Americans withdraw, will be used by Pakistan through its proxies who have been so strongly supported by it all along. Pakistan has refused to take action against these outfits in spite of immense pressure from the US, as it sees the US as an exhausted power tired of the Afghan misadventure and itching to get out. It sees the Afghan Taliban and other insurgents as its assets which will ensure that it alone determines the fate of Afghanistan in the post-2014 period. The Haqqani network have been allowed to establish and run one of the largest religious school (madrasa), namely the Drul Uloom Haqqani, well-known for supplying a large number of fighters for both the Afghan and Pakistani Taliban. Thousands of graduates from this school located in Akora Khattak, just an hour away from the capital, Islamabad. The Haqqqani brothers, Jalaluddin and Khalid and their sons openly move about the whole country, own several houses including at least one in the capital, visit military establishments and participate in the graduation ceremonies. They have links with both the Afghan and the Pakistani Taliban but the Pakistani establishment is unwilling to deal with this outfit as it regards them as its most valuable asset capable of influencing the post-2014 situation in Afghanistan in its favour. The threat of American aid—both military and civilian—drying up has so far not been enough to persuade Pakistan to stop its support to these bodies. Pakistan is also hell bent on ensuring that India has no say at all in Afghanistan and is using the Afghan Taliban as the instrument to achieve this objective. Pakistan has openly admitted that in the face of India, Iran and Russia trying to gain influence in Afghanistan through investments and projects, Pakistan cannot keep quiet and the insurgents are its only investments which can yield dividends in the post-2014 scenario. Pakistan is also apparently confident that China will bail it out financially and militarily in case the Americans finally turn against it. Pakistan calculates that its privileged position in Afghanistan will enable it to enhance its leverage with China when it comes to exploiting Afghanistan's rich mineral and energy resources. Pakistan is also confident that the support it has from China and Saudi Arabia will enable it to face down the US. The army which dictates foreign and nuclear policy in Pakistan seems to think that Pakistan is invulnerable as it controls NATO's supply line from Karachi to Kabul and it has a rapidly expanding arsenal of nuclear weapons. The army thinks that time is on their side, that NATO is doomed to give up in Afghanistan, leaving them free to act as they wish in Afghanistan. They want the Western powers to believe the war in Afghanistan is hopeless and encourage militia groups to speed up the withdrawal by launching more spectacular attacks. However, China will help so long it suits its own interests but may not go all out to rub the US on the wrong side. The Saudis, whose relationship with the US is very close, may support Pakistan only up to a point. So far at least, apart from subsidized oil from the Saudis, the aid from both China and the Saudis is very small compared to the vast military and economic aid of US which has given Pakistan some US $20 billion even after 9/11. In 2008, China did not loosen its purse strings but sent Pakistan to the IMF for a bailout package. China is unhappy as regards support by Pakistan-based militants to the Uighurs in Turkmenistan and there have been instances of attacks on Chinese workers. China has withdrawn from a US $19 billion project in southern Pakistan.

Many analysts are of the view that Pakistan does not really want a stable and secure Afghanistan with a credible system of government. It would prefer a Taliban controlled and chaotic country with a semi-permanent civil war condition. Pakistan feels that if normalcy returns and an independent a respected government is in position it may well reactivate the border dispute with Pakistan. No self-respecting Pashtun has ever accepted the Durand Line as the Pashtuns claim, with great justification that this border was imposed on them by the British in 1893. Their ambition is to have a "unique, unified and separate Pashtun identity and home land extending from Kandahar to Attock on the banks of the Indus". The late Khan Abdul Gaffar Khan it may be recalled showed his disdain pointedly for the Durand line by insisting that his body be taken across the Durand Line and buried in Jalalabad in Afghanistan. Surely a nightmare for the rulers of Pakistan and they will exploit every available means to avoid such an eventuality. Pakistan has not so far realized that if indeed the Afghan Taliban comes to power it may not be long before it tends to gravitate towards supporting the Pakistan Taliban (TTP) and its Punjabi associates including Lashkar-e-Toiba all of whom belong to the Doebandhi tradition, against mainly the Barlevi oriented establishment in Pakistan. There is already a chasm between the Pakistani establishment and the Taliban and other Deobandhi zealots on both sides of the Durand line.

The loss of export earnings and remittances, if relations with the US rupture on the other hand, can wreck its economy. Pakistan may consider itself safe with its growing nuclear arsenal and its army as well as the support of unconventional forces in terms of the Taliban etc. but a nation cannot live by nukes alone and the Haqqanis and the Taliban and especially the Pashtuns may have their own agendas. After upping the ante for weeks, Pakistan has started promising the US that it is ready to address its concerns regarding the Haqqani network. Many analysts believe that Pakistan cannot really afford to bring about a complete rupture of relations with the US. A lot of the anti-US rhetoric is an act of bravado by hot heads who do not understand the real consequences of their actions. There can be little doubt that the State of Pakistan is facing a crisis with bankruptcy looming ahead, being blamed by the US for engineering its defeat in Afghanistan, considered by the world as the epicentre of terrorism and critically dependent upon remittances and aid. The EU and even Canada have lost all patience with Pakistan's duplicity and questions are being raised as to why aid should at all be given to Pakistan, when all it does is to attack and kill soldiers of these countries in Afghanistan. Some are again talking of Pakistan's preparedness to 'eat grass' rather than depend on the US, as they did when in answer to India's acquisition of nuclear technology, in their anxiety to acquire nuclear weapons they made a similar boast. In this, they are ignoring the stark realities. Today economically Pakistan is, in a far worse position than what it was even 5 years back. With an increase in the percentage of people below the poverty line from 27 per cent to 33 per cent, more people are already probably eating grass. The fiscal deficit is up from 4.5 per cent to 8 per cent, the Pakistani rupee down from 77 to 90 per US dollar, inflation some 15 per cent and food inflation over 25 per cent, this proposition can be regarded as true. All this has happened even when aid from the US had not stopped; it can easily be imagined what can happen if the aid is indeed altogether cut off. Yes, the grass eaters are the poor and wretched and not the golf playing generals or the politicians or the corrupt judges and civil servants. The same Pakistanis who claim that they can rely on the Saudis know that the Saudis use Pakistanis to fight the Israelis through their proxies, kill Shias in Bahrain and treat the immigrants as slaves in Saudi Arabia. Very few complain about all this.

Pakistan's influence is basically with the Pakhtun segment of Afghan population which no doubt constitutes a major part. However, other ethnic components such as the Tajiks, Hazaras and Uzbeks have no love for Pakistan. It may be recalled that Ahmed Shah Masood known as the lion of Panjshir, the most competent Tajik commander who fought against the Soviets was killed by the ISI of Pakistan, as he was the commander of the Northern alliance which was successfully combating the Taliban. To work out an arrangement which is satisfactory to all these ethnic entities, as also to Pakistan will surely be a nightmare. Pakistan believes that just as it happened when the Soviets withdrew, the Taliban will sweep the whole country, and it will achieve its dream of converting Afghanistan into its client State. Whether the Afghans who suffered so much during the last rule of the Taliban are prepared for this, whether even if the Pakhtuns accept this, what will be the reaction of the other ethnic entities, what will be the reaction of the rest of the world which may face new threats, from a Taliban-controlled Afghanistan providing safe havens once again to Al-Qaeda and other radical elements, are all really worrying questions. Can the world afford to permit creation of another Somalia or Yemen from where every part of the world can be threatened merely, because Pakistan considers this to be in its strategic interest? The possibility of the situation degenerating into a renewed conflict among the various ethnic groups and reenactment of the scenario that developed when the Soviets withdrew from Afghanistan cannot be discounted. What is happening in Iraq after the withdrawal of US forces can happen in Afghanistan in a far more ghastly form.

India's security interests can be very seriously undermined by such developments. India needs to work with the saner elements in Afghanistan who desire a strong Indian presence and the rest of the world, to prevent such a development from taking place. India needs to confidently assert its right to play a constructive role in Afghanistan and need not be excessively sensitive to the so called interests of Pakistan. The future of Afghanistan no doubt, needs to be determined by its own people which means by all the ethnic groups. The Pashtuns form some 42 to 46 per cent of the population of Afghanistan and on both sides of the Durand line, number some 45 to 50 million. (No one has accurate figures, as conducting a census in this area has never been possible). The 13 Pashtun majority provinces out of a total of 34 provinces of Afghanistan account for some 30 million people. The Taliban has overwhelming presence in these provinces and hence, will have to be a part of any political settlement. None of the players who have a say in the future of Afghanistan can ignore these fundamentals.

There is understandable anxiety in the US to withdraw from Afghanistan and the process of handing over security responsibilities to Afghan forces has begun. Public support for the war in Afghanistan has been rapidly going down in the US. The memories of Vietnam and the forthcoming Presidential elections have hastened the decline. However, the security situation has not improved and the attack on the UN office in Kabul, the murder of Rabbani have shown that the potential for violence continues to be high. There has been a 39 per cent increase in violent incidents in 2010 compared to 2009 and a similar trend in 2011 as per the UN Secretary General. As India's permanent representative in the UN argued, the troop withdrawal by the US must be related to the ground realities.

President Obama in his sudden visit to Kabul on the 2nd of May, 2012 signed a protocol for long term security cooperation between the US and Afghanistan. While this signals that the Americans do not want to be seen as abandoning Afghanistan as they did when the Soviets withdrew from that country, however, means that there will be drastic scaling down of US presence and the limited number of advisers will be confining themselves to only two roles, namely counter-terrorism and training. The American presence albeit limited is now assured up to 2024. American or NATO troops will not be there to fight the Taliban and such a role is supposed to be that of the Afghan troops. Whether the Afghan national forces are sufficiently equipped, trained and motivated to fight the emboldened Taliban—which can claim that it has defeated one more super-power—is a worrying question. The possibility of some of them defecting to the Taliban for ideological reasons or plain bribery cannot also be ruled out. This has happened in the past and Pashtun loyalties and kinship may also encourage switching sides. It is also unclear whether the huge costs involved in running the Afghan manned security apparatus will continue to be borne by the US/NATO. The projected draw-down of American and NATO forces may be winning brownie points for Barack Obama in the forthcoming elections and indeed the time table for withdrawal seems to be designed to achieve this very purpose, there is growing nervousness about the future of Afghanistan not only among the security observers but among large sections of the Afghans themselves as they see the return of the Taliban as a disaster and an end for the relative freedom that they have been enjoying and the visible improvements they have experienced in their daily lives. The Taliban staged a suicide attack within hours of Obama's departure in Kabul itself. The ground realities do not it appears warrant any hasty withdrawal on the scale envisaged. The Pakistani establishment may be rejoicing to witness these developments.

In our immediate neighbourhood, the hostility of Pakistan with its claims on Kashmir and more recently, its efforts to radicalize Indian Muslims encouraging them to fight a Jihad and its efforts to draft the services of Bangladesh and Nepal to carry anti-India activities poses serious challenges to India's security. Bangladesh which had unfortunately emerged as a sanctuary for India's insurgents has recently taken a series of measures which have been very helpful to India. The influence of radical Islam has also been brought under control in that country.

However, in Pakistan and to a lesser extent in Bangladesh, there are still powerful elements whose very rationale for existence is hostility towards India. These elements which are able to raise enormous resources, particularly from the Middle East, are driven by a militant ideology, consider it their business to impose a heavy cost on India through low-intensity warfare, active support to anti-India elements and anti-India activities even in foreign soil. Terrorist outfits also indulge in widespread kidnappings for ransom causing a lot of insecurity even in cities like Lahore.

Pakistan which claims that it is a major victim of terror has created a number of Frankenstein's monsters which have not only bred more such monsters but have also now come to haunt the creator. Under international pressure, Pakistan does ban one outfit or the other but these manage to revive themselves under new names or spawns new bodies more radical than the previous incarnation. The Tehrik-e-Taliban Pakistan and others have found many ways to keep their activities practically undiminished and collection of funds, recruitment, training and indoctrination continue unchecked. The latest is the Ghazi Force named after Abdul Rashid Ghazi who was killed during the raid on Lai Masjid in Islamabad in 2007 and its declared objective is to violently overthrow the present regime in Pakistan as it is not sufficiently Islamic, an objective it shares with TTP and the Al Qaeda. Ayman-al Zawahari has recently called upon all the people of Pakistan to rise in revolt and get rid of the present regime and establish a truly Islamic State in Pakistan. These monsters are given a free run in Pakistan as it considers these as its strategic assets in dealing both with India and Afghanistan, though they are increasingly a threat to Pakistan itself. The State of Pakistan in now entering a new stage of instability and is facing a series of internal threats to its very existence. For some time now, a debate has indeed been going on if Pakistan will survive as a united entity, given the numerous sectarian, communal, religious, social and economic conflicts that are getting worse by the day and the failure of all institutions of governance to do anything about this. Pakistan has also extremely lax laws relating to manufacture and possession of the most lethal weapons and consequently for quite some time now, there has been a thriving weapon manufacturing industry in Peshawar and other cities along the Afghan border, where the most destructive Uzis and Kalashnikovs can be easily purchased at very reasonable prices—perfect duplicates of the original. Also, huge quantities of all kinds of weapons that the Americans flooded into the area to fight the Soviets are in the hands of various terrorist groups, all carefully and affectionately looking after them to be used happily against the very people who supplied these. Part of this huge cache was taken away by the army which also gives it to terrorist outfits which it favours. General Hamid Gul who was at the time of the Soviet invasion of Afghanistan the chief of the ISI and is considered the patron in chief of all Jihadis and the Taliban, was proud of the fact that he had facilitated the distribution of arms among the insurgent groups favoured by him. He said that weapons are the ornaments of men and will be useful for Pakistan to combat its real enemies including India. Hamid Gul is a leading light in a conclave of extremist elements called Difa-e-Pakistan Council (Council for the defence of Pakistan) who are opposed to normalisation of relations with India, resumption of supplies to the NATO forces in Afghanistan and support every kind of extremist activity both within and outside Pakistan.

As of now, the army is the only effective institution that can deal with some of these monsters and maintain a semblance of order but even when it does, it is highly selective and those outfits considered its long term assets against India are left untouched.

Pakistan has to also deal with a variety of separatist and secessionist tendencies. Apart from complaints regarding Punjabi domination, violence of an increasing order is becoming endemic in Pakistan because of Shia-Sunni conflicts, unrest in Baluchistan, in Gilgit and Baltistan, insurgency in the entire region bordering Afghanistan, conflicts between Sindhis and Mohajirs, between Pathans and Sindhis and Mohajirs and the expansion of the influence of Sunni-Wahabi systems leading to ill-treatment of the minorities of all hues. Since 2003, no less than 36,000 persons have met with violent deaths in Karachi alone the peak being in the year 2009 with 11,704 deaths. In 2011, till October, already 4,082 persons have been killed. Pakistan's share of violent deaths in the whole of South Asia is 80 per cent. As per the 'South Asian Terror Portal' in 2012 so far some 734 persons have met violent death. Till April 2012 there have been 201 bomb blasts in Pakistan. Life in Pakistan appears to be short and brutish and death sudden and violent. The targeting of Shias is on the increase and already in 2012, 150 Shias have lost their lives. Violence between Sunni sects has also been on the rise with the more liberal Barelvis being targeted by the radical Deobandhis. Of the terrorists arrested in Pakistan some 90 per cent are Deobandhis. While the population is growing at rapid and indeed unaffordable rates, the economy is in doldrums recording a meagre 2 per cent growth. Huge unemployment, power shortages, lack of diversification of the economy, poor education, and low literacy rates—all afflict the State. During 2011, there were repeated violent protests against endemic power shortages as well as shortages of gas. In 2012, as well Pakistan has started experiencing acute water and power shortages with power deficit estimated to be over 40 per cent and power cuts in rural areas extending up to 16 hours a day and up to 10 hours in urban areas.

The floods of 2010 which affected 20 million people adversely impacted agricultural production and huge swathes of the country have again been affected by floods in 2011. Even after more than a year, some 3.5 million of the displaced people are yet to be fully rehabilitated. As rightly pointed out, by thinkers even within Pakistan, people have occupied land that rightly belongs to the river due to population pressure and the river periodically reclaims this. Deforestation on a large scale due to demographic explosion has aggravated the problem.

The State of Pakistan, it appears, exists for only the upper crust comprising some 50,000 families who are landlords, hereditary tribal chieftains, the army, the civil service, the police, and the politicians. This powerful elite is linked by kinship and ever-changeable political affiliations. They take care of themselves by ensuring that one member or the other is in politics, the army, the civil service, etc., so that their interests are taken care of in one way or the other. The rest of the hapless populace is left to the tender mercies of religion reinforced by the linkages between the mullahs and the power elite. This structure is not designed to deal with the problems of modernizing a feudal economy in an increasingly complex international economic system. It has supported itself by repeated doses of international aid and has not attempted to become self-reliant even in sectors which are of vital importance for the life of the ordinary people. Its foreign policy is designed to ensure that aid keeps flowing, the military is continuously strengthened, and its perceived strategic assets are safeguarded, be it the nuclear deterrent or the insurgent network.

Lee Kuna Yew during a visit to Pakistan at the time of Zia-ul-Haq when asked about Pakistan's economic progress is reported to have remarked "How can we begin to think of economic progress of a people who consider life here in this world of no importance and feel that only life hereafter needs to be worried about."

Can this essentially unstable and elite-oriented structure meet the kind of internal challenges mentioned above and which have become worse with every passing year? Or will Pakistan as a unified political entity cease to exist and will its constituent parts break away as happened in the case of East Pakistan?

It will be worth noting that Pakistan itself is an artificial construct, a coming together of diverse elements, with no commonality in language, culture or ethnicity. Not all of these groups were fully committed to the idea of Pakistan and in fact, some of these elements, had indeed opposed the creation of such a State. Islam was the only unifying factor but this proved to be highly ephemeral. The idea of Pakistan was basically articulated and originated among the Muslims in central India and was backed by the Deobandh missionary school. It was also supported by the Barelvi School. Some in East Bengal became its vociferous supporters and in fact the Dhaka resolution is regarded as the real starting point for the demand for a separate Pakistan. The diverse elements that ultimately became part of Pakistan did not speak the same language, nor were they votaries of the same Islamic traditions. The Punjabis continue to speak Punjabi, the Sindhis, speak Sindhi and the Baluchs etc., and use different dialects or languages. Urdu, the official language of Pakistan is spoken mainly by the immigrant Mohajirs.

Pakistan took a long time to draft a proper constitution and this has been changed very many times with the army suspending this vital national instrument, quite a few times and for long periods.

In spite of all the negative elements—a weak State, a divided society and polity, etnnic, sectarian, communal conflicts, and an economy unable to grow even at a rate equal to the population growth, looming ecological disaster, etc., it appears that Pakistan will limp along for at least the foreseeable future. The reasons are that in spite of all the divisions and conflicts; no one really wants a total separation. Every player uses the divisiveness, as a bargaining chip to get more for his group, clan, and his relatives and for himself. Further, the State is held together very firmly by the one institution that still strongly believes in the idea of Pakistan and is powerful enough to have its say in most of the important matters, namely the army. It is widely believed that the army truly represents Pakistan and the faith of all segments of the population in the army remains fairly undiminished. It is said very rightly "No Army No Pakistan". Also, like what the British did and what the Romans advocated, for successful running of empires a combination of plain bribery, cooption into the system through patronage and use of brutal but effective force when required, has been practiced with considerable finesse by Pakistan, especially in dealing with groups such as the Baluchs and the restive tribes of NWFP and all along the Afghan border. While the Taliban had a great deal of appeal this seems to be on the wane after the indiscriminate attacks on civilian and much revered Sufi shrines. Strangely, the killing of Osama bin Laden did not generate the kind of widespread protests that were expected and the issue has more or less disappeared from the public discourse. But the danger of radicalisation is real, as the ideas that form the ideological core of Taliban have considerable resonance among the young and increasingly among the educated as well and needs to be very carefully watched.

More recently, anti-Americanism has emerged as a unifying factor based on sustained propaganda that America is against Islam and is not only interested in dismembering Pakistan but in collaboration with Israel and India, is planning to take control over the nuclear assets of the country. This kind of ill-founded but very useful propaganda is for purely selfish reasons supported even by the government and finds immediate resonance in the radicalized environment that prevails in Pakistan Both Al Qaeda and the Taliban have been able to poison the minds of a whole lot of people young and old, educated and illiterate with a set of lies which include: (a) The US has invaded Muslim countries—Iraq,

Afghanistan and intends to stay on permanently; (b) It is bent upon destroying Islam and Islam is in danger; (c) There is a conspiracy hatched by the US, Israel and India to dismember Pakistan and capture its nuclear weapons; (d) It is legitimate to target such invaders and it is the duty of Muslims to fight them; (e) The Pakistan Army is ordered by the US to fight against the Muslims and is hence a legitimate target; (f) The Taliban comprises pious Muslims and has established order, delivered quick justice, and enforced the Sharia, (g) The Taliban has not carried out any violence and it is the intelligence agencies of the US, Israel and India who carry out such attacks including those on the Marriot hotel and killings of civilians; and (h) Even the 9/11 attack was carried out by the Israelis and not by Al Qaeda.

This set of beliefs is found among university students and professors, and even lawyers and is actively promoted by the ISI and by the media. Recall when Salman Taseer, a cabinet minster, was killed because he had expressed sympathy for a Christian girl wrongly imprisoned on charges of blasphemy, by his own security guard the lawyers showered the accused with rose petals.

Only when the Taliban had taken over the whole of SWAT, Waziristan and even Buner some 70 kilometres from the national capital, the political establishment and the army, due largely to US pressure and for their own survival, launched successful operations in SWAT and other areas and reestablished their authority. The problem faced by Pakistan however is that while it will be happy to get rid of the Pakistani Taliban, it will not like to touch the Afghan Taliban and for that matter, all the insurgent outfits cultivated by it to target India. While the Afghan Taliban is under its protection, the Pakistani Taliban takes shelter in Afghanistan and both, along with other outfits, draw inspiration from the same ideology and have a high degree of commonality of objectives and cooperate with each other in a number of ways. The Taliban of both varieties are also basically of the same ethnic composition. The army's interest in protecting the Afghan Taliban is the main reason for its consistent refusal to launch any operations in North Waziristan in spite of immense pressure from the Americans. The successful operation in SWAT and the cooperation among various agencies of the Pakistani establishment, show how the Taliban can still be effectively dealt with provided there is a will. No doubt, the decline in public support caused by the violence indulged in by the Taliban and its destruction of much revered Sufi shrines also helped the establishment.

The thesis that Pakistan can avoid a collapse, may not however hold good if the army itself gets more radicalized and the society gets even more polarized. The biggest danger will be when a situation arises where a combination of population pressures, water shortages, energy shortages and ecological disasters overtakes the country and large swathes are filled with starving masses, without food or water. No institution, even if it is as effective as the army, can deal with such a situation. At present rates of growth Pakistan will have some 335 million in another 20 years, of which some 33 per cent can be below the poverty line and already there is an acute water shortage in areas such as Baluchistan and for large parts of the year, the Indus runs totally dry and vehicles are driven over the riverbed. As per recently released figures, the population of Pakistan has increased from 130 million in 1998 to 193 million in 2011. Punjab accounts of 47.50 per cent of this population. What is alarming is the fact that the average size of the household has come down by a tiny margin from 6.09 in 1998 to 6.08 in 2011, which means that population stabilization is not on the agenda of anyone. No one seems to have heard of Rev. Thomas Rabert Malthus and his dire predictions—famine, disease and war—and even if they have, he would in all probability be dismissed as an irreverant unbeliever worthy of elimination. It needs to be also noted that the population of Baluchistan has shot up by 139.3 per cent which clearly suggests that the government is deliberately encouraging demographic changes and attempting to reduce the Baluchs to a minority. The population of Sindh has also gone up by 81.5 per cent possibly due to the same reasons. Punjab has recorded the lowest rate of 24.1 per cent during this period of approximately 20 years. The Punjabis have been encouraged to settle in Baluchistan as well as places like Gilgit and Baltistan which has also witnessed a massive increase in population. Such increases in population combined with water shortages can cause serious inter-provincial conflicts and political instability. In a book just published entitled *"Pakistan on the Brink"*, Ahmed Rashid a well-informed observer of both Pakistan and Afghanistan is gloomy about the future of both Pakistan and Afghanistan and wonders which of these two will go down-hill faster. He is in fact more pessimistic about Pakistan as he believes that Pakistan's religious extremists and insurgents are well dug-in and the army will collaborate with them and avoid confrontation. Economic, environmental and demographic trends all suggest looming disaster. "These long-term problems, if not tackled immediately Pakistan may well plunge into the failed-state category" he concludes. He is particularly critical of the army and argues that the unaccountable army and spies set rotten policies, as hapless and thieving civilian politicians take the blame; the result is that Pakistan grows more fragile, posing an ever greater threat to the region. His thesis that Pakistan is in greater danger of a more rapid decline is perhaps justified if one takes into account the fact that by now Pakistan is far more isolated than Afghanistan, it is a known epicentre of terrorism and seems to believe that confrontation with the US, the West and India is the correct foreign policy posture. There are far too many hotheads, who have the support of the army and the ISI, who subscribe to the policy of confrontation and the State does not have the courage to control them.

The Jehadis and some radical elements, as usual point fingers at India for Pakistan's water woes and the looming ecological disaster. They threaten that if India does not provide water, blood will flow and Pakistan will answer with nuclear weapons. As it is, both India and Pakistan face severe shortages of water. As against the global average of water availability of some 8,200 cubic metres of water per person, an average Indian has just 1,730 cubic metres and a Pakistani even less, namely a mere 1,000 cubic metres. Water disputes may become a major source of conflict in the subcontinent.

To make matters worse, if Afghanistan goes into a tail spin of civil war post-2014 and there is a new wave of migration of Pashtuns as well as others into Pakistan, the situation can truly be beyond anyone's control. Warnings have indeed been sounded by many sane elements in Pakistan, especially as regards population control and ecological disasters but the hold of the mullahs is at the moment far too strong for any concerted measures to be taken to reduce birth rates, child marriages. A possible scenario is the breaking away of Sindh and Balochistan and their becoming independent and the Pashtuns on both sides of the Durand line coming together to become a unified political entity. Punjab may be separated from the rest of Pakistan. Such a development may sound farfetched at the moment but if this happens, the inhabitants of POK may have to make a choice as regards their own future.

For us in India, a chaotic and ungovernable Pakistan is already a big headache with anti-India elements having a free run and if the scenario that is likely to unfold does materialize, we may be faced with a huge problem on our western frontier as we may have to deal with the possibility of mass migration into India. Also, one cannot rule out the possibility of some hot head or the other launching another attack either directly or through proxies, to divert the attention of the population from the innumerable problems at home, which will not only at least temporarily unify the people but also have the support of the Taliban. The worst case scenario will be if the Taliban manage to take over Pakistan. This is their declared aim, and quite possibly if the Taliban takes over Afghanistan it can make Pakistan its next target. All the so called strategic assets of the army can facilitate such a take-over. Recently Pakistan has constituted a special force of 20,000 to protect its nuclear assets from the Taliban. It would appear that the Pakistani establishment itself does not altogether rule out such a possibility. The Taliban is intolerant of all those it regards as non-believers. In an interview to a correspondent of the Dawn one of the Taliban fighters, while declaring his hatred against non-believers including Shia's and Ahemedis, stated that the founder of Pakistan Mohammed Ali Jinnah was perhaps a Shia as his middle name is "Ali" and he does not consider Shias as Muslims and does not subscribe to the tolerance that Jinnah prescribed as the guiding principle for the state of Pakistan in his independence day address. Many analysts seem to feel that the situation in Pakistan can further deteriorate in the coming days and the outlook for 2012 is quite bleak. Is the country set to implode is a question being raised more frequently than before. With its confrontationist posture towards the US, the country can face further isolation. With foreign aid declining, the economy can experience turbulence and the ability of the country to meet its external obligations is under grave risk. The IMF which has been approached by Pakistan will no doubt impose new conditionalities. Its polity is being weakened by the rivalry between the executive and the judiciary, a President who has had psychological problems and was under treatment for unnamed cardiac problems and whom the army is bent upon ousting. He has been accused of siphoning off huge funds and the Supreme Court wants that he be investigated and charged. The reported explanation by the Prime Minster of Pakistan Gilani, that the President had to go to Dubai for treatment as he felt insecure about getting treatment within Pakistan shows the entire system in poor light. As of now, has suddenly returned looking quite healthy. No doubt, he has to face the Supreme Court which is looking into several charges against him. The Prime Minster Yusuf Reza Gilani has been hauled up by the Supreme Court for failing to act on its orders regarding the President's unaccounted funds slashed away abroad. The PM's claim that the President enjoys immunity has not been accepted by the Court and Gilani has been convicted on charges of contempt of Court and may have to resign. The army is also creating a huge embarrassment for the President by pursuing what has been dubbed as the 'memogate'. It has got rid of the country's ambassador in the US, Haqqani, a protege of Zardari holding him responsible for sending a memo asking for American assistance to avoid a coup by the army. Haqqani a career diplomat in recent interview to the BBC denies that he was the author of the memo but has had to run away to the US for his safety and claims that he needs health care. It is not safe for him to remain in Pakistan. He refers to the manner in which Salman Taseer was killed and how the judge who convicted the assassin had to run away as well to Saudi Arabia to show that Pakistan is unsafe for all those who are trying to do their duty. General Kayani has vociferously condemned this as a matter involving national security. Given the fact that both the judiciary and the army are gunning for him rumours that the President may quit the country had assumed great credibility. The President has now sought divine intervention by undertaking a pilgrimage to the dargah at Ajmer. He also donated some Rupees five crore to the dargah perhaps in the hope that these pious acts, may yet save him from both the judiciary and the Army. Many in Pakistan wonder as to from where the money is to come—not from the coffers of the State it is hoped. India went out of its way to welcome him and arranged a luncheon meeting with the Prime Minister Manmohan Singh, which as expected turned out to be a damp squib. The President, is in no position to address any of the India's concerns and known terrorists will continue to roam around freely. The visit which is summed up by some as 'he came, he ate, he prayed, and went back' has raised no expectations on both sides of the border.

The political class has, after a long time, mustered the courage to hit back at the army and the ISI, with Nawaz Sharif stating that if only the security establishment in Pakistan had confined itself to its prescribed role, Pakistan would have pursued different strategies including those with India. Prime Minster Gilani himself, while speaking to the National assembly in an unusually forthright speech hit out at the army stating "I want to make it clear that conspiracies are being hatched here to pack up the elected government. But we will continue to fight for the rights of the people of Pakistan whether we remain in the government or not." He added in a clear reference to the ISI that "there cannot be a state within the state". He went on to say, "All institutions of the country are answerable to the Parliament." This is even while the Defence Ministry of Pakistan conceded to the Supreme Court that it has no control over the army or the ISI. Gilani while expressing his chagrin about this added, "if they are not under the Ministry of Defence, then we should get out of this slavery, or otherwise, this Parliament has no importance, this system has no importance and you are not sovereign." He was highly critical of the army for harbouring Osama bin Laden and asked "On what type of visa was he living there? Why was security not taken care of if he entered Pakistan without a visa?" Extremely strong words indeed seldom spoken ever before in Pakistan by anybody and bound to be resented by the army which is already keen to get rid of Zardari. At the moment, the army finds that it is convenient for the civilian setup to remain, to take the blame for the mess that Pakistan is in and if the situation gets worse, as it is bound to, the army can step in claiming that it has to save the country. The only thing that is making the army hesitate is the possible adverse reactions from the international community, which is now more than ever tired of the shenanigans of the Pakistani military establishment. Also, the judiciary has intervened to state that it will not accept a military take over. Also even in the Arab world military backed dictators have been got rid of and elections are being held. The Army in Pakistan cannot ignore these trends.

The fact however remains that there is indeed an atmosphere of debilitating political and administrative paralysis in the country. A vacuum of this nature can provide scope for political Islam to make further inroads or the army to step in if things get worse. The Supreme Court in the meanwhile is getting to be increasingly assertive and has started questioning the role of the ISI in the unseating of Benazir Bhutto and acting as a "state within a state" behaving as an entity far above the law of the land. This new found enthusiasm of the Supreme Court for enforcing basic norms of a democratic polity and rule of law may augur well for the future of Pakistan. This and a relatively free press can encourage the political class, to regain the lost ground if only they can put their act together. The Supreme Court is also taking interest in the atrocities committed in Baluchistan and the cases of those who disappeared allegedly at the hands of the ISI.

The military seems to be bent upon a serious confrontation with the NATO, in the belief that this stance is supported by large segments of the population and will help the Afghan Taliban to gain ground. The Parliament has also supported such a stance and has laid down tough conditions for the relations with the US and NATO—no drone attacks, no night raids etc. Resumption of supplies to the NATO forces from Karachi is subject to these conditions. Militant outfits such as the LET have made it know that they will prevent resumption of supplies at any cost. Hafiz Sayed on whose head the US has declared a bounty of 10 million dollars has vehemently opposed any resumption of supplies.

The coming election in 2012 may complicate the situation further. The army would not like the PML (N) to come to power as Imran Khan has so far not articulated a coherent policy framework and his support levels are still low. The PPP is in disarray. A loose coalition may find it difficult to deal with the growing economic crisis.

Nepal has reached a stage where democracy has been taken over by the Maoists whose attitude towards India, in spite of all the help and support provided by India for democracy to take root in Nepal, is basically hostile. Baburam Bhattarai is a Maoist. In the process, the age-old traditions and spirituality of the Nepalese is being destroyed, as also its pluralistic and multicultural character. Thousands of lives have been lost and property worth millions has been damaged or destroyed. The Chinese who remained onlookers are now gradually but cautiously increasing their influence with the Nepal polity by building contacts with all the players. While they have been concentrating upon investments in infrastructure, they have also gradually increased their influence among the decision makers. Nepalese officials receive training from China and Chinese aid has been on the increase. The Nepal Government, due to Chinese pressure, has been particularly brutal in suppressing any protests from the small number of Tibetans in Nepal. Chinese agents have been allowed a free run in Nepal and they have infiltrated into the Tibetan community as well. Chinese agents have been allowed to follow the Tibetans, harass and threaten them and their e-mails and mobile phones are regularly hacked. In fact, before any protests are even staged, the Chinese officials instruct the Nepalese officials as to how to suppress these protests.

Unfortunately, the seven-party alliance is divided against itself and has not been able to present a cogent strategy against Maoist designs. The constitution is yet to be finalized and the task of reconciling the competing demands of various ethnic groups has been very difficult. The shape of the RNA will possibly be altered, with the Maoists insisting on incorporating their 7,000 strong cadre in the RNA while the Madhesias are also trying to get their own militia to become part of the RNA. Such changes may altogether transform the character of the RNA. The RNA has all along maintained intimate links with the Indian Army and it would be necessary to ensure its continuance. At the moment, the President, Ram Bharan Yadav is playing a stabilizing role and is a restraining influence on the Maoists. Pakistan is playing an important behind-the-scenes role and has been a major supplier of arms to the Maoists.

In this scenario, the agreement on 1st of November, 2011 with respect to the ex-Maoist fighters is of major significance. Nepal, which has suffered grievously due to the prolonged insurgency with some 18,000 deaths, requires peace more than anything else for solving its innumerable problems. The deal will result in nearly two-thirds of the 19,000 strong fighters getting hefty compensation (some US $11,500) for becoming civilians. The remaining will be given jobs such as forest guards or for disaster relief, etc. and those considered fit will become part of the RNA. The deal has to a certain extent avoided a dilution of the character of RNA and the PM Baburam Bhattarai has achieved this in the teeth of opposition. The deal has now been given effect to in the first week of April 2012.

Also, the process of making the constitution is to be speeded up and may be completed shortly. The difficult task of accommodating various interests is being handled with considerable finesse. The PM is also trying to achieve a better balance in relations with both India and China. An all party government is to be formed to see if the constitution making process can be completed by the end of May 2012.

The Sri-Lankan situation is also a matter of grave concern as India's position has been undermined by our perceived support to the Tamils and the LTTE. Both China and Pakistan have gained at our expense. China looks at Sri-Lanka as part of its strategy of encirclement of India. By building the port facilities at Humbantota and substantial investments, the Chinese have increased their presence and influence in that strategically located island, which commands the sea routes through the Malacca straits.

Sri Lanka has been recently under pressure with respect to its inhuman treatment of the LTTE. The killing of the young son of the LTTE supremo Prabhakaran, has received particular condemnation. India's decision to vote in favour of a UNHRC resolution demanding an enquiry into the atrocities has not been well received in Sri Lanka. Both China and Pakistan did not support this resolution on the ground that this can be construed as undue interference in the internal affairs of a sovereign nation. The Government of India seems to have, succumbed to pressure from the Tamil parties and Sri Lanka can be expected to take anti-India postures in conjunction with China and Pakistan in the future in international bodies. Already it has objected to the nuclear power plant at Koodankulam in Tamil Nadu going on steam on supposedly environmental considerations.

While our relations with China have improved, the fact that we have an unresolved boundary issue with China, that China is actively collaborating with Pakistan not only with regard to defence supplies but also with regard to nuclear and missile technology and is building the Gwadar Port, would underline the fact that China has no hesitation in playing a double game and ensuring that India continues to be troubled by her neighbours. India and China have a civilizational rivalry, a conflict of systems of economic and political management and competition for influence in South East Asia, in Africa, in West Asia and in Afghanistan.

Apart from Pakistan, China has assiduously cultivated Myanmar even when that country, because of its human rights abuses and action against Aung San Su Kyi had become an international pariah. China has made huge investments in the exploitation of its natural resources, in particular gas and oil. China has greatly strengthened its transport and communication links with Myanmar and is taking steps to establish its presence by building a port on its western coast in the Bay of Bengal. China's influence kept growing throughout the period of the military rule in Myanmar and it had turned Myanmar for all practical purposes a client State. China had emerged as Myanmar's closest strategic ally, nearest neighbour and biggest investor during the period when Myanmar was virtually a pariah to the international community. However, at a time when very few countries including the rich and the powerful dare to offend China, Myanmar's quasi-civilian government has started taking a more independent line and in what can be considered as an act of extraordinary bravery, it has suspended the construction of an enormous US $3.6 billion Chinese-backed dam on the river Irrawaddy in the north of the country inhabited by the Kachins. This, it appears, is caused by the Myanmar government at last listening to the voice of the people. There has been strong opposition to the dam from environmentalists and the local Kachins as well as from Aung San Su Kyi. Su Kyi the leader of opposition, is at last becoming freer than what she was in the past two decades of the military regime. The new semi civilian regime has started taking a number of measures which may gladden the hearts of liberal democracies, such as release of political prisoners and relaxation of press censorship. Sue Kyi has just won the election that she was permitted to contest. Hillary Clinton visited Myanmar and now the Prime Minster of UK as well. There is every possibility of lifting of longstanding sanctions by the West. These moves may restore the much desired balance in Myanmar's international relations and reduce her dependence upon China.

India, which had for a long time virtually cut off all relations with Myanmar, has for the past few years started reestablishing her contacts and has recently signed a number of agreements with the regime. India should take full advantage of the desire on the part of the people and the government to expand its relations with countries other than China. The visit of the Myanmar

President, Thien Sein along with his wife and a large delegation to India in October 2011 can be a significant step forward in building enduring multidimensional relations between the two countries. We may be looking at a historic opportunity to regain our influence in this area.

All of India's immediate neighbours have become in one way or the other linked to China, both economically and militarily.

China is fully utilizing its growing economic and military strength to increase its influence in the entire Asia-Pacific region. It is now competing with the US as regards economic and military influence and wants to ensure that it is in a position to effectively counter any India-US cooperation in this area. It is particularly wary of possible threats to the shipping lanes through the Malacca straits and the series of steps it has taken to expand its blue water capability are designed to deal with this possibility.

There is no doubt that China is poised to become a major economic and military challenge to the unique position that the US has enjoyed post Second World War and especially after the collapse of the Soviet Union. For the foreseeable future, China's growth story is expected to go forward without any major interruption whereas the US and the West are battling a series of economic crises. There has been serious slowdown in growth rates and a seemingly irresolvable debt crisis. Democracy and capitalism both seem to have failed in the eyes of many even within the US, with street protests against inequality and unemployment. The avarice of bankers and fund managers of the Wall Street have been particular targets of the younger generation.

One cannot, however, afford to ignore the many challenges that China does face both internally and externally. The authoritarian, one-party rule has for too long suppressed dissent and voices of protest have been ruthlessly stifled. Human rights violations are routine and imprisonment without trial widespread, even while corruption and illegal appropriation of land and property by the cadres has invited a large number of protests accompanied by violence. China has some 1.5 million people behind bars most without any chance of a fair or speedy trial. Recently, even relatively well-off and middle class homes have been subjected to such appropriations by real estate developers backed by party hacks and this has invited strong protests. Great damage to the environment is being caused by

China's mad rush for development at any cost. Problems such as aging population, the consequence of the one child policy rigidly enforced, serious and growing disparity between male and female numbers, disparity in levels of living between urban and rural areas and between the interior and the special economic zones all swept under the carpet for too long, can suddenly erupt into unrest and become a serious challenge to stability and progress. The regime which is so effectively in control, displays an unusual degree of nervousness and suppresses expression of dissent in any form, tries to control flow of information in every possible way and has been targeting the Internet and cyberspace through a variety of interventions.

The ruthlessly enforced one child policy may well turn out to be China's Achilles heel. In a study put out by the United Nations—February 2012. China's fertility rate in 2010 has come down to 1.56 below that of the US which was 2.08. The richer parts are showing even lower fertility rates. For example, Shanghai has fertility rate of just 0.6 in 2010 possibly the lowest anywhere in the world. Population growth during 2010-50 is expected to be a negative –3.4 per cent compared to a projected increase of 30 per cent in the US. The median age in China in 2010 was 34.5 compared to 36.9 in the US and this is slated to become 48.7 by 2050 while the median age in the US will be around 40—a clear sign that the population in China is ageing fast. More worryingly the population in the age group 20-24 which was 120 million is slated to go down to 63 million by 2050 in China which means that the really productive segment of the population will be drastically reduced with grave consequences for the continuance of the present high growth pattern. In the US during the same period the working group population 20-24 is slated to increase from 22 million to 30 million. There will also be significant changes in the share of population age group wise, in China. The under 15 group will decline by 5.5 per cent, the 15-64 age group by 11.4 per cent whereas the group above 65 will shoot up by 17.4 per cent. Such demographic changes may not only adversely impact on China's economic growth but also on her security related ambitions and her ability to dominate restive regions such as Tibet, Xinxiang, inner Mongolia etc.

The one child policy has seen some of the worst violations of human rights. The lid on this was blown off, by the revelations of the 40 year old blind activist Chen Guancheng who brought out that in his home province Shandong some 1,30,000 women were forced to get sterilized or undergo abortion. He campaigned against this practice. He was hounded for his revelations and imprisoned for four years followed by three years of house arrest. His escape from the heavily cordoned and watched home all the way to Beijing and his seeking refuge in the US embassy at the time of the visit of the US Secretary of State Hillary Clinton and Treasury Secretary Timothy Geithener was a huge embarrassment to the Chinese. Chen was pressurized to come out of the embassy get himself admitted into a hospital where he initially stated that he will not leave China but when he learnt of the torture being inflicted on his wife has asked for asylum in the US. The US has offered to permit him to come for a course in New York University. He may be permitted to leave to the US and his wife may also be permitted to go. If and when he decides to return whether he will be allowed to come back is doubtful. This episode has also brought out some staggering facts about the ruthlessness of the regime, not only with respect to the one child policy but as regards the way it deals with dissidence of any kind. Some 40 million forced abortions have taken place in China and an unknown number have committed suicide. It is an offence to have a second child and if one is expecting a second child the only course is to opt for abortion or lengthy incarceration.

China's mantra for progress and stability in the post-Mao era has been rapid growth, full employment, low inflation, price control and subsidizing of all essentials. This has kept all sections of the population reasonably happy and satisfied, even while China invested heavily on mega projects, politically important investments in Africa, Mongolia and in the Central Asian region. The search for energy security influenced a whole lot of investments. With growth slowing down, inflation going up, unemployment and inequalities rising, China may face serious difficulties in maintaining the kind of control it was able to exercise over its population for so long. The Asian Development Bank (ADB) has recently in its latest (2012) Asian Development Outlook report (ADO) estimated that the gini coefficient in China has gone up from 32 in the 1990s to 43 in 2010. The ADB report states that the figures show that worrying inequality has risen in China. It adds Inequality leads to a vicious circle with unequal opportunities, creating income disparities that in turn lead to dramatic differences, in future opportunities for families.'

Labour unrest has been taking place with increasing frequency and on larger scales, both in the State and non-State sectors. While some have been suppressed, in others the workers' demands had to be conceded and union leaders bought off. The huge labour force that had migrated from the rural areas to the towns and who was hitherto employed may be unwilling to return to the rural areas where it may find no work. With rapid growth of the Internet and increasing sophistication of transmission of messages and pictures through the growing mobile telephone network, and the rapid growth of micro blogs, especially the Chinese version of the twitter—weibo, used by nearly half of the 513 million Chinese who have access to the Internetnews of unrest spreads fast and efforts to control such spread of information by the party and the government have been often unsuccessful. China is set to effect major political changes even at the top levels, with the retirement of both Hu Jinto and Wen Jin Bao, constitution of a new politburo and a 300-member central committee during 2012. The Vice President Xi Jinping will replace Hu Jinto and Le Keqiang will take over from his boss Wen Jinbao. The new leadership will have its hands full with a host of internal and external problems. Increasing social unrest, lowering of citizens' satisfaction with their own lives and confidence in the government can be matters of serious concern.

Generally speaking, leadership changes in China have been orderly and well planned. However, this facade has been shaken by the removal from office of one of the most colourful and charismatic leaders namely, the party chief of the booming city of Chongqing. Bo is one of the 'prince-lings' the son of one of Mao's original revolutionary colleagues. Economic growth under his watch had notched up 15 per cent and he had also managed to control crime, improve civic services, etc. He was expected to rise high but has suddenly been cut down. The charges against him include his inclination to seek personal publicity but what made the top leadership nervous was his espousal of ultra leftist causes reminiscent of the Maoist Cultural Revolution. He is also accused of trying to block a corruption investigation into his family businesses particularly of his wife Gu Kailai. The police Chief Wang Lijun was abruptly transferred and he in turn fled to the

US embassy in the city of Chengdu. In the all too opaque system of China all such events generate a barrage of speculation. While Wang is presumably under arrest and Bo himself under some form of detention and he is no more a member of the politburo. Mysterious also was the death of a British businessman Neil Heywood in a Chongqing hotel. Neil Heywood was reportedly some kind of a fixer for the Bo family. Allegations have emerged that Heywood was poisoned with cyanide under orders of Bo himself on suspicion of his having an affair with Bo's wife Gu Kailai. A report in the Washington times indicates that his alleged to have been running an extensive wire tap operation extending right up-to members of the politburo and even Hu-jinto.

Bo's rhetoric held out hope of a more transparent political order and greater attention to bridging the growing inequalities. The Communist leadership which has been pursuing policies of unbridled growth, even if it results in huge disparities and whose 70 richest leaders have assets worth $90 billion, cannot it appears tolerate, at the moment at least, such heresy. It may be added that protests against inequality and corruption have been on the rise and some 300,000 protests large and small have been recorded in recent times. The Communist party greatly fears losing its legitimacy and credibility and dissent continues to be snuffed out. It is possible that Bo was trying to build a separate platform based on path of development and governance different from that espoused by the leadership and hence had to be cut down. These developments indicate that there is a serious power struggle underway in China ahead of the leadership changes scheduled to take place towards the end of 2012.

China has grave unresolved problems in Tibet and more recently in the Xinxiang province bordering Turkmenistan. There have been increasing instances of unrest in Xinxiang and the Uighurs who have been reduced to a minority by the influx of Han Chinese, have repeatedly expressed their anger through violence. Spread of radical Islam from Pakistan aided by Saudi financing, as well as resentment of the influx of Han Chinese into the area have fuelled protests and violence which has been suppressed with considerable ruthlessness. China had to sharply reprimand Pakistan not to meddle in this area. It has produced evidence to show that Uighurs get training and indoctrination in terrorist camps in Pakistan.

China keeps expressing its resentment at the respect commanded by His Holiness the Dalai Lama and is nervously watching recent developments where the Dalai Lama has very adroitly shed his temporal authority to democratically elected leaders. The Dalai Lama has also made it clear that it is he who will decide the question of reincarnation of the 15th Avalakotishwara after his departure. He has teasingly indicated that final decisions on all such matters will be taken when he will be 90. The present Dalai Lama is the 14th reincarnation. Recently, self-immolation by monks in Tibet and unrest in Tibetan-inhabited areas has become more frequent which China invariably condemns as inspired by His Holiness and his gang of 'splittists'.

It must be pointed out that India and Tibet had age-old intimate relations in the spiritual and cultural areas and Tibetan Buddhism owes a great deal to the teachings of great Indian Buddhist scholars. I had the privilege of having an enlightening conversation with His Holiness the Dalai Lama in 1997, when I was the Chief Secretary of Sikkim, when he spoke with great regard of the enormous contribution to Buddhism in Tibet by the great Indian masters Nagarjuna and Shantarakshita, whom His Holiness described as people coming from the land of the coconut, namely South India. The Tibetan script has close resemblance to the Pali script and in Sikkim as elsewhere, it is believed that Guru Padmasambhava known also as 'Guru Rimpoche' initiated Tibet to the tenets of Mahayana Buddhism. This great relationship was violently disrupted by China's armed invasion.

Could India have ensured that Tibet remained independent of China and continued to serve as a buffer between the two countries, as it had been throughout the British period and even earlier? Could India have avoided the presence of large Chinese forces right at our door step exposing our northern borders to an imminent threat? Could we not have averted the ecological consequences of China's exploitation of the river systems and the mineral wealth of Tibet?

Unfortunately, our Tibet policy has been full of contradictions and indeed, a series of backward movements, each having grave implications to not merely, the guarding of our northern borders but also to our national security. As summed up by Arun Shourie in his book *'We must have no Price'* (page 46).

The movement has been from:

- Regarding Tibet as an independent nation, empowered to enter into international treaties (This is what is the implication of our insistence on the validity of the McMahon line),
- to viewing Tibet as an autonomous region under overall Chinese 'suzerainty',
- to viewing Tibet as an autonomous region under China's sovereignty,
- to viewing Tibet as a region, as an integral part of China and recognizing its actions in Tibet as an internal affair, or
- accepting violation of Tibet's integrity by China which has sliced off parts of Tibet and incorporated these into other Chinese/Han dominated areas.

Well before China invaded Tibet and brutally suppressed whatever resistance there was, Sardar Patel in a letter, which is an eloquent testimony of his great foresight and clear understanding of the security implications of the Chinese takeover, wrote to Nehru on the 7th of November, 1950 describing how India has been taken for a ride by China's duplicity and how our own Ambassador in Peking, K.M. Panikkar had swallowed the Chinese line hook, line and sinker. This letter has been reproduced in Neville Maxwell's book entitled *'India's China War'* as also in Balraj Krishna's *"Sardar Patel—Bismarck of India"*. The Sardar lamented that while deceiving India through expressions of their desire to settle the Tibetan issue peacefully, they were all along getting ready for an armed invasion and this the Sardar felt "in my judgment little short of perfidy". He bemoaned, "the tragedy is that the Tibetans put their faith in us; they chose to be guided by us and we have not been able to get them out of the meshes of Chinese diplomacy or their malevolence." He was bitter that the Chinese accused India of complicity with Anglo-American machinations in Tibet, even when India was bending over backwards to express her friendship to China and in the teeth of opposition from the West, kept advocating Communist China's case for a permanent seat in the UN Security Council. At one point, India was offered this permanent seat, as at that time there was no other Asian power which had a reasonable claim but it appears we did not accept this, but kept supporting Communist China.

Though evidence on this matter is thin, if India had indeed intervened in collaboration with UK and USA even militarily, Tibet's independence may not have been lost. The Chinese State could not have afforded an armed confrontation with a combination of powers, as its internal consolidation was still incomplete and Chiang-Kai-Shek's powerful forces were still at its backyard. The PLA was not capable of war on two fronts. It had only recently battled Chiang's forces, as also the occupying forces of Japan. The support from USSR was quite half-hearted and in fact, the Russians had suspended supply of military spares due to ideological differences between Mao and Khruschev. China was also getting embroiled in the Korean War. In any case, India could have retained a powerful influence as to the future of Tibet.

Patel taking note of the armed takeover of Tibet wrote to Nehru, "We have to consider what new situation now faces us as a result of the disappearance of Tibet as we know it and the expansion of China almost to our gates." Patel suggested a series of steps to be taken to safeguard the frontier but unfortunately, these were not given the importance they deserved and in 1962, India was totally unprepared to meet the armed attack by China and suffered a humiliating defeat. This was an enormous blow, not merely militarily but psychologically as well and India is yet to fully recover from this humiliation. India had consequently lost a great deal of its stature and has for a long time been put on the defensive *vis-à-vis* China, on a whole lot of bilateral and multilateral issues. Patel had in his letter, in the face of the armed aggression committed in Tibet, suggested that we must not support the case of China any more for membership of the UNO. He felt that since China had played an active role in the Korean War, the Western powers may even "virtually outlaw" China. Even this advice was not taken and today, while we are going around seeking support for our membership to the Security Council of the UN, China is in a position to ensure in collaboration with Pakistan, that this does not take place. Our own actions have undermined our position in international affairs.

Taiwan continues to be a thorn in the flesh of China. The US has until now not yielded to threats to stop supplying both defensive and offensive arms to Taiwan and that country has managed to maintain its independent status despite all possible coercion and intimidation from mainland China. Its economic strength and prosperity, as well as democratic way of governance are serious challenges to the Chinese system and way of life. China has been increasing its defence expenditure and expanding its naval power. The primary focus of this seems to be to build up her ability to thwart any possibility of the US navy intervening in support of Taiwan. The idea is to deploy platforms capable of effectively preventing the US from using its missile power to come to the aid of Taiwan. Specific interceptor capabilities have been the focus of China's Defence Research and Development.

China has also laid claims to the entire South China Sea, disregarding the International Laws of the Sea and claims of other littoral states such as Vietnam, the Philippines, etc. The Philippines has sent its warships to the South China Sea recently to re-assert its claims in the area. China has also not unambiguously accepted international norms for sharing river waters with lower riparian States. It had even fought a war with Vietnam where the Vietnamese managed to give a bloody nose to the Chinese. In the whole of East Asia, the rise of China militarily and economically is viewed with considerable nervousness and a more confident and assertive China has been making many countries to seek better relations with India. They also do not want any scaling down of American presence in this region. India has realized the potential to build long-term and constructive relations with the South-East Asian nations and has been taking a more proactive and pragmatic 'look-east-policy'. It has built up growing, economic and commercial relations with Vietnam and trade and investments are being actively promoted.

India has age-old cultural and spiritual ties with a number of countries in the South-East Asian region—Thailand, Cambodia, Laos, etc., and has friendly relations both with Malaysia and Indonesia. India must take full advantage of the nervousness on the part of these countries *vis-à-vis* China and establish wide-ranging economic and strategic relations with all these countries.

China cannot afford any military misadventures and the international community will have to make China accept international norms of conduct in its foreign relations, as also bind China through multilateral institutional mechanisms.

In the far-east right up to Australia, the spectre of militant Islam posing a threat to security of nations, targeting economic assets, undermining tourism, causing damage to civil society and indulging in random terrorism, has been haunting many a nation. Japan, though relatively free from security threats, is wary of the rising power of China. While its economy is recovering slowly, its rapidly aging population, low birth rates (Japan's population may decline to 100 million from today's 128 million in the next 20 years) can undermine Japan's potential as a regional power. Apart from the economic crisis, Japan has had to deal with a series of natural disasters, accidents in its nuclear plants and continuous political instability. The continuous strengthening of the Yen is also affecting its exports. There is considerable concern in Japan about the rise of China and it is interested in furthering her relations with India, while reinforcing its strong ties with the US. A trilateral compact involving US, India and Japan has been mooted and it is up to India to grab this possibility and convert this into a certainty.

This brief survey can lead to the conclusion that a large part of the world is facing a new type of threat driven by factors which have been characterised as civilizational rather than ideological. The 20th century witnessed conflicts between democracy and dictatorship, between politico-economic ideologies of capitalism and communism. The current century seems to be drifting towards a clash of values, clash of belief systems and of civilizations. Except a few such as countries in Latin America, this clash has affected with varying degrees of intensity a large swathe of countries. Mention has been made of the challenges faced by the West as well as Russia, but it needs to be highlighted that countries from Algeria and Morocco to Egypt and Turkey to the Philippines all have been experiencing challenges from radical elements who threaten established order, forms of government and systems of conflict resolution. This issue will be covered in another chapter in full measure.

Against this background, we may now pay specific attention to the external threats to India's security.

Any discussion on this will have to focus inevitably on our immediate troubled neighbourhood and its external linkages, as India unfortunately faces the most serious security threats from her neighbours. The troubled neighbourhood is possibly becoming a dangerous neighbourhood. Pakistan poses the greatest threat to India's security as from the time of the partition; Pakistan's policies have been almost exclusively Indo-centric, calculated to undermine India's stability and security. For a variety of reasons, Pakistan considers India as an adversary and its policies have been formulated with the clear objective of weakening India by all possible means. Strong elements within Pakistan's establishment such as the army and the ISI can lose the rationale for their very existence, if there is no hostility towards India. While the Kashmir issue has been the long-standing bone of contention and confrontation, there have been persistent attempts to widen the ambit of conflict and indeed translating it into civilizational terms. The thesis that even if the Kashmir issue is resolved, to the full satisfaction of Pakistan, it may not shed its hostility towards India cannot be considered invalid. Recall the reported statement of the former Chief of Pakistan Army, Mirza Aslam Beg who stated that if anyone attacks Pakistan, he will attack India.

It would appear that Pakistan, on realizing that Kashmir cannot be taken away from India by force even after three major attempts, is resorting to a combination of Machiavellian and devious methods, drawing inspiration from its Chinese mentors, calculated to demoralize and sap the enemy, in this case India, of his strength and will to fight. These methods include a continuous upgradation of Pakistan's combat ability, carrying out a low-intensity warfare, training, arming, funding and motivating a number of Jihadi outfits, providing shelter to criminal elements from India, collaborating with Bangladesh and Nepal for creating problems in the North-East, providing shelter and training facilities to insurgent groups, subverting the Indian economy through smuggling activities including large scale induction of fake currency, establishing a number of ISI modules in various parts of the country and using every international forum and engaging lobbyists to agitate the Kashmir issue. Pakistan has built up an extensive military and technological relationship with China, which continues to provide technical assistance for upgradation of Pakistan's nuclear, military and missile capability and at the same time, Pakistan continues to get substantial military and economic assistance from United States as well. The triangular and unholy collaboration among Pakistan, North Korea and China in nuclear proliferation and missile technology is well documented.

More recently, Pakistan seems to be interested in undermining

India's economic and technological progress and has been encouraging Jihadist outfits to target vital economic and technological assets. Equally importantly, Pakistan has made determined efforts to destroy the multi-cultural and secular character of India by targeting Hindu religious institutions. It had actively aided Sikh militancy and sheltered many a militant in Pakistan who were advocating an independent Khalistan. While the Khalistan movement has died down, Pakistan has not altogether stopped its support. Periodic reports indicate that Sikh militants who have been provided shelter by Islamabad are being encouraged to revive militancy and violence in the Punjab and other parts of India. It continues to harbour a variety of anti-India elements including members of the underground and the mafia controlled by Dawood Ibrahim, who smuggle fake currency, arms and drugs. More worrying is the fact that Pakistan has been trying to influence some elements among India's minorities to radicalize their thinking, exaggerate their grievances and promote a victimhood psychology. Subversive literature, video and audio cassettes seem to flow across the border highlighting alleged atrocities on Muslims in several parts of the world and allegedly in Kashmir and calling upon Muslims to participate in world-wide Jihad. Bin Laden has been portrayed as a role model.

It would therefore appear that the challenge from Pakistan is becoming multi-dimensional and is posing a serious threat to the very fabric of India's multi-cultural, multi-religious and secular polity. India's economic success seems to excite the envy of elements within Pakistan.

At the same time, certain saner elements in Pakistan have started to realize that a continuous state of confrontation with India is causing considerable harm to the country and radicalizing its society. This it is felt is yielding no particular dividends. The policy of islamization of the society and the army, initiated by Gen Zia-ul-Haq, who proclaimed "Nizam-e-Mustafa", has it appears, caused considerable long-term damage to the country. Zia was supported by the Americans as they considered his assistance in kicking out the Soviets form Afghanistan as vital. They took no steps to halt his brazen attempts to build the nuclear bomb. They recognized that he was a liar and a "rascal" but did nothing excusing him as "our rascal" and a 'patriotic liar'. Pakistan's role in training Jihadis, who have been involved in a variety of terrorist acts in several parts of the world, has damaged Pakistan's image grievously. Pakistan's claim that it is a moderate Islamic country is finding less and less acceptance the world over and on the other hand, Pakistan is definitely regarded as a state which sponsors, trains and motivates a variety of terrorist organizations, which promotes Jihadi culture, has been responsible for illegal nuclear proliferation and is undemocratic with a poor record with respect to treatment of women and human rights. Pakistan has also, under heavy pressure from the US, the West and Afghanistan, been forced to deploy a huge part of its armed forces on the Afghan border to control the Taliban and Al-Qaeda. All this may compel Pakistan to see the advantages of building better relations with India. Some tentative steps seem to be on the way with the possibility of granting what is termed 'a modified MFN state', relaxation of visa restrictions, expansion of trade through enlargement of the list of permitted items for import, etc. Business interests which welcome such moves at the same time, are wary of the economic strength of India which is growing at around 8 per cent compared to a mere 2 per cent of Pakistan. Further India's GDP is over US$1.10 trillion, eight times more than Pakistan's US$ 207 billion. Even now, India's exports are some US$ 1.2 billion while Pakistan's exports to India, are no more than US$ 268 million. Smuggling across the border is estimated to be US$ 2 billion. There is no doubt the consumer in Pakistan will benefit a great deal from imports from India, especially with products such as drugs and pharmaceuticals and synthetic fibre and fabrics. Pakistan which is experiencing acute power shortages is keen to import power from India. One wonders if in the context of these developments Pakistan which, at least on the surface, co-operative with the West in its efforts to control international terrorism, will stop turning a blind eye towards terrorism calculated to damage India. So far Pakistan has been going into a denial mode with respect to terrorist camps, arming of militants, financial and ideological support, and providing shelter to criminals from India. Pakistan keeps demanding credible evidence to take action even against terrorists like Hafez Syed and all the voluminous dossiers presented by India are dismissed as inadequate. It is clear that Pakistan does not intend acting against any of these internationally proclaimed criminals.

Even with respect to co-operation in trade and economic

relations, Pakistan is at best half-hearted, being hesitant to open up markets and shies away from full-fledged participation in the SAFTA. Periodically, views are articulated that unless the Kashmir issue is resolved, there cannot be any progress in other matters. That such a policy is damaging Pakistan's own economy seems to weigh very little with its leaders. In sum, it appears that Pakistan will continue to be a very troublesome neighbour and our policies have to be so fashioned as to reduce the potential and ability of Pakistan to damage our interests.

With respect to Bangladesh, our main concerns are the radicalization and Islamization of Bangladesh, ill-treatment of minorities, shelter to insurgent groups and illegal infiltration.

Here again, several interest groups see anti-India rhetoric, postures and activities as vote-gathering and vote-winning strategies and such groups are invariably patronized by Pakistan. The rise of Islamic parties heavily influenced by Saudi Arabia with continuous financial support has aggravated anti-India attitudes. A lot of the initiatives which can promote bilateral trade have become hostage to short-sighted anti-India postures. Minor grievances are constantly harped upon and India is called upon to be generous to meet every demand of Bangladesh. The ISI was allowed to operate freely in Bangladesh and has managed to gain a strong hold over all Indian insurgent groups being provided shelter in Bangladesh. The insurgent groups have grown deep roots in Bangladesh with heavy investments in business ventures, hotels, etc. The money extorted by insurgent outfits in the North-East finds are invested in Bangladesh and profits used for procuring weapons. There has been, however, a sea change in the attitude of Bangladesh towards India with the Hasina regime taking a series of proactive steps to deal with all outstanding problems and effectively curbing the activities of insurgent groups lodged in that country.

With Nepal becoming a Maoist State, what is of very great concern is the fact that Nepal has provided a free hand to anti-India elements of Pakistan to cause immense harm to India's security interests. The ISI is known to be utilizing Nepal extensively for supporting insurgent groups, smuggling arms fake currency and funds and infiltrating terrorists into Indian Territory. Also, all along the Indo-Nepal border, there has been a significant demographic transformation along with growth of madrasas and mosques which have the potential of harbouring anti-India elements. Unfortunately, the concerned state governments have not shown sufficient awareness about these adverse developments and the need to deal with them in an effective manner. Nepal has weak institutions at the moment and this gives ample opportunities for lawless elements to function freely, a situation being taken full advantage of by Pakistan. Both Bangladesh and Nepal have been active partners in implementing Pakistan's policy of strategic encirclement of India.

Maldives, a group of islands in the Indian Ocean has recently witnessed a coup in which a regime which had been friendly to India has been replaced by one that is heavily influenced by Islamic ideology. Maldives may now become a haven for anti-India and extremist elements which can easily be exploited by Pakistan. Our maritime security may come under threat. Tourism which is the mainstay of the Maldivian economy may come under threat as well with adverse consequences for employment. The unemployed coming under the influence radical ideology can provide a fertile ground for recruitment by extremist elements. The ousted President has been appealing for Indian assistance but so far our reactions have not been positive.

The common thread running through the foreign policy posture of each of the countries showing distinct hostility towards India is a set of charges towards India accusing it of playing the role a big brother, hegemony, arrogance, attempting to dominate the smaller countries and lack of sympathy and consideration for the needs of smaller countries. That India has never been an aggressor and has never shown hegemonic tendencies is continuously ignored and every small incident is utilized to complain against India.

It would appear that in spite of concessions given by India and sensitivity displayed to the needs of the smaller countries, policies and practices are adopted by these countries calculated to harm India as much as possible. The primary reason for this is, the impression that India can be kicked on and off without any fear of retaliation. This can be called "Small Boy Syndrome" where a small country can afford to periodically kick the bigger neighbour without any real fear of retaliation. Unless this belief is effectively dealt with, India will continue to be hurt and policies and practices designed to hurt India will continue to be practiced.

The nexus between China, Pakistan, Bangladesh and Nepal has serious implications for the security situation in the North-East as this unholy combination can strangulate the region by targeting the narrow Siliguri belt called the "Chicken's Neck". The fact that this belt is also being inhabited by a large number of illegal infiltrators whose loyalty to India is at best untested is a matter of grave concern.

With respect to China, while we are still grappling with the unresolved border issue, China has agreed to maintain peace and tranquility on the border. Efforts have been on to expand economic, commercial, cultural and technological relations including opening up of the Nathu La border and the *de jure* and *de facto* recognition of Sikkim by China as an integral part of India. However, considerable unease is created by China's parallel strategy of undermining India's security and periodic reiteration of its claims over Arunachal Pradesh and parts of Ladakh. Its protests over the visit of even the Defence Minister to Arunachal Pradesh, refusal to give visas to residents of Arunachal Pradesh and issue of staple Visas for residents of Jammu and Kashmir are all irritants which compels one to take a suspicious view of long tern intentions of China. China no doubt, considers itself to be a member of a superior league with ambitions of becoming a superpower replacing the ex-Soviet Union. It does not regard itself as competing with India, but seems to be constantly endeavouring to contain and restrain India.

The fact that it has brutally suppressed Tibet, strangulating any sign of unrest or dissent, needs to be taken note of along with the fact that it has built an extensive network of roads and a railway to Lhasa and has plans to extend the railway line right up to the Indian border—all point to long-term calculations of China to be in a position to dominate the region. The population composition of Tibet has been perhaps irreversibly altered. China has stationed a large number of long-range missiles on the soil of Tibet, easily reachable to almost all corners of India.

What is also of great concern is the kind of military, economic and strategic relationship that China has built with all of Indian's neighbours. The long-standing economic, military, nuclear, missile and technological collaboration with Pakistan have resulted in substantial upgradation of Pakistan's combat ability. Pakistan is now intensifying nuclear co-operation with China, with a view to more than match any upgradation in India's capability in the nuclear field, consequent on the Indo-US civil nuclear co-operation programme. China is involved in the building of the Gwadar Port, which has the potential of posing a serious threat to traffic through the sea lanes out of the Persian Gulf. It is building extensive transportation links to the Arabian Sea through Pakistan-occupied-Kashmir and Baluchistan.

China has been supplying armaments to Bangladesh as well and is committed to huge investments in the energy sector.

China has built a variety of economic interests in Myanmar and has supported the military regime throughout. Extensive road network has been built with China's help and also a port on the Myanmar west coast in the Bay of Bengal.

While China is in the process of acquiring blue water navy, it has declared its intention to increase its presence in the Indian Ocean, a prospect which is unlikely to be relished by the Americans. Note must be taken of the fact that China is emerging as a world power, militarily strong, expanding economically at a rapid rate, a nuclear and a missile power with ambitions to have a blue water navy and capable of projecting its power in a much stronger fashion than ever before on the international stage. China is both respected and feared in the entire region. No doubt, it still has unresolved internal problems and is plagued by a high degree of corruption and decline in the moral appeal of the communist system and its cadres. China is trying to achieve a delicate but difficult balance between growing economic freedom and the perceived compulsion to keep tight political control and one-party rule. In a world more integrated and globalized, the question whether the communist party of China can continue to run a one-party dictatorship suppressing dissent and denying people basic human rights is debatable. The refusal to accommodate the growing aspirations of the people of China can undermine the long-term stability of China's polity, even while it is making a strong effort to emerge as a countervailing power to the US, replacing the erstwhile USSR.

Our response to the serious security threats, taking note of all the facts outlined in the above discussion, should be tailored to be in consonance with the changes that have occurred in the international security and diplomatic environment. It needs no emphasis that at the same time we must ensure that our internal strengths are enhanced and internal conflicts are resolved, so that we project an image of a strong united country with rapidly expanding economy and increasing technological capabilities. The issues that need to be addressed against this background will be examined in Chapter 6 which deals with foreign policy challenges.

4

EXTERNAL THREATS: RADICAL ISLAM

For over two decades now, the world which had been drained and exhausted by the two World Wars and then the cold war, has witnessed an altogether new form of violence which is termed international terrorism. Though terrorism has many colours and a variety of causes and motivations as for example, that perpetrated by the LTTE or the Naxalites or the Basque separatists and even the IRA, one form of terrorism derives direct inspiration from one of the major and rapidly growing religions of the world, namely, Islam.

Terrorism is a form of guerilla warfare, an informal non-declared aggression against the State and its people. It is practised by loosely-organized outfits whose objective is to overwhelm states established by law. Terrorism arises generally out of the failure to address specific grievances and has specific economic, political and social goals. It is an extreme expression of accumulated grievances, which have not been adequately addressed for a variety of reasons. It is also the result of the failure to remedy the grievances through the normal processes of democratic governance as well as through dialogue, accommodation, compromise and reconciliation. Systems which provide equity and justice do not allow grievances to accumulate and those which have established and workable methods of conflict resolution have, generally speaking, been free from terrorism. The terrorists while waging their wars do not observe any rules of warfare evolved by humanity and have no regard for human rights of any kind. Any method is acceptable to strike terror and cause maximum possible damage to lives and property. Terrorism respects no borders and is practised by what are called non-state actors, outside the pale of law.

Islamic terrorism, however, has besides some real and several artificial grievances that are considered legitimate by some, a specific set of religious objectives and has unhesitatingly championed and fought to achieve these in various parts of the world, continuously evolving its strategies and tactics, inventing new forms of attack; each more brutal than the other. It has assumed dangerous proportions and has already emerged as the single largest threat to the security and stability of a host of nations. Many countries have suffered due to the violence perpetrated by terrorists inspired by and deriving support from particular tenets of Islam.

India has been grievously hurt and the scale of damage seems to be increasing. Since 2004, India has lost over 4,000 lives to terror attacks—far more than the combined number of casualties suffered by North and South America, Europe and Eurasia. While without doubt, terrorism of this nature aimed at India originates from Pakistan, which for a variety of reasons provides every kind of support to terrorist outfits, what is a growing concern is the increasing evidence that such nefarious influences have started finding resonance in the minds of minorities within the country. This enables Pakistan to claim that terrorism in India is home-grown. Pakistan affords free run to a variety of terrorist outfits openly permitting them to raise funds, organize training camps, fund, arm, and provide logistic support to terrorists who are encouraged to target India to achieve not merely so called "liberation" of Jammu & Kashmir but also destabilize and dismember India as a viable economic and political entity. The direct involvement of the Pakistan's ISI and the army in these activities is now well-documented and recorded even in judicial proceedings—the Headly-Rana case—in the US. That the most notorious international terrorists have been provided shelter, with the knowledge and connivance of the State of Pakistan has been proved beyond all doubts by the killing of Osama Bin Laden in the very heart of a military cantonment. After denying that Pakistan is guilty of an such open violation of its international obligations under the UN charter and resolutions and its oft repeated commitment to fight terrorism and claims of being a victim of international terror, Pakistan dismisses the Osama episode as a mere and innocent intelligence failure! It is now known from the accounts of Bin Laden's wives, in particular his youngest wife from Yemen named Amal who has given detailed statements to Pakistani authorities and Najwa as well her son Omar that Osama was moving around all across Pakistan with absolute freedom along with his entire family and sired some four children through his youngest wife. Two of the children were delivered in government hospitals. No one can accuse Osama of idleness in any respect while it is clear that Osama was under official Pakistani protection all along. The account of Najwa and her son Omar is now published as a book called "*Growing up with Bin Laden*" written by Jean Sasson and published by Oneworld Publications in 2009. These accounts portray Osama in poor light as basically a cruel man who treated his wives as slaves and often beat his children. He wanted all of them to become Mujahideen and in fact, he was marrying one woman after another for the sole purpose of producing more warriors for Jehad.

That Mullah Omar is in Quetta and runs what is known as the "Quetta Shura" is now an open secret except that Pakistan pretends that it does not know anything about it. Another innocent intelligence failure! Mullah Omar plans and executes any number of terrorist acts and Pakistan is working assiduously to ensure that he gets an important position if not complete control in the post-2014 settlement in Afghanistan. It also actively supports the Haqquani network, as its pet insurgency outfit and would like to ensure that this body gains an influential place in the post-2014 set up. In the meanwhile, these two forces continue to create havoc in Afghanistan. It is essential to recognize that there is a mutually reinforcing relationship between the Taliban, Al-Qaeda, the 303 brigade of the Harakat-ul Jehadi Islami (HUJI) and the Haqqani network on the one hand and groups such as the Lashkar-e-Toiba, Hizbul Mujahiddeen, Jaish-e-Mohammed, etc. Pakistan which has been instrumental in creating or supporting each of these militant outfits, is unwilling and may even be unable to control these monsters as they have now a much wider agenda, namely world domination and fighting the West as much as India. Each one of these outfits derive their inspiration from the ideology of radical Islam and their objective is to establish an Islamic State of the highest purity first in Afghanistan, then in Pakistan and then in the rest of the world.

It is of great importance to understand the fundamental philosophical underpinnings of this religiously-oriented terrorism, its motivations, objectives and support infrastructure that it has been able to build up very effectively over the past few decades, posing great threat to our security as well as that of quite a few other countries. Apart from the US, parts of Europe as well as parts of Russia have suffered serious damage due to terror attacks caused by a variety of motivations driven by strong religious underpinnings. France, which has a large Muslim population estimated to be around 10 per cent and growing at a faster rate than the general population, has witnessed targeted attacks by terrorists trained and indoctrinated in camps in Pakistan and claiming to be part of Al-Qaeda. Terrorism of this nature has struck countries in South-East Asia such as Indonesia, the Philippines and even Australia. The Xinxiang province of China has witnessed terrorist activities allegedly by elements trained, armed and indoctrinated by outfits in Pakistan. However, the Western countries have not only fully grasped the grave import of the threat from this form of terrorism, but they have also initiated a series of measures which have fairly effectively contained, though not eliminated, this kind of terror. For example, the United States by taking a series of tough legal and administrative measures, has managed to avoid any terror attack after the infamous 11th September, 2001 World Trade Centre attack which killed some 3000 men women and children of many nationalities. More or less the same can be stated about the UK. The US enacted the tough Home-land Security Act in 2002, the Patriots Act in 2003 and the UK enacted the Prevention of Terrorism Act in 2005 and set up agencies to implement the provisions diligently and effectively. This spirit is reflected in the statement of General Norman Schwarzkopf (of Iraq fame), who with respect to the 9/11 attackers stated "Forgiving them is God's job. Our job is to arrange the meeting". The Patriots Act gives wide powers for search and surveillance and the right to search a suspect's house without notice-a power not given to the NIA of India even though; it was modelled on the FBI. In the US, the culprits are invariably identified quickly, apprehended and awarded exemplary punishments making it clear that the law of the land shall prevail. Surgical strikes, even if they violate the sovereignty of another nation have been undertaken to eliminate known terrorists—Osama in Pakistan, Anwar Aulakhi in Yemen, etc. China unhesitatingly deals with terrorism with unmatched ruthlessness and is least bothered by allegations of human rights violations.

Unfortunately in India, apart from the decline in the efficiency and effectiveness of all our institutions of governance, especially the law enforcement machinery, some political parties, seem to be inclined to deny the very existence of this serious threat to the stability and security of the nation, in the mistaken belief that by doing so they can win the favour of a particular religious community. The police have been prevented from taking effective action by some state governments against bodies who promote sectarian violence and who provide shelter and logistical support to terrorists.

This type of terrorism seems to be backed by enormous inflow of funds and seemingly endless supply of highly motivated, bigoted and committed foot soldiers who are prepared to blow themselves up, in the mistaken belief that by doing so, they are furthering a religious cause.

It is extremely disturbing to note that while on the one hand, terrorism with strong religious underpinnings, encouraged, abetted and supported by Pakistan and receiving almost limitless financial support from Saudi Arabia, has been gaining strength in the country, increasing its support base and by now establishing its presence in all the states including the deep south; on the other hand, there is a progressive weakening of the State machinery's ability and will to fight this form of terror. For example, in the state of Kerala there has been a virtual explosion of fundamentalism among the youth and organizations such as the Indian Mujahideen have been recruiting and training the young and the educated. While the SIMI continues to be banned, a number of alternative front organizations with different names have come up with the same objective of radicalizing the youth. The districts of Kasargode and Kannur have now become hotbeds of fundamentalist propaganda and people of other faiths have been facing threats and intimidation on an increasing scale. Hyderabad as well the west coast of Karnataka are known to harbour religiously oriented militant outfits. Unfortunately, while this is happening we witness a strange phenomenon where while the experience of countries fighting this type of terrorism shows the clear need for extraordinary laws, this country is engaged in deliberately and methodically de-fanging the entire enforcement structure, both the law and the implementing mechanism at the disposal of the State. Laws enacted earlier for dealing with terror of this particular variety such as the Maintenance of Internal Security Act (MISA), Terrorist and Disruptive Activities Act (TADA) and Prevention of Terrorism Act (POTA) have all been removed from the statute book. The over anxiety to take politically correct, safe and convenient stands has, in recent times, also made the Central Government deliberately deny some of the states the necessary legal powers to act decisively against terrorists. Every time a massacre of innocents takes place, there is a ritualistic response of condemnation and restatement of the old, meaningless and worn-out resolve to fight terrorism with all the might of the State. Appeals are always made to the people who have suffered repeatedly to remain calm and maintain communal harmony and peace.

Western democracies and even countries like Indonesia have realized the gravity of the threat posed by religious terrorism, and they have now enacted laws with strong provisions for dealing with terrorist acts, which *inter alia* include treating intercepts as admissible evidence (telephone, wiretaps, listening in to conversations about intentions to commit acts of terrorism), confessions before police officers, burden of proof on the accused, confiscation of profits from terror crimes and of course, provision for severe punishment for those providing logistical support to murderous Jehadis.

It needs to be underlined that as of now, the terrorists and their supports both within the country have been greatly emboldened by the support these terrorists receive from neighboring countries, the financial and ideological support from Saudi Arabia, the extremely weak and tepid response from the State every time a terrorist attack takes place and the ineffectiveness of every arm of the State machinery in dealing with heinous crimes. They are also encouraged by the recent phenomenon where political leaders, self-styled human rights activists, bleeding heart liberals and religious bodies' spring to their defence and the judicial processes seldom succeed in punishing the guilty. The Home Minster himself has been compelled to refer to this trend in conference of Chief Ministers in April 2012. When the perpetrators of terror gain the confidence that their crimes will not be punished in India and India lacks the will and the wherewithal to punish terror, they are prepared to commit even more brazen acts of terror even as they are openly sheltered by the State of Pakistan with impunity. Pakistan knows that India will not react and the terrorists know that they will not be pursued and punished even if caught. Those human right activists and liberals who misguidedly support the terrorists have no concern for the rights of those hundreds of innocent victims or for the nation's security, sovereignty or integrity. There is no deterrence worth its name in the entire country. The war on terror cannot be won merely by words and condemnations. Repeated assurances regarding the resolve of the State to fight terrorism lose all credibility if there is no effective follow up action. The action must be motivated by only one concern, namely the nation's security. The policies hitherto followed, which are nothing but a failure to safeguard the lives of innocent people who are killed by terrorists and føbbing off their relatives with words of sympathy and some monetary compensation, cannot continue.

For Pakistan, exporting terror to India is a low-risk and low-cost option. It is confident that India cannot and will not retaliate for fear of a nuclear retaliation. It is also sure that the US will pressurize India not to react beyond routine condemnations, as happened after the gruesome 26/11 attacks in Mumbai. That Pakistan has emerged as the epicentre of international Islamic terror is now well-documented, and every such incident anywhere in the world is ultimately traced to the training camps of the jehadis in Pakistan. So far, these disclosures have had little impact on Pakistan's behaviour, nor the fact that by now, this kind of terror has emerged as the most serious threat to the stability and economy of the State of Pakistan. Even after 26/11, there have been a series of terrorist attacks in the country but every time, our response is the same. This has now induced a sense of resignation in the minds of the people that nothing can really be expected from the Government as it steadfastly refuses to learn any lessons. The recommendations made by eminent administrators like RD Pradhan—the former Union Home Secretary—to deal with attacks more effectively and more importantly, to prevent such attacks remain in cold storage and those guilty of such lethargy and masterly inactivity, continue to occupy their offices and continue to be protected, even while the ordinary citizen is continuously exposed to danger.

Prompt and effective investigation followed by quick dispensation of justice resulting in punishment of terrorists is an important and major deterrent against terrorism and its perpetrators. There must be a high degree of fear that acts of terrorism will be dealt with effectively and expeditiously and it will be very difficult for terrorists to get away. Unfortunately in our country, major incidents of terrorism remain unresolved and perpetrators remain at large, to commit more daring acts of terrorism. They can easily escape to neighbouring countries and our efforts to get at such criminals have not only been half-hearted but entirely ineffective. We seem to be emerging as a major regional power but display extreme helplessness in dealing with our neighbours who seem to get away repeatedly after kicking us in the pants. Apart from the inexplicable withdrawal of deterrent laws (MBA, TAD A, POT A), and unwillingness to come up with an effective Central Act in the face of ever increasing threats to internal security, repeated acts of terror including planned, deliberate attacks on places of worship and massacres of innocent, the Centre does not even want to enable the States to enact effective laws. Witness the refusal of the Centre to accord the assent of the President to effective pieces of legislation enacted by the states of Gujarat and Rajasthan even while states like Maharashtra and Andhra Pradesh already have similar laws on their statue books. That there should be such discrimination between states by the Centre and such inexplicable unwillingness to provide the law-enforcing machinery with the necessary legal instrumentality, does make one wonder if the Indian State is already a hostage to vested interests who have some kind of empathy and kinship with terrorist outfits. This is in spite of repeated declarations that we are a secular State and are not influenced by religious considerations. The absence of effective legal framework is a grave handicap and every time the Centre convenes a meeting of state police chiefs in its anxiety to show that it is serious about combating terrorism, the states have repeatedly emphasized the need for bringing back laws such as TADA. Unfortunately, these exercises have become nothing but rituals and frustratingly, no effective follow-up is taken.

What is also impossible to understand is the reluctance of the Centre to even mete out the punishment to terrorists which has been awarded by the highest court of the land in the mistaken belief that inaction even in such cases in politically correct. Take the case of the attack on the country's Parliament where the death sentence awarded to Afzal Guru upheld by the Supreme Court has not been implemented. It is deplorable that while the Centre acts in this manner which can only be interpreted as encouragement to terrorism, furthering the belief that terrorists do not get punished in India, and there are any number of so called intellectuals and liberals who keep up the pressure on the Government not to act in the name of human rights or some mistaken notion of liberalism. Even state assemblies have had no hesitation in passing resolutions opposing capital punishment to terrorists, in total disregard of constitutional norms or judicial pronouncements by the highest court of the country. It is a sad commentary on our polity and the state of the nation, that today one has to be extremely wary even to go to a place of worship and our places of worship are unsafe and need to be protected by armed police.

Mention must be made in this context of the pathetic failure on the part of the Government to protect the nation's international borders. Political considerations have played an extraordinary role stalling all efforts to prevent illegal immigration into the country. Measures to contain this menace from the then East Pakistan were implemented with considerable degree of sincerity. After the creation of Bangladesh, however, illegal immigration from that country is, for all practical purposes, uncontrolled. Corruption and lack of adequate manpower has gravely undermined the effectiveness of the Border Security Force which has unfortunately earned the opprobrium of being described as the border security farce. One comes across arguments advanced by certain vested interests and bleeding-heart liberals that illegal migrants are poor people and deserve sympathy, as if this country does not have enough poverty-stricken masses with some 300 million below the poverty line and 500 million without sanitation. More importantly, that the illegal immigrants form a substantial vote bank has influenced a number of political parties to not only turn a blind eye to this demographic aggression or silent invasion but has also encouraged initiatives to enact legislative measures to actually protect these illegal immigrants. Even when the Supreme Court held that the IMDT (Illegal Migrants Determination by Tribunals) Act, is unconstitutional, the Central Government passed an amendment to the Foreigners Act with the same objective of protecting illegal immigrants from Bangladesh. Even this has been struck down by the Supreme Court but the Assam Government has taken no measures to detect and deport illegal migrants. Consequently, the share of Muslim population in Assam which was around 20 per cent in 1971 has gone up to 31 per cent. The illegal migrants have now spread to all parts of India and their numbers are estimated to be in millions. Unfortunately, given their poverty, illiteracy and religious inclinations, they provide extremely fertile ground for recruitment of jehadis. The enormous amount of funds that flow from the middle east and a militant ideology has been used unabashedly to influence the poverty-stricken, insecure immigrants. Bangladeshi outfits such as Harkat-ul-Jihad-e-Islam (HUJI) and Pakistan's Jaish-e-Mohammed (JEM) and Lashker-e-Toiba (LET) and their Indian arm, the Students Islamic Movement of India (SIMI) and Indian Mujahideen find easy resonance in this reservoir of man power who can be counted upon to provide foot soldiers, shelter, logistical support, etc., to terrorists, home-grown or otherwise.

In spite of growing evidence of the fact that Bangladeshi and Pakistani terror outfits have been able to establish cells all over the country and are responsible for acts of terror and killing of innocents, no effective action is taken to detect and deport illegal immigrants. Thousands of Pakistani entrants simply disappear when their visas expire. Even in Assam, where the entire students' agitation which started in 1979, was primarily against illegal immigration, action against illegal immigrants is nonexistent. With regard to the Students Islamic Movement of India which openly preaches hatred against India and would like to destroy India's liberal belief systems and considers itself to be in a state of perpetual jihad, it is treated by our political establishment with velvet gloves. The ban imposed on this dangerous outfit which is now known to have been involved in a number of terror attacks, was removed, enabling the organization to gather strength. This ban has had to be been re-imposed, in spite of opposition from a number of political parties. Terrorist outfits now use technology on an increasing scale, to spread their lethal message and more and more educated people are getting recruited. Such well-equipped and well-supported bodies would, if they study the decline of our institutions, their increasing ineffectiveness, the attitude of our political parties, the indiscipline that is displayed in our legislatures and lack of any commitment to deal with problems facing the country can easily and justifiably conclude, that this country is rotting at the core, is progressively dismantling its internal defences and can be targeted with impunity with little or no fear of punishment and reprisals.

While there is an immediate need to bring in an effective law against terrorism, to my mind, it is equally important to improve the effectiveness of law-enforcement machinery, i.e. both the police and the judiciary. The police in every state has been reduced to pathetic levels, infected as it is to the core by widespread corruption, incapable of defending the ordinary citizen while invariably being used by the ruling party for its political purposes. The police is so demoralized by rampant political interference that functions such as crime control, local intelligence gathering, effective investigation, in a word what is normal police functioning, for which the police are fully empowered under existing laws to be autonomously exercised as per law, have all have been totally neglected and have perhaps reached a point of no return. Cases are not unknown where politicians-turned-criminals or criminals-turned-politicians exercise control over the police, in some states and have taken over the function of transfers and postings. Consequently, the policemen are busy looking after the interest of such politicians. When the ordinary policeman finds that criminals can get away with their crime by being part of the political establishment and there is nothing called equality in the eyes of law and equal protection under law, he has no motivation to take action against the other criminals. Moreover, he is not held accountable for the failure to perform functions which he is expected to do as per law and for which he has been appointed and for which he is paid from the public exchequer. What is tragic is that the political establishment has completely destroyed the principles of hierarchy and accountability in the police, without which no organized machinery can effectively function. The constables and station house officers who are really the cutting edge of the entire machinery are no more answerable to the district superintendent of police and the SPs themselves can get away without being answerable to their superiors. The office of the DGP has become ornamental and in most states, has been almost totally defanged. One is entitled to be amazed at the strange spectacle of our politicians who interfere blatantly in the functioning of the state police and undermine its effectiveness, rendering it all but useless, demand that they be protected by the CRP or SPG/Black Cats, showing their own lack of trust in the state police. What hypocrisy and what expression of confidence in their own machinery! Almost every politician is 'protected' in one form or the other and on an average every politician is protected by at least three men in uniform whereas there is just one policeman for every 1750 citizens of this country.

While this is true of the police machinery, even in the unlikely event of the police managing to file charge sheets, we know what happens in the courts and how effectively the culprits utilize every legal loophole to delay cases and escape punishment. As mentioned above, even when justice long delayed is delivered; it is effectively thwarted by political considerations.

If this is the state of the ability of the state to deal with terrorism of any type, it is no wonder that this country is such an easy target for highly motivated and ideologically bigoted terrorists.

What must be done along with fundamental police reforms and removal of political interference in the functioning of the police is to give powers to the NIA for preemptive investigation and search. The NCTC should be made more effective and fully operationalised. It is indeed strange that the very same parties which had earlier accused the Centre of lack of commitment in tackling terror are now resisting the operationalisation of the NCTC. It is unfortunate that the operationalisation of the NCTC has become a turf war between the centre and the states. To a certain the Centre is to be blamed, as it has often misused central agencies—CBI, IB—for political purposes targeting the opposition parties, going slow on friends and tightening the screws when friends turn foes. The undue delays in according Presidential assent to legislations of opposition ruled states often deliberate and motivated has caused great discomfort to the states. There is a growing trust deficit between the centre and the states. This should be addressed decisively. The NCTC cannot and should not be viewed as a state *versus* centre problem but as an effort to ensure greater centre state coordination and state to state co-ordination in effectively combating what are truly existential threats to the whole nation. The NCTC when it is set up will pool all the intelligence inputs from different agencies, draw a balanced assessment and disseminate this to all security formations for proper preventive and investigative action.

In addition there should be a separate ministry for internal security manned by officers with specialized experience and training in internal security. Counter-terrorism should also be placed in the concurrent list so that both the Centre and the states can act in tandem. For all this to happen, there should be clear recognition of the existential threat that terrorism poses to the nation and mustering of the necessary political will by all the players to deal with the situation urgently and decisively. Partisan and petty electoral politics will have to be totally eliminated. As is the case in the US certain crimes which have multistate implications and national as well as international dimensions such as international terrorism, Naxalism, fake currency, arms smuggling, drug trafficking etc. should be classified as federal crimes and the Centre empowered to act without being fettered by jurisdictional problems and the specific police acts of the states. An organization such as the NIA modeled on the FBI should be empowered under a Parliamentary enactment such as the Prevention of Terrorism Act POTA. We are only too aware of the limitations of the state police machinery, the high degree of politicization they have suffered and the fact that politicians have never hesitated to interfere even in the case of terrorists, if that suits their electoral calculus. The state police cannot be trusted to effectively investigate serious crimes especially of an inter-state nature and those with international linkages. The centre has a definite responsibility to safeguard every citizen from internal and external threats. The centre after all consists of people who are all from one state or the other and cannot surely be regarded as inimical to the interests of any state. India is without doubt a union of states.

We may now analyze the fundamental ideological underpinnings of Islamic extremism, so that all action that is initiated takes into account the strong fundamentals that drive this world-wide threat.

The Al-Qaeda has emerged at the most significant perpetrator of this type of terror. It enjoys a safe haven in the territory of Pakistan, in spite of Pakistan being a party to United Nations resolutions to combat terror, as also in lawless States such as Somalia, Sudan and Yemen. This outfit has acquired worldwide reach and has been able to find recruits in almost all parts of the globe. It is able to provide training grounds, weaponry, support systems and no doubt, limitless finances. It has provided the ideological *raison d'etre* for an entire gamut of terrorist activities based on Islamic tenets, spawning a variety of outfits which are able to take root and thrive in those environments which are loosely termed as failed States. They are invariably financed by Saudi Arabia's various trusts or they take control of natural resources and exploit any and every avenue for drug trafficking or arms smuggling. Yemen, Nigeria, Somalia, Afghanistan and Sudan are prime examples. Somalia specializes in piracy as well, taking advantage of its location on the vital sea lanes leading to the Suez Canal through which a major part of the world's energy resources are transported, besides other goods.

Pakistan continues to provide a base for this outfit and also protects it officially and unofficially with impunity. Though widely acknowledged, Pakistan's role in promoting international terror is yet to be taken seriously enough and dealt with by the world community. Pakistan has been able to get away by claiming that it is a victim of terrorism and is seriously combating terror by deploying its armed forces. By apprehending minor players, it has sought to carry conviction with the international community while continuing to protect the main perpetrators. It suits Pakistan to keep up this farce as it keeps getting American money to fight terrorism and Saudi money to spread fundamentalist beliefs and expand terrorist infrastructure. Such a strategy enables Pakistan to keep up the pressure on both Afghanistan and India to achieve its long-standing strategic objectives of gaining critical depth in its backyard while punishing India and keeping Kashmir on the boil and if possible, seize Kashmir forcibly out of India's hold. While undoubtedly greatly disillusioned by Pakistan's duplicity, the Americans seem to be caught in a dilemma. They feel that it is dangerous to allow Pakistan to collapse and be taken over by Islamic extremists who will take control of its nuclear assets. It has been keeping the tap open, in the fond hope that one day Pakistan will be able to put its house in order. The Americans do have, it appears, a contingency plan to take over the nuclear assets in case of a collapse, but this fuels anti-Americanism and makes a nervous Pakistan take protective measures to thwart any American moves. Conspiracy theories that India, Israel and the US are in cohorts to take control of Pakistan's nuclear assets find easy currency in paranoid Pakistan. The unemployed in Pakistan and those who study in madrasas established with Saudi Arabian finance, provide a fertile ground for recruits. It is stated that the family of a suicide bomber is given something like Rs. 20 lakh. For a family with excess capacity and expendable lives, a promise of this nature is highly tempting, especially when it is combined with heavenly rewards.

International terrorism has now spawned a number of outfits which in one form or the other pose grave threat to internal security of several countries. Bodies such as Lashkar-e-Toiba, Lashkar-e-Jhangvi, Hizbul Mujahideen, Hizbul Tahirir, Hizbul-Jehadi Islami, Hizbollah, Muslim brotherhood, all draw their ideological inspiration and sustenance from the same religious-oriented fountain, based on a belief system that advocates a world vision where Islam alone will prevail. Added to this are a set of so called grievances, alleged injustices meted out to the believers and occupation of Muslim lands. Some of these outfits aim at recreating the ideal Islamic State that is supposed to have prevailed at the time of the Prophet and his companions. This idea, promoted by the Salafist movement and backed by the Wahabi school, does not spell out in precise terms what is to be recreated and whether it will be possible at all to march back some 15 centuries negating all the scientific, technological, economic and political as well as social progress that humanity has achieved. This fundamentalist ideological framework derives inspiration from religious texts, which according to this interpretation provide the basis for universal political organization and international terror. Radical Islam rejects claims to national sovereignty, based on secular state models and its reach extends to wherever significant populations profess the particular faith. Some scholars are of the view that devout Muslims dream of the recreation of a global caliphate—a seat of religious and political authority holding sway over the whole Islamic world, and ideal form of governance deriving its authority from the Almighty. In Islamic literature there is huge reverence for the first four caliphs who succeeded the Prophet (though not by the Shias). That three of these were murdered is seldom mentioned. The West is blamed for the abolition of the Caliphate in 1924 after the defeat the Ottoman Empire in the First World War though in reality, it was Kemal Ataturk who abolished the Caliphate. In such a scheme democracy as such which derives its authority from the people may have no place. Since neither the current international system nor the internal structure of existing states has legitimacy in the eyes of radical Islam, its ideology leaves little room for modern notions of negotiation or of equilibrium, notions which have been evolved over-time by humanity as conflict-resolving mechanisms. Indeed, followers of the radical version are prepared to sacrifice all modern notions of civil society in order to pursue creation of the apocalyptic Utopia. The highly conservative and radicalized belief system seems to fear any progress as dilution of faith, and zealously advocates concepts unsuited to the modern world such as cross-border loyalties to an Islamic "UMMAH". This system believes in total rejection of all other belief systems and indoctrination of minds with an ideology which discourages debate, discourse and dissent. This ideology even advocates use of unlimited violence, legitimizes murder of innocents and aims at creating a vague Utopian world based on a fuzzy vision of a distant past, calling for the revival of archaic values, laws and practices. This ideology is nihilistic, bereft of any idealism and is in direct conflict with forces of moderation, tolerance, modernization and progress. It poses a direct challenge to systems of international management evolved over a long period of time, designed to avoid conflicts, avoidance of the use of armed power and violence and evolution of solutions to the problems of humanity through dialogue, discourse, accommodation, compromise and acceptance of a variety of viewpoints.

While there are a number of terrorist outfits, quite a few of which have been named above, what needs to be noted is that they all derive their inspiration and motivation from the same ideological fountain, have broadly the same objectives, believe in violence and martyrdom and their tactics are not dissimilar. Suicide bombing is now practised by all of them. Increasingly, they have been able to attract the educated and are now capable of applying the latest technological solutions to perpetrate terror in order to achieve their objectives. The madrasas, particularly in Pakistan, contribute many of the foot soldiers but the educated are also drawn towards militancy because of its ideology and the role of the mosque and the mullahs. The mosque is a vibrant and effective platform for the propagation of a militant ideology and the Friday prayer is a potent instrument to encourage violence, tap into and incite the latent sense of injustice, build up grievances and create a sense of victimhood, while blaming a host of external forces for the present state of affairs.

Since 9/11, the Americans and the Europeans have spent a lot of their time and resources in fighting the Al-Qaeda and its affiliates. It is claimed that hundreds of operatives have been killed or captured and a whole lot of plots have been thwarted. Osama himself has been killed and quite a few of his top lieutenants have also been eliminated. America has invaded both Afghanistan and Iraq. In spite of all this and the huge cost of these wars 6,000 American troops and a large number of allied soldiers, 1,37,000 civilians killed in Iraq, Pakistan and Afghanistan, US$ 4 trillion spent, and 7.8 million displaced as per a study by the Brown University—success seems to be nowhere in sight. The money spent is equivalent to the US budget deficit during the period 2005-2010. Al-Qaeda can easily and justifiably derive satisfaction of seriously damaging the American economy. The objective of the Al-Qaeda and its affiliates to involve the US and the West in 'bleeding wars' in Muslim lands has, it appears, also been achieved. Al Qaeda has now spread its tentacles to new countries in Africa and its presence is noticed in many European countries where it is capable of planning and executing acts of terror. Germany reportedly has detected the presence of no less than 1,000 sleeper cells influenced by Al-Qaeda. More importantly Al-Qaeda has now become a virus which mutates continuously into new forms and has managed to not only poison the minds of a whole lot of Muslims, in a whole lot of countries, all of whom are becoming increasingly suspicious and hostile to other belief systems but also poison relations between nations. They tend to blame the West for their ills, for poverty and of course for not helping in the destruction of Israel.

This kind of hostility displayed openly and often in violent forms has now started generating increasing intolerance in several Western nations. Islamophobia has even influenced the political class which is nervous of voters becoming impatient with attacks and demanding ever stricter measures. In France the increase in the appeal of Marie Le Pen of the far right and that of Wilders in Holland are signs of this trend. It cannot be denied that this kind of a threat has kept many societies on edge and governments are compelled to continuously increase their vigilance against attacks, with ever-increasing budgets and more and more intensive surveillance and security measures causing a good deal of inconvenience to ordinary citizens.

The death of Osama Bin Laden has it appears been a setback, but the infrastructure of terrorism is now well established in many parts of the world especially in those countries called failed states, where there is no governance worth the name. Osama's death has also not resulted in any reduction of violence or terrorist attacks in any country already infected by his militant and violent ideology. There is a unity of purpose among many groups with clear loyalty to ideas which provide the underpinnings to Al-Qaeda. Take the case of Ilyas Kasmiri who was killed in June 2010 by a drone attack. He represents what can be termed as the intersection of several groups—the Al-Qaeda, the Afghan Taliban and the Pakistan Taliban as well as outfits such as LET, Hizbul Mujahideen etc. Ilyas Kashmiri had managed to put together a shadowy army, Lashkar-e-jil bringing together Al-Qaeda and Taliban fighters. What is frightening is the conclusion of the Pakistani journalist Syed Saleem Shahzad, who was killed allegedly by the ISI and possibly under the direct orders of the Army Chief of Pakistan, that Al-Qaeda was directing most of the Jihadi operations in Pakistan and the Pakistan Taliban is the creation of Al-Qaeda. He also claimed that the Al-Qaeda ideology has now widespread appeal among a major section of the society and even the Pakistan Army. Witness the lawyers showering rose petals on the assassin of Salman Taseer whose only 'fault' was to defend a Christian girl detained for blasphemy. In fact, it appears that Shahzad's guilt was to have revealed the involvement of several officers in the lethal attack on the naval base in Karachi which resulted in the destruction of three very valuable US made P3 Orion surveillance aircraft. It is known that Hizbul Tahirir has many adherents in the Pakistan Army and quite a few ex-army and ISI officers are active members of this body. The Pakistani Taliban functions under the leadership of the

Haqqani network which is part of the Al-Qaeda and which is a favourite of the Pakistan Army. The debate has it appears shifted from the Talibanisation of Pakistan to the Pakistanisation of Taliban. This disease has now taken heavy toll on human lives in Pakistan and over 35,000 people have been killed since 9/11. An article in the *Dawn* Newspaper (31st August, 2011) argues that the number of deaths due to attacks and suicide bombings show dramatic increases every Friday and for the past year every Friday witnesses on an average ten times more deaths than all other days of the weak. Does this indicate that radicalization takes place in mosques and Friday prayers are used to preach violence?

A host of regional satraps have now emerged to further the cause of Al Qaeda. Apart from Aiman-al-Zawahiri, the heir of Osama and Saif-al-Adel (the military leader), there is Abdul Shakoor who operates in Afghanistan's Waziristan area, the well connected Quetta Shura led by Mullah Omar, Hafiz Majid, Hassan Akhund, Hassan Rehmani and others, there is also now the Al-Qaeda of Arabian Peninsula led by Abu Nasir Wuhayasi. The spiritual leader of this group was Anwar al-Awaliki. There is also the Al-Qaeda in Mahghreb led by Abu Musad Wadud, the Al-Qaeda of Iraq and of Indonesia—all subscribers to the same ideology and pursuing the same objectives. These regional groups while basically following the ideology of Al-Qaeda and its violent and brutal techniques are not under the direct control of any central authority and often follow their own local objectives. Osama in his last days bemoaned the fact that some like the Pakistani Taliban are killing Muslims, much against his own diktats on such matters.

Basically Islamic extremism and its offshoot of international terrorism, springs from the following principles:

a. That a particular belief system is the only true belief system
b. All other belief systems practised by various segments of humanity are not only false but deserve to be destroyed.
c. Believers have a duty to destroy the false belief systems. Some like the Salafists believe that non-believers should either accept Islam and if they do not they deserve to be killed Wajib-ul-Qatl.
d. Believers cannot be expected to owe loyalty to a

particular state, as they belong to a wider international trans-border group of believers, who derive their belief systems from divine revelations, contained in religious texts.

e. Believers must work towards re-establishment of an old world order which commanded the loyalty of believers namely, the Islamic Caliphate.
f. Believers have a right to live by their own divine law wherever they live and cannot be expected to comply with laws enacted by human beings, in particular states where they happen to live. However, they see no problem in taking advantage of the protection, freedom and equity afforded by modern societies and their legal systems where they happen to live.
g. Believers must work towards establishing the world of Islam "DARUL-ISLAM" which is equivalent to the world of peace "DARUL-AMAN"—and—until this is achieved, believers have to live in the world of conflict-"DARUL HARB" in which they have to carry a relentless struggle to achieve "DARUL-ISLAM".
h. In the world of Darul Islam, non-believers have no rights and indeed no place and if at all they are tolerated, they have to occupy the position of Dhimmies or people who are subservient.
i. In order to achieve success in efforts to establish Darul Islam, jihad or holy war is permissible and those who engage in such holy wars are entitled to special heavenly rewards.
j. It is the duty of believers to struggle to recover what has been termed as *"Muslim Lands"*. The fact that some Muslim conquerors had reached the gates of Vienna in Europe, as well as Spain and the fact that Islamic rule prevailed at one time over most of India and also the Philippines, are all advanced as reasons for recovering these lands back for Muslim rule. That these lands earlier belonged—to those human beings who were not Muslims for centuries, that they were subjected to forcible conversion, widespread violence and repression, and that their places of worship were destroyed, are all of no account.
k. It is the duty of believers to avenge alleged ill-treatment

of Muslims and killing of believers in various parts of the world—Palestine, Chechnya, Kashmir etc., being examples.

l. It is legitimate to target the US, Israel, and India for so called atrocities on believers.

This entire system of beliefs is derived from a number of verses in the Koran itself which are explicit in their commandments. As Sam Harris argues in his *"End of Faith"* these commandments are divine and leave not an iota of doubt in the minds of the believers, as to their intent and the action to be taken by the believers. These commandments were indeed the inspiration for all Muslim conquerors to destroy and pillage religious institutions in conquered territories. Muslim historians of the period invariably extol such acts in glowing terms, glorifying such destruction as legitimate, carried out in the service of believers and in compliance with the commandments. No doubt there are commandments, which do speak of religious tolerance but the scriptures make it very clear that such earlier revelations are negated by later commandments and the believer is left in no doubt which of the commandments, he is expected to obey and carry out. Dr. Ambedkar in his *"The Decline and Fall of Buddhism—Writings and Speeches"* Vol. III, Government of Maharashtra (1987, pp. 229-38), who is an icon of liberal intellectuals, has in detailed accounts described the destruction and desecration of monasteries and the butchery of monks by Muslim invaders. The great Nalanda University in Bihar was razed to the ground by such marauders.

In displaying this kind of behaviour, Sam Harris points out, the followers of Islam are no different from the Christian proselytes, who carried out the inquisitions against the heretics and killed innocent women, branding them as witches. The great library at Alexandria which contained all the accumulated wisdom of the ancient world—of the Greeks, of the Romans, the Egyptians, the Phoenicians and whose works had recorded great knowledge in philosophy, astronomy, mathematics etc. establishing that the Earth is a sphere and it and other planets are part of the solar system going round the Sun—was wantonly destroyed and the priest, who killed the last librarian, a lady scholar of repute, was canonized. Great and advanced civilizations—the Aztecs, the Incas—were all destroyed by

Christian crusaders. Brutal wars were waged against the Muslims and of course throughout the ages, Jews have been murdered by Christians. The Koran does contain a lot of the elements which are part of the commandments of the Old Testament which inspired the Christian zealots. Concepts such as levy of interest being considered unethical are common between Islam and Christianity. In many parts of Christendom money lending was left to the Jews. The church held that usurers by charging for the duration of a loan were not trading in goods but in time, which belonged to God. It was declared that bankers will inevitably go to hell.

The problem arises basically from the fundamental belief propagated by the Semitic/Abrahamic religions, that their followers alone will have the unalterable right to enter heaven, while all others not only have no right, however noble their character and behaviour may have been, to come anywhere near the gates of heaven but are condemned to suffer eternally in hell. Even a Gandhi or a Buddha had no prospects to enter heaven. Take the following verse from the Koran which is one of the most famous and is taught in all madrasas in the first semester: "The believers and the faithful shall enter paradise and the unbelievers shall be condemned to eternal hellfire". Thomas Friedman relates the story in his book *"The World is Flat"*, as to how during a visit to a madrasa on the Afghanistan border he was made to listen to a bright student recite this verse with the right cadence and was complimented by the teacher for the devotion with which he recited this verse. Such dogmatism may be contrasted to the wide catholicity of the teachings of Swami Vivekananda which aver that "Each soul is potentially divine. The goal is to manifest this divinity within by controlling nature—external and internal. Do this by work, or worship, or psychic control or philosophy by one or more—or all of these and be free."

Both the Old Testament and the Koran place the 'chosen people' above the rest of humanity—the Israelis in the Old Testament and the Arabs in Islam. In the Hadis, the Prophet of Islam declares, 'God chose as the best the children of Ishmael, the son of Abraham. From Ishmael's descendents, God chose the Quarish (the tribe of the Prophet)—as the best people; from the Quarish God chose the Banu Hashim (the clan of the Prophet) the best of people and from the Banu Hashim, God chose Muhammad as the best of all men.'

The Prophet instructed his followers to respect the Arabs, for the is an Arab, the Koran is Arabic, and the inhabitants of paradise speak Arabic. One cannot disagree with Dr. S Radhakrishnan, when he wonders if such a concept of exclusive concern of the God of the Universe for a small minority of inhabitants, in one of the smallest and most insignificant of planets, in the outer periphery of the Universe, can be reconciled with modern notions of creation and knowledge of the Universe and equality in the eyes of God.

However, today Christianity has grown out of the savagery of the middle ages and in fact, there is growing interest and appreciation of tolerance, catholicity and universality of Eastern and non-Semitic belief systems. Swami Vivekananda's message has found resonance in many parts of the world and his 150th birth anniversary will be celebrated during 2013 by some 3 million Americans. Maybe, in the same manner one hopes sometime in the future, Islam will also be transformed. Another renaissance can take place and a new Voltaire or Spinoza may bring about the desired transformation. In the meanwhile however, one must take note of the fact that Christianity's damage potential was determined and limited by the weapon systems it could command, basically swords and spears and gun powder. On the other hand, today's Islamic terrorists can access weapons of mass destruction. The Chinese and the Americans have done grave disservice to humanity by conniving at, aiding and abetting development of these weapons in Pakistan. In particular, the Chinese have caused great harm to international security by promoting the tripartite unholy collaboration with North Korea and Pakistan which has resulted in it acquiring both missile and nuclear technologies of increasing sophistication. Pakistan has also tried to transfer these technologies to other mainly Muslim countries. While this broad ideological framework is projected as the philosophical support system for Islamic extremism, particular reasons against particular countries add to the volatile mixture. The United States is singled out as the most important target as it supports Israel and has waged war against Muslim countries—Iraq and Afghanistan, it has stationed troops of unbelievers in the holy land, exploited Muslim resources and is generally a great threat to Islam and its belief system. The Israelis are regarded as equally legitimate targets for having established a Jewish state in Muslim lands, rendering Palestinians as refugees and carrying out almost daily killings of believers in all countries surrounding Israel. Ill-treatment and killing of Muslims is also a charge against Russia, India and the Philippines. The radical elements do not spare even purely Muslim countries including Saudi Arabia as in their view, these countries are not being governed according to the pure Islamic tenets, the sharia law is not properly and fully implemented, are guilty of modernizing their countries accepting Western notions of democracy, system of governance, gender freedom and educational systems which do not promote radical Islamic values. Scholars such as Sam Harris (*End of Faith*) have argued that many other people have much more serious grievances against the US the Vietnamese or the Cambodians or the people of Laos and for that matter the Tibetans against the Chinese—but they are not going around promoting terrorism, suicide bombings or targeted attacks on innocent civilians, who have nothing to do with the so called atrocities and in fact, may be conscientious objectors to some of the policies. What is so special about the grievances, articulated by the Islamic terrorists that justifies violence on such a scale and is such a mindless manner, is the question that must be raised.

The philosophical underpinnings discussed above are also reinforced and supported by the teachings of Islamic scholars, primarily from the Middle East.

The most important and influential thinker is the founder of the Wahabi Sect of Sunni Islam. This was founded by the 18th Century cleric named Ibn-Al-Wahab. The school is an extremely austere and strict system rejecting other Islamic sects, describing these as apostates and totally rejecting Christians and Jews. In its interpretation of monotheism, the Wahabis have shown no hesitation in condemning the practices of other Islamic sects and destroying many cemeteries in Saudi Arabia including that of the Prophet himself. Prayer at the graves of Imams and saints of Islam is prohibited. In particular, the Wahabis show great intolerance towards the Shias, periodically attacking some of the holiest sites of Shia Islam. What is of great importance is the fact that the Wahabi school is becoming more and more assertive in the international arena and is able to spread its influence more effectively, given the fact that the Wahabi sect collaborated in the establishment of the kingdom of Saudi Arabia and the Saudi royal family has been promoting the Wahabi school in particular and Sunni Islam in general. This family has used its enormous resources for promoting this school throughout the world. The oil exporting countries of the Middle East have benefited greatly by the continuous increase in oil prices and Saudi Arabia is a particular beneficiary. The IMF estimates that these countries run a current account surplus of some US $ 600 billion compared to just 180 billion of China. The current account deficits of many countries including the US have been rising due primarily to the rise in oil prices. Saudi Arabia has been instrumental in establishing a large number of madrasas and mosques in countries like Pakistan and unhesitatingly promotes a jihadi culture. Particular mention needs to be made of the role played by Saudi financers backed by the extremist Wahabi ideology in the current conflicts raging all along Pakistan's border with Afghanistan. The Taliban and the Al Qaeda as well as many terrorist outfits are the off-shoots of this extremist ideology. The Taliban hold that, the Sunni creed is the only true and pure version of Islam and all other sects such as Shias, Ahmedis etc. are unbelievers and deserve to be killed—wajib-ul-qatl. The Deobandi set of religious institutions which accept the Sunni Wahabi traditions, receive both financial and ideological support from Saudi Arabia and its madrasas, have been the largest source of jihadi warriors all along the Afghan and Pakistan border. The Israeli Ambassador to United Nations, Dore Gold in his book entitled "*Hatred's Kingdom*" has fully documented the role played by Saudi religious institutions, Saudi charities and the Saudi royal family, in promoting and financing a wide variety of terrorists in various parts of the world. Bodies such as the World Assembly of Muslim Youth (Riyadh), International Islamic Federation of Students Organizations (Kuwait) have provided huge funds in support of militant ideology, to recruit and train jihadis. Such unlimited flow of funds and militant ideology finds ready response in the huge reservoirs of unemployed in Pakistan and elsewhere, where the State has failed to provide modern education or health care or employment opportunities while the population has been growing at a fast pace. Pakistani rulers like General Zia-ul-Haq actively promoted religious extremism in the belief that Pakistan will achieve its strategic objectives of creating a friendly client State in Afghanistan, punishing India in a variety of ways and capturing Kashmir. This lethal combination of enormous financial resources, militant ideology and unlimited supply of motivated foot soldiers considers India as a legitimate target as it is a land of unbelievers and has allegedly ill-treated Muslims in Kashmir.

One of the Wahabi prelates who were able to exercise an influence far beyond Saudi Arabia in recent times was the blind cleric Abdullah Bin Baz who died in Mecca in 1999. At the time of the Gulf War, he issued a fatwa against women drivers, Saudis and Americans and even declared in a fatwa that those who held that the Earth was a sphere were atheists. He was patronized by the Saudis and became the Chancellor of the Islamic University of Medina and President of the General Presidency of Islamic Research. He also chaired many committees such as Muslim World League, the Supreme Committee for Islamic Propagation and the World Supreme Council for Mosques, all dedicated to the cause of export of Wahabi teachings.

One of the students of Bin Baz was Abdullah Azam, was a Palestinian who can be regarded as one of the biggest contributors to Jihad in Pakistan. He moved to Egypt where he came into contact with the Muslim Brotherhood and absorbed its mission to spread the central message of the essentiality for Islam to combat non-Islamic ignorance (jahiliya). He had to flee Egypt and sought shelter in Saudi Arabia where he was given the post of a lecturer and in the process, absorbed even more deeply the Wahabi creed and the teachings of Bin Baz and Ibn Taymiyya. He came into international prominence by issuing a fatwa entitled "Defence of the Muslim Land" in the wake of the Soviet invasion of Afghanistan in December 1979 in which he declared it obligatory for all Muslims to wage jihad against the Russians in Afghanistan and the Israelis in Palestine. He moved with his family to Pakistan taking as his inspiration the declaration of the Prophet that "a few moments spent in jihad in the path of Allah are worth more than 70 years praying at home" Abdullah Azam along with Osama Bin Laden played a crucial role in mobilizing an international Islamic force to fight the Soviets. His political philosophy is summed up in his message, "Jihad and the rifle alone; no negotiations, no conferences, no dialogue". He wrote "Jihad continues until Allah's Word is raised high; jihad until all the oppressed peoples are freed; jihad to protect our dignity and restore our occupied lands. Jihad is the way of everlasting glory." He was a firebrand preacher who carried his message through his speeches and his publications which were lapped up in many countries. He can be termed as the god-father of jehad in the sub-continent.

That it is the very same ideological underpinnings and training to inculcate this ideology in establishments in Pakistan that has produced a large number of jihadis to fight battles against the West and carry out bombings elsewhere has now started receiving increasing attention all over the world. The role played by Saudi Arabia is of critical importance, and the Saudi war chest for carrying out international jihad is expanding all the while given the soaring world oil prices. No doubt, Iran is also playing an important role but its reach is somewhat more limited compared to Saudi Arabia. World opinion, however, is highly squeamish and cautious in pointing fingers towards Saudi Arabia. Even when it is known that the majority of the suicide bombers of 9/11 were from Saudi Arabia, were highly educated but driven by the militant ideology, it is only a courageous few who were prepared to speak about it. No government has taken any worthwhile action in this regard.

The other influential Islamic scholar who followed a literalist, text-based interpretation, was the medieval scholar, Ahmad-Bin-Taymmiya who advocated a return to the ideals of the original Muslim community of Arabia established by the Prophet himself. In fact, Bin-Taymmiya should be regarded as the original author of the Wahabi school. He was born in 1263 and grew at a time when the Mongols centred in Persia evolved a tolerant inclusive Islamic civilization rooted in Sufism and predominantly Shia. This was anathema to Taymmiya and others who followed the Hannabali code of jurisprudence—the strictest of the four schools. They considered the practices introduced by the Mongols as an insult to God and wanted a return to the days of the Prophet. His interpretation was of pure monotheism and did not permit practices such as worship at the graves, mausoleums etc., which was condemned as heresy. He showed extreme intolerance towards non-Muslims and unbelievers, asserting that "Muslims have the right and indeed, the duty to revolt against non-believers and wage jihad". He rejected the idea of drawing a distinction between lesser jehad (jehad kabeer), i.e. warfare against infidels, etc., and greater jehad (jehad akbar), namely moral struggle for conquering inner self, and advocated unrelenting campaign against all those whom he considered apostates, heretics and infidels. Ibn Taymmiya is a highly venerated figure in today's Saudi Arabia.

This doctrine is copied by Egyptian extremists such as Sayid Qutub who established Egypt's Muslim brotherhood. The Muslim brotherhood was established in 1928 by Hassan-al-banna. This group used violence on a large scale including assassination of the Prime Minster of Egypt in 1948. Qutub used the word "Jahiliyyah" (the term used for describing the pre-Islamic world, a period of ignorance) to describe the modern world. He condemned the decadent culture of the West as well as the dictatorial and un-Islamic governments of the Muslim world. He saw the West as a historic enemy of Islam and the elite in Muslim countries as corrupt. He advocated a violent, offensive and armed jihad in order to create a new Islamic community. It needs to be noted that the teachings of Ibn Taymmia and his followers literally put the clock back as regards Islamic societies, taking them back to the 7th century AD. It may be recalled that when during the middle ages Christian zealots were busy destroying the accumulated knowledge of humanity from the time of the Greeks, Islamic scholars were the ones who preserved the works of Plato, Socrates and Aristotle and translated these into Arabic and much later, these could be accessed by the Europeans after the renaissance. But for such Islamic scholars, this ancient wisdom may have been permanently lost to the world. It is, therefore, a matter of great regret that a society which had attached such great importance to the value of knowledge and had developed respect for learning and free expression of dissent, had to suddenly reverse direction. It is yet to regain the lost thirst for knowledge and open its windows once again to the flow of wisdom from every direction.

In the Indian subcontinent, the leading light of extremism is Maulana Maudoodi who founded the Jammat-i-Islami. He condemned the rise of nationalism in South Asia; as a western-imposed ideology calculated to weaken and divide the world-wide Muslim community with individual nationalism based on language, ethnicity and locality. He strongly advocated waging of relentless jihad as a struggle to bring about Islamic revolution capable of uniting the entire Muslim community of the world. The military dictator of Pakistan, Zia-ul-Haq was an avid follower of Maudoodi's teachings and is held responsible for the radicalization of Pakistan's Army, polity and major segments of its society. With Saudi financing he promoted the establishment of thousands of madrasas which have emerged as jehadi factories of today.

Osama Bin Laden had been inspired by all these thinkers and had fashioned his war on this militant ideology. He exploited the poor unemployed youth of the subcontinent and of Afghanistan as well as the southern republics of ex-USSR and applied his enormous resources and ideology to convert them into warriors capable of causing great damage to organized societies. More importantly and dangerously, his violent message has found resonance in even the educated and talented as well the techno-savvy, who have used their considerable skills and energy to achieve higher levels of sophistication in the planning and execution of acts of terrorism.

India has become a victim and while the foot soldiers are available in plenty from our neighbouring countries, unfortunately, segments of our own population have been providing support for carrying out terrorists activities. While for a long time Kashmir has been the focus of jihad, supported, financed, trained and armed by Pakistan in recent times, the network of terror has spread to almost all parts of the country and the militant ideology of targeting India as the country of non-believers, is playing an increasingly important role. The ISI and its extremist creations in Pakistan have often articulated the view that India is a legitimate target, the main enemy of Pakistan and must be punished by a thousand cuts. The aim clearly is to destroy the Indian nation and bring about its balkanization by continuous attacks. Children in almost all schools of Pakistan are taught that India is a land of non-believers and an enemy.

The other aims of militant extremism are:

a. To destabilize this country politically.
b. Bring about total communal polarization and destroy the country's secular ethos.
c. Seriously damage the economy of the country.
d. Destroy investor confidence in India's stability and security.
e. Target educational institutions and knowledge industries which have contributed to the growth of the nation's wealth and intellectual capital.

f. Attack its institutions of governance—the Parliament, the courts and high profile business establishments etc., so that widespread fear psychosis is created with continuous threat of violence and the faith of the people in the country's institutions is undermined.

That India has been able to record much higher rates of economic growth; than its Islamic neighbours and today, the country's international profile and importance has been greatly enhanced, that it is a sought-after investment destination and as a strategic partner by countries such as the US, have caused envy in the minds of jihad groups and they want to inflict as much damage as possible. Hitting soft targets has recently become more prominent. The aim of hitting soft target seems to be as follows:

a. The jihadis want to demonstrate their ability to hit in any part of the country, not only cause damage but also increase insecurity and spread terror.
b. They want to discredit the government and destroy the faith of the people in the police, security agencies and systems of governance.
c. They would like that security agencies over-react so that sections of the community are alienated.
d. Attacks are often termed as revenge—for so called perceived atrocities committed by the government towards the members of a particular community.
e. Most importantly, everyone of the acts of terrorism makes life more difficult for the ordinary citizen and the government has to continuously upgrade the mechanisms to even provide minimal security to its citizens and this means that precious resources are diverted towards unproductive expenditure, diminishing the ability of the government to spend money on economic and social development or accelerate the growth process.

It is clear that by now a wide arc of countries starting from Algeria and Morocco and extending throughout the Middle East, Afghanistan, Indian subcontinent including Pakistan and Bangladesh and parts of Indonesia, Malaysia and the Philippines, have all become victims in one way or the other to this brand of international terrorism. The whole of Middle East has been recently in ferment and longstanding dictators have been sent packing. Whether this will necessarily result in the establishment of benign, genuine and participatory democracies which are capable of protecting human rights, rights of minorities, and of women is at the moment, very uncertain. Whether they can accept the present systems of international economic and security management and emerge as constructive partners is open to question. The dictators had often brutally suppressed radical Islam in the entire Arab world. Whether the Middle East will now see full scale revival of bodies such as the Muslim brotherhood and Salafists, whether militant Islam will take over the States to establish Islamic systems of governance and justice, is being watched with considerable nervousness. That this area's stability is of critical importance to the entire world's economic well-being as it has the worlds' largest reservoir of hydro carbons adds to the problem. The dictators invariably failed and indeed refused to see the point in creating effective, secular institutions of governance. They have left behind none of the essential instruments of governance, the judiciary, the civil service, etc., which can run the country, provide basic services and take care of orderly conduct of the affairs of the society. The army, if at all, is the only viable institution in all these countries.

On the other hand, the Islamists are relatively better organized, with dedicated, highly committed and motivated cadres, backed by an ideology which derives support from the word of God. A legal system, the Sharia, a control and command system, namely the vast network of mosques, all constitute a readily available organizational framework for running a State system and governing a society. The example of Iran is a clear pointer, especially if the modern idea of separation of the church and the State is given the go by. The Islamic concept of charity can also be a very useful supplement to the system for providing a variety of services. Education can be taken care of by the mosques and the madrasas. As to resources, at least for now and the foreseeable future, the huge oil wealth will suffice. In this entire area the Western model of democratic governance is highly discredited and Western society is viewed with suspicion, and regarded as arrogant and immoral. Unless therefore, those who have inherited the mantle of leadership in these countries evolve a new system which avoids the infirmities of an Islam-based polity, guarantees human rights, rights of women and minorities, there is the real danger that a system which the Islamists advocate, may come into being in these countries. The violent attack on the Israeli embassy in Cairo destroying its compound wall is possibly a pointer of the way things may turn out. The attacks on Coptic Christians in Egypt and reports of threats against secular symbols, and rapid increase in the number of women who have taken to the veil and the hijab are all uncomfortable pointers. One can only hope that it will not be a replication of what happened in Afghanistan under the Taliban.

The fact, generally speaking, that the level of education in the Middle East is far higher than that in Afghanistan, and women's education in countries such as Tunisia and Egypt had reached high levels, that this region has been exposed to western influences for a long time now and except in Saudi Arabia the status of women had been improving, offers the hope that the Middle East will not go the Afghan way. Also, today more than ever, with the Internet and worldwide communication and data transfer systems, one cannot close any society from getting infected by superior ideas. Writers like Ohran Pamuk, Ayan Hirsi Ali and Edward Said who have gone through the experience of living in Islamised States as well as, in liberal democracies, write freely of what can be the blessings for ordinary people, especially women, if liberal ideas are the norm. Edward Said has courageously spoken of the Arab world as being 'disfigured by a whole series of outmoded and discredited ideas and shortcomings which included political failures, human rights abuses. and the fact that alone of all the modern peoples they have receded in democratic and technological and scientific developments'. Edward Said also chastises the West for all the injustices and the pro-Western dictatorships in Muslim countries for many of today's ills and resentments.

A fine model is available to the Middle East, namely Turkey but to get to this model you have to recreate a Kemal Ataturk, but at the moment Ataturks are in seriously short supply. Worryingly however ever since the so called 'mildly Islamic' party under Recep Erdogan assumed power 'mildness' is evaporating at a fairly rapid rate. Erdogan has been pandering to the Islamists by ramming through legislation allowing middle school students to enroll in 'imam hatip' schools where Muslim clerics are trained and to study the Koran in state schools. He is also tailoring his foreign policy to be more supportive of Sunni regimes trying to create arc of Sunni Muslim countries spanning Africa, Asia, the Balkans and the Middle East. The objective is suspected to be to counter America and Iran. While he was earlier supportive of Bashir Assad he has now changed tack and is asking for a regime change and is coddling Syria's Muslim brotherhood. Is Erdogan dreaming of a neo Ottaman empire?

The question as to why so many Muslims are so keen to migrate to the West and not anxious to return to their homelands cannot be avoided. A recent survey in Pakistan brings out this reality, as so many respondents expressed the view that their best hope for the future was to run away from Pakistan.

It needs, to be recognized that international terrorism inspired by radical Islam, is a new type of war being waged by highly motivated groups with no identifiable territory, operating in small groups, with a diffused command and control system, almost totally invisible but unified by one motivating purpose, namely changing the existing order in almost all countries, to be replaced by a medieval system considered to be the answer for all of humanity's problems of today. It is of little import that the change that is desired and which motivates the terrorists will take humanity backwards by almost 1,500 years and negate all the scientific, technological societal and cultural progress; that the world has recorded. The fact however remains that these are groups who are operating mostly below the surface, seem to be capable of seriously damaging if not destroying the existing order in many countries and India is a prime target. This is an undeclared war and hence, the rules evolved by humanity over the years for, what can be termed as a 'civilized wars'-such as the Geneva Convention, not killing innocent civilians, humane treatment of prisoners of war, etc., do not apply. It is mindless destruction for the sake of destruction, to spread terror, spread insecurity, propagate the belief that the existing order has taken humanity on the wrong path and those who have made humanity traverse on this wrong path deserve to be eliminated.

Terrorism of this kind is fundamentally a challenge, which can only be managed and, it appears, cannot altogether be eliminated with any degree of finality. It is a war that cannot be won in the conventional sense. Unlike most wars, it has neither a fixed set of enemies, nor the prospect of coming to a conclusion through a decisive victory on the part of one of the parties. Counter-terrorism can at best be compared to the effort of public health authorities to combat particularly virulent communicable diseases, where success is often temporary and the disease causing organism mutates itself, to become more drug resistant. It is a threat that cannot be defeated, at least as of now, but only reduced, attenuated and to a degree, contained and controlled. But even to achieve this, what is required, as argued above, is an effective, swift and organized response with a clear understanding of the nature and gravity of the threat and a clear commitment to deal with it, without so called political compulsions complicating the situation. Effective laws, efficient enforcement mechanisms unfettered by political interference and extraneous considerations working under able leadership can achieve this end, as has been demonstrated in some of the countries in the West and in China.

Terrorism of this kind is a serious challenge to the present world order and at the moment, it enjoys some very distinct advantages. These are (a) the fact that the population of believers is growing at a more rapid rate, than all other segments of humanity, especially of the Western advanced economies. (b) The Western civilization is seen as losing its moral authority, (c) The economic clout of the West is perceived to be declining, (d) International terrorism is backed by a militant ideology which is triumphalist in character and is convinced that it alone will ultimately win the battle, (e) It is able to command a vast network of institutions, the mosques and madrasas and a number of militant outfits to supply foot soldiers and suicide bombers including children and women, to carry out its missions of carnage, (f) It disregards all modern notions of human rights, women's rights, conventions of war and is capable of indulging in mindless violence. It is a no-holds-barred war of attrition to exhaust and wear out the enemy without being squeamish about the quantum and nature of violence and about moral considerations. It believes that the ends clearly justify the means, (g) It has accumulated a host of grievances for which it seeks revenge, (h) It takes full advantage of the rights available in liberal democracies to further its cause while increasing its demands for separate rights, and (i) Its resources are, at the moment, limitless based on the oil wealth of the Middle East.

If the present world order has to effectively answer this growing challenge it has to, more than anything else, drastically reduce its dependence on hydrocarbons. This no doubt, also happens to be an effective answer to the problem of global warming and hence, an end to be pursued in itself. The drying up of flow of funds in support of terror will, within a short while, diminish the threat and arrest its growth very effectively. The second weapon is the use to the fullest advantage, the strength of technologies that can be employed to detect each and every terrorist plot, the location of terrorist and their training grounds and to destroy these and punish those who are members of various outfits. The West's greatest advantage is its technology and its ability to come up with more sophisticated technology-oriented responses, to which the terrorists steeped in medieval theology have no effective answer. Witness the effectiveness and lethality of drone attacks on the Taliban and Al Qaeda. International cooperation and bringing on board countries like Pakistan and China to fight terror will be of great importance.

In sum, the urgent need is to recognize the grave danger posed to many countries especially to India, by this new type of terror that the world seems compelled to confront and to improve our ability on all fronts to combat this menace. Its real character, the forces that support and sustain it and its ability to strike, the forms it can be take and its capacity for endurance even after repeated assaults—all need to be clearly understood. The question therefore is, how do we defeat this terror. As mentioned above, there cannot be a final victory in the conventional sense but the threat can be contained and controlled and the damage, to a very large extent, minimized. But for this to happen, internal systems of security management in India, executive as well as judiciary, have be vastly improved and sufficient political will must be mustered. Tepid and ineffective responses and statements without any action cannot and will not yield any results and there will be only a worsening of the situation. That a nation can be defeated from within, even before it is defeated from without is a lesson that history offers and we would be very stupid, if we do not learn and take warning from the historical experience of a host of countries like France during the Second World War. In addition,

India must work in all forums and in all possible ways to garner international cooperation to deal with this world-wide menace.

Fortunately, there is at least the beginning of a realization, within the Islamic world that it would be counterproductive to permit the forces of regression to triumph. Indeed, some scholars believe that forces which support modernization, educational reform, individual freedom and human rights combined with greater freedom for women are beginning to make their presence felt. At the moment, the forces of modernization and the forces of regression are aggressively competing with each other. The moment oil wealth starts depleting, societies will have to find other avenues of progress and the inexorable laws of economics will compel these societies to modernize. No society can afford to be at a standstill or travel backward towards an idealized version of a state of affairs in the distant past. In fact, as mentioned earlier, it is the Islamic scholars who rescued the great wisdom of ancient Greece by translating the works of Greek philosophers into Arabic and ensuring that this wisdom did not get lost due to the overzealousness of Christian fundamentalists.

History teaches us that fundamentalist theocracy does not last for long, as it is basically untenable with the progress of human thought. It may secure footholds in societies which are isolated and ignorant but rarely does it last its main propagator. Its usual course is to fragment into splinter groups, each accusing the others of heresy. Each group usually accuses the other of not being radical enough. The present phenomenon of the spread of radical Islam is primarily because of the immense backing it has received from Saudi Arabia and Iran and the resources that have been poured into it by both. This is quite possibly an exception. If the oil-based resources dry up, the momentum will be lost and that is why it is so important for the world to get out of its addiction to fossil fuels--fuels form hell-and rapidly switch over to fuels from heaven—solar, wind, hydro, etc.

In a world where knowledge is becoming a more potent source of power and wealth, the present importance of oil wealth cannot be taken for granted, especially as the oil reservoirs of the Middle East do have a terminal point and possibly even before this century is over, humanity would have learnt to live without oil. In the meanwhile, it also appears that the world's overwhelming reliance on the Middle East Arab world for energy may after all be going down with new discoveries of hydro carbon reserves in many areas. The US is now dependent on oil from the Middle East only to the extent of 10 per cent. Huge amounts of natural gas have been found in deep waters of Israeli Mediterranean Sea and Israel may be able to extract synthetic oil from kerosene-rich rock fields near Jerusalem. From the Arctic waters of Norway, shale oil fields of Argentine Patagonia, oil sands of Canada, and deep water wells off Angola, giant oil or gas fields may be mined and exploited quite profitably with new and emerging technologies. Put together, these fields should bring billions of barrels to the market. These, combined with greater emphasis on energy conservation and progress in the use of non-conventional sources of energy actively promoted by the environmentalists can dramatically change the energy supply outlook, even with the rise in demand for energy from the emerging markets.

All this can improve the chances of the world ultimately overwhelming the threat from radical Islam.

5

INTERNAL THREATS—JAMMU AND KASHMIR, NORTH-EAST ETC.

Right from the time of our independence, the nation had had to battle threats from within to its security, unity, sovereignty and territorial integrity. Unfortunately, the gravity of these threats has been increasing. India has been called a land of thousand mutinies. It cannot be denied that the country's unity and integrity have been preserved with considerable difficulty and at great cost. The nation has been a victim of separatist and sectarian conflicts fuelled by social, political, religious and economic causes. There is, to my mind, a distinct correlation between the multiplication of these internal conflicts and decline in the effectiveness of systems of governance. Distrust, disillusionment and disaffection result when the people's grievances do not get addressed speedily and fairly, their basic necessities are not met and the system is seen to fail them repeatedly, while those who are elected to govern them and provide them these very reliefs and services, are seen to be taking care of themselves and only themselves very well. While we claim to be a democracy, the system which we established has degenerated into what can be termed as 'Kleptocracy', that is, where a set of people capture the system and use it for enriching themselves at the expense of the people who put them in power.

The growing disconnect between those who govern and those who are governed, undermines the faith of the people. They are then forced to look for alternative systems. The disillusioned also consider resort to violence as justified, to uproot what is perceived as an unjust, incompetent and rapacious system which is high on promises and low on deliveries. Such a situation provides a fertile ground for forces inimical to the country, to intervene and exploit the same, for their own interests and weaken the nation further.

Such a situation should not arise in a participative democracy which recognizes the rights of the people, the right to dissent, the right to free expression, the right to demonstrate peaceably and where those who are given the right to govern by the people, cannot afford to be insensitive to the needs and aspirations of the people, and if they are, they can be thrown out of power through peaceful means. This is the underlying principle of democratic governance and implies that performance and delivery on promises is the main plank on which elections are contested and it is the main if not the only criterion for winning elections and getting reelected. Once this fundamental principle is diluted, as has happened repeatedly in India, a host of problems follow.

In this Chapter, I shall deal only with the major internal security challenges which have plagued this country, which have so far doggedly defied solution, namely Jammu and Kashmir, the North East and Naxalism.

The state of Jammu and Kashmir is of great strategic importance to India bordering as it does—Pakistan, Tibet Autonomous Region of China and Afghanistan. It is the gateway to the entire Central Asia region. Unfortunately, the state has witnessed armed insurgency and invasions from Pakistan and China almost from the very first year of our independence. Since 1989, the situation in this state has deteriorated sharply due to this armed insurgency aided, and abetted by Pakistan. The rebellion is confined to the six districts of the Kashmir valley. The demand articulated by the Muslim segment of the population is for separation from India. Some want merger with Pakistan but the majority wants independence. The cry is for "AZADI". It has posed a serious threat to the internal security of the whole country and to the very integrity and unity of our nation. Under the British, it was administered in the very same manner as any other princely state of British India. Under the Indian Independence Act, passed by the British Parliament in 1947, it was to be given the same option as all other princely states, namely to join either the Indian Union or Pakistan. It must also be stressed that the option to be so exercised was the prerogative of the ruler of the state and no one else. This was indeed the choice exercised by each and every ruler of every princely state which was part of British India without a single exception. The Maharaja of Jammu and Kashmir exercised this choice in full faith, out of his own free will and with due diligence and not due to any coercion by India on the 26th of October, 1947. He acted in accordance with the provisions of the Indian Independence Act and this accession was accepted by the then Governor General of India, Lord Mountbatten who was earlier the Viceroy of India and more than anyone else, responsible for implementing the Indian Independence Act and the Partition of India.

The Maharaja could have acceded to Pakistan, as was the case with many other princely states but he did not. There can be no question about the legality or legitimacy of this act by a ruler empowered by law to do so. It may be added that the state had been part of the Maharaja Ranjit Singh's domain ever since 1810. A brief chronology of events outlining the long history of the region reproduced below shows; the close and intimate links the state has always had with the multi-faceted, rich and ancient land of India.

The Muslims and Hindus of Kashmir have lived in relative harmony and friendliness since the 13th century, when Islam first became the majority religion in Kashmir. The Sufi-Islamic way of life that ordinary Muslims followed in Kashmir complemented the *rishi* tradition of Kashmiri Pundits (Hindus), leading to a synergetic culture where Hindus and Muslims revered many local saints and prayed at the same shrines. Since 1989, however, this liberal tradition has come under grave threat due to open interference by Pakistan which has aided and abetted an armed insurgency and sent any number of terrorists imbued with a radical Islamic ideology to 'liberate' Kashmir. Pakistan has made it a religious struggle to liberate Kashmir from the hold of infidels and the Sunni-Wahabi cult has been assiduously promoted in an effort to supplant the prevailing Sufi oriented belief system. In this Saudi Arabia has played a very important role pumping in enormous funds and flooding the valley with wahabi literature. The target has been the youth of the valley, some 60 per cent of whom have been in one way or the other infected by this extremist virus. The Deobandhi school has been a valuable ally in all this effort to convert the population of the valley to the wahabi cult. Recently, as a reaction to this the Balrevi School has stepped up its activities in an effort to win back the valley's youth. The Wahabi's are violently opposed to worship of saints, pirs, and in shrines. The famous Hazratbal shrine has recently been targeted by the wahabis. Such attacks may not go down well among the population in the valley

Periodically however, there have been rulers and leaders who have had a narrow view of Islam, and have subjected Hindu minorities to great cruelties and discrimination. The current armed secessionist movement in Kashmir mostly derives its inspiration from such extremist interpretations of Islam.

A canard is being spread in the past few years by the secessionists, terrorists and their sympathizers that in the 1990s Kashmiri Pundits left Kashmir willingly, having been "tricked" by the then Jammu and Kashmir Governor Jagmohan. Nothing could be farther from the truth. The fact is that Kashmiri Pundits were driven from their homeland after a campaign of intimidation and harassment was launched against them by the military-wing of the secessionists. Kashmiri Pundits were forced from their hearths and homes at gun point. The objective of this ethnic cleansing was to create a minority-free Kashmir valley where the goal of Islamization could be easily forced on the ordinary people. In this both the Saudis and Pakistanis have played a predominant role.

However, the history of Kashmir proves beyond doubt that Kashmir has a long history of intimate association with the rest of India. It will be useful to recapitulate the historical chronology of Kashmir.

Historical Chronology of Jammu and Kashmir

App. 3000 B.C.:	Kashmir clan is named in Mahabharata.
2629-2564 B.C.:	Rule by King Sandiman.
2082-2041 B.C.:	King Sunder Sen rules Kashmir.
1048-1008 B.C.:	King Nara rules Kashmir.
250 B.C.:	Shrinagari (today's Srinagar is located about three miles from Shrinagari) near the ancient capital Pandhrenatha is founded by Ashoka the Great.
7th century:	King Lalitaditya builds the famous Sun temple and forms the city of Pharihaspura.

813-850:	Pampore founded by Padma, during the rule of King Ajatapida.
855-883:	King Avantivarman builds the town of Avantipur and the famous Sun temple.
883-902:	King Shankaravarman builds Shankarapura-pattan (now known as Pattan).
1128-1149:	Reign of King Jayasim. mid-12th Century: Muslim invasion of Kashmir.
1322:	Turks, under ferocious Zulkadur Khan, first invade Kashmir.
1394-1416:	Central Asian ruler, Sikander invades Kashmir and brings about mass conversion to Islam. After the tyranny of Sikander was over, only eleven Kashmiri Hindu families survive.
1540:	Mirz Haidar, a relative of Humayun (of the Mughal invader dynasty) conquers Kashmir. Kashmir gradually absorbed into Mughal.
1810-1820:	Maharaja Ranjit Singh, one of the greatest rulers of India, regains Jammu and appoints his Dogra feudatory Gulab Singh to rule the state Empire.
March 16, 1846:	The present state is created by a treaty between the British East India Company acting on behalf of the British Government and Maharaja Gulab Singh in Amritsar.
1931:	One of the worst communal riots led by Sheikh Abdullah and his Muslim Conference.
1939:	Muslim Conference becomes the National Conference.
Aug. 15, 1947:	India gains independence. The ruler of Kashmir, Maharaja Hari Singh yet to make up his mind regarding accession.
Oct. 22, 1947:	Pakistan violates the Standstill Agreement by preventing essential supplies to the state, then hoards of armed Pakistani tribesmen entered Kashmir.
Oct. 26, 1947:	Hari Singh signs the instrument of accession, it is no different from the one signed by over 500 other rulers. The accession of Kashmir accepted by the Governor General of India, Lord Mountbatten.

Oct. 27, 1947:	The first Indian forces arrived in Kashmir to defend against Pakistani troops.
Dec. 31, 1947:	A highly unconstitutional offer of plebiscite made by Prime Minister Nehru in the U.N.
Jan. 1, 1948:	India under Nehru declares a unilateral cease-fire and under Article 35 of the U.N. Charter, India files a complaint with the U.N. Security Council. Pakistan still controls 2/5 of the state.
Jan. 20, 1948:	The U.N. Security Council in its resolution establishes the United Nations Commission for India and Pakistan (UNCIP).
July 1948:	Mohd. Zafrulla Khan, then the Foreign Minister of Pakistan and principal Delegate of Pakistan in the U.N. admits to the U.N. Commission for India and Pakistan that the Pakistani Army had been in Kashmir.
Aug. 13, 1948:	UNCIP adopts a resolution on Kashmir accepted by both India and Pakistan. Pakistan is blamed for the invasion of Kashmir and is instructed to withdraw its forces from Kashmir.
Jan. 1, 1949:	Amidst great tension, one minute before midnight, India and Pakistan conclude a formal cease-fire agreement.
Jan. 5, 1949:	Almost a year after Nehru's offer of plebiscite, the UNCIP passes a resolution that states that, "The question of accession of the state of Jammu and Kashmir to India or Pakistan will be decided through the democratic method of free and impartial plebiscite". However, Pakistan has yet to comply with the earlier part of the resolution—an essential precondition for the plebiscite—and withdraw from the state. Also, Pakistan is now busy changing the demographic composition of the state.
1949:	Notwithstanding opposition by several authors of the Constitution of India, including Dr. Ambedkar, its chief architect, Article 370 inserted in the Constitution of India. This article is meant as a temporary measure, to be in effect until the formal constitution of Jammu and Kashmir is drafted.

June 1948: Sheikh Abdullah declares, "We, the people of Jammu and Kashmir, have thrown our lot with Indian people not in the heat of passion or a moment of despair, but by a deliberate choice. The union of our people has been fused by the community of ideals and common sufferings in the cause of freedom."

1949: Following the cabinet decision taken by the Abdullah Government, Hari Singh steps down. Hari Singh's son, Karan Singh is named his successor.

Apr. 1950: UN Security Council appoints Sir Owen Dixon as the UN representative in place of UNCIP to find expeditious and enduring solution to the India-Pakistan dispute over Kashmir.

Oct. 1950: General Council of the National Conference demands elections to create a Constituent Assembly.

Sep. 1951: Elections for the Constituent Assembly are held. The National Conference wins all 45 seats unopposed.

Oct. 1951: Constituent Assembly of the state of Jammu and Kashmir is inaugurated.

Nov. 5, 1951: The Constituent Assembly is given four tasks by Sheikh Abdullah which include accession to India.

Nov.-Dec. 1951: Karan Singh steps down as the ruler, and is elected by the Constituent Assembly of Jammu and Kashmir as Sardar-i-Riyasat (Governor)

1952: Jana Sangh begins campaign called "Ek Vidhan Ek Pradhan" (One Constitution, one leader) and demands that the state of Jammu and Kashmir be totally integrated into India and that people from other states be able to visit Jammu and Kashmir without a passport.

1952: Jana Sangh leader Shyamaprasad Mukherjee dies in a Kashmiri Jail under mysterious circumstances.

Aug. 9, 1953: Sheikh Abdullah is arrested. He had turned corrupt and autocrat. He tried to hold India to

	ransom by giving increasingly anti-India speeches to preserve his power.
Feb. 1954:	Under the leadership of Bakshi Ghulam Mohammad, democratically elected Constituent Assembly of Jammu and Kashmir ratifies the state's accession to India.
May 14, 1954:	The President of India promulgates the Constitution (Application to Jammu and Kashmir) Order placing on a final footing the applicability of the other provisions of the Indian Constitution to Jammu and Kashmir.
1956:	Constitution (Seventh Amendment) Act, 1956, the category of Part B State is abolished and Jammu and Kashmir is included as one of the states of India under Article I. However, Article 370 of the Constitution of India is still retained.
Jan. 26, 1957:	After the formal inauguration of its constitution, the Constituent Assembly dissolves itself.
1958:	All-India services extended to J & K through an amendment in Article 312.
1964:	Sheikh Abdullah is released from prison.
1965:	Pakistan attacks India, in operation code named Gibraltar. The defeat of Pakistan results in the Tashkent Agreement between the two countries.
Mar. 30, 1965:	Article 249 of Constitution of India extended to Jammu and Kashmir whereby the centre can legislate on any matter enumerated in the state list (just like in any other state in the Union). Designations like Prime Minister and President of the state are replaced by Chief Minister and Governor.
1971:	A Pakistani attack on India results in the third war between the two countries. Pakistan is completely defeated, over 90,000 of its men surrendered.
1972:	India and Pakistan signed the Shimla Pact. The Two agreed to convert the cease fire line into a line of control and eventually into the international border in effect partitioning the state.

	This is however not recorded at the request of Bhutto.
Feb. 24-25, 1975:	Following an accord signed by Prime Minister Indira Gandhi and Sheikh Abdullah on February 24, 1975, Jammu and Kashmir is made a "Constituent Unit" of India on February 25, 1975. Through this accord, Indian Parliament reaffirms its right to legislate on any matter concerning the territory of the state
1977:	National Conference wins the first post-Emergency elections.
1982:	Sheikh Abdullah nominates his son, Farooq Abdullah as his successor setting up a political rivalry between Farooq Abdullah and his brother-in-law G.M. Shah.
1986:	In one of the most shameful acts of religious massacre, several ancient and historical Hindu temples are destroyed and scores of Hindus killed in the city of Anantnag. Chief Minister G.M. Shah loses power to his brother-in-law, Farooq Abdullah.
1990-1991 onwards:	In the continuing terrorist violence, thousands have died so far, and 400,000 people have been driven out of their homes. Pakistan's involvement in this carnage of violence is beyond doubt.

Unfortunately Pakistan, which created itself as the homeland for Muslims in India has been allowed to keep alive its claims on this state and has repeatedly tried to seize this territory away from India through armed invasion and use of force in one form or the other. For reasons which are difficult to fathom, we ourselves have yielded ground and become more and more defensive on the so called 'Kashmir question' and have permitted Pakistan by many an act of omission and commission, to have a say on this matter. Pakistan has been allowed to agitate this matter in every international forum and blatantly interfere in India's internal affairs. This has been happening even while we claim that the state of J&K is an integral and inalienable part of India and the Parliament of India, through the expression of its collective will (with MPs from J&K participating) of the entire people of India, declares that the state is an integral part of India and that the Parliament has the authority to legislate on matters concerning the state. The Constituent Assembly of the State of J&K while enacting a separate Constitution for the state, makes it clear that the State is an integral part of the Indian Union and shall always remain so. We ourselves have been obfuscating vital facts and diluting our strengths and too many people, in particular the communists, the left-leaning intellectuals and bleeding heart liberals have been muddying the waters, while coming out in support of religious bigots, secessionists and traitors. Truth and facts considered inconvenient are often deliberately concealed to suit vested interests.

Our own pusillanimity has allowed Pakistan, so far at least, to occupy the moral high ground and until recently, the world was listening to Pakistan much more, while India was made to adopt a basically defensive position. The forces of religious bigotry have been given a free run, while the real issues and fundamental facts have been forgotten or at least not stated with the emphasis they really deserve. The Kashmiri Pundits have been driven out and the Christian minority which is minuscule lives in fear. The only pastor in Srinagar was summoned recently before a Sharia court, charged with imagined crimes and expelled from the valley. The Christians may not even be able to hold the revered Christmas mass. We have been willing to sacrifice our basic national interests; while pandering to narrow, sectarian, secessionist and anti-national forces, bent upon dismembering this country. An added complication is the poor standards of governance in the state of J&K and extreme corruption at all levels, leading to erosion of faith in the ability of the system to deliver even the most basic of services and ensure that justice and fairness prevails.

The state of Jammu and Kashmir has been treated as a special category state with massive infusion of funds and package after packages have been offered; but this has not been able to diminish the levels of dissatisfaction or unrest and the ordinary tax payer in the rest of India has to continuously bear the burden of ever increasing allocations of both plan and non-plan funds to the state. Indeed in my view, insurgency, as in the case of the states of North-East, is a convenient tool for extracting money from the Centre. The money of course benefits a select few much more but nevertheless, the ordinary resident of J&K is far better off than anyone in UP or Bihar and the human development indices of the state are in many respects superior to many states.

Let us examine the real issues that matter and analyze how wittingly or unwittingly, we have allowed forces inimical to our security interests to occupy the field and start dictating the agenda.

Pakistan believes doggedly that the princely state of Jammu & Kashmir by right belongs to it and irrespective of the fact that the Maharaja of J&K signed the instrument of accession with India and not Pakistan, the whole state should be handed over to it on a platter. It has been parroting for a long long time that J&K is an unfinished agenda of the process of Partition, and in fact Pakistan is not complete without this state. In the meanwhile, that part of the erstwhile princely state of J&K which was occupied by Pakistan by armed force is being treated by it as if it owns the place. It has shown no hesitation in drastically altering the demographic composition of the occupied areas including federally administered Gilgit and Baltistan by settling people from the mainland of Pakistan on a large scale. It has deliberately induced the Sunnis to settle in Gilgit and Baltistan so that the Shias are reduced to a small minority.

Pakistan's position is based on the so called principles of Partition namely: (a) the population composition of the state, i.e. whether its majority is Hindu or Muslim and (b) geographical contiguity. It is, my view that both these contentions are invalid *ab-initio* in the case of the State of J&K.

Let us dispose of the question of contiguity. If this is of such fundamental importance, then Pakistan could not have claimed East Bengal as part of the new State of Pakistan. Secondly, it is known that Jinnah was openly encouraging the princely state of Hyderabad which had a Muslim ruler to accede to Pakistan and India saved the day only because of the resolute action of the great Sardar in the face of reluctance of the Prime Minister and resistance from the then Army Chief, General Roy Bucher. As recounted by V.P. Menon, Patel had to walk out of the crucial meeting of the Defence Committee of which Nehru was the Chairman, as Nehru was not in favour of armed action. V.P. Menon also walked out and this shook Nehru out of his complacency and in a subsequent meeting presided over by the then Governor

General, C. Rajagopalachari, the decision to order troops to march into Hyderabad was taken. This episode is narrated in Balraj Krishna's book entitled '*Sardar Patel the Bismarck of India*'. Contiguity was of no account as far as Jinnah was concerned, when it came to interference in Hyderabad.

As to the issue of population composition, this again was invalidated at the time of partition itself, as a large Muslim population stayed back in India. This population which was around 35 million at the time of Partition today exceeds 180 million. They enjoy a higher degree of peace and prosperity than those living in Pakistan and successive governments both at the Centre and the states; have been going well out of their way to take all possible measures for the welfare and prosperity of this segment of population, as they by now form a very substantial vote bank.

This principle perished once and for all with the separation of Bangladesh from Pakistan in 1971 after the brutal treatment that was meted out to that area by the rulers of Pakistan. No less than three million people, most of them Muslims, were killed by the Pakistan Army.

Apart from this, the established principle of partition was not the question of minority or majority of the whole state but in each of the districts. This again was the signal contribution of Patel who insisted on this principle, when Jinnah had claimed all the area east of the then Calcutta for Pakistan and the people of Assam and the adjoining areas were appalled at the prospect of becoming a part of Pakistan. This indeed is the principle that led to the partition of the provinces of Punjab, Sindh and Bengal.

That religion can be the basis of nationhood is totally anachronistic and outdated and is not acceptable even in Islam, which talks of the world-wide Islamic Umma and of a caliphate. All countries in the Middle East will lose their sovereignty if this principle is applied.

Pakistan did not have a case at all under the Indian Independence Act, which conferred the prerogative to the ruler and the ruler alone and once the choice had been exercised by him and in this case the Maharaja of Jammu & Kashmir Hari Singh, there can be no going back on it.

It is worth noting the statement made by the then Prime Minister of Pakistan, Liaquat Ali Khan, published in the *Statesman* dated 21st September, 1947 and quoted by Lord Mountbatten, the then Governor General of independent India, in a detailed memorandum that he drew up after meeting Jinnah who had assumed the office of Governor General of Pakistan and the final arbiter of all matters in Pakistan, in Lahore on the 1st of November 1947. The statement of Liaquat reads as follows:

> "The correct position is that the Indian Independence Act of 1947 has left all Indian states completely free to join either one Dominion or the other, or to enter into treaty relations with either. Legally and constitutionally, there can be no question of putting limitations on this right of the states. Muslim League leaders before 15th August and the official spokesman of the Pakistan Government thereafter have publicly declared their agreement with this view; and have since rigorously stood by it. No objection has been raised by Pakistan to any state acceding to the Dominion of India."

Mountbatten records that he read out this statement of the Prime Minister of Pakistan to Jinnah who was ill and was bedridden and asked him if he stood rigorously by his Prime Minister's stand. In Lord Mountbatten's words "He looked somewhat uneasy but admitted that it represented the correct legal position."

The full text of the note recorded by Lord Mountbatten is reproduced in the book on Patel written by Balraj Krishna mentioned earlier. This note is a historic and revealing document, one of extraordinary importance as it buries a number of myths, falsehoods and canards that have been spread all these years and have confused and muddied the debate on Jammu and Kashmir. This note firmly, unequivocally and finally establishes that Pakistan had no claim whatsoever at any point of time, over the princely state of J&K and our own actions enabled Pakistan to claim a role and become an important player. Both Jinnah and Liaquat Ali Khan, by their own statements and actions had forfeited any claim on this state in 1947 itself.

It is worth having a close look at the note recorded by Lord Mountbatten after his visit to Karachi to meet Jinnah who was bedridden. The visit of the Governor General who was accompanied by Lord Ismay took place on the 1st of November, 1947 when the question of accession of three princely states, Hyderabad, Junagadh and Kashmir had not been finally settled. The three states had one common feature, namely the ruler belonging to a different religion, other than that of the majority of its population. Junagadh and Hyderabad had Muslim rulers with a Hindu majority, whereas J&K had a Hindu Dogra ruler with a Muslim majority. In each of these cases, Pakistan was creating difficulties in the hope of getting the rulers to accede to Pakistan and not to India. In the case of J&K, armed raiders had been sent and in the case of Hyderabad, the razakars were being supported with arms and finance by Pakistan. The matter had engaged the attention of the Indian Government and in fact, Prime Minister Nehru himself was to travel to Lahore (Jinnah was ill and bedridden) but at the very last minute, Nehru took ill and could not travel. The Governor General was dispatched to hold the discussion and Jinnah complained that if Nehru could not come, why no other minister was deputed.

Lord Mountbatten's long memo covers all the three states and it will serve our purpose, if the main points are taken note of.

a. Mountbatten makes it clear that the proposals he had placed before Jinnah were made by him in good faith, more in his capacity as the ex-Viceroy responsible for the partition and in the belief that these ideas may be accepted by the cabinet if Jinnah's views could be obtained.
b. He did not carry a full authorized brief from the cabinet and he had not discussed the ideas that he was proposing to Jinnah with the cabinet.
c. He was making the proposals, as he was anxious that his actions regarding partition did not result in any harm to either dominion.
d. If the ideas he projected were acceptable to Jinnah, then he may be in a position to persuade the cabinet to accept these as well.

Given the similarities in the situation between Junagadh and Kashmir, Mountbatten suggested that in the two cases, plebiscite should be held under the UNO. Jinnah rejected the idea as in his view, a plebiscite was redundant as it was clear that the states concerned should go according to the wishes of the majority of the population. He reiterated his non-acceptance of the idea if it was applied to all the three states, namely Hyderabad along with J&K and Junagadh, since the Nizam of Hyderabad did not wish to join either of the two dominions and he (Jinnah) could not be a party to coercing him to accede to one of the dominions. When Mountbatten reverted to the subject of plebiscite, with specific reference to Kashmir and enquired as to why Jinnah 'objected to plebiscite so strongly'. Jinnah stated that the National Conference under Sheikh Abdullah would pressurize everyone not to vote for Pakistan.

It is crystal clear from the note of Mountbatten, which can be taken without doubt as a true, impartial and accurate account of his conversation with Jinnah that the very idea of plebiscite was not acceptable to the founder and ruler of Pakistan from the very beginning, for reasons which are now very clear. He did not want that the wishes of the people should prevail, in the case of Hyderabad and Junagadh as the strict adherence to the Government of India Act which vested the power of accession in the ruler only, suited him. He was confident that in the case of Hyderabad, with his encouragement and supply of arms as well as support from Britain, the Nizam will be able to carry the day and will either accede to Pakistan or remain independent and become a thorn in the flesh of India. The Nizam and his razakars could be his agents for all kinds of nefarious purposes. He did not care much for Junagadh. In the case of J&K, he thought that the ruler who was vacillating, could be tempted, induced or coerced to accede to Pakistan. His raiders were already wreaking havoc in Kashmir and in a few more days, they could have occupied the capital Srinagar, if they had not indulged in rape and looting. In Mountbatten's note, it is recorded that when the question of raiders was raised by him, Jinnah made it clear in unequivocal terms that they were under his complete control, showing that Pakistan was guilty of complicity in attacking the state of J&K. Zafrullah Khan had admitted as much to the UNCIP. The Maharaja of J&K was bargaining with both the dominions and promises were being made to both, while he dreamt of an independent Kashmir playing a grand role in international affairs, given its strategic geographical position. Jinnah was also apprehensive that the people's wish will not be in his favour, given the hold of Sheikh Abdullah and his antagonism to Pakistan at that time. Such being the facts of the case, it is indeed difficult to understand as to how we have landed in a situation where the nation's security is imperiled because of unrest and insurgency in J&K, both China and Pakistan merrily interfere in the state, parts of the state are under foreign occupation and the issue is the subject of UN resolutions. The area has become a play ground for a variety of international trouble mongers to pillory India, while sucking in an endless flow of precious resources. A large number of lives have been lost and our armed forces are tied up almost endlessly, while Pakistan has launched a proxy war against us and its agents are causing havoc in every part of India. It has been turned into a holy war—a Jihad. Pakistan cleverly claims that the real reason for growth of terrorism is the unresolved dispute in Kashmir and this gives rise to Muslim anger. International think tanks often characterise Kashmir as a major flash point and possibly the most dangerous part of the world, given the fact that both the interested parties are nuclear armed. India is under continuous pressure to settle the so called Kashmir dispute at any cost and we ourselves have been yielding ground, agreeing to discuss the 'Kashmir issue' with Pakistan and allowing separatists, secessionists, traitors and ant-national elements to dictate terms to the Government of India. Our Parliament was attacked, a plane was hijacked and any number of terror attacks, even on our temples have been staged—all in support of the Kashmiri separatism. Pakistan has funded, trained and armed a number of outfits to specifically fight jihad in Kashmir, while we continue to be passive in our responses. We hesitate to act, even where our vital national interests are involved and when our unity, integrity and sovereignty is under continuous threat.

Could we not have solved this matter once and for all as we did in the case of Junagadh or Hyderabad?

A dispassionate examination of facts indicates that the decisions relating to the state of Jammu & Kashmir were taken by the Prime Minister, Pandit Nehru. Sardar Patel had the responsibility of dealing with all the princely states and he handled all the 560 princely states with unequalled firmness and competence, keeping the nation's interest alone above everything else. He ensured that both Hyderabad and Junagadh were fully and irrevocably integrated with the Union of India. He did not leave behind any legacy of intractable problems for the future.

The subject of Kashmir was taken out of the portfolio of Patel by Nehru in December 1947 and placed under Gopalaswamy Iyengar. This was done without prior consultation with Patel and this affront hurt Patel deeply. Patel wrote to Nehru, acknowledging his letter of 23rd December, 1947 stating that it had caused him great pain. He tendered his resignation indicating that the letter of the Prime Minister (taking away J&K from his portfolio) made it clear to him that he must not and cannot continue as a member of the Government. Patel was persuaded not to insist on his resignation by both Gandhi and Mountbatten.

This action to divest Patel of the responsibility of dealing with J&K was taken by the Prime Minister under pressure from Sheikh Abdullah, despite the fact that it was Patel who took the decisive steps of securing the Maharaja's accession to India and sending the Army into the valley for driving out the tribal raiders. He flew into Srinagar on the 4th of November, 1947, against the advice of the then Army Chief, General Roy Bucher and in highly inclement weather. He gave clear orders to evict the raiders and arranged to airlift the required troops within 24 hours. In this again, he had to overcome the Prime Minister's vacillation who was worried about international opinion. According to Field Marshall Manekshaw who was then the Brigadier Military Operations, "Panditji's long exposition about accession of the state and the United Nations, was cut short by the impatient Sardar Patel with the question, 'Jawahar, do you care for Kashmir or not?' 'Of course I do', thundered Panditji. The Sardar turned to me and said, 'Go, you have your orders'. Thus Sardar Patel was able to beat back the raiders and would have cleared the whole state but for the unfortunate and ill-advised and ill-timed cease-fire." This episode is related in Balraj Krishna's book referred to above.

Patel wanted the entire state to be regained, even if it meant a war with Pakistan. He did not like the idea of ceasefire, was against a reference to the UN and never supported the idea of a plebiscite. It must be underlined that as mentioned above, when Mountbatten went to meet Jinnah in Lahore on the 1st of November, 1947, he did not have any mandate to offer a plebiscite to Jinnah. On the contrary, when the matter was discussed in the cabinet on the 28th of October, Patel expressed his opposition in strong terms, comparing it with Neville Chamberlain's visit to

Godesburg to appease Hitler in 1938. Mountbatten seems to have acted out of his own volition in offering a plebiscite to Jinnah.

The decisions of the Prime Minister to (a) call for a cease-fire even while India's armed forces were fully prepared to liberate the entire state, (b) to refer the matter to the UNO, (c) agree to a plebiscite, and (d) grant—special status to the state of J&K under Article 370; were all taken under pressure either of Sheik Abdullah or Mountbatten. Both of them saw to it that Patel was out of the picture at the crucial times these decisions were taken. Each of these decisions had grave long-term consequences and Panditji himself regretted having agreed to refer the matter to the UNO. These decisions have made the state of J&K a veritable millstone round the neck of India.

The reference to the UNO was particularly unfortunate, as it in effect internationalized the issue, sucked India into the vortex of international politics and worst of all, enabled Pakistan to acquire a firm foothold, in what was an issue to be settled within the framework of the Indian Independence Act. A whole lot of busy bodies, human right activists, interlocutors, etc., have been enabled to muddy the waters.

The decision to ask the Army to halt and to refer the Kashmir issue to the UN was almost entirely due to the influence exercised by Mountbatten, even when he was no more the Governor General of India. Also, even when he had at his own initiative, unbriefed and unauthorized by the cabinet and against the express wishes of Patel, made the offer of plebiscite to Jinnah who himself rejected it, he forced Nehru to accept the idea. One is amazed as to why so much importance was give to Mountbatten by Nehru and as to why he was allowed to have such a decisive say in affairs of such vital importance to the nation even while he held no office.

Equally inexplicable was the blind faith of Nehru in Sheikh Abdullah. According to Stanley Wolpert, the biographer of Jinnah, Nehru believed that the fate of Kashmir was tied to the fate of the Nehru family—their intertwined destiny. He quotes Nehru as having said, "Kashmir is of the most vital significance to India. We have to see this through the end". Nehru somehow believed that only Abdullah and no one else could help him achieve this. He was Nehru's anchor in the Muslim dominated valley. In the process, the interests of the Hindu Dogras of Jammu, the Buddhists of Ladakh and even the ethnically different sects of Muslims such as the Gujjars and Bakkarwals were all sacrificed. Both Jammu and Ladakh have half the state's population and 89 per cent of the area. Nehru supported the Sheikh in his agitation against the Maharaja and when he was arrested, he got him released. On his release, the Sheikh swore unswerving loyalty and allegiance, of himself and his party to the Maharaja but forgot all about this very soon. Nehru advised the pandits of the valley to support the National Conference, which was the Muslim Conference earlier and responsible for communal riots, if they wanted to live in the valley. They were nevertheless booted out of the valley in 1991 with no prospects of returning.

The Sheikh fully exploited this weakness of Nehru and the Prime Minister having yielded ground to the Sheikh for long, was compelled to imprison him when his true colours become evident. He was at last getting tired of the deceit and duplicity of the Sheikh, who spoke different languages in New Delhi and in Srinagar and had started hobnobbing with Pakistan. By this time a lot of damage had already been done.

The Sheikh had a role to play in calling for the ceasefire, as beyond the line that the Army had reached at that point of time, the National Conference did not have any following and Abdullah's objective was to be the undisputed and uncrowned king of the state. He managed to kick the Maharaja out of Kashmir even though was as much a native and a part of J&K as the Sheikh. With the active assistance of Nehru, the Sheikh, got a semi-independent status for J&K, with a separate constitution and Article 370 of the Constitution which gives special and separate status to J&K. No other state of the Union has been given this kind of treatment.

This was not favoured by either the Sardar or the Constituent Assembly or even the Congress party. The subject of J&K having been taken away from the Sardar who was the Home Minister and who was also the Minster of States and had successfully handled the integration of all the other 560 princely states; the Sheikh could dictate Kashmir policy and he brought immense pressure on Nehru to incorporate Article 370 in the Constitution of India, which was in the making. Nehru, who was to travel to Europe, entrusted the task to KM Munshi and Goplaswami Iyengar. The draft prepared by these two was not satisfactory to the Sheikh and instead of supporting the draft, he decided to go back to Srinagar but was stopped by Patel. In fact, he walked out of the Constituent Assembly in protest.

Both in the Congress Parliamentary Party and the Constituent Assembly, the need for such a special provision for the state of J&K was hotly contested. Panditji had to go to great lengths to explain repeatedly that the provision had to be made as a part of the state was under occupation and some time was needed to restore normal conditions, and this was a purely temporary and transitory provision and can and will be done away with at the earliest opportunity. He kept repeating in Hindi "Ye gisthey gisthey chale jayega". But the fact is that the Sheikh got his way and even after 65 years, the provision has remained and has been misused by successive administrations in J&K to further their own interests. This has enabled the administration to enact laws and retain laws which are discriminatory, which are violative of the principles of natural justice, and against the fundamental rights granted to all citizens by the Constitution of India. It has bred separatist tendencies and has prevented the Government of India from taking many a step which are essential for the nation's security. It is clear from the language of this particular provision that it was a purely temporary device, transitional in character and the Constitution makers' intention was, that it should be removed at the earliest opportunity. It was a stop-gap arrangement meant to pave the way for full integration sooner than later and there was no intention other than it being a passing show. This is what the Prime Minister himself intended and promised. There is a clear provision in this article itself for its demise, as the President of India is empowered to declare that this article shall cease to be operative through a public notification. No doubt, the recommendation of the Constituent Assembly of the state of J&K is necessary before such notification. Since the Constituent Assembly dissolved itself after framing the Constitution of J&K, the necessity for a recommendation ceases to be operative. In spite of all these no Governmant in India has had the courage to get rid of this nefarious article and on the contrary instead of fully integrating this state with the rest of the country, we have allowed separatism to grow.

It is, therefore, amazing that some keep harping on the point that there has been an erosion of the special status and this has raised the level of dissatisfaction in the valley, giving rise to insurgency, when this so called special status was nothing but a temporary and transitional arrangement, meant to be thrown out at the earliest. Strangely, any one making this point is pilloried as anti Secular.

This article has placed the Central Government at a disadvantage in conducting its foreign policy, safe-guarding internal security and compelling the Government of India to waste precious resources to enrich a select few. The separatists have posed a grave threat to internal security and to the unity, integrity and sovereignty of the nation. India is under intense pressure to settle the so called Kashmir issue when the only real solution is to achieve full integration of the state, get rid of Article 370 and repeal all discriminatory laws of the state.

Pakistan has given no special treatment to the area under its occupation and has treated it as its integral part. That it occupied this part of the erstwhile kingdom of J&K through armed invasion, is a matter of minor detail which Pakistan does not bother itself about. Pakistan has succeeded in burying this inconvenient fact and ensured that its act of armed aggression does not figure in the debates in any forum. India has also never forcefully pointed this out failed capitalize on this act of naked aggression. Nor does it capitalize on the brutal treatment being meted out to Shias in Gilgit and Baltistan and the fact that Pakistan has flooded this area with settlers from the mainland of Pakistan reducing the Shias to a small minority.

Could Patel have settled the Kashmir problem for good? He himself provided the answer while talking to H.V. Kamath stating that 'if Jawaharlal and Gopalaswami Iyengar had not made Kashmir their close preserve, separating it from my portfolio of Home and States, I would have tackled the problem as purposefully as I had already done in Hyderabad.'

When Pakistan's repeated efforts to take over the entire state through armed aggression did not succeed, from about 1989, a new form of offensive has been launched, namely fuelling insurgency. Pakistan claims that the people of the valley desire integration with Pakistan on religious grounds. It has created a number of insurgency outfits and unabashedly trains them, arms them and enables them to cross into the valley to create mayhem. The composite culture of the valley has been destroyed and replaced by an entirely Sunni oriented religious ethos.

This provision incorporated to serve the interests of one individual and satisfy his personal ambitions, has stood in the way of full integration of J&K with India, even though we keep proclaiming that the state of J&K is an integral and inalienable part of India. It has also created a number of anomalies. Apart from the fact that the laws enacted by the Parliament, do not automatically apply to J&K as in the case of every other state, it has established a one-way relationship between the state and the Centre. It has provided a convenient leverage to J&K to exploit the Centre and the rest of India while getting very little if at all in terms of reciprocity. J&K benefits from Plan finance and the awards of the Finance Commission while contributing so little to central revenues. Strangely, a citizen of J&K is automatically a citizen of India but a citizen of India is not a citizen of J&K. A citizen of J&K enjoys all the rights conferred by the Constitution of India, buy property, do business, have all the fundamental rights and enjoy the protection of the courts whereas this is not so when it comes to a citizen of India. A women citizen of J&K, if she marries an Indian stands to lose all her property rights and her J&K citizenship. This does not apply to a male J&K citizen who can marry any number of Indian females.

In keeping with the provisions of the Article 370, with the consent of the state a number of Central legislations have indeed been extended after 1954, i.e. after the incarceration of the Sheikh. These include statutes covering subject such as, central excise, customs, civil aviation, jurisdiction of the C&AG, census and posts and telegraphs. In 1960, the appellate authority of the Supreme Court was applied to the state of J&K. In 1964, Articles 356 and 357 empowering the Central Government to promulgate President's rule were extended to the state. The All India Services Act as well as the jurisdiction of the Central Election Commission were also extended. How do these very desirable actions undermine the language, culture, identity or the economic and political aspirations of the Kashmiris? It may be added that the Indira-Abdullah Accord in 1975 ratified all these actions but unwisely gave the freedom to the state to ask for the withdrawal of any of these extensions. So far however, in all these years, no proposals whatsoever have been made for withdrawal, as all the extensions without exception were beneficial to the people of state.

Sadly, there are repeated suggestions for going back to the

pre-1953 position and the interlocutors appointed by the GOI who are so called liberals and who it is revealed have been participating in anti-India seminars and conclaves organized by ISI supported outfits, are again talking of undoing the so called erosion of autonomy without understanding the lethal consequences this will entail. To start with, the state will become bankrupt if the financial integration is undone and the huge central infusions are stopped. If there is break down of the constitutional machinery or if the state refuses to comply with any direction concerning foreign relations, defence or communications, there can be no intervention under Article 356. Residuary powers under Article 248 empowering the Parliament to make laws, to control insurgency or for prevention of terrorists attempting to overawe the Government, alienating any section of the population, disrupting the sovereignty and integrity of the India or attempts at secession, insulting the national flag, the national Anthem, acquisition of land property etc. cannot be exercised. No one has cared to consider how putting the clock back promotes the welfare or progress of the state. Why should the nation bend over backwards to please a set of anti-national, religious bigots and hot heads backed by Pakistan.

Going back to the pre-1953 position will also mean abrogation of the relatively liberal 1957 J&K Constitution, and return to the regressive 1939 Constitution which means no fundamental rights, no concessions to the disadvantaged, a committed judiciary, no appeal to a higher court, and a malleable Sadr-e-Riyasat elected by the state legislature. In a word a retreat from, democracy to autocracy. There can be no doubt this will sound the death knell for the unity and integrity of the nation.

There can be similar demands from the states of the North-East or for that matter from Tamil Nadu. How can the country handle such challenges if it listens to self-styled liberals, out to please separatists and traitors who are known to be agents of Pakistan and in its pay?

It is strange that no one talks of the real issues of autonomy which, to my mind, are in the sphere of economic and financial management. Greater economic freedom, freedom to raise resources, more taxation powers; powers to attract investments and reduction of the present overdependence on the Centre, are the issues which can enable the states to progress faster. Such freedom can introduce competition among them States to excel. A strong Centre having adequate powers in other areas, is necessary to preserve the integrity, unity and sovereignty of the nation and as corrective to the narrow chauvinism in several states. It can also look after the interests of the smaller states who may require central financial assistance.

The state of J&K sends MPs to the Parliament but the laws made by this very Parliament in which MPs of the state sit and are paid for, do not apply automatically to that state. Secondly, these MPs from J&K are eligible to become Ministers in the Union Cabinet and are entitled to make policies and programmes which apply to the whole of India and impinge on the lives of everyone in this country. Yes, we have even had a Home Minster from J&K. Fortunately, his disastrous tenure was short lived. Thirdly, given the fractured nature of our polity and thin majorities enjoyed by the governments in power, the MPs from J&K have a decisive say in the formation of the Government at the Centre and indeed in the continuance or otherwise of the Government. The very stability of the Central Government can be determined by these MPs. Recall that the Vajpayee Government was voted out by just one MP.

When this state has been allowed to have such a decisive say in the affairs of the whole nation, why should the Central Government and the nation's Parliament suffer from the limitations imposed on them by the temporary and transitional provision of Article 370?

For the past 20 years now, Pakistan has promoted, supported, financed, trained and armed a set of insurgents whose objective is not merely the forcible separation of the state of J&K from the Indian Union but dismemberment of India as a political entity. India has unfortunately made matters worse; by conceding that Pakistan has a say in this matter, by appointing pliant, inefficient and corrupt Chief Ministers one after another, rigging elections and allowing a collapse of all standards of governance. Corruption on humongous scale is taken as the norm in J&K. No wonder, there is no faith in the efficacy of any of the institutions of the system.

What the Kashmiris want is apparently 'Azadi' or independence and not merger with Pakistan. This view is of course not shared by the people of Jammu or Ladakh or even some segments of the population in the valley. To achieve 'Azadi', they have had no compunctions in accepting assistance from Pakistan and becoming religious zealots. Pakistan tries to exploit this weakness to further its agenda of Kashmir becoming part of Pakistan. In the process, the valley has lost its ancient culture which was a mixture of Hindu and Islamic traditions and slowly but surely, has become a victim of religious/Islamic extremism and that too of the Sunni/Wahabi tradition. A host of players have entered the fray and Saudi Arabia has acquired an influence which it had never before, and is pumping in huge amounts of money. The preachers from north Indian madrasas, belonging to the Deobandi School have taken over the mosques and madrasas, poisoning the minds of young and old alike. Pakistan has managed to convert the issue into a religious struggle between the believers and others.

Independence is totally impractical, as within two days, the Pakistan Army will walk in to take over the state followed by the ISI and the Taliban. Those who demand independence have never thought through the viability of this option nor its lethal consequences. Why should Pakistan guarantee Kashmir's independence, as it is interested only in total annexation of Kashmir?

With Pakistan descending into chaos, its very survival in question and it being regarded as the epicentre of international Islamic terror, world opinion is unlikely to support any change in the *status quo* in favour of Pakistan. With religious extremism and Islamic terror becoming totally unacceptable to the international community, a religion-based demand will not be backed by the international community. India should, therefore, deal with this issue in a resolute manner with confidence, without any hesitation and keeping national interests uppermost.

Unfortunately, we have a weak Central Government which is prepared to sacrifice national interests in order to please some vested interest or the other.

Historic opportunities to solve the problem created by Pakistani invasion, in the past were squandered away, first by Nehru who could have ensured liberation of the entire state by the Army and again in 1971, when Pakistan was on its knees after the comprehensive defeat it had suffered. In Simla, Zulfiquar Bhutto had agreed to the conversion of the ceasefire line into the permanent international border, forfeiting his claims on J&K. Unfortunately, Mrs. Gandhi did not ensure incorporation of this commitment of Bhutto in the agreement at the request of Bhutto who promised to abide by it as a gentleman. Since there is nothing on record, Bhutto took no steps to live up to his commitment and Pakistan reneged on the word of its leader. He himself perhaps never intended to keep his word. However, for the next 17 years, Pakistan dared not raise this issue either bilaterally or in international forums and India's attempts to get the promise of Bhutto implemented were met with evasion. We could have sorted out the problem ourselves and Pakistan could not have raised a finger. On the contrary, Mrs. Gandhi only created a new difficulty in the shape of Sikh insurgency which opened the doors to the crafty Zia-ul-Haq to merrily interfere and support Sikh extremism, resulting in years of strife and bloodshed.

Today another historic opportunity knocks at our door. Our stature and importance for the world community is at an all time high, with the West and the countries in the entire South East looking to India as a valuable countervailing power to China and a valuable ally to fight Islamic extremism. On the other hand, Pakistan is an international pariah, considered untrustworthy, a promoter of international terror and a nuclear proliferator. Madeline Albright, the US Secretary of State under President Clinton, characterized Pakistan as "an international migraine". Can we expect our leaders to seize this opportunity and not allow it to slip away once again?

Also today, the Kashmir insurgency has degenerated into a simple money game as elaborated in Wiki leaks which quotes extensively the US Ambassador, Timothy Roemer. Money is paid by Pakistan to the separatists who also take money from India. There will be no insurgency if there is no support from Pakistan. Money flows from Saudi Arabia as well. American think tanks have pointed out that the Hurriyat Conference and all its members are controlled, supervised and funded by the ISI of Pakistan. Syed Ali Shah Gilani a prominent pro-Pakistan separatist openly espousing an extremist, sectarian, secessionist and communal agenda has been charge-sheeted by a Delhi court for indulging in havala transactions running to crores of rupees. He is also being investigated for murder charges to which the Hurriyat Confernce has protested.

Shiekh Abdullah first invented the art of milking New Delhi and his successors have further refined and improved his technique. Every other player,—the army, the paramilitary forces, the civil servants-all benefit from insurgency, in huge monetary terms. Whatever ideology there was in the beginning has by now, totally evaporated. There are a whole lot vested interests who do not want to see the end of insurgency.

If determined action is taken therefore, the so called problem of Kashmir can be once and for all solved and the nation will be spared the trauma of a seemingly unending insurgency, the huge monetary costs and loss of lives. Both Pakistan and India can cut down on military expenditure and both can reap a handsome peace dividend. Trade and economic relations can vastly improve.

What needs to be done is, simply make Pakistan abide by the commitment given by Bhutto in Simla in 1971, convert the LOC as the permanent international border, repeal Article 370 and fully integrate the state with the rest of India. When 180 million Muslims live in India and have lived comfortably for all the 65 years and who are given special attention by the government at all levels, there is no reason why the Kashmiri Muslims cannot do so.

The North-East

The basic causes for continued turbulence in the North-East of India can be summed up *inter alia* as the three 'E's—'Ethnicity', 'Economic Development' and 'Elections'.

Over the centuries, Assam and the North-East have been the recipients of a variety of immigrants, each with a distinct ethnic identity. A process of assimilation had been going on for a long time with the tribes getting used to the idea of being regarded as part of the mosaic of Assam, accepting the Assamese language and adopting a lot of the region's cultural practices and religious modes. Even the Naga tribes use Assamese as their lingua franca. Unfortunately, however this process of assimilation and absorption has been not only halted but is being reversed. This has been caused by two factors. One is the growing competition for resources, land in particular, and for livelihood and employment, caused by leaps in population density, with no matching expansion and diversification of the economy. This is accompanied by the revolution of rising expectations. This has made the groups view others with suspicion as undesirable competitors and rivals for the limited resources and opportunities. Assertion of one's separate ethnic identity is a means to safeguard one's interest to ensure cohesiveness to collectively meet the challenges from others. Demands for separate statehood and indeed nationhood are considered a means by which a particular ethnic group can ensure its dominance, reduce or indeed eliminate the challenge of other groups. Everyone, therefore, is busy identifying themselves as a separate ethnic or linguistic and religious entity. Safety is sought in building a separate identity and carving out a little piece of real estate in and from which others can be dealt with from a position of strength.

The Central Government has, from the very beginning, been making efforts to satisfy the economic, political and social aspirations of the ethnic groups, particularly the tribals. Within the composite state of Assam, the hill tribes were permitted to have autonomous district councils under the Sixth Schedule of the Constitution. These councils were well funded, with considerable executive and even judicial powers. This did not deter the tribals from demanding a separate hill state which was also granted. Such pandering to narrow loyalties has now unfortunately bred even narrower loyalties. In Meghalaya, which was created as a state for the hill tribes, now the Khasis fight the Garos who have their own insurgency outfit and who complain of unfair treatment by the Khasis. The Garos in turn treat the poorer Rabhas very badly and have kicked out thousands of them out of Meghalaya. The district councils which have outlived their purpose with the creation of tribal states continue to exist, delivering nothing, but sucking in Central funds. Mizoram has had the sense to wind up the district councils. In these newly created tribal states, the so called outsiders—those from the rest of India are actively discriminated against and periodically subjected to violence.

These tendencies have been further reinforced by the second factor, namely the poor progress recorded by the states on the economic front. Public investment, which was the major factor in promoting development, has become increasingly inadequate, in spite of the Centre pouring more and more money into the area because of the decline in the efficiency with which the funds are utilized, diversion of development funds towards non-productive expenditure, failure of investments to generate any returns and widespread corruption. Added to this is the fact that a good part of the funds is taken away by the insurgents. Nothing is left for either maintenance of assets or building of new assets. To be sure, successive administrations have thoughtlessly expanded the bureaucracy with no regard for the workload and have created an impossible burden on the states 'exchequers, consuming more and more Central funds for maintaining the ever increasing establishment. This was a politically convenient device to relieve themselves of the continuous pressure for employment opportunites.

As to private investment, except Assam, the other states were never the favourite destinations. With turmoil in Assam, no one is now prepared to invest there. Those who remain, like the tea gardens, have to pay the insurgents regularly. Private enterprise will not thrive if there is no freedom of enterprise which means sanctity of contracts, security of investments, freedom of choice with respect to personnel and raising of funds, availability of talent, sufficient markets and reasonably good infrastructure. None of these are there in the North-East and narrow chauvinism, poor educational standards and an environment of fear has ensured that the North-East does not benefit from the dynamism of private initiative which has done so much in the rest of India. Governmental efforts must address these concerns first and foremost but unfortunately, the region has only leaders who have no knowledge or imagination on such matters and whose only concern is to win elections through vote bank politics.

Even where the Central Government tries to execute projects, the insurgents interfere to extort funds, forcibly extract contracts for their members, who either do not execute the project or do such shoddy work that the project gets delayed and its economics goes haywire. Execution of projects becomes a nightmare. The staff posted for supervision is under continuous threat. The ONGC's efforts to expand oil exploration and exploitation of uranium reserves in Meghalaya have suffered because of these factors that are further exacerbated by narrow chauvinism. Influences inimical to India's growth easily exploit such misguided elements enabling them to hold up these very vital efforts, while spineless state governments who are guided by electoral considerations alone, turn a blind eye.

The North-East, therefore, is in the firm grip of a vicious cycle of low investment leading to its failure to create economic opportunities and unemployment, which in turn breeds ethnic divides and dissatisfaction, disillusionment and unrest, leading to insurgency, which again drives out investment. It needs to be noted that Mizoram was also in the grip of an insurgency, but wisdom prevailed and a durable peace accord was concluded. Today, Mizoram is reaping rich peace dividends. Sikkim is another example where peace has attracted investments, created employment and vastly improved living standards.

It must be stated with emphasis that the Partition of India and the creation of East Pakistan was a very cruel blow to the long-term prospects of the whole of the North-East. The economy of this region which was closely integrated with the Bengal area and through it with the rest of India, with good transportation links fully utilizing the river route, were suddenly and violently disrupted. This has done incalculable damage to prospects of progress of the North-East. Our recent efforts to improve relations with Bangladesh and Myanmar and further progress in our 'look east' policy may address this issue in a satisfactory manner.

The third factor is the present system of electoral politics where each aspirant to office appeals to voters on the basis of tribe, caste or community considerations. This reinforces the cry for separate ethnic, cultural identities leading to separatist-movements. The electoral system that we have adopted, particularly the first-past-the-post method of winning elections, encourages our politicians to think in terms of winning and retaining the loyalty of a narrow segment of the electorate in a constituency and for this purpose, appealing to sectarian considerations based on caste, tribe, language, creed, etc., and generating and aggravating a sense of grievance and insecurity among different segments^ These politicians present themselves as the sole defendants of the interest of the particular segment, while presenting an exaggerated version of the so called hostility and nefarious designs of other contestants. National interests are mercilessly sacrificed in the process.

Unfortunately, insurgency has assumed a self-perpetuating character, with interests actively working against end of insurgency.

It must be added that it is politically convenient for all state parties to exaggerate the economic difficulties and blame the Centre, in-spite of the fact that the Centre has shown a great deal of sensitivity to the needs of the North-East. The per capita development expenditure in the states of the North-East all of which enjoy special category status is much higher than very poor states like Bihar. They also have little no repayment liabilities. The Centre finances the entire plan expenditure of these states with 90 per cent as grants. If only the money available had been properly utilized and no part of it taken away by the insurgents, there would have been far better progress than what has happened so far. It cannot be denied that the general living standards in the North—East are far superior to that in quite a few parts of India. The kind of abject, soul destroying, gut wrenching and life threatening poverty one sees in parts of Bihar or UP does not exist in the entire North-East. Further, right from the time of the framing of the India's Constitution, the founding fathers and the leadership at the national level have been acutely conscious of the ethnic diversity in the entire North-East and the political and economic aspirations of the peoples inhabiting the area. A large number of measures have been initiated to preserve the identity, culture, traditions, etc., of the tribals, to give them a higher degree of autonomy than other states and generously promote all round socio-economic development of the tribal societies under the Sixth Schedule of the Constitution and Article 371. The composite state of Assam has been progressively reconstituted, creating new states for each of the ethnic groups. The state of Nagaland was created in the year 1963 (Under the British it was a district of Assam) and as of now, we have six separate states. None of them is economically viable or sustainable. Each of them have separate governing structures, on par with any state in India, with strong representation in the Parliament and other governing structures in the Centre. Special efforts have been made to promote indigenous culture and preserve traditional laws and practices. Any Parliamentary act which abridges, negates or interferes with any of these matters cannot be enforced without the consent of the state government. Further, autonomous district councils were created right at the time of adoption of India's Constitution devolving a wide range of powers relating to economic and social development including administration of land and forests and even administration of justice. These arrangements are backed by special allocation of funds. That this noble experiment of democratic decentralization has largely failed to live up to expectations and the district councils have become infamous for their inefficiency and corruption, with marked lack of accountability and do not command the confidence of the people for whom they were created, is a sad fact.

Further, the system of reservations in the services, education and legislatures, benefits the tribals of the North-East, very substantially.

In addition to this, to promote a degree of economic integration and execute large projects which involve utilization of resources in two or more states and whose benefits can be available to two or more states, a North Eastern Council (NEC) has been created with substantial and regular flow of funds. The Centre has also been investing large funds for centrally executed projects in the area of hydropower, hydrocarbons and establishment of institutions of higher-learning—Central Universities, IIT's, Institutes of medical sciences and even research and development centres. Unfortunately, each of the initiatives is viewed by vested interests in a negative way, one group claiming that this is inadequate and the other group viewing it as a nefarious attempt to exploit the states' resources for the benefit of others. Also, narrow chauvinism has taken a firm grip over all these institutions and if better talent from the rest of India is invited, agitations are launched. The Khasi students union, a body which actively promotes narrow chauvinism and which can unleash considerable violence, has for example stifled the healthy growth of many a central institution by insisting on a 'locals only' policy and has ensured that Meghalaya's uranium reserves are not made available to the country's nuclear energy programme. The Centre and the state seem to be helpless in stemming the rot that has set in, in many of these institutions.

One must also refer to the widespread sense of alienation that seems to pervade the North-East. The feeling that the system has failed to deliver, that it has been unable to solve the problems of the people, that very few are better off, that promises are never kept, that there is all-pervasive corruption and inefficiency, has bred dissatisfaction all-round. Interaction with student groups, who visit some of the more advanced states, reveal that they find that while there is visible progress in these places, their states have remained backward and are probably deteriorating. The usual allegation of 'neglect by the Centre' is often articulated. That a great deal of the present situation is the result of the turbulence and instability in the region compounded by narrow chauvinism is not acknowledged and somehow, our leaders are not able to and seem to be unwilling to explode this myth of "neglect by the Centre" and tell the people the stark truth. This sense of alienation is no doubt exploited to the full by anti-national forces within and without. The practically unchecked illegal migration from the erstwhile East Pakistan (now Bangladesh) has generated a high sense of insecurity and xenophobia, with fears that the original residents are being reduced to a minority in their own state and that very soon, they will lose control over their political authority. There is great disillusionment with the Centre and even the state government for their abject failure to detect and deport illegal immigrants and going to the extent of protecting them by enacting the Illegal Migration (Determination by Tribunals) (IMDT) Act. Great damage has been done to the North-East's demographic profile by these failures. The AASU and others have had to fight for nearly 10 years to get this Act declared as unconstitutional by the Supreme Court and even after this, action to detect and deport illegal immigrants from Bangladesh has been halting and at best sporadic. The Assam High Court has come down heavily on the government on this issue and as of now, the AASU has threatened a new agitation and some reports indicate that the people in some areas have taken law into their own hands and are identifying illegal immigrants and asking them to leave. If the matter is not handled well, one more cause for violence may emerge. On account of such unchecked illegal migration, three or four districts in Assam have now become Muslim majority districts and extremist outfits as well as the ISI have found it possible to establish footholds in these areas. Attempts to clean up the electoral rolls to weed out non-citizens and prepare a correct national register of citizens have been thwarted by groups who favour illegal immigration, through open violence. Recently, the office of the Deputy Commissioner of Barpeta was attacked where the process of preparing correct NRC was being undertaken and the effort had to be stopped. The Government of Assam cannot muster enough courage to go forward in this vital matter. A student outfit called AAMSU (All Assam Minority students Association) is active in this regard and has no hesitation in indulging in violence. The illegal immigrants have forcibly displaced a whole lot of poor tribals even from tribal belts and tribal blocks.

By now, there has also developed a brotherhood of insurgents having a common purpose, a common enemy. Some reports indicate establishment of linkages with the Maoists of Central India and even the separatists of J&K. Each provides the other with support, shelter and training. All show a distinct tendency to take advantage of the legal procedures that the country has and also exploit the concerns of human rights activists to place the security forces on the defensive. None of them have, it appears, paid any attention as to what exactly will be the shape of things if they do get their independence. Economic viability, ability to defend themselves in this hostile world are matters which they seem to blissfully ignore. Some glibly talk about certain small European nations, ignoring all the violence and carnage that Europe has gone through in the first part of the 20th Century and how boundaries have been drawn and redrawn through bloodshed and how these small countries have suffered through so many wars. Europeans have traveled a long way in submerging interests and identities, and have opted for economic integration, a common currency, a common defense system and even a degree of political integration by surrendering their legislative powers to the European Parliament at Strasbourg.

Fortunately, the overall security scenario in each of the states of the North-East has in the recent past, shown some improvement even though new issues keep cropping up born out of the same factors mentioned earlier, namely the anxiety to preserve ethnic identity and improve the ability to garner economic opportunities. Pointed and determined efforts to deal with the problems, with a view to finding enduring solutions are yet to be fully worked out, leading to an intensification of dissatisfaction, disaffection and disillusionment. There is disproportionate faith being placed on pouring in more Central funds into the region as an easy way out, and this seems to suit all concerned, especially the insurgents who take away a substantial segment of Central funds for their nefarious purposes. The efficacy and efficiency of the delivery systems have been neglected for a long time. With leakages all round, there are a select group of beneficiaries, but the fundamental problems of the region remain without lasting solutions. There is continuous decline in governance standards and the generous assistance from the Centre does not generally speaking benefit the common man. Widening of disparities has also been noticed. These issues need urgent attention.

It will be worth having a closer look at the situation in the worst affected states.

I. Assam

Peace and progress in Assam is of fundamental importance to the situation in the entire North-East. While the ULFA had some appeal among the Ahoms, Mataks and some ethnic Assamese, it has by now lost much of its support base except in some pockets. Its confused political and economic philosophy of "sovereignty for Assam" and freedom from "Indian capitalist exploitation" has lost its relevance. However, the ULFA continues to retain to an extent its damage potential and more significantly its ability to indulge in widespread extortion activities. Self-styled civil liberties and human rights groups are conveniently utilized by ULFA for justifying its existence. Practically everyone in Assam is subject to extortion and threats and in particular, tea gardens and the business class. The government has been entirely ineffective in affording protection against such extortion activities. The impression unfortunately has gained ground that the government is soft towards ULFA. Also, the entire police machinery has become moribund making it impossible for the ordinary citizen to get any relief from this organization. Corruption on a large scale has permeated all layers of the society.

The ULFA (United Liberation Force of Assam) is the offshoot of the agitation launched by the students in 1979 against illegal immigration into Assam. While its main targets were the immigrants from Bangladesh, it degenerated into a movement to oust all considered non-natives. The Assam Accord paved the way for the end of the agitation and the student leaders who formed their own regional party—the Assam Gana Parishad—won the elections. The student leaders had no experience in governance and could not keep any of their promises. There was also considerable infighting and corruption seeped in. The ULFA attracted the more radical elements in the student body advocating armed revolt as the means to achieve their objectives. During the AGP rule, the ULFA was permitted to take over parts of the state and collect levies at will from traders, trucks, etc. The economy of Assam suffered a great deal and along with violence, pervasive atmosphere of fear was created. The police was effectively defanged.

The AGP which did nothing to stop the illegal infiltration, lost the next election due to misgovernance and corruption. Firm steps were taken to suppress the ULFA and those who abjured violence and surrendered were given generous financial assistance and offered alternative employment. The hard core however escaped to forests in Bhutan and then to Bangladesh, where they were captured by the ISI. Begum Zia's pro-Pakistan Government treated ULFA with kid gloves allowing it to set up training camps, procure arms and launch operations in Assam. Targeted killings of mainly people from the rest of India were carried out along with blasts to damage vital installations. The ISI had found one more ally to impose "a thousand cuts" on India. Killing labourers from the rest of India who come to execute projects financed by the Centre, was calculated to promote demand for illegal immigrants from Bangladesh. The ULFA had been able to carry out widespread extortion and occasional kidnappings for ransom and the local administration was quite helpless in preventing this. The ULFA had, at one point of time, become so powerful that it was being wooed by political parties who were prepared to pay the ULFA for permitting conduct of elections or for active assistance to win them. The support that ULFA enjoyed from the general population at one time has in the meanwhile, evaporated and its ability to extort money remains its only strength.

In the past three years, with the surrender of the main leaders and the active assistance of the Hasina regime in Bangladesh, the ULFA menace has possibly reached its end. The surrendered leaders are in the process of negotiations with the Centre and it appears they do not any more insist on their core demand of "sovereignty" for Assam, an idea which has never been clearly defined. Reports that the ULFA's self-styled C-in-C has amassed assets worth millions of dollars and had deep business interests in Bangladesh, will surely undermine whatever credibility he still has. Sadly, a whole lot of young lives have been sacrificed for what was an impractical and indeed a stupid idea.

In Assam, the extortion fever has now spread to other insurgent outfits. In the Bodo Territorial Council Area, armed cadres of those who were not part of this Bodo peace accord regularly collect taxes on the highway and trucks carrying goods have to pay. One report indicates that even government servants have to part with a share of their income to the rebels. Extortion is now a well-organized industry in Assam.

In Assam, in order to satisfy the economic aspirations of various plain tribals, tribal autonomies councils were established for the Bodos, Rabhas, etc., but in each these areas, the tribals themselves are a minority. Consequently, the non-tribals inhabiting these areas are deeply dissatisfied and periodically indulge in violence. Recently, in the Rabha and Bodo autonomous areas, immigrant Bangladeshi Muslims took to violence causing widespread damage.

Further West towards West Bengal, another group of tribals, namely Koch Raj Bangshis are demanding a separate Kamtapur state and to reinforce their demand, periodic bandhs and blockages of transport arteries occur frequently.

In the hill districts of Assam, new outfits, demanding greater autonomy and separate states, with links with NSCN (IM) indulge in violence directed against labourers from the rest of India who are brought in by labour contactors and earn a living doing an honest day's work. There has been for the past 10 years or so, repeated incidents of violence perpetrated mainly by United Peoples Democratic Solidarity (UPDS) which has been fighting for a separate state for the Karbi tribe. Since this district has other inhabitants including tribes such as the Dimasas (known also as Kacharis) Bodos, Kukis, Tiwas, Garos and Rengmas, all of whom are living together though not in contiguous areas, the Karbi armed gangs have often attacked these non-Karbi tribes. The Dimasas have their own armed cadre, Dimasa Halam Daogah and a more radical Black Widow faction.

In an effort to bring peace and create conditions for economic progress, the Central Government has negotiated an agreement (25th November, 2011) with the UPDS which in effect upgrades the present district council into a more autonomous territorial council with enlarged number of members—50 against the earlier 30, provides an economic package of Rs. 350 crore, promises improving transportation links, rehabilitation of armed cadres and setting up of village councils. Though a very desirable step forward, it is difficult to predict if this will bring about enduring peace or stability in the area which has been rocked by mindless violence for a long time. The state government seems to be unhappy with this agreement. There is secondly the apprehension that the conflicts between the Karbis and all other tribes in the area as well as the Assamese may become exacerbated. The armed wings of the Karbis, the Karbi Longri NC Hills Liberation Front (KNLF) and the Karbi People's Liberation Fighters (KPLF) have not accepted this agreement and disarming them may prove very difficult. The KNLF chairman, Pongbi Dilli has rejected the agreement and wants to continue the fight for a separate state outside Assam. The Assam Government is concerned that the conversion of the UPDS to a political party and the failure to provide any safeguards in the territorial council to other inhabitants of the district, is bound to generate new tensions. Also, the problem of creating a proper accountability mechanism to ensure proper utilization of funds; under the new economic package and for ensuring that this is not siphoned off by the insurgents, needs urgent attention.

A more recent manifestation of the phenomenon of ethnicity and economic aspirations is the demand for Scheduled Tribe status by tea garden labour groups. They migrated to Assam more than a century ago from Orissa, Santhal Parganas, Andhra Pradesh, etc., and are recognized as ST in the states from which they came. This demand of the tea garden labour is over a decade old and has recently taken more strident tones. The capital of Assam witnessed great violence when these groups descended on the capital to press their demands. Other groups which already enjoy ST status such as the Bodos are against this demand and the scene is set for one more dose of inter-group rivalries and conflict.

The Barak valley of Assam is a forgotten corner of India, but it is the only gateway to Tripura, Mizoram and Manipur. This area is neglected by the Government of Assam as it is inhabited by Bengalis; with uninterrupted flow of migrants from Bangladesh, the demographic character of this area consisting of three districts has drastically changed. It has become a Muslim majority area and we may see the spread of fundamentalism and even demands for separation.

The tragedy is that all this ensures that the pace of economic development remains halting, while population keeps increasing, unemployment grows and dissatisfaction builds up. Those who are victims of extortion, particularly the business class, recoup their expenses through higher prices and it is the common man who ultimately suffers. The government loses valuable revenue, while its expenditure for non-productive purposes keeps on going up. Also, capital costs in the entire area are much higher than the rest of India, as for executing any project the insurgents have also to be paid, while getting reliable technical personnel becomes more and more difficult. Consequently, there is no flow of private investment into the entire region.

The common thread running in all these separatists and insurgency movements is the dissatisfaction and even anger about the abject failure on the part of the system, including those mechanisms that have been created specifically for satisfying the economic, political and social aspirations of the ethnic groups as well preservation and promotion of their culture, such as the district councils, to provide the most basic services to the people and create employment opportunities which can match the growth of those who enter the labour market. Land, which was the basic means of livelihood of many especially the tribals, has been misappropriated by the immigrants who are generally more hard working and who have been enabled to buy off the land even in violation of the regulations, which granted the tribals only heritable and not transferable rights, especially in tribal blocks and tribal belts by bribing the land revenue officials. Well-conceived programmes for tribal welfare called intensive tribal development programmes have mostly floundered in the face of ineffective delivery mechanisms. To my mind, all this is a resounding failure of governance, caused by the malaise that has afflicted the whole of India, namely decline in the effectiveness, efficiency and responsiveness of all systems of governance and the politics of divisiveness, that is practised for winning elections.

I, who has served in the North-East for long years, have seen how the land revenue machinery has suffered grave neglect, how the land records staff often connives with the immigrants to deprive the tribals of their land rights, how in the areas declared as Intensive Tribal Development Blocks money is either wasted or eaten up and permanent assets are seldom created and even if they are, poor maintenance ensures that they do not provide enduring benefits to the people. I have also seen that facilities such as hospitals and dispensaries created at great expense and with much fanfare, fall into disuse as the doctors and para-medics do not attend to their duties and in fact, avoid such postings and even if they are transferred, hardly ever take up their posts. There is an all pervasive lack of commitment and spirit of public purpose. Young officers of the All India Services find that they have to run the place with very few officers of the right quality and their efforts to get officers to man all the posts created to serve the area are thwarted due to political interference.

II. Manipur

The state of Manipur continues to be in ferment and it would be no exaggeration to say that the Constitution of India applies only nominally to the state. Over a dozen insurgency outfits have carved out their own fiefdoms and carry out unbridled extortion activities, levy taxes, etc. Even government servants are not exempt. Many politicians are part of one outfit or the other and violence is endemic and in spite of presence of armed forces, peace is elusive and development is nowhere on the horizon.

The main demand of all the insurgents of Manipur, is independence from India as according to them, before the British take over Manipur was a separate kingdom. They also are critical of the parting of a fertile valley to Burma which was part of the kingdom. Manipur is inhabited by a number of tribes and ethnic groups. In the plains there are the Meitheis, while the hills are inhabited mainly by the Thankul Nagas. Some areas are occupied by the Peitheis as well. The NSCN (IM) claims the area inhabited by the Thangkuls (Muivah the NSCN IM supremo is a Thankul Naga) and wants this area; to be incorporated into the Nagalim—greater Nagaland. This Naga tribe is in conflict with the Meitheis as also the Kukis, another hill tribe. With economic development halted by continuous insurgency, the only avenue of occupation is to take to the gun, become an insurgent and extort money from everyone. Periodic road blockages are organized by one group or the other for long periods, cutting off essential supplies creating severe shortages and imposing heavy costs on the economy. Prices of essential items soar and great hardship is caused to everyone.

Those who carry essential supplies to the state are the main targets while the money poured in the by the Centre is also either wholly or partly misappropriated. The Constitution of India has been converted into a convenient device to get money from the Centre by creating a farce of a government where every minister is allegedly a member of one outfit or the other. It is often said that they are ministers by day and insurgents by night. If any minister is seen to violate the dictates of the militants, he is promptly disposed of. With nothing to do except extort money, there is widespread use of drugs and this state has the highest incidence of HIV and AIDS. The border with Myanmar which is poorly policed on both sides offers full scope for arms smuggling and drug running which finds it way to other insurgency groups across the country. It is a sad fact that even after 65 years of independence, this problem remains unsolved. Very few if any in New Delhi seem to have the energy, time and inclination to fully understand the real nature of the problem and find a lasting solution with the involvement of all the stake-holders.

Let us note certain special aspects of the Manipur scenario which are as follows:

a. Manipur has a very advanced civilization with no caste system, deeply influenced by Chaitanya Mahaprabhu's version of Vaishnavism. It can indeed be considered as the eastern-most extension of the finest aspects of Hindu philosophical system. The Manipuri language is written in the Bengali script.
b. The people have a great history and a fine heritage of which they are very proud. Lack of respect for this invites considerable anguish and anger.
c. Ethnically they belong to the same Tibeto Burman stock as the tribes inhabiting the Myanmar area adjoining the state. The Kangla fort has the same architecture and characteristics as the fort at Mandalay.
d. The Manipuris consider their accession to India as flawed and believe that their Maharaja was coerced, though there is no evidence to support this.
e. Since independence, possibly due to lack of understanding, a series of missteps were taken which have caused deep resentment. These include, making

Manipur a Chief Commissioner's province and a group 'C state instead of treating it on par with other princely states, non-recognition of Manipuri language for over 20 years, occupation of the Kangla Fort by Assam rifles, application of the Armed Forces Special Powers Act, surrender of a large tract of land which was part of the Manipur kingdom to Myanmar.

f. The formation of a separate state of Nagaland in 1964 sent shock waves in Manipur leading to the conclusion that armed insurgency yields results and Delhi can be bent through violence. The formation of the UNLF roughly coincides with the formation of Nagaland. The PLA (Peoples Liberation Army) is an older outfit.

There has been a continuous deterioration in the situation for decades with insurgency now degenerating into a pure extortion and employment generation activity. Everyone in Manipur is involved in the racket and even the periodic blockades are often a device to generate a black market to make a killing out of supplies hoarded by someone or the other.

The economy has suffered grievously, with no infrastructure in major parts of the area, most villages unconnected even by rudimentary roads, and people deprived of even the most basic needs including drinking water, education and health care. Large funds, poured regularly by the Centre, go into the hands of a few and the insurgents are known to have benefited substantially and invested huge amounts in Bangladesh and elsewhere. The local leadership is part of this racket and come to Delhi only to get more funds but have no time or inclination to sit and discuss enduring solutions.

Large numbers of inhabitants have come out of the state to find work in Delhi, Bangalore, etc., as also for education and seem to display a high degree of entrepreneurship. Manipur also contributes handsomely to the sporting talent of the country in the fields of wrestling, archery, weight lifting, etc. Women seem to be particularly gifted.

Fortunately, there seem to be saner voices emerging, especially among the younger generation who have had the benefit of education in the rest of India and wider exposure to the great pan-Indian mosaic of culture and who are articulating the need for a life with dignity, well being and respect. They desire that the political class be made accountable for the mess that they have created and have started feeling that they have been taken for ride for too long. They are becoming aware that a few people for their self-interests have been holding the entire state to ransom. The recent blockade called by leaders who have a following among their tribes has caused immense hardship for all the people. This generation is now calling for a change and it will be desirable to listen closely to the message they are trying to convey and build on the possibilities that this offers.

If the decision makers can find the political will, the issue can be dealt with and enduring solutions can be found.

The steps can be as follows:

a. The serious feeling of injustice and alienation that seems to permeate all layers of society needs to be recognized and concerted efforts made to achieve reconciliation and regaining of trust.
b. Harmony between the warring tribes needs to be promoted. There has been a tendency to pit one tribe against the other leading to increased violence.
c. The AFPSA can be withdrawn from Manipur to begin with in some districts and the kind of protection asked for by the Army can be provided through other means. This may be symbolic but will be of great significance and may end the fast of Irom Sharmila. India has unnecessarily drawn a lot of flak from the international community and from human rights activists on this score.
d. Instead of large investments in projects which do not get completed and which provide fertile ground for siphoning off funds by the insurgents and politicians, community-based projects to cater to the local requirements such as decent roads, water supply, irrigation systems, schools, dispensaries, electricity solar energy, etc., need to be promoted and quickly and efficiently implemented through community participation. Also, specific steps to improve agricultural productivity and promote small and medium enterprises to produce goods which are brought through the very

tenuous transport network will not only generate gainful employment but also bring down costs.

e. The connectivity to Manipur and communication facilities need to be upgraded, in particular a rail line to Jiribam and on to Imphal needs to be completed.
f. Sports talent of the state needs to be harvested through well-designed scholarship, training and talent promotion programmes.
g. Provision of basic services at all levels and deeper penetration of the administrative system needs to be ensured.
h. The insurgent, politician and contactor nexus needs to be broken.
i. Trade channels with Myanmar can be broadened and this will generate new employment on a substantial scale. The 'Look East' policy now being promoted with some vigour needs to be expanded as this will greatly benefit the entire North-East. So also improved relations with Bangladesh. This can possibly undo the damage done to the North-East by the Partition of 1947.
j. Tourism, especially village, adventure and eco tourism, can serve as a very useful instrument for greater integration and employment generation.
k. Comprehensive improvement in standards of governance and control of corruption can go a long way in improving trust and confidence.
l. Greater degree of economic integration can be promoted with neighbouring states of the region. For example, Tripura produces substantial quantities of gas and rubber while Mizoram can produce large quantities of electricity. These can generate a viable set of industries in the field of plastics, rubber, etc.

III. Nagaland

The demand of the insurgent groups in Nagaland, mainly the NSCN (IM), is for the separation of so called Naga nation from India and creation of an independent nation. It needs to be emphasized that the demand for a separate Naga nation (Nagalim), is a post-independence and wholly artificial construct which has no historical basis. The British had carved out a district out of their empire in India, purely for administrative reasons and named it the Naga hills district, though the so called Naga tribes inhabited not only this district but nearby Manipur as well as Burma (now Myanmar). Within this district (which later became the state of Nagaland), no less than 16 separate tribes (recognized in the Indian Constitution as Scheduled Tribes) exist and there are quite a few Naga tribes in Manipur and Myanmar; all these tribes have separate languages, traditions and cultures. With no common language, a corrupt form of Assamese is used as the lingua franca. There is no written script for any of the languages. For long years, these tribes were at war with each other adopting gruesome practices such as headhunting. Those in the border area of Assam used to indulge in violence and the British had no hesitation in conducting reprisals, often brutal, with punitive raids. The Ahom kings had built a long earthen embankment in the districts bordering Naga inhabited areas, to prevent Naga incursions and depredations. This embankment known as the "Dodar aali" can be seen to this day and was reportedly made by putting to work idle characters and possibly conscripted labour.

It would appear that the Nagas were quite comfortable under the British, who ruled with an iron hand for over 150 years and it is only after the independence of India that they suddenly discovered a common but artificial identity and developed demands for independence. It cannot be denied that the missionaries, particularly of the Baptist Church, have played an important role in creating separatist attitudes among the Nagas. That the Nagas who belong to the Tibeto Burman stock, have a separate ethnic origin, different customs and languages from the rest of India, is an argument which can be applied to several tribes and communities in India, as after all, India has been the recipient of streams of humanity from many parts of the world for centuries.

The NSCN (IM) which has emerged as the most militant, well armed and trained insurgent outfit, has utilized the ceasefire to consolidate its position and spread its influence. Though the ceasefire has created a constituency for peace, with its strength augmented continuously through levies and taxes, the NSCN (IM) can prove to be a tough nut to crack if the ceasefire breaks down. In the meanwhile, this outfit runs a parallel administration in those areas where it has its hold. It has tried to expand its influence into the state of Arunachal Pradesh and the areas inhabited by Tangkhul Nagas in Manipur. Its demand for Nagalim includes all these areas and even some parts of Assam.

It is unfortunate fact that whole of North-East has been turbulent for a long time now and external forces are aiding and abetting the insurgency. It has to be realized that the people in that entire area suffer grievously due to lack of adequate job opportunities and inadequate investment, as the private sector is extremely wary of investing in the area. That this area is surrounded by India's international borders enhances seriously the security threat to the nation.

What can be the way forward? Several measures can be initiated.

a. Given the fact that plan funds are poured into the area, what is required is to ensure that results are achieved through efficient utilization of funds and elimination of all leakages.
b. The unholy nexus between the contractors, politicians and bureaucrats as well as, the underground should be broken.
c. Widespread extortion which keeps the insurgency alive must be ruthlessly eliminated.
d. All round improvement in standards of governance is required to restore peoples' faith in the official machinery. Efficiency and effectiveness of the police can be improved easily, if they are permitted to exercise the powers vested in them by law and respect for hierarchy is also restored.
e. A disproportionate number of the police force is deployed, to guard various functionaries and consequently, normal policing has ceased to exist. Corrective measures must be taken in this regard by augmenting the police force substantially. Smuggling of arms and infiltration through international borders must be effectively stopped.
f. Local resources such as jute, bamboo etc., can be developed to create large scale employment opportunities.
g. Vocational training needs to be expanded and special measures taken to promote local entrepreneurship.

h. The issue of alienation must be addressed squarely through well organized psy-ops programme. It must be recognized that real battle is for the winning of the hearts and minds of the people.

The campaign should emphasize the following:

- The people, particularly the tribals have their own states.
- That they choose their rulers and enjoy the liberty of throwing them out if their performance is not satisfactory and if promises are not kept, provided they use this right wisely and without being influenced by narrow considerations.
- That they participate in the governing structures of the whole country.
- That they enjoy reservation in all government services and in public sector undertakings.
- That they have been enabled to occupy some of the highest offices in the country (Supreme Court judges, Secretaries to Government of India, Chief Election Commissioner, etc.).
- Their land rights, culture, ethnic identity, etc., have all been fully protected and encouraged to flourish.
- That the people enjoy a higher standard of living than that in many parts of India.
- They have been provided quotas in educational institutions which ensure generation of much needed skills for socio-economic development.
- That their external security is taken care of.
- The whole of India belongs to them and is indeed their homeland and they can move freely anywhere in India, buy property, get employment, educate themselves and set-up businesses while in their own territories they enjoy a high degree of protection. Ordinary Indians do not have such rights in the North-East region except Assam.

i. The isolation syndrome should be removed by improving the transportation and communication links with the rest of India. Strong cultural links must also be built and the people made to realize the futility of violence which only retards progress.

j. Peace talks such as with the NSCN (IM) cannot go on indefinitely. Such attention to one particular insurgency group alienates other groups. The NSCN (IM) does not command the loyalty of several tribes.

k. It must be made clear to the insurgent groups that ceasefire and dialogue cannot be used for improving their combat capability and expanding their reach as is being done by the NSCN (IM) which is spreading its tentacles to the peaceful state of Arunachal Pradesh. It must be made clear that there cannot be any compromise as regards the sanctity of the Constitution and the question of granting "independence", "sovereignty", etc., cannot be considered at all.

l. The support from external sources which is currently enjoyed by NSCNIM and ULFA must be cut off once for all.

m. It needs to be recognized that in the whole of the North-East, tribal loyalties, clan and kinship relations are more important than adherence to rules and regulations. With the exception of Assam and Meghalaya, the British oriented Westminster system, has not taken roots in this area and the administration will have to make the necessary adjustments to factor in such considerations.

A macro view of the situation in the entire North-East, based on personal experience of working in that area for long years, would suggest that the present policy of buying peace by throwing money all-around cannot be a continued indefinitely. This has by now become a punishment for all honest, hard working people in the rest of India, who by their honest efforts, contribute handsomely to the GDP and pay their taxes. Why should this money instead of being well spent for improving standards of administration, building infrastructure, generating power, etc., and upgrading the security systems and effectively dealing with external and internal threats, be wasted on a set of people who have perfected the art of blackmail? This disproportionate faith in largesse and plain bribery has created a milieu where honest hard work is at a discount. It has prevented a whole set of people from developing the DNA for acquiring the main drivers of real and enduring social and economic development, namely education, particularly technical education, skills for a modern economic system, the spirit of entrepreneurship, individual initiative and innovation. It results in these societies developing a massive dependency syndrome and destroys their self-confidence, self-esteem and the urge for competing and excelling. It has also created highly distorted notions in the mind of the leadership of what real development is all about. The leadership ignores the essentiality of creating the best possible environment for fostering the real drivers of sustained development, namely human resource development, individual initiative, entrepreneurship, innovation, etc., along with ecological conservation and relies mainly on distribution of official largesse.

We are encouraging a culture of violence and so long as everyone carries a gun and keeps getting trained to use it, the society's psyche is distorted and it is made to believe in the efficacy of violence. Faith in peaceful resolution of conflicts through dialogue, negotiation, compromise and accommodation is eroded. Violence breeds more violence and this kind of ethos is totally alien to our culture which has articulated the concept of "*Ahimsa paramo Dharma*". It is out of tune with the basic ideals and principles of our Constitution, Gandhiji's teachings and our democratic ideals. This is also a direct assault on the basics of rule of law. And so long as there are guns around, the army and para-military forces have to be deployed and this leads to a self-perpetuating cycle of violence, with all concerned developing a vested interest in the continuation of the unsettled conditions as has happened in J&K. More importantly, if the nation has to face external aggression, these areas can be targeted by the enemy for disruption, sabotage, etc., with the cooperation of the insurgents who have received the support of potential aggressors, at one point of time or the other. There are far too many guns and too many explosives in the wrong hands in this area and can come in handy to perpetrate widespread sabotage and undermine the efforts to combat external aggression.

We are also undermining the long-term economic prospects of this region and its ability to participate in the growth story of India. That the North-East has some very important natural resources that the country needs, e.g. hydro power, coal, hydro carbons, uranium, etc., cannot be ignored. Instead of benefiting from the leveraging of these resources, this part of the country has become dependent upon the rest of the country. It has the potential to become a net contributor to the GDP of the whole country but so far it has only drawn away the surplus generated by the other parts.

Very importantly, given the strategic location of the North-East, instability in the area is an open invitation for powers inimical to India to interfere and exploit this to their advantage. It is alarming that the insurgents of the North-East have been striving to develop links with the Naxalites as well as separatists of J&K, along with forging a brotherhood among the rebels of the North-East itself for providing mutual support, shelter, training, gun running, financial assistance, etc. Some reports indicate that such cooperation among anti-national forces already exists and they have hatched plans to target the hydroelectric projects under implementation in Arunachal Pradesh.

We need also to remind ourselves that throughout our history, at times when the central authority weakens, the peripheral areas have shown a distinct propensity to revolt and break away. In post-independent India, the makers of our Constitutions did realize the great importance of a strong central authority and made a number of provisions for creating such a mechanism. When one party ruled the whole of India and strong leaders with an all India appeal, a Nehru, a Patel or Indira Gandhi were on the scene, this system operated very well. In fact, both Nehru and Indira Gandhi basically ran a Presidential system and the people voted for Nehru or Indira rather than the party or an ideology. However, since then, there has been perceptible decline in the ability of the Centre to enforce its writ and many states act more in interests of the ruling party or state's interest than in the interests of the nation, even on national security and foreign policy issues. Take the case of the defiance of the Chief Minister of West Bengal with respect to the sharing of Teesta waters with Bangladesh—an external relations issue and the exclusive preserve of the Union. The Prime Minister was placed in an awkward position and what could have been a massive diplomatic triumph, was robbed of its significance in a major way. The Chief Minister has disregarded her constitutional obligation under Article 257 which specifies "*The executive power of every state shall be so exercised as not to impede or prejudice the exercise of the executive power of the Union and the executive power of the Union shall extend to giving such directions to a State as may appear to the Government of India to be necessary for the purpose."* Does not the conduct of the Chief Minister who has sworn to uphold the Constitution and the laws of the land amount to violation of the Constitution and failure to carry on the administration of the State in accordance with the provisions of the Constitution? Is this not a case warranting dismissal of the State under Article 356 of the Constitution? Surely the Centre is undermining its own authority by failing to act as per the Constitution.

With the kind of coalition politics, the decline in the appeal of truly national parties, the decline in the calibre of leaders and the rise of regional, caste-based parties; who thrive on narrow electoral politics at the cost of national interests, there is the real fear, indeed danger, that we may find the strength of the Centre being eroded continuously and the states becoming more assertive and indeed unreasonable, if not uncooperative even on matters of supreme national interest. Also, such leaders who are basically regional satraps or caste chieftains, do not have the time, the energy and the knowledge to pay detailed attention to the complexities of the North-East and we may find that the possibility of finding lasting solutions to the problems of this area becoming more difficult and more remote.

We cannot allow the situation in the North-East to drift and every possible measure must be taken to solve the insurgency problem to restore peace, along with full enforcement of the Constitution in all the areas. Insurgents cannot be allowed to run parallel governments and the writ of the constitutional system must apply to all parts. Also, the greater the economic integration with the rest of the country, the better are the chances of peaceful coexistence, as everyone develops a vested interest in peace and progress.

The history of many an empire from the Roman times, shows that when the centre starts getting weaker, it is the periphery which becomes more and more uncontrollable. Chanakya warned the Mauryas to keep a wary eye on the periphery at all times. We cannot allow such a situation to develop in our North-East. There is the ever present danger of foreign interference if the area becomes unstable. This should make us redouble our efforts to sort out the problems of the North-East once and for all.

The Naxal Problem

The other major menace to the unity, integrity, welfare and progress of the country is Naxalism. It would be noted that it has taken strong roots precisely in those states and parts where there has been a comprehensive failure of governance. Eastern India and small parts of Maharashtra, Madhya Pradesh and Andhra Pradesh have been affected and as of today, some 223 districts out of 620 of the country are wholly or partly in the grip of this menace.

The Naxal movement which originated in the Naxalbari area of West Bengal was inspired by Maoist revolutionary ideology which considered the CPI and CPM not radical enough to root out the capitalist and bourgeois system of economic and political management and advocated violence as the only viable method to achieve its objectives. Mobilization of the peasantry to destroy the existing system through armed action and then surrounding and taking over the urban areas was the strategy advocated. This was the classic Maoist strategy which enabled Mao to establish his version of the dictatorship of the proletariat in China. Years of violence were gone through by West Bengal before the movement was brutally suppressed. In the meanwhile, the movement spread to other states. In Bengal itself, it has lost much of its appeal though pockets of influence remain. The main bases are in Orissa, Chhattisgarh, Jharkhand, and parts of Maharashtra. In Andhra, where at one time the movement was very strong, determined, well planned and executed action by the administration combining armed action with development has reduced this menace to a very large extent and if the present strategy and tactics are continued, the state can get rid of this problem altogether. Even today the main leadership of the Maoist movement comes from Andhra Pradesh. I have worked in the field of tribal welfare both at the Centre and the state level and have visited the areas inhabited by tribals and affected by the naxal menace. I consider that this movement has its roots in the total and continuous failure of the administration to provide even the most basic services to the people and take care of their welfare and progress. All the institutions of governance have failed these people most comprehensively, while they have been exploited by middle men with political links.

Many in these areas, even after six decades of independence, barely survive with daily earning insufficient to satisfy the most basic of needs. For long periods in a year, even this is not available, as large numbers live by collecting what is called minor forest produce, which is seasonal. They are often harassed by the forest officials and exploited by middle men who pay prices well below that fixed by the government and get away with it because of political connections. There are no roads, no electricity, no education, no health care and even if the buildings have indeed been constructed, the doctors do not come, medicines get stolen and schools are dysfunctional. They have no land rights and corrupt land revenue officials have no time for them, while they are exploited by landowners with impunity. There is no way they can fight for their rights given the nature of justice delivery system. There is little or no presence of the administrative system in this area which is seen by the tribals as remote, unsympathetic, unresponsive and beyond the reach of these people. They perceive the system as not in the least concerned about them in any way. While they continue to wallow in abject poverty, they see that their rulers who come at election time with tall promises, that are never delivered, live in luxury surrounded by barbed wire and security guards. Gandhiji had time and again advocated and practised simple living and high thinking, an ideal advocated by all our traditions. Our leaders have forgotten this and are doing exactly the opposite. Many are also seen by the poor and disadvantaged as thoroughly corrupt, with no moral scruples in exploiting the nation's mineral and other resources, to enrich themselves and their families. Even in the North-East where the Centre has taken special interest and allocated huge funds, the Naxals have managed to infiltrate and exploit the peoples' dissatisfaction or create artificial grievances to stifle economic development. Their objective clearly is to destroy the Indian State which in their view is nothing but a parasite created to benefit a select few, by any and every means.

The huge administrative void in many areas has been successfully filled by the naxalites who have, while promising to remedy all the ills, want that the tribals be part of the violent revolution which they consider as absolutely essential, if the lives of these people is to improve. In fact, they want the tribals to be part of a nationwide uprising to wipe out the present system of governance as it is, in their view, unjust and exploitative. Anyone who has seen no improvement in his life in decades under the present system is an easy convert to this militant ideology. The Naxal lives among these people, talks their language and seems to bear the very hardships they have been victims of for years. He delivers rough, ready and often brutal but speedy and inexpensive justice. The naxalites for example, were able to build a substantial following in areas such as the Telengana region of AP, as they redistributed thousands of acres of land to the landless.

The naxals have also managed to build a network of front organizations, which contain several left leaning intellectuals who take advantage of the new found enthusiasm for human rights, civil rights and civil society activism. These include university professors and members of the literary world. Organizations such as the Peoples Union for Civil Liberties are basically fronts for the Naxalites.

While the naxals have indeed succeeded in awakening the exploited tribals and the downtrodden, carried out armed attacks with brutal violence, it cannot be denied that they are advocating an economic strategy which has failed resoundingly all over the world and in particular in China itself. China was chained and held back by Mao and once it broke free of this restrictive and oppressive system which had killed millions, rapid progress was recorded and today, China is in a position to overtake the US in terms of GDP mainly because it abandoned the path of Mao and warmly embraced Deng Xio Ping.

Violence has driven out all investments from the Naxal infested areas and with it the prospects of growth, generation of new employment and progress. The nation has been deprived of opportunities of exploiting precious natural resources and minerals and millions of jobs have been lost. The tribals have become captive to an outdated economic philosophy and entrapped in seemingly endless violence without any real progress in the very areas where they need advancement. The naxalites while indulging in widespread extortion and violence have pitted themselves against all progress. They have not built any roads or bridges, or schools or health facilities and indeed, they actively prevent any development from taking place.

Such a situation cannot be allowed to continue as it is harmful for the very people the naxals claim to be fighting for and is damaging national interests. The Naxals are using every opportunity to stifle India's growth, encouraging tribals to agitate against acquisition of land for the establishment of large projects, be it in the area of mining or steel production or power generation. The huge investment by the Koreans for the Posco project in Odisha has been delayed by years. The Naxalites very conveniently use concerns regarding environment to mislead people and make it difficult to acquire land or implement projects. The Naxals' ability to violently prevent exploitation of rich mineral resources at a time when the country is poised to accelerate its growth process can seriously undermine India's growth prospects and destroy investor confidence. The states seriously affected by Naxal violence are repositories of a great deal of the country's mineral and forest wealth. For example, Chhattisgarh has 44 per cent forest cover and has 17 per cent of the country's coal and has deposits of 28 major minerals, including iron ore, lime stone, dolomite, bauxite and diamonds. Jharkhand has 30 per cent forest cover and is the largest producer of coal, mica and copper. Orissa has 37 per cent forest cover has 70 per cent of India's bauxite (sixth largest in the world), 90 per cent of its chrome ore and nickel and 24 per cent of coal. Since the state has not been able to protect them, the mining companies have started paying protection money to the Naxals and this can increase their lethal potential and ability to buy weapons.

They have now infiltrated into the North-East to collaborate with the rebels in that area to obtain arms and ammunition and in exchange provide the rebels training in combat. They are also agitating against large hydro generation projects and misleading the locals by exaggerating their grievances and creating artificial grievances. The Maoists have been in the lead to form this pan-India insurgency movement with the Indian State as the common enemy. Their intention is to co-opt not only the rebels of the North-East but the separatists of the J&K as well. These are truly dangerous developments and need to be dealt with, with determination and urgency.

What needs to be done is to emulate the AP model of raising special forces that are fully equipped, trained and committed to combat this menace. Improvement of intelligence to target the leadership, ensuring systematic reestablishment of all wings of the administration led by able, incorruptible and motivated officers, who are given the freedom to act against the naxalites and execution of development programmes which directly benefit the tribals all need to done. It is necessary to bring up educated tribals to play the leadership role and ensure that they work for the welfare of the people. In addition, there ought to be clarity of purpose and commonality of policy. There cannot be a situation where one state goes after the Naxals, while a neighbouring state adopts a soft policy and initiates a dialogue process. The Naxals exploit this and take shelter in the state which is soft. The Home Ministry must ensure a consensus among the states and implement a uniform policy, as this menace is doing great damage to the economic prospects of the country. It is necessary to take a firm line as regards hostage taking and demands for ransom and release of jailed Naxalites. The Odisha Government has tied itself into knots by vacillating on this issue and yielding to the demands of the Naxals. So has the government of Chhattisgarh. Once and for all we must decide that there can be no negotiation with terrorists of any kind under any circumstances. Mrs Thatcher set the right tone in refusing to negotiate with terrorists, when she was Britain's PM with respect to hijacking of planes and brought to an end this menace.

Above everything else, the Centre and the states must display the political will to wipe out this menace. The fundamental issues of land reforms, providing land rights and forest rights and a clear policy on land acquisition and tribal upliftment need to be speedily addressed while the penetration and strengthening of the normal administrative machinery and building infrastructure is given top most priority. It must be realized that the Naxalites have declared a brutal war. They have no regard to the human rights of others, even while they use every possible legal and other means to demand their rights and enlist the support of sympathizers to fight their battles in the open, while they carry on their own violent agenda through guerilla tactics.

There have recently been some very significant successes in the ongoing battle against the naxalites with the killing of Kishenji who was a rare and versatile leader, a great ideologue an organizer and one of the most articulate leader, giving telephonic interviews to the media. For the Naxalites the elimination of Kishenji, within a year of the killing of another top leader Cherkuri Rajkumar *alias* Azad, is a definite set back. Further, a number of leaders are behind bars and it is estimated that the Maoists have lost some 150 leaders in the past year or so. Some 20 central committee members including those of the Politburo, such as Kobad Ghandy, Amit Bagchi, Narayan Sanyal and Sushil Roy are in jail. This loss has affected many regions though Dandakaranya remains a safe zone. While "operation green hunt "of the Government, has met some significant successes, this needs to be intensified along with a massive development effort. Release of Naxalites against hostages needs to be put an end, A mass contact programme by all political parties and NGOs with a stake in the long-term development of India needs to be carried out to convince the people that the naxalite view of India as a semi-feudal and semi-colonial state is flawed and totally outdated and their strategy of liberating the village and encircling Delhi cannot succeed. It had failed resoundingly in Mao's own home-land and that country has prospered by drastically changing course and has now gone far far away from Mao. The tribals have themselves have suffered a lot under the Naxalites who have been ruthless in torturing and eliminating their rivals and so called informers or police agents. It is strange that political parties, who talk endlessly of the welfare, empowerment and resurrection of the down-trodden have been so hesitant to get to the grassroots, to combat this menace at the political level. They prefer to let loose the police and then accuse the police of excesses.

In addition to these major problems, the nation is also beset by divisive tendencies, casteism, regionalism, centrifugal and separatist tendencies, linguistic chauvinism and communalism. All political parties practise divisive politics, in one form or the other, as they find that winning and retaining the loyalty of a narrow segment of the electorate, combined with money and muscle power is more than adequate to seize power.

If the nation is to deal with all these multifarious problems, we need to ensure that all the institutions of governance recapture their lost vigour, stature and their effectiveness, efficiency and responsiveness. It is also very important to have a strong Central Government which was what our founding fathers worked for, realizing how our history is full of instances where internal strife has made us vulnerable to external aggression and we have lost our freedom. For this to happen, we need leaders of stature, who command the respect of the country and not sectarian satraps, who have only electoral arithmetic uppermost and their self-interest or the interests of the party far above national interests. The Centre should deal with all the states in a non-discriminatory manner irrespective of the party in power. The Centre cannot and should not play partisan politics. All its policies and programmes should be not only fair, just and equitable but seen to be so in the most transparent manner. It must be noted that States which are better administered and which have been recording rapid growth, such as Gujarat have been free of Naxalism or insurgency of any type.

It would be, in this context, worth recalling the words that Somerset Maugham who, saddened by the inglorious capitulation of France in 1940, wrote a perceptive piece in May 1940. Mangham's concern was with the importance of moral and ethical values that should permeate all layers of a society. Shocked by the collapse of France at the hands of the German Army in less than three weeks, he wrote, "While not ignoring factors such as the conflict between the general staff and the Illrd Republic's leadership, the sloth and conceit of the French Generals, the treachery of the politicians, or the fear of Bolshevism of the rich who preferred German rule to communism and the conflict between the working class and the employers, I strongly feel that these contributory factors were only symptoms and effects of a far more fundamental cause namely the general lack of morality in France of that period. No doubt there were thousands of French men and women who were honourable, upright, and patriotic. There were, however not enough. Too many politicians were unscrupulous, too many newspapers were venal, too many employers were crafty and tyrannical, and too many working people were dishonest, selfish and avaricious. France was defeated from within, well before she was defeated from without on the field of battle by the German army." Maugham cautions, "That we should be very stupid if we do not take warning from the fate of France."

Throughout our history, we have succumbed to foreign aggression because of internal weaknesses and loss of our moral fibre. Any number of instances can be cited in our sad history, where a ruler or a general had been bribed or promised a new office which he had coveted and he switched his allegiance. Armies which could have very successfully defeated the adversary or invader, simply laid down their arms and melted away, leaving the door open for the invader to conquer and pillage. Today, in the face of the challenges from within and without, unless we become internally strong and united and reinforce the moral and ethical underpinnings of the nation, peace and prosperity will remain distant dreams.

6

FOREIGN POLICY CHALLENGES

The contours of a country's foreign policy are determined by a number of factors which include its geographical location, its strategic vision, economic and security interests and the role it wants to play with respect to the world community. Broadly speaking, foreign policy should concern itself with all matters pertaining to the nation's relations with other countries, more particularly its neighbours and international bodies. Foreign policy is also governed by certain fundamentals which determine international relations namely, congruence or convergence of interests and conflict of interests.

The objectives of foreign policy should clearly be to increase the country's influence in world affairs, increase the number of friends it has, reduce the number of enemies it has or at least reduce the effectiveness with which its adversaries can harm its interests. The Romans had long ago understood the basics of international relations by emphatically stating that "If you want peace, be prepared for War" and our own Chanakya had averred, "If you want to be strong, you must keep your enemies weak and divided." These are eternal truths valid to this day. So also "Your enemy's enemy is your friend". Such advice assumes great importance when we consider the fact that while most countries have managed to secure their internal peace and stability by declaring the State established by law as the monopoly power, which is empowered by law to use force, at the international level there is no such monopoly. Despite all the arms control negotiations, in international relations 'might continues to be right' and the victor has seldom to answer any questions. Adolph Hitler famously stated, "If you win, the war you don't have to explain anything but if you lose the war, you should not be there to explain anything." There continues to be huge competition to acquire the latest arms among all nations and international stability is tenuously maintained, primarily by building up credible deterrence against perceived enemies and entering into alliances with perceived friends.

Foreign policy by its very nature cannot be static and has to be kept under continuous review, in consonance with the changes in the international security, political and diplomatic environment.

Before independence, India's foreign policy was determined in London and was meant to serve the imperial interests of Britain. India gained independence just after Second World War, which was a conflict of global dimensions, characterized mainly as a struggle between democracies on the one hand and fascism and dictatorship on the other, though Stalin was an ally of Western democracies, albeit temporarily. The Western world characterized the struggle as one in favour of individual freedom and participative democracy as opposed to total subjugation of citizens by the State. However, even before this struggle was brought to a successful conclusion, a new struggle between Western capitalist, liberal democracies and Communism had emerged creating dramatic increase in international tension and conflicts, including armed conflicts such as the Korean War and the war in Vietnam. Europe was turned into two opposing armed camps and actual conflict was avoided primarily because both the camps had reached a MAD situation, namely Mutually Assured Destruction through nuclear arms. Eyeball to eyeball confrontation, however, continued for decades.

India's foreign policy had to be crafted in this atmosphere of tension and potential conflict. India was anxious to preserve the values of liberty and individual freedom and safeguard its core interests, while embarking on a process of rapid economic and social development designed to eradicate age-old poverty and deprivation. A policy of neutrality termed as "non-alignment" with a high degree of independence in taking positions on international issues, was the hallmark of our foreign policy. It cannot, however, be denied that in practical terms, India had a distinct tilt towards the Soviet Union, even as relations with China deteriorated. The Soviet anxiety to expand its influence in Asia was taken advantage of and substantial benefits were reaped in terms of support for the armed forces, economic co-operation and support for our position on the Kashmir issue in the United Nations as well as with respect to our relations with Pakistan. India had to lean on the Soviet Union to counter Pakistan's successful efforts to gain the support of Western countries particularly United States as also that of China. In the process, India became somewhat unwittingly, a victim of super-power rivalry in the area. Both the United States and China took a series of initiatives to bolster Pakistan by providing massive amounts of foreign aid, military supplies and in the case of China, active assistance with respect to development of nuclear weapons. The Americans, in spite of their declared nuclear non-proliferation declarations, kept turning a blind eye to the covert programme of Pakistan to develop nuclear weapons as also missile capability. The Saudis bank-rolled Pakistan's nuclear weapons programme, buying the argument of Pakistan that Islamic civilization must acquire nuclear capability in a hostile world, where all other religious entities had already acquired such capability. Pakistan deftly played upon American fears of Communist expansionism and reaped a host of benefits by co-operating with the United States in booting out the Russians from Afghanistan. That in the process, religion was used unabashedly for combating Communism and this in turn has now boomeranged to haunt the United States in the shape of radical Islam, is another story. Pakistan managed to keep its relations with China intact, while avowedly combating Communism, taking full advantage of the United States' inclination to befriend China as a strategy to counter-balance USSR. Throughout this period, the equation of India and Pakistan to achieve a high degree of balance of power in the subcontinent was the basic underpinning of the policy of Western powers. This was also the strategy of China. In the case of China, the added factor was to contain India's growth as a regional power.

India had to deal therefore with a complex situation created by hostile neighbours, who were bent upon undermining the security of India in all forms and in all forums and using every diplomatic stratagem to reduce India's strength. The policy of non-alignment with a distinct tilt towards Soviet Union helped India to a very large extent, in withstanding the enormous pressures brought upon it by this unholy combination of Pakistan, United States and China and the territorial claims of both China and Pakistan.

The world has changed vastly since these times, and in the foreign policy context, one must note the following highly significant developments:

1. The cold war has effectively ended and the Soviet Union as a countervailing power to United States has ceased to exist. The USSR has fragmented into a number of separate and independent countries. It's satellites such as Poland, Hungary, Czechoslovakia, Bulgaria, Rumania etc. have all broken away from the communist bloc. Ukraine and Georgia have become independent. The Southern republics such as Kazakhstan, Turkmenistan, and Uzbekistan have also become independent nations. Today, it is a power that is weakened territorially, geographically, militarily as well as economically. It is struggling to resolve internal problems, primarily economic and retain its influence among its erstwhile satellites. Its political structure is also facing serious challenges with a whole lot of people dissatisfied by the continued denial of true democratic values and the dominance of Vladimir Putin through manipulated electoral processes. Its population is ageing and declining and disparities in income is widening alarmingly. It has lost its influence almost completely in Eastern Europe, Middle East and Africa. Though still a permanent member of United Nations Security Council, its voice has been greatly weakened. Nevertheless, Russia, with its huge natural resources, particularly energy and as one of the fastest growing economies of the world is endeavoring to regain a good deal of its lost influence in world affairs.
2. The recent developments both in the US and in Europe clearly indicate that the long period of the West's dominance politically, economically and technologically is drawing to a close. Gone are the days when the fate of millions inhabiting various parts of the world was determined in London, Paris or Washington. Institutions for managing the world's security and economics

dominated by Western countries will have to change. The pendulum has swung distinctly eastward and we may see the emergence of a multi-polar world.

3. On the other hand, China is emerging as a world power, militarily strong expanding economically at a rapid rate and a nuclear and a missile power. Its navy is getting transformed into blue water navy. China is today capable of projecting its power across the oceans, in a much stronger fashion than ever before, on the international stage. China is both respected and feared. No doubt, it still has unresolved internal problems such as the wide economic disparities between the urban and the rural sectors and between regions, growing unrest in several parts of the country and as some analysts point out, the lack of institutions capable of addressing the growing aspirations of its people. It is also plagued by high degree of corruption and a decline in the moral appeal of the Communist system and its cadres. China is trying to achieve a delicate but difficult balance between growing economic freedom and the perceived compulsion to keep tight political control and one party rule. In a world more integrated and globalized, the question whether the Communist party of China can continue to run a one party dictatorship suppressing dissent and denying basic human rights to people is likely to assume greater importance. This can undermine the long-term stability of China's polity. China also has prickly relations with Japan and its smaller South-East Asian neighbours, who seek security from perceived hostile nature of Chinese intentions through traditional alliances with the West. China continues to have problems in Tibet and with Taiwan.

   Nevertheless, one cannot ignore the increasing international profile of China and its potential to emerge as a countervailing power *vis-à-vis* the United States capable of replacing the erstwhile USSR.

4. The third issue relates to the fundamental change in the manner in which international relations are conducted. It would appear that open armed conflicts, with forces crossing national borders and occupying territory is no

more the currency fashionable in international relations. The threat to use force rather than actual use of force is the stratagem more in vogue. While armed strength continues to be important, economic and technological strengths have assumed much greater importance. Conflict management has assumed a new character with nations endeavouring to impose their will on an adversary through a combination of measures, economic, technological, and diplomatic and through subversion. Intelligence therefore plays a much more important role. Consequently, nations watch each other much more closely, constantly monitoring every development which can have security-related implications. The nature and character of leaders, their personality, their will power, their intentions, strengths and weaknesses along with developments in the fields of technology, particularly military-related technology, and armed strength are all monitored very closely. "Coercive diplomacy" with a view to subvert the will of the opponent, to reduce if not eliminate resistance and his will to fight, is the name of the game. Wars are today fought and won not so much in the field of battle but across conference tables. Consequently, the strength and effectiveness of institutions of governance assume enormous importance.

5. The next development to be noted is the growing conflict of civilizations. In spite of the fact that the "HUNTINGTON THESIS" of "clash of civilizations" is much derided, particularly by those who want to be politically correct, nevertheless, the fact remains that there are powerful interests bankrolled by huge oil-related revenue from the Middle East who have declared a war against all non-Islamic civilizations. The West has tried to combat this growing menace which has hit the West primarily in the form of periodic terrorist attacks, by creating an international alliance against terrorism. The Americans have shown no hesitation in directly attacking terrorist targets even if it violates the territorial sovereignty of nations such as Pakistan or Yemen, Sudan or Somalia. The US justifies its actions with the argument that there is indeed a warlike situation created by terrorists through

attacks on American targets and American citizens, without an open declaration of war and without observing internationally accepted codes for waging war and hence, territories which harbour such elements hostile to the US are legitimate targets under US laws.

6. In India, radicalization of Islam and the support it receives from oil rich kingdoms of the Middle East and Pakistan as well as Bangladesh has more sinister dimensions. Such an alliance is calculated to destabilize India, undermining its democratic traditions, her multi-cultural and pluralistic ethos and creating widespread communal conflict. It also seeks to achieve territorial expansion into the North-East for creating the so called "Lebensraum" to relieve population pressures of Bangladesh. There have been consistent attempts to infiltrate India's minorities, create disaffection and recruit candidates for terror and jihad, and finance anti-national activities. These efforts are being continuously intensified, trying to exploit the nation's fault lines and failure of systems and institutions of governance in parts of the country. The country's electoral system is also being taken advantage of, to intensify divisive and centrifugal tendencies.

In this context, as evidence of the validation of the thesis of "clash of civilizations" one must take note of pronouncements by Iran's leadership of what constitutes their declared policy. This policy contains a clear threat to wipe out Israel from the world map, as also open hostility to the US. Iran accuses the West to be a "World of Arrogance" and declares, "We are in the process of a historical war between the 'World of Arrogance' and the 'Islamic World' and this war has been going on for hundreds of years". Iran maintains that Israel is a front for the "World of Arrogance" in the heart of Islamic World. "This means that the current war of Palestine is the front line of the Islamic World against the World of Arrogance." Iran's leadership speaks of the struggle between the Islamic world and the world of infidels and condemns all those countries—"Egypt, Jordan, etc.", who have come to an understanding with Israel stating that such powers "will burn in the fire of the Islamic Ummah".

Such extreme views come not from any sundry cleric or terrorist, but the leadership of a nation, with enormous oil wealth and with a declared interest in acquiring nuclear weapons and an active uranium enrichment programme. Such a policy declaration can have grave implication for those targeted. It is well known that both Iran and Saudi Arabia compete with each other to finance religious outfits in India to promote extremist ideas and widen their influence among India's Muslims.

7. Note must also be taken of the fact that India herself is undergoing a vast transformation. For a long time from the time of our independence, we were regarded by the international community as a poor country dependent on foreign aid, unable to resolve its internal and external conflicts (Pakistan and China), pursuing wrong economic policies while its population was steeped in poverty, deprivation and ignorance. "An indigent, violent and ungovernable country" was a statement often featured in the Western media. India was also accused of trying to play an international role disproportionate to its economic, political and military strength, primarily based on the personality and stature of its strong leaders. For the past 10 years however, there has been a sea change in the manner in which India is regarded by rest of the world. India is now acknowledged as an emerging economic power backed by a huge and growing middle class, offering markets for a variety of western products. Today India has a rising number of super rich, and is in the process of opening up its economy, commanding the attention of the world through its intellectual attainments. For the first time, in its post-independence history, India is wooed by a variety of western countries, who consider India as a potential partner not only as regards their economic interests but also to a certain extent their security interests. It would not be farfetched to suggest that India is being regarded a possible ally in the longtime clash of interest between the Western world and China as also the Western world and radical Islam. There is congruence of interests between India and several countries in the West as also Israel and Japan with regard

to the major security challenges, both with respect to China and radical Islam.

8. It must also be recognized that the stratagem of working towards achieving a balance of power in the sub-continent, has undergone drastic changes in the recent times. The United States and Western powers while continuing to treat Pakistan as an important, though often unreliable ally, particularly with regard to fighting terrorism, have given up the objective of equating India with Pakistan. A number of policy pronouncements from Western capitals clearly indicate that they recognize India as belonging to a different league, an emerging economic and technology power. Indirect recognition has been accorded to India as a nuclear weapon power, though not a signatory to the nuclear non-proliferation treaty (NPT) through the Indo-US civil nuclear cooperation agreement. The strength of her armed forces, her nuclear and missile capability, her economic and technological strengths, are all being given due recognition. The US has initiated a number of steps to build a strategic partnership with India and has gone to the extent of calling India as an "ally". China however continues to play the balancing card and it would not be surprising if Pakistan manages to obtain from China a deal with respect to nuclear development, not dissimilar to what we have been able to get from the United States. China continues to support Pakistan in all her nuclear programmes as also for enhancing her military strength.
9. One must also take note of the fact that today we are living in a far more integrated world—on account of the phenomenon of globalization—where developments in one part have an impact on another part. The 21st Century can be stated as being deeply influenced by both globalization and global warming as also the unprecedented and fast-paced changes in global technology and its global impact. Financial crisis in Europe or the US, affects almost all economies linked with the West in terms of exports and imports as well as financial inflows or outflows on a global scale. Global warming accelerated by actions of one country can impact

on a whole lot of countries. There is growing convergence of interests in dealing with such problems. Financial contagion will require international mechanisms to deal promptly and effectively with the problem and global warming will entail cooperation on an even wider scale. At the same time, technological progress offers perhaps for the first time in the history of mankind, an excellent chance to wipe out poverty altogether. As Jeffrey Sachs sums it up in his seminal work *"Economics for a Crowded Planet"*,—"the fundamental reason for believing that prosperity can spread to all corners of the world is that the very science and technology that underpin prosperity in the rich world are potentially available to the rest of the world. He argues that if rich countries are rich because they adopted these improved technologies—power-generations, medicine, transportation, construction, communication and much more—the same improved technologies can also be readily adopted by today's impoverished countries within a much shorter time cycle. This is because technology has this wonderful property of being non rival; each person, business or country can adopt the technology without limiting the ability of others to adopt the same technology as well. Unlike a given number of barrels of oil which are available either for you or for me, but not for both, the fruits of scientific advancement such as genome or Internet are available, without the need to ration the knowledge. Moreover, for many advanced technologies-the Internet, computer operating systems, vaccinations, etc.,—the benefits are greater when more and more people use these technologies. Such technologies are often called net-work technologies, and the benefits of mass use are called network externalities. Fittingly, we live in a networked age where the advent of such technologies is soaring."

10. In recent times, the world is also witnessing a new type of conflict known as cyber wars. In a world where information and communication technologies have penetrated every system of management, ways are being devised constantly by "hackers", sometimes backed by official agencies to paralyze command, control, and

communication systems through cyber attacks. Such attacks are capable of disabling everything—military, energy, and transportation and security systems. New varieties of virus which can get into computer systems silently and stealthily are being manufactured and fed into the worldwide information highway for disabling targeted countries or institutions with lethal consequences. The Government of China is often accused of openly supporting such intrusions.

11. The recent past has also underlined the fact that there will be increasing competition among nations for the energy resources of the world and the emerging economies have to take special care to ensure uninterrupted supplies of energy at reasonable prices. China's economic diplomacy has invested a lot of time on this question. Russia has also been using this instrument to regain its hold on some of the countries such as Turkmenistan, Kazakhstan etc.

The biggest challenge facing India as argued earlier, on the foreign policy front, is our extremely strained relationship with some of our immediate neighbours. While Bhutan continues to be friendly and our relations with Sri Lanka are manageable, we have been experiencing serious problems with respect to Pakistan, China and Nepal. Recent developments have the potential of vastly improving our relations with Bangladesh. With respect to Myanmar as well the prospects for a mutually beneficial relationship have started growing.

Pakistan is now regarded by the world community as a state which supports a variety of terrorist organizations, promotes Jihadi culture, has been responsible for illegal nuclear proliferation, and is undemocratic with a poor record with respect to treatment of women and human rights. It is terrorist state in all but name.

The nature of the threat that India faces from Pakistan, its efforts to seize the state of Jammu and Kashmir, the ascendancy of radical elements who have started influencing Pakistan's policies towards India, Afghanistan and the West and the fact that the army retains the decisive say in Pakistan's foreign and nuclear policies have been adequately discussed in the chapter on

International Security Environment. We have also seen how the US is disenchanted with Pakistan's duplicity and is continuing a troubled relationship only because it is capable of harming US's interests in Afghanistan. The Americans would like to reduce Pakistan's ability to cause mischief in Afghanistan and in the wider region.

It will be in our interest to work with United States and other Western countries with the objective of ensuring that Pakistan does not and cannot support cross-border terrorism and is forced to wind up all training camps and ensure that flow of funds is completely stopped. The developing internal situation in Pakistan deserves to be watched very closely. The possibility of Pakistan getting fragmented or being taken over by the Taliban cannot be ruled out. Its economy is in crisis and it has a looming demographic and ecological crisis.

However, despite these adverse developments, Pakistan continues to orchestrate anti-India policies, encouraging militancy in J&K and infiltrating insurgent groups into several parts of India. The Pakistani establishment continues to espouse the cause of destabilizing India and undermining its sovereignty and integrity.

It is necessary for India to be far more confident and assertive in dealing with Pakistan especially with respect to its open role in promoting terrorism and blatant interference in the internal affairs of India and Afghanistan. We need not be apologetic about the role we play in Afghanistan as we have a vital stake in the future of that country and a peaceful, prosperous and modern as well as liberal Afghanistan is definitely in our interest.

It is necessary for us to bear in mind that we have been repeatedly betrayed by Pakistan. There is a history of Pakistan failing to keep its word and commitments both at the bilateral and international levels. Pakistan has repeatedly failed to keep its commitments to the UN with respect to harbouring international terrorists. It extracts huge funds from the US in the name of fighting terror but not only diverts this money for its own purposes but actively supports those terrorists it considers as its assets. Recall that even when Vajpayee was getting promises of peaceful coexistence from Nawaz Sharif, after his historic bus journey, his army chief Musharaf was planning the Kargil attack. Recall also the 'peacenik' Prime Minister Inder Kumar Gujral, in his misguided enthusiasm to build peaceful relations with

Pakistan ordered dismantling a whole lot of intelligence assets that had been painstakingly built up over long years and all that Pakistan did in return was to further shore up its assets in India and launch several attacks through its proxies. Initiatives such as *'aman ki asha'* are no more than cosmetic exercises and cannot yield any enduring results. This is because the real rulers of Pakistan who determine every strategic move in Pakistan—the army and the ISI— have no interest in peaceful relations with India. The rationale for their existence will disappear if there is no hostility towards India. The recent statements by the army chief General Kayani after some 140 soldiers lost their lives in Siachen that he wants 'peaceful coexistence' with India and it is necessary to 'dimilitarise' this glacier, are just an eye wash made primarily to placate the restive Shias of Gilgit as all those killed were Shias belonging to the Northern light infantry regiment. This is the same regiment that was sacrificed in Kargil and Pakistan refused to accept the bodies of the hapless soldiers. We cannot trust Pakistan—at least not yet.

With respect to Bangladesh, our main concerns have been the radicalization and Islamization of Bangladesh, ill-treatment of minorities, shelter to insurgent groups and active promotion of illegal infiltration. The influence of radical Islam in the armed forces is also a matter of serious concern. Many in the Bangladesh army are allegedly members of the radical Hizbul Tahirir who are unhappy with the present policies of the Hasina government, especially its efforts to build friendly relations with India. The recent attempted coup by elements in the army, though thwarted by timely action, calls for a high degree of vigilance with respect to the activities of radical and pro-Pakistan elements in Bangladesh. The Hizbul Tahirir has many followers among the young and the educated and since the army in Pakistan is known to harbour such elements; the ability of such a body in Bangladesh to derive support from similarly inclined elements in the Pakistan army, requires to be taken seriously and ruthlessly dealt with by Bangladesh.

The illegal infiltration of both Hindus and Muslims from Bangladesh into Indian territory is influenced by economic and religious considerations. The Hindus come mainly as refugees seeking shelter in India to escape the continued ill-treatment of minorities in Bangladesh at the hands of radical elements. For some time now, Muslim infiltration is proportionately more than Hindus resulting in radical alteration of the demographic composition of several districts in Assam, West Bengal and Bihar. This needs to be checked effectively by better border management and hastening the process of preparing accurate and reliable National Register of citizens. It will be desirable to ensure that those whose citizenship is doubtful do not get the UID as any official document is a ground for claiming citizenship by illegal infiltrators.

In Nepal, the problem is caused by the failure on the part of the political parties to establish durable and effective systems of governance. There are also reports of growing disenchantment with the Maoists because of violence and extortion activities. The Maoists, who are now an integral part of the governing system, need to get their act together and attend to the basic problems of development and security. The economy and in particular, the tourist industry has suffered immensely resulting in further immiserisation of the population and growing unemployment. Anti-India feelings are promoted by each of the players to promote their particular agenda.

What is of very great concern is the fact that Nepal has often provided a free hand to anti-India elements of Pakistan to cause immense harm to India's security interests. The ISI is known to be utilizing Nepal with great intensity for supporting insurgent groups, smuggling arms and funds and infiltrating terrorists into Indian territory. Also, all along the Indo-Nepal border, there has been a significant demographic transformation, growth of madrasas and Mosques—all having the potential of harbouring anti-India elements. Unfortunately, the concerned state governments have not shown sufficient awareness of these adverse developments and the need to deal with them in an effective manner.

What needs to be underlined is that such anti-India policies have the potential of undermining the security and integrity of the nation, while encouraging separatist tendencies. These also impose heavy costs on the country, in terms of need for continuous heightening of vigilance and augmentation of the nation's internal security apparatus resulting in diversion of precious resources from much-needed nation building activities.

Contours of India's Foreign Policy

Taking note of all the above developments and the discussion in the chapter on international security environment, the fundamental features of India's foreign policy are suggested in the following paragraphs. It needs to be recognized that a nation's foreign policy stance can only be an expression of its own personality, in terms of internal cohesion, economic and technological strengths, economic progress, military capabilities both defensive and offensive, strengths of its institutions and ability to cope with challenges. The personality of its leaders, the competence and reach of its intelligence and security agencies are also of great importance.

The objectives of foreign policy should include:

- Safeguard India's security interests, both internal and external, in all their dimensions.
- Protect India's integrity, sovereignty and territorial integrity.
- Protect our trade and economic interests, maritime security and safeguard sea lanes and EEZs.
- Increase our circle of friends and reduce the number and effectiveness of our adversaries.
- Identify congruence and convergence of interests, as well as conflict of interests in order to exploit congruence of interest, to manage and if possible eliminate conflict of interest.
- Safeguard India's external investments.
- Work towards achieving energy security.
- Safeguard interests of overseas Indians.
- Play a constructive role in international bodies to expand her influence in world affairs, increase India's ability to cope with her problems and deal effectively with adversaries.

Any discussion on the foreign policy must be based on a clear understanding of external and internal threats to India's security.

As mentioned above, our relations with Western world and China have shown very distinctive change. India's profile in the world has gone up. However, the major threat comes from our neighbouring countries, particularly Pakistan and to a lesser extent from China. While there is an active interest in segments of Pakistan's polity in favour of improvement of relations with India as beneficial to Pakistan, this is confined to a very thin upper crust of English-educated elite, while the vast majority, fed on a daily diet of hate dished out by the Urdu press, still regards India as enemy number one. The US has possibly taken the number one position more recently but India continues to be regarded as a more immediate threat. What is truly saddening is that the entire educational system, not merely the madrasas but even the government-run schools, as also some of the elite institutions, indoctrinate the youngest of minds with anti-India rhetoric and teach them about Jehad and martyrdom. India is often portrayed as an enemy country in-habited by non-believers which has attacked Pakistan several times.

Our relations with Pakistan and Bangladesh also have serious implications with respect to internal security environment and this link should be clearly recognized. Pakistan continues to interfere in our internal matters and support Jihadi forces, while its focus has been the so called "Kashmir dispute" but it has in the past meddled in Punjab and has shown a distinct inclination to spread violence in all parts of India, cultivating and promoting radical Islam, creating disaffection among the minorities. There is also the continuing collaboration between agencies of Pakistan and Bangladesh, in destabilizing India, spreading the influence of radical Islam, and in sponsoring and promoting terrorist outfits.

The elements of the nation's foreign policy should be tailored, to be in consonance with the changes that have occurred in the international security, political and diplomatic environment.

We should taking into consideration all the above mentioned factors, take full advantage of the United States' and West's new-found enthusiasm to deal with India on favourable terms. There is now a convergence of interests in several areas, namely

a. Combating international terrorism, particularly that which is backed by radical Islam.
b. Build-up of a countervailing power combination *vis-à-vis* China.
c. Expansion of trade, opening up of markets, and economic co-operation.

d. Collaboration in the fields of education, culture/science and technology, as well as increase in the effective use of India's soft power.
e. The democracy consensus or alliance for democracy.

This convergence of interests must be cultivated to achieve the following specific objectives:

a. Obtain technological and investment inflows to accelerate the process of economic and social transformation of India.
b. Reduce and in the course of time, eliminate the potential for mischief by Pakistan.
c. Deal with China from a position of strength which can be enhanced if strategic ties with the US, Japan and Australia are ramped up.
d. Increase bilateral co-operation in the field of education, scientific and technological development.
e. Increase co-operation in combating international terrorism, including obtaining sophisticated technologies and intelligence sharing.
f. Co-operate in stabilizing the situation in Afghanistan and enable that country to achieve orderly economic and social advancement.
g. Enhance defence and strategic ties.

It must be emphasized that in the Western market-driven economies and polity, in determining foreign policy initiatives, every government gets influenced by business interests. China is a classic example, where the United States has moderated its posture, with respect to a number of issues (Tibet, Human Rights, Democracy, etc.) so as to ensure that the interests of her MNC's which have huge investments in China are adequately safeguarded.

The fact that the West is viewing India in a new light is apparent from, the very significant statement of the US Secretary of State, Hillary Rodham Clinton contained in an article in the *'Foreign Policy'* journal which signals a new orientation in US foreign policy. She suggests that India would be the linchpin of the US's new vision of an economically integrated and politically stable South and Central Asia. She says *inter alia* that China, India and Indonesia are the key allies of the US in the Asia Pacific region. Harnessing Asia's dynamism and growth is central to American economic and strategic interests in the region, as this area offers unprecedented opportunities for investment, trade and access to cutting-edge technology. Hillary Clinton is of the view that the US must invest the same resources, time and energy in the Asia-Pacific region as it had done in the post Second World War period in Western Europe, as the future of the US is intertwined with Asia Pacific. India, regarded as a vibrant pluralistic democracy, now appears to be of prime importance to the US policy makers. Noting President Obama's speech in the Indian Parliament, Mrs. Clinton avers that the relationship between India and the US would be a defining partnership rooted in common values and interests. The US according to her is making a strategic bet on India's future, India's role will enhance peace and security and Indian advances in science and technology will improve lives, while advancing human knowledge. There has never before been such a positive and indeed ringing endorsement of India's position in world affairs by the US. The US ambassador to New Delhi Nancy Palosi has gone to the extent of declaring that India is now an ally of the US. The US's reaction to the successful test-firing of the long-range Agni V was subdued and there was just one comment which stated that India is a responsible nuclear power. The US had at earlier times actively dissuaded India from going ahead with this missile launch. It has also now loosened control on the transfer of a whole lot of "dual-use" technologies.

The US and Japan as well as Australia seem to realize that China's growing might will have to be handled by a combination of powers who have strategic interests in the region and would like India to be an integral part of this effort by participating in the India-Japan-US strategic discussion. India should unhesitatingly participate in such a dialogue and take necessary follow-up action without being unduly worried by China's reaction. China's policy makers have been ruthless in safeguarding their interests and its new found aggressiveness in the Indian Ocean (establishing a base in Seychelles) needs to be countered with a deterrence mechanism. India needs also to expand its co-operation with Japan in the nuclear, space and technology fields and intensify its contacts with Taiwan as well.

Along with the congruence of interests with the West, Japan and Australia, we should continue to leverage our healthy relations with Russia to obtain advantages with respect to our economic, security and technological interests as also our energy requirements, particularly nuclear energy. Russia has an abiding concern with respect to terrorism and radical Islam and we should work with Russia to achieve common objectives of effectively combating terrorism, expanding economic relations and military and technological cooperation.

With respect to China, our main concern relates to resolution of the border problem and China's covert and overt support to militarization and nuclearization of Pakistan. We should ensure that Pakistan's efforts to get a favourable nuclear deal from China similar to that obtained by us from the United States do not succeed through international pressure and the co-operation of the IAEA. Pakistan is not a signatory to the NPT and cannot legally procure Uranium from any source. Tangible progress on the settlement of the border issues, while expanding our trade, economic, scientific and technological co-operation can yield rich dividends. At the same time we should greatly enhance our ability to defend ourselves in case there is any armed threat from China. Our border defences especially in the eastern sector require to be vastly upgraded with superior transport and communication networks, much larger deployment of defence forces, upgradation of air power and very importantly our deterrence capabilities.

While dealing with Pakistan, the objective should be to reduce its potential to harm India's security interests and in this context, we need to intensify our efforts to strengthen our relations with Afghanistan. The fact that Pakistan has to now reconcile itself to a neutral Afghanistan which is not interested in furthering Pakistan's fundamentalist agenda, that Afghanistan has cultivated friendly relations with India, that Afghanistan has not hesitated to blame Pakistan for many of its ills, that the West has now an abiding stake in peace and prosperity of Afghanistan and does not want a return of Taliban in the area, that Pakistan has had to commit some ten divisions on its borders with Afghanistan to combat the Al-Qaeda and Taliban, that Pakistan is under great pressure from the West to stop its support to all fundamentalist and terrorist outfits, that Pakistan is now deeply apprehensive that the radical forces it had unleashed are now going to be its own nemesis, capable of undermining its own sovereignty and territorial integrity are all factors that need to be taken into account. Recent events, where Afghanistan has received investments to the tune of $2 billion from India and several agreements have been concluded including one for security cooperation and training of Afghan National Security Forces, augur well for the future even if these are bound to raise the hackles in Pakistan. Indo-Afghan relations cannot be determined by Islamabad and the two countries have a long history of friendship and co-operation. The Indo-Afghan relations can now assume a more comprehensive character, covering economic, political and security co-operation and will be a fitting response to the growing Pakistan-China nexus. Indian investment can flow into Afghanistan for all-round economic development and this can open the doors for extension of Indian co-operation with the neighbouring region which includes Uzbekistan, Turkmenistan, Tajikistan and even Iran. For a moment, it is worth pondering over the consequences of Pakistan's unabashed support for the likes of Haqqani and the Taliban, in the hope that these outfits will be able to take over Afghanistan and convert that country into a client State of Pakistan. Did not the Afghans, in particular women, suffer enormously when last time the Taliban had assumed control of Afghanistan and did it not pose a threat to the rest of the world? Does Pakistan want a repetition of all these horrors? The Haqqanis may be great fighters, but are there any in their ranks who can be called nation builders, planners, development economists, doctors, engineers, legal and constitutional experts? The answer, I am afraid, is a resounding no—as all these fighters possess only one type of knowledge derived from the madrasas they have been to and from the militant training camps that they attend. It is also know that the likes of Haqqani are basically criminals known to indulge in smuggling, gun running, drug trafficking, kidnapping for ransom, etc. They come from an area where the British discovered, as recorded by British officers, 'that the Pathan pride goes hand in hand with Pathan violence and it would seem that the spirit of murder is latent in the heart of every man.' The British also found 'murder in all its phases: unblushing assassinations in broad daylight, before a crowd of witnesses; the carefully planned secret murder of the sleeping victim at dead of night, murder by robbers, murder by rioters, murder by boys and even women, sword in hand. Crime of the worst conceivable kind is a matter of almost daily occurrence among the Pathan people.' The British after some attempts, left these people alone as ungovernable, who regularly fight among themselves and unite instantly in the face of anyone perceived as an enemy occupier, who may interfere with their way of life.

What kind of a future is Pakistan planning to condemn the Afghans to, particularly the women, all for the sake of its own selfish interests? Why does Pakistan think that it must determine the future of Afghanistan? Is this not open interference with the sovereignty and integrity of another independent nation? Is not Pakistan aware that a Taliban/Haqqani controlled Afghanistan will surely infect its own polity, even further than what has happened so far? Does it not realize that a Taliban-controlled Afghanistan may once again pose a grave threat to the security and stability of the rest of the world by becoming a safe haven for all radical forces bent upon violence and exporting terror? India must convince not only the Afghans but the rest of the world of the grave implications of Pakistan's efforts to get the so called 'strategic depth' by making Afghanistan a client State. As has happened in Iraq, does Pakistan want the withdrawal of the NATO forces to be followed by sectarian strife and untold misery for the common man with the Taliban assuming control over Afghanistan?

India must be wary of the possibility that a Taliban controlled Afghanistan will surely descend into chaos and this may well be followed by a Taliban controlled Pakistan. This will mean that the Taliban will be right at our door step. The Air Chief, Air Chief Marshal Browne, echoed this very thought recently when he stated that the Taliban can treach Wagah border. Our western defences can be severely tested by such developments. President Obama while signing the long term strategic relations agreement with President Karzai stated that the stability of Afghanistan was contingent on the dismantling of safe havens of the Taliban in Pakistan.

Apart, from the fundamental clash of civilization between Pakistan's brand of Islam and Hinduism, Pakistan has based its policy towards India on the issue of Kashmir which according to it should have become part of Pakistan during partition. Having failed to seize Kashmir from India through armed conflicts and low intensity war for over a decade, Pakistan is now seeking a solution through dialogue, while at the same time continuing to sponsor terrorism. Due to international pressure, Pakistan may be reducing its support to terrorist outfits but given the fact that the ISI is a government within government, has never been answerable for its policies to the political establishment and has an agenda of its own, it will be difficult to imagine a situation where Pakistan stops its support altogether to the innumerable terrorist outfits it has sponsored and cultivated with huge investments for a long time now.

Given, however, the change in the international scenario, the following issues relating to the so called "Kashmir problem" need consideration. These have been dealt with elaborately in an earlier chapter on internal security and are summarized below:

- We have been unduly defensive as regards our position with respect to the state of Jammu and Kashmir.
- We have failed to highlight the fact that as in the case of all other princely states of British India, as per the provision of Indian Independence Act, the Maharaja and the Maharaja alone had the right to decide on the question of accession to one of the two dominions namely India or Pakistan.
- The Maharaja exercised such a choice of his own free will and since this as an act irrevocable under law; there is no question of going back on this basic position.
- If the Maharaja's decision is to be questioned then the whole plan of partition and the creation of two dominions in the subcontinent will be unravelled.
- The act of accession which is valid in law has been fully endorsed by the people of Jammu and Kashmir, who enacted their own Constitution through a constituent assembly which was elected on a free and fair basis. The very first part of this Constitution states that state of Jammu and Kashmir is an integral part of India and shall always remain so.
- That religion cannot be the basis for creation of nation states and even if this principle was accepted for the sake

of creation of Pakistan in 1947 at the time of independence, after the separation of Bangladesh, this principle cannot be valid even with respect to the subcontinent.

- If religion is to be accepted as the basis for creation of nation states, the minorities will have no place in the state of Jammu and Kashmir and similarly, minorities may not have any place in the whole of India.
- The idea of a plebiscite which was offered as a composite package for solving the problem of integration of three princely states, namely Junagadh, Hyderabad and J&K was firmly rejected by Jinnah, the founder of Pakistan and its first Governor General himself, when this was made to him by the then—Governor General of India, Lord Mountbatten and cannot be revived selectively to please Pakistan.
- Pakistan claim is totally untenable not only on the basis of all the above arguments, as also fact that it entered the state of Jammu and Kashmir without permission and remains in the area forcibly and illegally occupying one-third of the state through armed intervention.
- The political entity that was recognized as the State of Pakistan in 1947 by the international community, which was the creation of the Indian Independence Act and which was the party recognized by the original UN resolution on Kashmir (which *inter-alia* called upon Pakistan to withdraw its armed forces from the territory of Jammu and Kashmir) ceased to exist as of 1971. The part which calls itself Pakistan is not the Pakistan recognized by the UN in 1947 and cannot by right claim to be entitled to any action required by the UN resolution.
- It is impossible to put the clock back by 65 years.

Therefore, while projecting clearly the untenability and non-sustainability of Pakistan's claims on Kashmir given the geopolitical realities, it would be appropriate to strive for a solution to the so called Kashmir problem. One solution is to make the LOC the *de facto* and *de jure* international border. International opinion is at least half inclined to accept this position. If we achieve this, this should be followed by full integration of Jammu and Kashmir with the rest of India ensuring that the displaced population from Kashmir valley is properly rehabilitated. Zulfikar Ali Bhutto had indeed given his consent to making the LOC the permanent international border in 1972 in the Simla Conference, but out of consideration for his internal difficulties, India generously but ill-advisedly permitted him to get away, without ensuring that this agreement is recorded. Pakistan lost no time in going back on Bhutto's commitment.

It would be in the interests of both India and Pakistan to strengthen and expand economic, trade and commercial ties as also cultural links. Once important segments of the population in Pakistan see distinct advantages in improving relations with India; through commercial and trade exchanges, as also in the field of education, scientific and technological co-operation, there can be a substantial constituency in favour of stable, normal, long-term relations between the two countries. The Jihadi elements can be effectively neutralized. At the same time, back channel diplomacy can be carried forward with the clear objective of cleansing the minds of substantial segments of the population, which have been corrupted by sustained, poisonous and vicious propaganda about India and its people. It is heartening to see some positive developments in these areas and the reported preparedness of Pakistan to grant after long delay the reciprocal MFN status to India. Such improvements can also help in removing the tendency of Pakistan to blame India for all its ills. Pakistan should be made to realize that while it has often failed to fulfil its bilateral and multilateral commitments—fighting terrorism, the Simla accord, etc.—India on the other hand, has always kept to all her commitments. Studies by scholars point to the fact that even with respect to such a critical issue as sharing of river waters, India has scrupulously observed its obligations, despite grave provocations including wars and terrorist attacks. Pakistan's water woes are attributable to its own bad water management practices and the relentless pressure of population.

Given the tendency of Pakistan to keep up pressure on India through the proxies ithas nurtured for a long time, for the time being our policy should be one of containment, to eliminate Pakistan's ability to harm India while we continue to strengthen ourselves internally and externally, to deter that country from doing anything against our interests.

As to other neighbours, the Nepal situation requires

immediate and much greater attention from our policy makers. It will not be in our interest to have a failed state on the other side of our northern border. It would be in our interest to collaborate with Americans and the European community to work towards establishment of multiparty democracy in Nepal. We must encourage collaboration between the seven-party alliance and the Maoists to work towards drafting of a new Constitution. The RNA is an important factor in ensuring stability and there are age-old ties between the Indian army and the RNA which need to be leveraged. We cannot permit a situation to develop where the Chinese have a decisive influence in all aspects of Nepal's polity and economy. This can complicate even further the situation on the entire border. Recent developments leading to an arrangement under which the maoist cadres have been provided compensation and alternative jobs while a small number is to be directly absorbed into the RNA augur well for the future.

As regards Bangladesh, the recent positive initiatives should be continuously reinforced and the support that we have been able to garner widened. As in the past, regime changes should not be allowed to affect Bangladeshi policy towards India. Fortunately, Pakistan is discredited not only in the eyes of the world but also in Bangladesh. The atrocities committed by the Pakistan Army and the fact that its agents were responsible for the assassination of the father of the nation, Sheikh Mujibur Rahman, have not been altogether forgotten. Pakistan's hands are tied by its international image, as a sponsor of radical Islamic terror and it is busy with the multifarious internal problems and its uneasy relations with Afghanistan and the US. We must take full advantage of the reduction in the mischief potential of Pakistan and build effective and enduring ties with Bangladesh covering the whole gamut of diplomatic, economic, commercial and cultural relations. Indian investment in vital areas to forge durable links, create substantial employment and bring about all round development can be of great value. There is a historic opportunity to build lasting and durable relations between the two democracies. There is substantial constituency in Bangladesh which sees the advantage of friendly relations with India and at the moment, anti-India voices are very subdued.

With Myanmar our policy has taken a right orientation and the ties need to be strengthened and widened. Similarly with countries in East Asia our relations can be upgraded given their wariness of the intentions of China.

It needs to be emphasized that the profile and effectiveness of a country's foreign policy postures are, to very large extent, determined by its internal strengths. Internal cohesiveness, a strong economy, technological progress, military capabilities, sound and effective institutions of governance, are all vital elements in the successful implementation of foreign policy. As of today, unfortunately, our innumerable internal problems and lack of cohesion, insurgency in parts of country, the depredations of Naxalites, lawlessness and continuous decline in the efficiency of our institutions, create the impression that in spite of India's democracy and credible progress on economic front, India cannot sustain itself in the face of mounting internal and external challenges. Unfortunately, internal political compulsions have made even foreign policy a hostage to narrow political considerations of certain political parties. Foreign policy must at all times be based on national interest and cannot be subjugated to the passing fancies of political leaders, whose only concern is to garner votes of particular constituencies.

A matter of grave concern is the efficiency of our governing institutions. This has to be looked at in the context of the fact that today's wars are fought and won across conference tables and the negotiating ability of a country's institutional mechanisms, to safeguard the country's core interests is of paramount importance. If a country lacks; internal cohesion, if the institutions are ineffective, if they are infiltrated by hostile elements and are prone to corruption, that country can face defeat even before the actual battle starts. While military strength is of great importance in today's world, the country's economic, scientific, technological strengths, the personality of its leaders, the strength of its institutions, its ability to withstand pressures and its competence to negotiate the turbulent and treacherous waters, at the bilateral and multilateral levels are all becoming increasingly important. One notices that for some time now, the quality of intake into the Foreign Service has been declining. Till the 1980s the Indian Foreign Service was preferred even over the IAS and usually, the top-most rank holders joined the IFS. There was considerable glamour and prestige attached to a career in the IFS. That the IFS officers were relatively free from low-level political interference and they had diplomatic privileges were distinct attractions. Today, however, the IFS has lost much of its appeal and even lower rank holders need to be persuaded to join the service. The revenue services are preferred over the IFS.

This matter needs to be addressed at once and measures taken to ensure that the service attracts the best available talent. We cannot allow India's external relations be handled by incompetent hands, who are unable to deal with the increasingly complex world full of pressures and where "coercive diplomacy" is widely practiced.

7

THE ARCHITECTURE OF GOVERNANCE

Having surveyed the myriad challenges that we as a nation have to face and vast variety of problems that need to be overcome and having argued that to effectively deal with all the challenges and problems, it is of utmost importance that the governing system should be fighting fit, it is appropriate to briefly study the system of governance, that we the people have established through our Constitution. This will provide the necessary backdrop for exploring issues such as what constitutes good governance and the relationship between governance, security and development.

The Constitution of India is the foundation for the entire architecture of governance that we have in the country. It is by any standard a noble instrument enshrining a whole lot of the most advanced principles and concepts of democratic polity and good governance. This great instrument is to my mind, an extraordinary product of creative genius. The framers of the Constitution, Sir Benegal Narasimha Rao, Alladi Krishna Swamy Iyer and Dr. B.R. Ambedkar were men of great learning who studied the Constitutions of a number of countries and drew lessons from the vast body of thought generated by Western political thinkers and philosophers, as well as from ancient Indian wisdom articulated in our classics. The Constituent assembly had as members, stalwarts of the freedom struggle who in their own right were eminent scholars and legal luminaries. The debates in the Constituent assembly make delightful reading, evoking admiration for the high standards of debate and the kind of knowledge that the participants brought to bear on these, the extraordinary degree of concern, which they displayed to evolve a constitutional system that truly reflected the will of the people and their hopes and aspirations. They were anxious to create an enduring system capable of answering the needs of a multi-cultural, multi-religious and multi-ethnic country which had to solve a large number of economic and social problems, while maintaining its unity and integrity. It had to achieve a peaceful transition from the colonial system without violence, especially in the aftermath of a vivisection of the country, with the creation of Pakistan. In all the debates, the fundamental commitment to the idea of nationhood, the principle that the nation is above everything else and that the rule of law must prevail dominated all the deliberations.

The principles our Constitution enunciates, the institutions it creates, the processes, procedures and practices it prescribes have indeed kept the country going in spite of the many vicissitudes the country has faced, including external aggression and internal unrest. It has enabled the country to avoid the kind of travails that have befallen many of the newly independent countries in Africa and the countries in our own immediate neighbourhood. There has been no occasion for the army to assume power or for martial law to be promulgated. The system has managed to resolve conflicts in a reasonable manner though several problems have been allowed to linger on. The spirit of accommodation, compromise, assimilation and the freedom for various points of view to coexist and resolve conflicts through dialogue and reconciliation, which is the very essence of the great Indian civilization, permeates every layer of the Constitution.

The Constitution prescribes the maintenance of a fine balance in the working of all the institutions and demands the full and faithful observance of all the norms and principles that are enshrined in it. Unfortunately this has not often been the case and the very functionaries who swear to uphold the Constitution, have repeatedly failed to observe these stipulations and consequently, a whole lot of distortions have crept in the working of the system leading to an erosion of faith in the system. Institutions created by the Constitution have been under assault and their independence, efficiency and effectiveness have been continuously undermined for short term political gains. Short-term electoral considerations have often taken primacy over the need to adhere to the provisions and principles of the Constitution. Many an amendment has been carried out for purely short-term electoral considerations or to please some vested interest. The expectations from such a fine Constitution and the excellent benefits that the country and its people could have reaped from it have not been fulfilled in many respects, resulting in great disillusionment and dissatisfaction.

The vital importance of well conceived, well organized institutions which function with high standards of efficiency and integrity and in accord with widely accepted norms and limits, for the organized and orderly conduct of all aspects of a society's affairs and to assure peace and prosperity is now well accepted and well documented. All institutions need to play by the rules and adhere to their prescribed roles. This was what our founding fathers envisaged of and what our Constitution lays down. Each society functions within a set of economic and political rules created and enforced by the state and the citizens collectively. Economic institutions shape the incentives: the incentives to become educated, to save and invest, to innovate and adopt new technologies and so on. It is the political process that determines what economic institutions people live under; and it is the political institutions that determine how this process works. It is the political institutions that determine the ability of the citizens to control politicians and influence how they conduct themselves. This in turn determines whether politicians are agents of the people or are they able to abuse the power entrusted to them or they have usurped, to amass their own fortunes and pursue their own agendas which may be in fact be detrimental to their own citizens. As the character and quality of institutions and the character and quality of those who man these, influence and determine the welfare and progress of the society, it is they that forge the failure or success of nations. Failed states invariably have failed institutions or have destroyed their institutions. Noam Chomsky in his book "*Failed States*" suggests that even a democracy with a fine constitution can become a failed state if it suffers from what he terms as "democracy deficit" which means depriving of the formal democratic structures of their real substance. This has I am afraid happened already in our country.

While it will not be possible to discuss the entire Constitution, our purpose will be served if a brief survey of its main features is presented. Basically, our Constitution makers opted for the British parliamentary system, following the essence of the Government of India Act of 1935. A multiparty democracy with adult franchise, regular elections with the right to change the government with its performance being the primary guiding consideration were considered suitable for adoption even in a multi-religious, multi-cultural, multi-lingual country with low levels of education. A federal structure with a unitary bias was felt to be essential to maintain the unity and integrity of the nation which had so often been the victim of disunity. The Central Government and the Union Legislature enjoy far greater legislative, financial, economic and administrative powers than the states and under Nehru and Indira Gandhi, there was continuous accretion of power and authority in the hands of the Centre, with the Centre assuming powers to interfere in the states in many areas, by including several subjects originally in the state list in the concurrent list. The Centre also showed a distinctive tendency to dismiss the state governments at will under Article 356 of the Constitution. Indira Gandhi dismissed state governments 39 times in eleven years and Morarji Desai 9 times in three years.

The Constitution provides for threefold division of institutional authority—the legislature, the executive and the judiciary. The executive consists of two parts: the political executive—the Cabinet/Council of Ministers and the permanent executive, namely the civil service. The system operates in accordance with the principles of checks and balances and separation of powers. The functions to be performed by each of the arms are clearly defined. The legislatures are expected to legislate and hold the political executive accountable as to the propriety and constitutionality of all its actions. The executive is expected to function in accord with the Constitution, laws made by the legislatures and the rules made thereunder. Conscious of the need to ensure the highest standards of propriety and probity in managing public funds, the Constitution takes special care to provide specific mechanisms for sound financial management with high levels of supervision and control, such as the process of budget approval by the Parliament, and accountability to watch-dogs such the C&AG, the PAC, the CVC, etc.

The judiciary has been provided the most exalted status in the Constitutional scheme with absolute independence and charged with the responsibility not only of delivering justice but also the complete compliance with the provisions of the

Constitution, by the other two arms of governance as well as safeguarding the fundamental rights of the citizens.

That the entire structure derives its authority from the people and is accountable to the people is made clear unambiguously in the Preamble itself which states: "We the people of India having solemnly resolved to constitute India into a sovereign democratic republic and to secure to all its citizens, justice, liberty, equality of status and opportunity and fraternity assuring the dignity of the individual and the unity and integrity of the Nation. Give unto ourselves this Constitution." This is the essence of democracy, as the Constitution as well as the instruments and institutions it creates derive their legitimacy and authority from the people and are answerable to the people. The mechanism for such accountability is the periodic electoral process through which the people are enabled to express their will, their approval or disapproval of the manner in which the system of governance has performed and conducted itself.

Given the complexities of the Indian polity, and its multi-cultural, multi-ethnic and multi-religious character, special efforts have been made to cater to the political and economic aspirations of special groups through the constitution of a variety of bodies and making special provisions for their social and economic advancement and political empowerment. For the past 20 years or so, such measures have been expanded and intensified and more and more schemes and programmes are being churned out. The ambit of reservation in public services has been enlarged and there is an ever increasing clamour for further enlargement and more and more groups see advantage in being classified as backward. Even while proclaiming the secular character of our polity and in violation of the most fundamental and basic principles of the Constitution, which enjoins upon the government to ensure equality in the eyes of law and equal protection under the law and which prohibits discrimination on the basis of caste and creed, the government has displayed no qualms in extending reservation to specific religious groups. The special treatment to be given to certain segments of the Hindu society was provided for, taking into the account the historical fact that certain groups had indeed suffered discrimination in the past. This is a rare exception to the fundamental right to equality and equality of opportunity and was meant to be basically a temporary device (originally for just 15 years). But this basic principle—of reservation being a rare and temporary exception to the fundamental rights of equality, equal protection and equality of opportunity—has now been buried deep, in the face of ever increasing demands from caste or creed based groups, supported by vested interests. The original intent and purpose have been forgotten in the interest of purely electoral considerations. Every political party has entered the fray and there is an unholy competition to demand more reservations in every sphere for every group, especially if it is considered electorally beneficial.

Electoral considerations have now persuaded the governments to consider extension of reservation to religious denominations. Subterfuge is being employed to give them reservation claiming that certain people in the religious group are socially and economically backward. They are sought to be clubbed with other backward castes of Hindus.

This is totally and unequivocally against the basic structure of the Constitution, against secularism, and the very basis on which this nation is constituted, namely complete prohibition of discrimination on the basis of religion, race, caste or sex. Article 16 clearly lays down, that there shall be equality of opportunity for all citizens in matters relating to employment or appointment to any office under the state. Article 16 reiterates the country's commitment to secularism by stating emphatically that, "No citizen shall on ground of religion, race, be ineligible or discriminated against in respect of any employment or office under the State." The only exceptions are for the State to make special provisions for the advancement of any socially and educationally backward class of citizens or for the Scheduled Castes and the Scheduled Tribes (Article 14) and the provision for reservation in favour of any backward class of citizens who in the opinion of the State is not adequately represented in the services of the State (Article 16).

The important points to be noted are: (a) Nowhere is there any provision for reservation on the basis of religion, (b) Discrimination on the basis of religion is expressly prohibited and hence such discrimination is violative of the fundamental rights guaranteed to all citizens in the country and against the basic structure of the Constitution as well as our polity. Any law which contains such a provision is *ab initio* void and unconstitutional, (c) Both Articles—14 and 16—talk only of backward classes and not castes, (d) Article 14 talks of only special provisions for the advancement of socially and educationally backward classes and not specifically of reservation, (e) Article 16 clearly indicates that reservation for backward classes will be for only those who are not adequately represented in the services of the state. It is, therefore, not a blanket permission for all those claiming to be backward castes to ask for reservation and weak governments yielding to such unreasonable and unconstitutional demands mainly for electoral gains. Also the presumption is that the moment any particular class gets adequately represented, the benefit of reservation should be taken away. In a word, it is a temporary crutch to be provided to enable the beneficiary group to stand on its own two feet at the earliest, (f) The word "classes" has been deliberately misrepresented as "castes" so that certain powerful groups can take advantage of this and perpetuate the advantage for themselves but suddenly, when it comes to non-Hindu groups, the political class conveniently reverts to the real meaning of "class" even when it resists doggedly any attempt to apply the economic criteria for conferring benefits of reservation.

All this is happening because of the clout that has been acquired by small regional and caste-based parties, who keep claiming all the while that they are truly secular. Also, this contagion is spreading despite the fact that the religious denominations which are clamouring for reservation, had all along been loudly proclaiming that there is no discrimination at all in their belief systems, that there is absolute equality in them and indeed, this is their unique quality, the USP which enables the Hindus to be freed from discrimination and the shackles of the Hindu caste system and that is why conversion is so desirable. Suddenly, they change their tune and admit that there is discrimination even after conversion and there are backwards among them and there is a caste system among them, all for the material advantage to be obtained through reservation. The government is only too ready to swallow this canard for the sake of ephemeral electoral gains. This is indeed, a real tragedy and a dilution of the concept of secularism and by the very parties which claim be the most ardent champions of secularism.

Some state governments have already provided for religion based reservation and the Central Government has planned to follow suit. Once such a policy is accepted, there will be demands for increasing the percentage of reservation and that too in proportion to the size of the population. As numbers increase of any community, a demand for increase in the percentage of reservation will follow. This can be an endless process. This will surely be an incentive to have larger families and destroy all policies and prospects for population stabilization. The Centre has also succumbed to the pressure of caste-based parties to carry out caste census after 65 years and once the figures are revealed; there will be much greater demand for more and more reservation. We are entering a very dangerous territory where selfish politicians for the sake of electoral advantage seem bent upon destroying the unity and integrity of the nation.

Today, no one seems to remember that the Constitution lays down in Article 335, that reservation must not result in compromising the efficiency of the governing system. The article states, "The claims of the members of the SCs and STs shall be taken into consideration, consistent with the maintenance of efficiency of administration, in making of appointments to services in posts in connection with the affairs of the Union and the States." The Preamble of the Constitution itself emphasizes that it seeks to secure justice for all and equality of status and opportunity. No one also recalls that Gandhiji who was realist, a true patriot, whose concern for the weaker segments was second to none, whose efforts to uplift the poor and the down-trodden was unparalleled and who more than anyone else understood the needs for building a just society and a brighter future for all of India, clearly realized that efficiency in the services of the government is of paramount importance. He had no hesitation in laying down, "For administration to be efficient, it must be in the hands of the fittest. There should certainly be no favouritism. If we must have five engineers, we must take the fittest five, even if all of them were Musalmans or Parsis. The educationally backward communities will have a right to favoured treatment in the matter of education in the hands of the National Government. But those who aspire to occupy responsible posts in the Government of the country can, only do so if they pass the required tests." A clearer enunciation of the basic principles on which good governance should be grounded can hardly be made. No Indian before him or after has done more for the liberation and advancement of the disadvantaged segments of our society, but his message, as in so many other matters in our national life, has been conveniently forgotten by the very people who claim to be his staunch followers and who have no hesitation in misusing his hallowed name for winning elections.

On the eve of every election, the ghost of reservation is resurrected with demands for inclusion of more categories and minorities. Unfortunately, this has now become a convenient tool for competitive populism and touted as the sure-shot remedy that is capable of solving all the problems faced by the disadvantaged. If this were indeed so^ with 65 years of reservation there really should have been no backwardness in this country. The truth is that reservation does not even touch the outer fringe of the myriad problems faced by the poor and the disadvantaged.

There are some four lakh jobs in the Central Government and some 11 lakh in the states. The number may go up to 20 lakh if the public sector undertakings are taken into account. Out of this, 50 per cent are already reserved for one category or the other. Out of this total of 20 lakh, the annual vacancy due to retirement, etc., may be something of the order of two or three lakh and reservation can apply to around just 1,50,000 jobs. Can this be the solution, the magic wand, for all the ills afflicting the poor and downtrodden who number something like 500 million or more? In reality, reservation is the last resort of netas who are suffering from an acute case of bankruptcy of ideas and is indeed a convenient cover for their myriad failures to do anything worthwhile for the poor. Reservations do not result in more or better roads, more or better education, or better health care or provide electricity or clean drinking water, nor does it automatically make the poor rich overnight. On the contrary, reservations result in a compromise on the quality of the delivery system and actually lead to decline in standards of delivery of those very basic services which are needed by the poor and the down-trodden.

These arguments will expose me to the charge of lack of sympathy for those who have suffered discrimination in the past, or caste bias or worse. All that needs to be pointed out is the fact that the very netas who daily clamour for reservation and more reservations, are the ones who run to the nearest well-run private hospital when they fall sick, where there are no reservations and competence of the doctors is the only thing that counts. They also prefer to go away to the US or Singapore for treatment, send their children to private English medium schools or send them abroad for higher education. Do they not express a resounding no-confidence in the government-run institutions, which they are doing so much to ruin by compromising standards at every turn? The poor have to suffer at the hands of negligent doctors (who though paid by the government indulge in private practice) supply substandard drugs, blood and fluids which are poisonous, and also pay for everything because everyone is so corrupt. Hundreds of babies die due to negligence regularly in government hospitals. Why is it that the netas do not have the time to remedy these fundamental ills, which will benefit the poor and the disadvantaged, far more than reservation? Indeed, to my mind, indefinite extension of reservation is one of the causes of the neglect suffered by our public services and as Gandhiji so rightly pointed out, you should not compromise on standards when it comes to holding positions of responsibility. Our netas are declaring that the poor and the disadvantaged do not deserve first class services, while they themselves have no hesitation in availing of the very best. They are doing great disservice to the poor and the downtrodden, even while claiming that their hearts bleed profusely for them alone and their whole life is dedicated to serving the poor. Unfortunately, the people who vote get so carried away by the rhetoric of positive discrimination that they have been blinded to real facts. Those who point out the reality are condemned as anti—poor and anti-people.

The real reason advanced in favour of reservation is the severe discrimination suffered by certain segments of the Hindu society in the past. It is this that made the framers of our Constitution; make a specific departure from the fundamental principle of equality and equal opportunities in favour of the scheduled castes and scheduled tribes and that too as a temporary measure for a period of 15 years. This special dispensation has now been extended repeatedly and no government can muster the courage to terminate this provision. In India, once a concession is given, vested interests emerge around this measure, which ensure that it is never withdrawn. It needs to be pointed out that many groups who have never experienced any discrimination of any sort and who are economically, socially and educationally far more advanced than many other segments of the society, have been enjoying the benefit of reservation for all these years. For example, the Mizos of the North-East or the Bhutias of Sikkim have never suffered any discrimination of any sort and are very well off educationally and economically. The Mizos are mostly Christians for the past two centuries and the Bhutias were the ruling class of the Kingdom of Sikkim till the merger of 1975. Reservation has been, in a word used and is being used continuously, as an instrument of appeasement. The result is that such educationally and economically advantaged groups corner the benefits and deprive the truly deserving in other parts of India. We have also the strange spectacle of sons and daughters of cabinet ministers, MPs, high officials who get the best of education and do not suffer any discrimination, and may have never suffered any discrimination, continuing to enjoy the benefits generation after generation. Why should not reservation be limited to the first generation only and the creamy layer concept properly applied so that the truly deserving also benefit?

The policy of indefinite extension of reservation has now created in India, a new privileged class, which is truly forward in every respect but does not want to let go the privileged treatment they have enjoyed and want that the benefits should accrue to them alone and not percolate to the truly deserving. We have now created semi-permanently a category which regards certain dispensations as their birthright and hence are demotivated from making any effort to deserve the offices they get appointed to, because of the privileges they have been enjoying. A psychology of inferiority is created and when any one gets a position as a right, he forgets that the position carries certain responsibilities. Instead of fostering the spirit of competition among the disadvantaged, we are discouraging them from being competitive and destroying all incentives to rise above their level and excel. When you give a set of people the feeling that a particular job or promotion is their right and not something for which they should strive and excel, you knock out the most important impetus for them, to put in their best. Also, in the unholy competition to confer special rights, we lose sight of the effects it will have on the whole system and the entire community. That compromising standards affects the community and the poor in particular has been ignored.

Such measures taken in total disregard of the fundamental

principles of the Constitution have implications for the quality of governance, as they compromise on standards and prevent those who are truly the fittest from occupying positions of responsibility.

We have also, in pursuance of these policies, constituted a whole lot of commissions to supposedly promote the welfare and progress and advance the interests of the many disadvantaged segments. We have the SC, ST and OBC commissions, the Women's commission, the Minorities Commission, etc., both at the Central and the state levels. The watch word is empowerment, which in practical terms has only meant privileged treatment in all matters, more reservation and disregard of the fundamental principles of equality in the eyes of law and equal protection under the law. What was eminently justified with respect to those specific castes which had indeed suffered discrimination in the past has been distorted to benefit a whole lot of classes who have not suffered discrimination and in any case, and whose economic and social status does not justify any such special dispensation. The word 'class' in the Constitution has been misinterpreted to mean caste and benefits taken by groups who can influence elections by their numerical strengths. While the Supreme Court after a good deal of deliberation upheld reservation for other backward classes (OBC), it specified that the creamy layer should be excluded from such favourable and special treatment. Again, those who have benefited from such special treatment have ensured that they continue to benefit by continuous revisions of what constitutes the creamy layer by increasing the upper limit of income of those to be excluded in the benefits of reservation. The Central Government recently revised this limit upwards from Rs. 2 lakhs to Rs. 4.5 lakhs per annum even though the average per capita income in India is still nowhere near even Rs. 1 lakh per annum. A new class of privileges has been created and the really deserving have been deprived of the benefits of this entire policy of reservation. The poor of so called forward castes are discriminated against while the rich of the backward castes continue to enjoy favourable treatment. Suggestions that economic criteria and not caste should be the basis for special treatment and positive discrimination are dismissed with disdain as these may not deliver votes. Demands for reservation in the private sector have been vocal and may gather force if jobs in the government become more scarce.

Reverting to the structure of governance from this what I feel essential digression on the issue of positive discrimination, the political executive, the governing arm of the structure, referred to above is constituted from the party or combination of parties which command the majority in the Parliament and is accountable to the Parliament. This designated as the Council of Ministers may include members from both the houses of Parliament.

As to the permanent executive, this consists of the All India Services (the IAS, IPS and IFS), the Foreign Service, the Central Services (IAAS, IRS, etc.) and various specialized professional services. At the state level as well there are the state civil and police services, as well as specialized professional services. This entire body of public servants is protected by the Constitution under Article 311 which lays down that no public servant can be punished except in accordance with the prescribed laws and regulations. All aspects of the management and conduct of this body are governed by clearly laid down rules, regulations and procedures.

The nation owes a deep debt of gratitude to the iron man of India, Sardar Vallabhbhai Patel who more than anyone else appreciated the essentiality of a neutral, efficient and impartial civil service, for good governance and orderly conduct of affairs of the nation and the society. This was at a time when the freedom fighters who had been jailed or ill-treated by the British bureaucracy, as well as its Indian members, had deep distrust of and indeed resentment against the civil service and the police and wanted to get rid of these. Krishna Menon at his acerbic best had described the ICS as "neither Indian, nor civil and had never been a service".

When one witnesses the travails of many a country trying to transit from one system to another after wars or revolutions, experiencing violence and suffering that afflict the general populace, and the breakdown of law and order that takes place, one can easily appreciate the need for an organized system of administration which can competently handle the transition and allow the leaders the time and freedom to reorganize the country. That India was able to handle the huge problems of transition during the post-independence period with relatively little violence or disorder and provide the much needed relief and rehabilitation to all those who were displaced because of the partition of the country, while laying down the foundations for a new Constitution and for orderly economic and social development, is certainly due to the fact that there existed a structure which could handle all the tasks of normal administration with great competence and which earned the trust of the new rulers by the standards it set.

It was only Sardar Patel who could, in appreciation of the unifying role the civil service could play, force down the throats of reluctant Chief Ministers the concept of the All India Services. Patel was farsighted and grasped in full; the essential requisites of rule of law. He argued in the Constituent Assembly on the 10th of October, 1949, "The Union (of India) will go, and you will not have a united India, if you do not have a good All India Service which has independence to speak out its mind." Patel considered "an efficient, disciplined and contented service. a *sine qua non* of sound administration under a democratic regime."

Patel was clear in his mind that the civil service should be impartial and neutral. He said, "A civil servant cannot afford to and must not take part in politics. Nor must he involve himself in communal wrangles. To depart from the path of rectitude in either of these respects is to debase public service and to lower its dignity." He added that, "It would be a bad day if people did not look up to officials holding high positions. Ministers come and ministers go, but the permanent machinery (the civil service) must be good and firm and must have the respect of the people." Patel had been convinced that the civil service was a bastion against chaos and disintegration of the country and an essential part of the system of checks and balances to ensure that the political leadership is advised not to go beyond the limits and norms laid down by the Constitution and the laws of the land as well as the fundamental principles of equity and justice for all.

Patel in my view was the tallest of the founding fathers of independent India. Lord Wavell, the then Viceroy, had called him India's Bismarck and Mountbatten the 'strong man' of India. JRD Tata, the doyen of Indian industry had this to say of him. "While I usually come back from meeting Gandhiji elated and inspired but always a bit skeptical, and from talks with Jawaharlal, fired with emotional zeal but often confused and unconvinced, meetings with Vallabhbhai were a joy from which I returned with renewed confidence in the future. I have often thought that if fate had decreed that he instead of Jawaharlal would be the younger of the two, India would have followed a very different path and would be in better economic shape than it is today." It is a mystery to this day as to why Gandhiji preferred Nehru over Patel, to don the mantle of leadership of independent India, overruling the opinion of the Congress, where Patel enjoyed overwhelming support.

It is interesting to note that across the border, Jinnah had expressed these very thoughts while addressing the civil servants of Pakistan. He stated, "You should not be influenced by any political pressure, by any political party or individual politician. If you want to raise the prestige and greatness of Pakistan you must not fall victim to any pressure but do your duty as servants of the people and the State, fearlessly and honestly. Service is the backbone of the State. Governments are formed and may be changed, Prime Ministers come and go but you stay on and therefore, there is a very great responsibility on your shoulders. Make the people feel that you are their servants and friends, maintain the highest standards of honour, integrity and fair-play."

The civil service structure is, primarily a meritocracy which is designed to ensure that the system operates in accordance with certain well established principles with the objective of delivering justice, fair play and equity for all citizens and promoting all-round welfare and progress. It creates a body of persons who are chosen for their proven competence based on objective criteria in a fair manner based on the principle of equality of opportunity. The best of talent is to be recruited for the very obvious reason that when you are dealing with the affairs of the whole nation and especially a nation that has all the complexities one can imagine, you need the best of brains, the creme de la creme. They are expected to be imbued with the highest ideals of public service, patriotism, nationalism and prepared to dedicate themselves to the service of the nation. They are trained and motivated to give out their very best in discharging all their responsibilities and make public service as their sole career. They should be prepared to serve in any part of the country and bring a national perspective and broad outlook, even while they deal with regional and state level problems. Their loyalty is to the country and the Constitution above everything else and they are expected to be totally neutral as far as political beliefs are concerned. They are expected to render impartial, professional and expert advice in an independent and fearless manner to their political masters and carry out with dedication the policies that are laid down. They do play an important role in policy formulation with their knowledge, professionalism and expertise in the field of public affairs, so that the best possible results are achieved and the interests of the nation and the people remain paramount. Needless to say, that they are expected to be honest to the core and ensure that the highest standards of financial probity are always observed. They are expected to provide the right advice, even if their views are not in conformity with those of the political masters. Sardar Patel rightly felt that a civil servant is paid to provide independent advice without fear or favour. The great Sardar very correctly anticipated that there will surely be occasions when politicians will give greater importance to the political advantage of the particular party to which they belong, which may or may not be in tune with national interests and short term electoral gains may dictate policy. They may like to favour those who vote in them or their party and discriminate against those who did not. The civil service, the Sardar held, should act as an effective check against such tendencies. How important this is, in a multi-party democracy when governments may come and governments may go and in a multi-ethnic, multi-cultural and multi-religious society hardly needs any emphasis. This principle assumes greater importance when we see the phenomenon of small political parties representing a small segment of the electorate, in a particular constituency, having a disproportionate say in the affair of the nation and they are often seen to use the offices they occupy to exclusively further the electoral interests of themselves or their party or the particular group they represent.

The entire body of civil servants is selected by impartial independent bodies, namely the Union and State Public Service Commissions, through open competition with merit and achievement being the fundamental guiding principles. They are provided adequate avenues of career progression where once again merit, performance and achievement are of fundamental importance. They are expected to be adequately trained to perform their duties and are expected to constantly upgrade their knowledge and skills through continuous in-service training.

The civil servant, apart from his loyalty to the Constitution and commitment to upholding the rule of law, is to my mind, more than anything else answerable to his own conscience and should be able to inspire the confidence of the public through his knowledge, competence, and expertise, ability to serve the public with speed and with high sense of justice. His expertise is based on strong theoretical foundations, training, motivation, continuous upgradation of talent, and specialization in specific fields. He is accountable for his performance. There is a system of rewards and punishments and the civil service is expected to be imbued with a pervasive spirit of public service. A civil servant must appreciate the changing role of government as it is today, more an enabler and a facilitator, and show the ability to continuously reinvent himself and go through a process of self-renewal. The increasing role of technology must be appreciated and the ability to apply these innovations to improve the quality and speed of delivery systems must be acquired. The essentiality of an efficient civil service, in an increasingly complex internal and international environment can hardly be overemphasized. This is so especially because today's wars are fought and won not in the field of battle but across the conference tables where the strength of institutions and the quality of those who run them are of overwhelmingly importance.

Throughout their service life, the civil servants to my mind are more than adequately compensated and enjoy considerable degree of prestige in the society. They are also well insulated against the ravages of inflation through a system of regular increases in compensation. There have, been many an occasion when the general public has protested against the premature transfer of an official who had served them well and who had acted impartially and was moved out because of political pressure. Their welfare and career advancement is taken care of through well defined rules and procedures with a high degree of transparency.

The important point is that for the civil service to be truly effective, impartial and neutral, it must be equipped and empowered to discharge its functions without fear or favour, enabled to effectively enforce the authority vested in it. The civil service must be able to ensure full compliance with the laws of the land by all citizens, while everyone receives equal protection under the laws. The well established principles of governance, namely (a) that all governmental actions should not only be fair but seen to be fair, (b) that all efforts of the government should result in the greatest good of the largest number, and (c) that in spending government money, the same degree of prudence must be observed as that observed by an individual while spending his own money, must be the "*mool mantra*" that permeates all layers of the administration.

The importance of an efficient, neutral, and independent Civil Service has been appreciated by many advanced countries. Countries which have achieved rapid progress in all fields invariably boast of an efficient and neutral civil service with a high degree of integrity. The UK is a prime example as also France and Italy. It may be recalled that in the post-war period after 1945, when political instability was endemic in France and Italy, it is the civil service which held these countries together and attended to the post-war reconstruction programme. Nearer home, both Hong Kong and Singapore have extremely efficient civil services which deliver with speed and are very well rewarded. In my view, for good governance, an efficient, effective, responsive and independent civil service is absolutely essential. It is no coincidence that Singapore has now a per capita income of US$ 60,000 and Hong Kong nearly $70,000. In Africa, country after country has suffered as there is no stable machinery to look after the people's basic needs. Tony Blair, the former British Prime Minister and patron of the Africa Governance Initiative has bemoaned the fact that continuous infusion of aid has failed to relieve Africa's poverty, disease or malnutrition. Poor standards of governance, and absence of institutions and delivery mechanisms which function with a modicum of efficiency and honesty, have stalled any progress and as of now, aid has failed to save lives or have any credible impact of combating dreaded killers such as HIV, or malaria. In areas such as Africa's Sahel near famine conditions have been prevalent for years. An efficient, impartial and independent civil service is a *sine qua non* for both peace and prosperity.

In India, while policies after policies are formulated with considerable care and expertise to achieve this objective or the other and a large number of programmes are launched especially with respect to poverty alleviation and inclusive growth, most of these flounder because of poor delivery standards. The public distribution system is a telling example of inefficiency and corruption which are now endemic. Projects do not get implemented in time, electricity is not generated, roads do not get built or maintained, water supply is not available, health systems are inefficient and teachers do not teach or even come to the school but get paid, all because the delivery mechanisms have become rotten to the core. In a word, everything that the government does from top to bottom is today both inefficient and corrupt. Let me add that it is the poor and the deprived that depend upon the government almost wholly and it is they who suffer because of the inefficiency of the governmental system. The rich look after themselves very well and are now totally independent of the government even for their own security, leave alone for electricity, health, transport or education. They now also often manipulate the system for to their own advantage.

The efficiency of any organized system is contingent upon certain fundamental factors. These are the quality of those who man the system, their knowledge and expertise, their training and motivation, internal systems of accountability, performance audit and a system of rewards and punishments. Also, the best man for the job, a clear mandate, clear and adequate delegation of authority, freedom to choose his team, powers to hold them responsible against specified outcomes, reward them for outstanding results and he himself being accountable for his own performance and delivery of results are all well-established essentials for the efficiency of any system. The fear of losing one's job or not making the next grade, if prescribed performance standards are not met can all be important factors in promoting all round efficiency. While job security is no doubt desirable, too much of it is not. The 'iron rice bowl' syndrome should not be promoted.

The civil service system that we inherited at the time of independence did indeed have all these features built in. It served the interests of the British very well, and it enabled them to administer a nation of some 400 million, with high level of efficiency and impartiality with some 2,000 ICS officers, 3,000 IP officers and 10,000 army officers. There was high degree of acceptability for this system among the people, as this was seen as a big improvement over the previous unjust, partial and often cruel rule. The British could not have ruled such a vast country and so diverse a population without the tacit consent of a majority of the ruled and the loyalty of the locals, who became part of the system. No one doubted the quality of the officers, their impartiality and their sense of justice and fair-play. It was a meritocracy, a rewarding profession with a high status, commanding the respect of those who were governed, with impeccable standards of integrity.

This was the model that the great Sardar tried to replicate in creating the All India Services and in the first decades of independence, the system he established answered these very considerations not wholly perhaps, but very substantially. Even today, when this structure is allowed to function with a high degree of independence and in accord with set rules and procedures, it does acquit itself very creditably. Take the case of conducting of general elections, when the entire machinery is granted a high degree of independence and is galvanized to conduct elections on a scale far greater than any country in the world. The structure is placed directly under the control of the Election Commission and is generally free from undue political interference. The machinery delivers time after time and shows itself in the best possible light. Even the US cannot match the standards that we have achieved. Successive Election Commissioners have reformed and refined the methodology, processes and procedures, to improve the performance levels and the quality of results. They have zealously and even ferociously guarded the independence of the Commission and even when political considerations influenced the appointment of some of the members of the Commission, the systems were so well set, that they could not alter the basic rules and procedures or do any substantial damage to the reputation or credibility of the machinery.

I may add that when the country had to deal with the problems associated with the birth of Bangladesh in 1971, along with the breakout of hostilities, the civil service rose to the occasion and provided the entire range of relief and rehabilitation services to some nine million refugees, who crossed the border into India. I myself as the Deputy Commissioner of the remote district of Cachar in southern Assam, right on the border with the then East Pakistan, looked after some three lakh refugees, providing them food, shelter and medical services and education to the children. It was a district dependent upon one metre gauge rail link and one narrow road subject to disruption, for all its needs as the only linkage with the rest of the country. These two slender lifelines had to feed and fulfil every need, not only of my district but also the state of Tripura, parts of Manipur and the then district of Mizoram. With tensions building up on the Indo-East Pakistan border, this life-line was what served the armed forces as well. My small team of officers and I managed the tasks, even while ensuring that the normal administration of the district carried on undisturbed. The entire administration was galvanized and no one raised a finger at the integrity or efficiency of the administration.

However, from about the mid-1970s, the basic principles upon which an efficient civil service is built have been tampered with and standards have been continuously diluted and compromised. During the Nehru era, the civil service continued to be in fine fettle and some of the outstanding officers went on to earn distinctions in world bodies. Sir B.N. Rao and Dr. Nagendra Singh were judges in the International Court of Justice and Shri C.V. Narasimhan was the Under Secretary General on the United Nations. The civil servants from India even today are to be found in many international bodies winning the admiration of those who work with them.

The damage started with Indira Gandhi's call for a committed civil service and characterization of corruption as a universal phenomenon. The greatest damage was done by the worst Prime Minster the country has ever had, namely V.P. Singh who for the sake of short-term electoral gains extended the policy of reservations to those called other backward classes. He totally ignored Article 335 of the Constitution and sacrificed at one stroke, the quality of the intake into the services, depriving the meritorious of equality of opportunity. He undid with one fell blow, all that had been achieved by the founding fathers of the nation to promote a casteless society. In one thoughtless act, he damaged the unity and integrity of the society and the nation. He introduced casteism in the services and undermined the loyalty of the services to the nation and the Constitution. Since that lethal blow, competition for caste based reservation in everything has become the main forte of a variety of political outfits and caste is now the dominant consideration in many government policies and programmes. In India, once a concession is granted, it is impossible to undo the damage and no political party can muster the strength or courage to reverse what has been granted.

Compromises in the quality of intake have also been

introduced one after another, in the totally misconceived and misguided belief that the services should not be elitist, should get more candidates from the rural areas and from a broader social background. The personality test, which is very important in evaluating the fitness of the candidate to deal with determination and finesse, the myriad problems that an officer may confront in his service life, and in ascertaining whether the candidate does posses the qualities required for functioning as the leader of a multidisciplinary team at various levels, has been continuously devalued. There used to be 400 marks assigned for this test and that too as a separate minimum, which meant that mere bookish knowledge and ability to do well in a written examination was not considered adequate and one had to satisfy minimum standards with respect to the many qualities which determine the personality of an officer. Not only was the separate minimum removed but the maximum marks were progressively reduced right down to 250 but have now been increased to 300. Secondly, the maximum eligibility age which was 24 has been progressively increased and is now 35 years in the case of certain categories. The number of attempts to qualify for recruitment into the services which was just two, has been again increased and now, one can make no less than seven attempts if you belong to certain categories. Peculiar difficulties can arise for a young district collector who had got into the service in the first attempt at the age of 23 or so, when he has to deal with his trainee assistant commissioner who is above 35 years, possibly married and with children. With the salary at that level, it is difficult to support a family and the possibility of the elder officer compromising on standards cannot be ruled out. Also, at the age of 35 or above, one is basically set in one's ways, with declining ability to learn and upgrade one's skills and family responsibilities becoming a burden. It is difficult to mould the officer to absorb the particular culture and ethos of the civil service with a spirit of concern for the public. Due to all these compromises in standards, there has been a perceptible decline in the quality of intake in the past two decades. Such officers, who get into the service at a late age, also have a relatively short service life and cannot hope to make it to the top echelons. This leads to certain level of frustration.

Till the 1980s, for getting into the All India Services and the Foreign Service, one had to pass a larger number of examinations, in the light of the fact that generally speaking, officers of these services have to bear much heavier set of responsibilities and it is appropriate to test those aspiring for these services more rigorously. For example, a young sub-collector or a district collector has far more onerous tasks to perform than for example an officer recruited for the postal service at an equivalent level. This very desirable distinction has been done away with and there is now a uniform set of written examinations which one has to pass and allocation of service is based purely on the rank one achieves. To get into the All India Services, no special effort is required except to do well in a given set of examinations. No doubt, considering the very large number of aspirants who appear for the competitive examinations, a two stage process has been introduced—the preliminary examination, meant to filter out a whole lot, who may not be answering even the basic minimum requirements and a second examination confined to only those who clear the preliminary examinations.

Also, with the vast growth of more attractive alternative employment opportunities in the private sector and the increasing fascination for technical education and in particular for IT education, the best of talent is no more interested in the civil services. The younger generation is only too aware of the vicissitudes of a career in the civil service or the police service, with rampant political interference. The brighter minds, justifiably believe that even if they do very well in the competitive examinations, their chances of getting selected have declined, as someone less meritorious will be preferred on purely caste considerations, whereas their merit and achievement is readily appreciated and rewarded handsomely in the private sector. The meritorious also find their way abroad where again talent is sought after and rewarded with greater equity and justice. They are recruited on the basis of their merit and ability to perform and nothing else and their career progression is based upon performance and achievement. Performance is rewarded while non-performance is punished. There are any number of professors and CEOs in other countries, particularly the US, from our country whose merit is recognized and rewarded. Even those who get into the services tend to leave the service after 10 or 15 years, as they find that the idealism that inspired them to get into the services is of no value and there are intolerable levels of corruption and political interference. Their experience discourages all the other potential aspirants. In the deal, the nation is being deprived of valuable talent which could have done so much for the welfare and progress of the nation and especially for the poor and the disadvantaged.

Apart from reservations for the Scheduled Castes, etc., at the induction stage, a dangerous measure which almost completely destroys the principle of merit, performance and achievement as fundamentals to career progression, is now in practice, namely reservation in promotion. Theoretically, this is supposed to apply only upto a certain level in the hierarchy, but is known to happen even at the higher levels. Even when applied to levels where it is officially supposed to be, this pernicious principle destroys all incentive to perform, to excel and to achieve. It demotivates those who are genuine performers, as they find that even when they keep performing and earning outstanding reports, someone else gets promoted not because he is better suited for the higher post, judged on the basis of objective criteria, merit or seniority, but on the sole consideration of the accident of his birth in a particular community. This has played havoc with the entire system. On the whole, one finds in all departments, since those who deserve do not get just rewards, the level of service to the common man has deteriorated. To get into the government and into higher positions, merit, performance and achievement have all ceased to be of any importance and all-round demoralization and decadence is evident. To occupy offices of joint secretary and above in the Government of India, there is a selection process which is supposed to be on the basis of merit and seniority. In theory, this is very desirable and in fact, at the state government level as well, such a screening process needs to be introduced for all posts which require higher management skills. The selection is to be primarily based on the performance record of the officer and the depth and width of his experience. In practice however over the years, this process too has become more and more opaque, subject to political pressure and an informal system of who are your contacts and who can influence the decision in your favour, is very much the order of the day. Considerations of merit and achievement have been sacrificed to a large extent. Since the considerations upon which the performance appraisal reports are recorded vary from state to state, if you are unlucky to be part of a state where those who record your CRs are conservative, then your chances can be affected. Also, there is now the increasing tendency to write bland CRs, never enter adverse remarks especially with respect to officers who belong to the reserved categories as you may find yourself accused of bias, or favouritism and worse. These days, one has to be particularly careful while dealing with lady officers. The performance appraisal system as such, has fallen into disuse and has ceased to be the kind of effective instrument of internal control that it was and was indeed meant to be.

The empanelment process has also been politicized and many who do not deserve are able to manipulate the system to get into the panels, by utilizing their political contacts. The system, generally speaking, favours those who are from the larger states which have more ministers at the Centre and more powerful politicians. Off the record and informally, there is also the tendency to ensure so called adequate representation at the highest levels of bureaucracy for the disadvantaged segments and for minorities. At the state level, there is also the bias in favour of the locals.

There is also the trend where it is believed that areas of administration that deal with special programmes meant for the welfare of backward classes, should be in the hands of members of these classes. This introduces the pernicious principle that justice to the backward classes can be expected to be done only by an official who himself belongs to the particular community. This is an expression of no confidence in all others to be just and fair to everyone, which is the very basis of our Constitution-based governance structure. Unfortunately, this nefarious principle is now being sought to be introduced in higher level statutory and constitutional bodies through reservation.

The problem with all these policies which are called, positive discrimination, is that they violate the principle of equality of opportunity, guaranteed by the Constitution, sacrifice principles of merit and achievement, lower standards all-round and encourage sections of our society to believe that they are by birth, entitled to certain privileges, that they do not have to strive, compete and excel to get a whole lot of benefits, they can advance in service without any effort on their part and they will not be held accountable for their performance or lack of it and no one can punish them for their errors and misconduct or misdemeanour. What was a temporary device to uplift the truly backward and the disadvantaged has now become an impenetrable armour for some. They enjoy a special status which places them above ordinary norms.

While in every other country, especially developing countries, all people are encouraged to believe that they can do better than others and everyone is competing and taking pride is becoming more advanced and going forward everyday in every way, in India we have the strange and unedifying spectacle of people wanting to be declared backward. India is perhaps the only country in the world where there is a fierce and growing competition to be classified as backward, more backward or even most backward. Agitations are launched and *'rail roko'* and *'jail bharo'*, *'andholans'* are organized to get one group or the other classified as backward. All this, for the sake of a few benefits that are handed out by the government and for the few jobs in the government. There is an unholy and fierce competition to be backward and remain backward, generation after generation even though materially, many are what can be called super rich and cannot be called economically, socially or educationally backward by any standards.

No one today cares to remember that there is in the Constitution Article 51-A which lays down what are called fundamental duties cast upon every citizen of India. To my mind this is of equal importance to the provisos on fundamental rights, if not more important. And of these I regard subsection (j) as the most important which states that it *shall* be the duty of every citizen "to strive towards excellence in all spheres of individual and collective activity so that the nation constantly rises to higher levels of endeavour and achievement." It is indeed a great pity that most of our leaders have forgotten that such an Article is an integral part of our Constitution and the duties listed therein are expected of all citizens. Most of our citizens are perhaps unaware that there is such an Article, as all the while they are made conscious of their rights alone and not their duties.

In this context, it would be worth relating an experiment, conducted by a management guru in the US which offers valuable lessons on consequences of sacrificing the principles of merit and achievement and the deleterious impact this has on the entire system.

An economics professor at a college made a statement that he had never failed a single student before, but had recently failed an entire class. That class had insisted that Obama's socialism worked and that no one would be poor and no one would be rich was a great equalizer.

The professor then said, "OK, we will conduct an experiment in this class on Obama's plan"? All grades will be averaged and everyone will receive the same grade so no one will fail and no one will receive an A. After the first test, the grades were averaged and everyone got a B. The students who studied hard were upset and the students who studied little were happy. As the second test rolled around, the students who had studied little, studied even less and the ones who had studied hard decided they wanted a free ride too, so they studied little. The second test average was a D! No one was happy.

When the 3rd test rolled around, the average was an F.

As the tests proceeded, the scores never increased as bickering, blame and name-calling all resulted in hard feelings and no one wanted to study for the benefit of anyone else.

To their great surprise, ALL FAILED and the professor told them that socialism would also ultimately fail because when the reward is great, the effort to succeed is great, but when the government takes all the reward away, no one will try or want to succeed.

There are possibly the 5 best sentences you'll ever read and all applicable to this experiment:

a. You cannot legislate the poor into prosperity by legislating the wealthy out of prosperity.
b. What one person receives without working for, another person must work for without receiving.
c. The government cannot give to anybody anything that the government does not first take from somebody else.
d. You cannot multiply wealth by dividing it.
e. When half of the people get the idea that they do not have to work because the other half is going to take care of them, and when the other half gets the idea that it does no good to work because somebody else is going to get what they work for, that is the beginning of the end of any nation.

These are the reasons as to why socialist experiments all over the world failed so resoundingly. This experiment and the principles mentioned above, however, needs to qualify by one caveat, namely it assumes that there is equality of opportunity and everyone has an equal chance of succeeding. This was the case in the class room but may not be the case in actual life where despite Constitutional guarantees, equality of opportunity may not be available in an adequate manner. This is what our Constitution makers sought to address. My thesis is not against positive discrimination as such, but the indefinite extension of this policy both in terms of time frame and more importantly to those classes who are manifestly undeserving and who are exploiting this feature of our polity to their advantage, depriving the truly deserving and the needy. Also, my complaint is that this has by now resulted in a weakening of the system and consequently, those very people, who are dependent upon the government, are being served poorly.

The other important instrument of internal control and accountability is the implementation of Government servants' Conduct rules and Discipline and appeal rules. With the protection afforded by Article 311 of the Constitution and the numerous judicial proceedings bringing to book recalcitrant, non-performing and corrupt officials has become a nightmare and a near impossibility. Proceeding against an officer for non-performance is, for all practical purposes, non-existent. As mentioned above, giving a bad chit to a useless officer requires great courage and determination to face the consequences. Political contacts can ensure that at the level of the CM, etc., the remarks can be deleted and in fact the officer who made the adverse entry, pilloried. Given the procedures involved, taking departmental action is very lengthy and the officer who frames the charges can often be accused of bias of one type or the other. The officer who is suspended has all the time to fight the case and go to the courts whereas the officer who initiates action has his normal responsibilities which cannot be neglected. Most, therefore, look the other way and allow things to drift. There is never the fear of losing one's job in government and accountability is now almost nil.

Let us briefly examine the other arms of governance, namely the legislature and the judiciary before looking at the serious infirmities and distortions that have progressively crept into all the institutions of our constitutional system as well as the manner in which these have damaged the capacity of the nation to effectively and efficiently deal with all the challenges faced by it.

The constitutional system expects all the players to play by the rules and perform their roles in accord with the principles that are the basis for each and every provision of the Constitution. Constitution makers were guided by some of the noblest ideas that humanity has developed over the centuries as principles that must govern the conduct of rulers and the ruled for orderly progress of the society and the welfare of its citizens. Apart from the unique concept of '*Dharma*', an unparalleled contribution of our civilization to human thought and advancement of moral values, the Constitution also incorporates the principles of *Satya* (truth), *Ahimsa* (non-violence), *Swarajya* (independence), *Antyodaya* (upliftment of the poor), *Anrishmasya* (compassion) and *Sarvodaya* (welfare of all). "*Ahimsa paramo dharma*" is basic to India's spiritual thought and tradition. India is and has always been one of the greatest treasure troves of what can be termed as the moral wealth of nations as evidenced by the extraordinary thought processes that resulted in India's ancient spiritual literature—the Upanishads, the Vedas and epics and our unmatched heritage. In the *Mahabharata*, the grand sire Bhishma while addressing Yudhisthira, who is greatly distressed at the carnage of war and desires to abandon the kingdom that he has just won, lays down the principles of governance and his own *Svadharma* that is the duty of Yudhisthira as a King. These are, while justice must be done to all, there can be no hesitation on the part of the ruler to punish the guilty. Moral perfection does not mean abandonment of the use of the rod as the prime responsibility of the ruler is to protect the innocent and if this implies the use of force, so be it. The King must be prudent and follow the middle path and his *swadharma* is to govern the country, protect its people and guard the frontier. The *Mahabharata* is wary of both the pacifist position of Yudhisthira and the amoral view of Duryodhana. Its overall position is the pragmatic evolutionary principle of reciprocal altruism: adopt a friendly face, but do not allow yourself to be exploited. Turning the other cheek sends a wrong signal to cheats and enemies who have no scruples. The great law giver, Manu lays down that 'the happiness of the King derives from the happiness of the people.' The *Bhagawat Gita* also stresses that rejoicing in the welfare of all creatures and working for the welfare of the world '*Lokasamgraha*' is the sign of nobility and is part of the *Raj Dharma*.

The legislatures, both at the national and the state levels, were designed to represent the will of the people who, through the electoral process, have given them the mandate to frame the laws of the land. They as the representatives of the people are also to hold the government—the political executive-accountable for its performance. The litmus test is whether all the actions are ultimately in the interest of the people and in the interest of the nation. To perform such lofty tasks, the legislator should be duly qualified, fully acquainted with the Constitution, the laws of the land, patriotic and always mindful of the welfare and progress of the people. He should be a person of impeccable integrity and should have a good track record of service at various levels. He should be a person of high moral stature and not be a person with a criminal record, accused of heinous crimes, or misuse of public funds. Nor should he be only interested in a narrow segment of the electorate. Once he is elected and especially when he becomes part of the political executive, he has to consider himself as serving all the people of the country at all times and not only his party or the particular group of electors who made him a legislator. He must display a national outlook and a national perspective in dealing with all questions that are to be considered by him. Above all, he must be true to the oath he takes at the time of his assumption of office, namely to uphold the Constitution and the laws of the land. Such a mindset and attitude can come only if the legislators are highly educated, in the real sense of the word, imbued with a great sense of public service, have adequate experience in public life and truly nationalistic in outlook. Pride in being Indian and a high degree of patriotism will be very desirable. John F. Kennedy rightly observed "Leadership and Learning are indispensable to Each other." He meant that to become a leader a person must be learned, but this principle is not observed in India of today.

However, this was indeed the picture in the first years of independence, when national interest took precedence above everything else. The Parliament and several state legislatures were studded with stalwarts of the freedom struggle and legal luminaries, learned men with high sense of patriotism. But this was but a passing show and today, while the Parliament does have a high percentage of educated members; the state legislatures are filled with people whose levels of education are minimal. Some have had no education at all in the true sense of the word. From my own personal experience at the state level, I can say that very few are equipped to understand the intricacies of governance, economic management or security or even the basics of the Constitution itself. The first generation of leaders, all of whom were educated and idealists allowed the system to work and listened to and respected the advice of officials. Sardar Patel's relations with the civil service are indeed a great example, of the way the machinery was designed to function. When the question of reorganization of the states of the Union of India on linguistic lines had come up for consideration in the Congress party, both Nehru and Patel had approved this. Gandhiji himself had accepted the idea but H.V.R. Iyengar, the Home Secretary, had grave reservations and when the matter had to be submitted to the Cabinet, Iyengar was hesitant and told the Sardar about his reservations but the difficulty of recording his views in the Note to the Cabinet, as he knew that both the Prime Minister and the Home Minister had expressed themselves in favour of the proposal in the party meeting. The Sardar berated him by saying that he (Iyengar) was the Home Secretary of the country and was being paid a huge salary not to say yes to everything but to provide objective and impartial advice and if Iyengar had reservations, he should state these in clear terms without any hesitation. In the event, Iyengar's detailed objections carried the day with the Sardar agreeing with him and the issue of linguistic reorganization was indeed put on hold. It was later when Potti Sriramulu immolated himself for the creation of a separate Andhra Pradesh that Nehru's hand was forced to accept this demand. The Sardar was not there to act as a check, which he had done so many times in the past.

Even those with relatively low levels of education, were sensible enough to understand that the officials are trained to run the State and should be free from undue interference. However, from the late 1970s, the new breed have become insensitive to the basic requirements of good governance, see the advantage of caste-based and divisive politics and consider that performance is not necessary for winning elections. Money and muscle power are more important and money can be made more easily once they start interfering in executive functions. A large number are of those who face criminal charges in one court or the other of even the most heinous crimes. No less than 25 cent of those elected to the Parliament in 2004 face criminal charges. The civil service and the police are regarded by them as tools to meet their particular ends and if some officers insist on acting in accord with principles, they are thrown out by the way side.

More pointedly, especially after the damage done by V.P. Singh's narrow-minded politics, today many of the MPs are only interested in furthering their caste interests, as they find that this is the surest way for them to get elected, to capture power and retain it. Progressively, party interests are paramount in all actions of the government, even if it means sacrifice of broader national interests. Cultivating and advancing the interests of a particular caste group or religious group is the order of the day so long it is perceived as improving the electoral prospects of the ruling group. Also, elitism is frowned upon in the anxiety to reflect a pro-poor image. The civil servants are regarded as elitist and hence often subjected to ill-treatment. Witness the antics of some Chief Ministers who go out of the way to browbeat high ranking civil servants and humiliate them in the public eye—the exact opposite of what Sardar Patel wanted. Today, we witness a combination of ignorance and arrogance in many a politician.

Some parties join or support the government only to exploit their offices, to garner resources even through highly questionable means or to serve their own business interests, and to use the money so acquired to further their electoral prospects or enrich themselves. They make their support contingent upon the allocation of certain 'lucrative' portfolios and coalition governments have been invariably held hostage by such parties. The recent telecom scams show how some of the parties have used this kind of strategy causing immense damage to national interests and huge financial losses to the public exchequer, while enriching themselves. Self-interest above national interest and party above government is the prevailing *'Zeitgeist'*.

Have the legislatures served the purpose for which they have been created and empowered by the Constitution? For all the money being spent and for all the privileges conferred upon them, what has the nation got in return and what benefits the society has derived? The record of even the Parliament with respect to legislative business is very poor and one sees frequent interruptions, lawless behaviour, rushing into the well of the houses at the slightest excuse, adjournments at the drop of a hat and huge waste of time on matters of trivial importance. All of this is being televised today. Compare this to the kind of dignified conduct of business by the British Parliament where the standard of debate is always very high and concern for public welfare and national interest is paramount.

The state of affairs in the state legislatures is far worse, to say the least, with fisticuffs and violence occurring frequently. Indiscipline of a high order is the order of the day and any criticism of their conduct within or even outside is not tolerated. Many of our legislators are extremely conscious of their privileges and are ready to take up cudgels against those who voice the most legitimate criticism. Witness the sorry spectacle of MLAs demanding free passes for cricket matches in Karnataka. They seldom transact any legislative business with the required attention and seriousness of purpose, but the one legislative business that is transacted with the greatest speed is that relating to enhancing their emoluments and privileges.

As to the other important responsibility, namely holding the political executive accountable for its performance and fulfilment of commitments and budgetary control, our legislatures have, generally speaking, failed to exercise the kind of vigilance that was expected of them. Huge amounts asked for as demands for grants are passed without any discussion and even when some of the grants are indeed discussed, the level of debate seldom reflects a clear understanding of the larger and complex macro-economic issues like inflation control, budgetary deficit, and the relationship between fiscal and monetary policies. The criticism is on party lines, or reflecting the sectarian interests of the particular legislator. For example, the Communist parties have always criticized every budget as anti-poor and anti-people, whereas the ruling party always claims that the budget is pro-poor and now-a-days, for the '*aam admi*'. If the required degree of vigilance was indeed exercised by the Parliament or the state legislatures, the kind of illegalities that have happened, the huge waste of public money that has become endemic, the huge and deteriorating fiscal balances and the failure to achieve the objectives for which the money is granted by the Parliament may not have taken place. Notice what happened to T.T. Krishnamachari, the then Finance Minister in Nehru's cabinet for what, by today's dismal standards, was a relatively minor violation of law.

The question hour, the other important instrument for enforcing accountability has been going down in importance. Questions are often asked on behalf of some vested interests and even business interests, to elicit information which may be of use for a particular business venture. Very often, the MP who has asked the question is busy elsewhere and the question does not get answered.

It is known that many legislators merely sign the registers for the purpose of marking their attendance and obtaining the allowances due but remain busy elsewhere. Some so called backbenchers spend their whole term without asking a single question or contributing anything worthwhile to the debates, but mange to get re-elected. Performance or non-performance as a legislator is of no importance for fighting and winning elections in our country.

A particularly virulent and potentially lethal disease, that has take hold of all legislators in recent times is the role, they play in purely executive functions. Instead of performing the functions that are supposed to be performed, namely legislate for the good governance of the country and hold the political executive accountable for its performance on behalf of the people, the legislators interfere in transfers and postings to ensure that officers who do their bidding are placed in their fiefdoms, award of contracts, distribution of relief, and in the selection and implementation of the plethora of schemes now being administered in the country. Roads are built without assessment of the traffic load, or where none is required, contracts are awarded without competitive tendering, to favourites of a legislator (who often takes a cut), quality is compromised and advances are given and payments made on the recommendation of the legislator even in cases where no work has been done at all. Public money is wasted and the intended benefits never accrue to the people. In Karnataka recently flats built for slum dwellers who were displaced, have been occupied forcibly by others at the behest of

MLAs and who enjoy their protection. The intended beneficiaries are left homeless and hopeless. Some MLAs interfere in the distribution of title deeds for those granted land and allegedly need to be bribed.

In most states, projects are started as these can be publicized as achievements, but no one bothers about completion. Huge amounts are locked up in incomplete projects and the people for whom the projects were first conceived are left high and dry. In state after state, the landscape is dotted with such incomplete projects as tangible evidence of the incompetence and neglect of the administration. In a small state like Sikkim, over Rs. 500 crore is locked up in incomplete projects. This happens because the states in order to please the legislators start too many projects, without regard to fund flows and there is little synchronization between implementation and release of funds. Completion of ongoing projects and ensuring that the intended benefits accrues to the people is given little importance in the scheme of things; all because political expediency rules the day and techno economic considerations are thrown out of the window.

Generally speaking, starting a project and even completing a project is relatively easier, as the funds are provided in the plans, which in the case of all the special category states (the North-East States, J&K, etc.) are to the extent of 90 per cent and that too as grants, from the Central Government but maintenance is neglected as the funds have to be provided by the states which are left with little or no surplus after meeting their unavoidable non-plan liabilities such as salaries and interest payments. States do not bother to manage their finances in a competent manner as this requires greater control of infructuous and wasteful expenditure and raising of revenues is considered electorally undesirable. Why bother about such trivialities as all that matters is winning the elections at all costs?

To my mind, the damage was done by the unfortunate decision of the Narasimha Rao Government to start a new initiative called the MPLADS (the Members of Parliament Local Area Development Scheme) under which each MP was provided Rs. 1 crore—subsequently increased to Rs. 2 crore and now to Rs. 5 crore, for supposedly undertaking programmes in their respective constituencies for creating tangible and beneficial assets to the community. This interfered with the normal development functions of the states, consumed some Rs. 2,500 crore, and was an open invitation to legislators to play the role of development programmers and administrators. Each state has followed this with its own MLA schemes where again huge funds are handed over to the MLAs. Though there are guidelines for implementing the schemes, the idea contravenes an important and indeed fundamental principle of the constitutional system as it mixes up the functions of the legislators and the executive. Apart from taking away precious resources from much needed programmes such as creation of infrastructure or power generation; it has introduced a new avenue for nepotism, favouritism, patronage and corruption. In the states I have worked in, I have seen no great benefit that the society has derived from this kind of legislator oriented initiative. Many MPs do not utilize the funds or even when it is actually utilized, no enduring assets are created and no tangible benefits flow. Techno economic considerations do not play a role and economic or social returns are not evident. It is seen as a device to please the legislators. Unless an impartial audit establishes the desirability of these programmes, on the basis of objective techno economic considerations, there is no justification to continue these programmes. Bihar has realized this and has scrapped the scheme altogether. Other states should follow very quickly.

When legislators start exercising executive functions, it is but inevitable that party considerations will predominate and undermine the basic principle of democracy, namely that government programmes should be designed and implemented for the benefit of all citizens. All expenditure from the 'Consolidated fund' of both the Centre and the states has to be for the common good of all the people. This is of fundamental importance in a multi-party democracy and the basic rationale for a neutral civil service which observes the fundamental principle of right to equality. Everyone is a tax payer, in particular indirect taxes in this country, everyone contributes to the loans floated by the government and everyone suffers from inflation caused by government's deficit financing and borrowing programmes. Inflation is indeed an indirect form of taxation. The resources from the consolidated funds of the State which include taxes, borrowings and deficit financing cannot and should not, therefore, be used for the benefit of a political party or an individual MP or MLA. This is a fundamental objection to the very idea of providing funds directly to the MPs and MLAs.

The civil service finds itself in an embarrassing and difficult position where purely executive functions entrusted by law and rules to it are sought to be exercised by functionaries who are not authorized to do so. It has a grave and adverse impact on the morale and efficiency of the civil servants. Apart from the fact that such unauthorized actions can primarily benefit a particular party or a group of voters, such non-executives who spend the money cannot be held accountable for the money they spend and if things go wrong, invariably it is the civil servant who is put on the mat, especially if there is a public outcry. The public representative can get away by saying that he had only requested for a particular action but the responsibility is that of the authority empowered to act under the law. Unfortunately, since the civil servant cannot be sure of protection from his own superiors, leave alone his political masters, when he does not agree with the public representatives—he is termed as tactless and rule minded—many adopt the policy of least resistance and swim along the current. Today, it requires a great deal of courage to cross swords with the local MLA. I may add that in all my years in Assam, I was never popular with the local MLAs or ministers, whose bidding I could not and would not comply with and consequently, at least one Chief Minister downgraded my ACR. Sikkim was a different story and fortunately my work was appreciated by both Bhandari and Chamling.

The chief ministers who depend upon the MLA's for reaching the high office and want their supporters to remain loyal to them, are happy to allow the MLAs to blatantly interfere with the executive and give greater weight to the views of the legislators than that of the officers. If in the process there is growth of inefficiency and corruption, so be it. Today, except in a handful of cases, no chief minister can take effective measures to control political interference. The era when the PM or the CM had mass appeal and it was on him/her that the MPs/MLAs depended for winning elections and the people voted not only for a charismatic leader but for a credible programme, which could deal with their problems and concerns and which carried with it a credible record of achievement and fulfilment of promises, does not seem to exist. There is also the perennial anxiety of keeping your flock loyal and away from poaching by rivals from within the party and from other parties, all hungry to grab power at any cost. Anything that will keep your flock intact will do and if in the process, institutions are debased and the constitutional principles are sacrificed, it matters little.

In the smaller states, defeated party members can also be a nuisance and need to be kept happy. They may go off to rivals or form a dissident group, or even a separate party. Hence, they are made chairpersons of various public sector undertakings and chairperson of some commission or the other. In some states, they are made chairperson of even regular governmental departments, even where there is a cabinet minister in charge of the department. They all have to be provided a whole lot of perks and kept happy in one way or the other. All this, results in huge increases in establishment expenditure without any benefit to the state. The legislators have no competence to man any of these offices and more importantly this constitutes one more blatant violation of the constitutional principle of separation of powers between the legislature and the executive. The legislators are being provided an opportunity to play a role which rightly belongs to the executive. Many Public Sector Undertakings have suffered due to blatant, partisan and politically motivated interventions by the politician chairpersons.

When the head of the government is so vulnerable to the demands of the MLAs, the legislators start feeling powerful enough to interfere in every aspect of the administration. Merely being legislators is not lucrative enough, when there is a veritable beehive in the area of executive action ready to yield rich dividends, which can now be tapped with profit and with impunity. The officers are virtually defenceless against this onslaught, even though all laws empower them to act and they are ultimately responsible for results. The CM who listens to the legislator and not to the Chief Secretary or the DGP and who depends upon his survival on the legislators, who in the first place put him where he is, is more than ready to listen to the complaints of legislators against officers, who are unwilling to do their bidding even if the action is against the rules or principles. He cannot get rid of such officers but can transfer them and more damagingly, enter adverse remarks in their performance appraisal reports and this can seriously affect their career progression. There are very few safeguards against this for an upright officer who wants to function in the manner expected of him under the laws.

The problem is compounded by the fact that for every officer who stands by the rules and principles, there are two or more who are prepared to bend the rules be accommodative, look the other way and gain favour with the political bosses. Quite a few have now crossed the limit and besides violating the law and rules, actively participate and profit from the decline in standards, in the firm belief that their political masters will protect them, even if the law catches up with them.

Let us now turn our attention to the other arm of governance, namely the judiciary.

An independent, efficient and effective judicial system is a *sine qua non* for a civilized society. While law making is the function of the legislature, the enforcement of the law in terms of punishing those who violate the law is essential for civilized and orderly conduct of affairs in any society. Rule of law which is the most important element of any organized society and which ensures the safety and security of every citizen, his assets and the society, can prevail only if the courts of law function effectively and dispense speedy justice to all. The society can breakdown if the courts do not function properly, criminals do not get punished and the law is not enforced strictly and impartially. Lawlessness and chaos will surely follow. Societies which have been unable to establish systems of judiciary and rule of law based on principles evolved by humanity through long experience and on theories and principles enunciated by legal luminaries, thinkers and philosophers, bring down immense suffering upon ordinary people and do not permit orderly growth of the society and the economy. Poverty, squalor and disease stalk the land and the law of the jungle takes over with armed bands roaming the streets. Such a vacuum invites foreign interference and as has been seen in recent times, terrorist outfits find safe havens in such places to establish themselves, recruit cadres, run training camps, and start implementing their pogroms of violence against their perceived enemies. Peace and prosperity have no chance at all and what is more worrying is that such a situation develops into a major threat to international stability and security. Countries in the horn of Africa—Somalia, Yemen, Sudan—, Afghanistan and parts of Pakistan—are prime examples of this dangerous phenomenon.

A well organized, efficient judicial system along with an effective police system is therefore the very basis for civilized and orderly progress of any society. Keeping in mind these very important considerations, our founding fathers did place the judiciary on a high pedestal and gave it primacy above the other two arms of governance. A society can be run if and only if there is both respect and awe for the rule of law. The principle to be observed is 'howsoever high thou are the law is above you.'

The rule of law, along with high rates of growth eliminates the causes of unrest, dissatisfaction and disaffection, thereby creating conditions for peaceful and orderly conduct of affairs of the society and its sustained advancement. An environment is created where through participative arrangement between those who rule and those who are ruled, peace and prosperity are secured. When you wish to foster responsible behaviour in the people, apart from the reciprocal responsibility on the part of those who rule and those who are ruled and adequate regulations and their fair and just enforcement, you need also to inspire and enlist the support of the people through a set of acceptable values. People and societies need to be governed both from outside through compliance of rules and regulations and from inside, inspired by shared values. That is why a high sense of self-discipline in every society is so valuable. In addition, a society generated, society-oriented and self-regulated system of checks and balances is also essential for peace and prosperity. The society can be expected to develop such a value system if the rulers set an example worthy of emulation by their own conduct and character.

Also, as has been established by all prosperous nations, efficient systems for enforcement of the rule of law is the best guarantee for ensuring sanctity of contracts and providing adequate mechanisms for speedy resolution of disputes and conflicts. Such a system enables investors to gain the necessary confidence in the safety and security of investments and creates the preconditions for sustained growth. This is why the rule of law is such an essential precondition for sustained progress and prosperity in every society. As will be argued in a subsequent chapter there is a positive correlation between rule of law and economic and social development. Those countries which have attained high standards of living are invariably those which have established in their societies all the elements of rule of law.

Unfortunately in India, even this institution, so fundamental for orderly progress of the society and rule of law, has experienced a precipitous decline. Grave deficiencies have developed with respect to all aspects of judicial administration and the kind of high standards of integrity that is so essential seems to be evaporating.

For the first time in our history, a judge of a High Court has been impeached by the Parliament. On an earlier occasion, another judge was allowed to get away on caste considerations. Even some Supreme Court judges have faced serious allegations of misuse of office, lack of impartiality and questions have been raised about their integrity.

While no doubt, the higher judiciary has, to a large extent, discharged its functions with a high degree of impartiality and safeguarded the interests of the common man delivering exemplary judicial verdicts, there has been an increasing tendency to interfere in purely executive functions. A lot of time is taken in dealing with high profile public interest litigations. This no doubt, is the result of the failure of the executive to attend to the requirements of good governance. Nevertheless, this does stand in the way of speedy discharge of normal judicial functions and delivery of justice to the ordinary litigant.

The lower judiciary has however witnessed an extraordinary decline in standards. It is almost impossible to get any justice in the lower courts, leave alone speedy justice. There are serious shortages in the number of judges at all levels, infrastructure is woefully inadequate and the procedures both with respect to civil and criminal matters are extremely lengthy, cumbersome and time consuming. Efforts to amend the procedure codes have met with stiff resistance from lawyers, who are the prime beneficiaries of the current state of affairs.

Vacancies at all levels of the judiciary do not get filled up as the processes for filling up vacancies are unduly long and there is declining interest in the so called elevation from the bar to the bench. As of now, the courts are short of 3,000 judges out of the sanctioned strength of 17,000. This strength itself is highly inadequate if one looks at the volume of work and huge numbers of pending cases. The process is highly politicized as well. For a long time, the question of constituting an All India Judicial Service has been debated but without any decision. The selection process is not transparent and since the Chief Ministers have to be consulted for appointment as High Court judges, there is great scope for nepotism and favouritism. CMs would like "friendly" judges and when a judge owes his position to the CM, he cannot be expected to be totally impartial. Caste and regional considerations have started playing an increasing role in the appointment of judges.

Generally speaking, all our courts are housed in poorly maintained dirty unhygienic, old and overcrowded buildings with creaking furniture. They rob the system of any dignity and there is no aura of authority in any of the courts. With criminals in hand-cuffs and litigants milling around and a huge amount of noise all round, the atmosphere can drive any normal person round the bend. The way the court records are handled is a pitiful sight. The problem is that no one, neither in the Law Ministry nor the judiciary itself, nor the state governments, has shown any anxiety to remedy this state of affairs in such an important arm of governance. Our prisons are indeed pathetic and crime within prisons is rampant. Ministers and Chief Ministers, who spend huge sums to beautify their official residences, build monuments at public expense and live luxuriously, do not find the resources for improving our courts or prisons. Since 2007, only Rs. 412 crore, have been spent on the much needed upgradation of court infrastructure, against the pitifully low target of Rs. 669 crore. The Supreme Court had estimated that per year the funds required for infrastructure are at least Rs. 2,162 crore.

The pendency of cases in India's judicial system has now reached levels which no system can deal with. As of June 2010, in the Supreme Court alone, 54,562 cases were pending, while in all the High Courts, no less than 4.1 million. The situation in the lower courts is truly horrifying with pendency of 26.8 million cases of which 19 million are criminal cases and 7.8 million are civil cases. Even a superhuman effort may not be enough to clear such a backlog. It may take over 300 years to dispose of all the pending cases even if for arguments sake, no further cases are filed in any of the courts. Our system has also one of the lowest rates of conviction in the whole world. Some studies suggest that it is as low as 6 per cent which means that some 94 per cent criminal go scot free. This may be mainly attributable to poor quality of investigation, incompetent prosecuting lawyers and plain corruption. In the case of high profile criminals it has also been found that witnesses are threatened or are afraid of deposing in favour of the prosecution in courts of law. This happens also in cases where powerful politicians are the accused.

The entire system seems to have become wholly dysfunctional. How can anyone have faith in such a system? To my mind, this is one of the important causes for the spread of left wing extremism which dispenses justice quickly, even if brutally. Growth of insurgency and terrorism can also, at least partly, be traced to the failure of our judicial system and law enforcing mechanisms. Recent studies by the University of Surrey (UK) and the Duke University on the economics of crime suggest, on the basis of empirical evidence, that crime control becomes easier (and this applies to all types of crimes including terrorism) if the costs of committing crime in terms of quick detection and deterrent punishment is increased and rewards and incentives for not committing crimes, namely gainful employment combined with high quality education are also increased.

I am also of the view that the separation of the judiciary from the executive at the district level was premature in a country like India. When the head of the district was also the district magistrate, dealing actively with criminal cases, empowered to dispense justice, he was placed in a better position to contribute more effectively to crime control, and prevention of crime with a better appreciation of the overall law and order situation in the district.

Urgent steps are therefore necessary to fill up all vacant posts in the judiciary, vastly improve the infrastructure and bring about necessary amendments in the procedure codes to speed up trials in both criminal and civil cases. The question has also been raised if it is not time that we replaced the present adversarial system of trial by the inquisitorial system that is prevalent in countries such as France and Germany. Even Australia and the UK seem to be considering a switch over to such a system in order to improve the rate of conviction and to speed up trials. The French system applies primarily to serious cases such as murder and rape as also complex cases such as misuse of public funds, corruption and misappropriation. While in the adversarial system the judge is basically a neutral umpire, does not actively try to get at the truth, and does not participate in the investigative process. In the inquisitorial system the judge actively participates in the investigative process and seeks the truth. Many against whom there is inadequate evidence get discharged at this stage itself. The chances of conviction vastly improve as the investigative court obtains irrefutable evidence and the guilt of the accused is more or less established. The long delays that take place, for example in our system by the investigative process undertaken by the police, who in many cases do such a shoddy job, is eliminated. The actual trial comes after the process of investigation by the judiciary itself and the burden of proof basically shifts to the accused, instead of the prosecution. In France because of such a system the rate of conviction is around 95 per cent and trails are over in a matter of days if not weeks. I feel we should switch over to such a system especially as regards serious crimes such as murder, rape, misuse and misappropriation of public funds, as also terrorism, membership of bodies declared unlawful, sedition, secession and waging war against the government by law established. Crimes investigated by the Lok Ayuktas and the Lok Pal should also be subjected to this procedure.

In sum, we have now reached a stage where all the agencies of governance are in an advanced stage of decline. Most importantly, the principle of accountability which should apply to all the institutions is nowhere to be seen. Has anyone been held responsible for the many accidents that take place on our railway tracks, the numerous terrorist attacks, for the failure to tackle insurgency, for the mess that we have created in the North-East or Jammu and Kashmir, for the innocents who are killed, for the failure to protect our citizens, for the failure to provide even the most basic needs to the common man, in a word for the grave failures in the system of governance? Gone are the days when a conscience-stricken Lal Bahadur Shastri had resigned. Yes, the Home Minister, who so comprehensively failed during and before the 26/11 Mumbai Carnage, was made to vacate his office but far from punishing him, he has actually been rewarded with gubernatorial office and is possibly trying to stage a comeback.

In this Chapter, I have not discussed the decline in standards of our security apparatus and the police system as this requires separate and specific attention. I have reserved this for a later chapter.

Is it any wonder, when we have actively decimated the efficacy and effectiveness of every institution and every aspect of governance, that today we are unable to combat effectively the combination of internal and external threats, that terrorists are able to strike at will our cities and our citizens with impunity and innocent people die, our Parliament is attacked, that one out of every four teachers do not attend to their classes and an equal number just do not teach, that one out of five doctors in government hospitals do not show up, that a large part of medicines are stolen, children die due to negligence and every police man has to be bribed and farmers cannot get their titles without bribing the revenue officials?

Does not the nation as a whole gets weakened and loses a bit of its soul due to such comprehensive and all pervading failures even if every time one party or the other gains a pyrrhic victory?

How are we going to arrest the decline and recapture the lost ground? Can we restore a modicum of efficiency and accountability in every wing? Can we afford to allow the present situation to continue any longer? These are issues we will examine in the subsequent chapters.

8
GOOD GOVERNANCE

Having surveyed the challenges that we as a nation face and having elaborated the reasons as to why the challenges are becoming more unmanageable and having highlighted the extraordinary significance of high standards of governance for improving the ability of the nation to successfully overcome the problems and travel towards peace and prosperity, we may now turn our attention to examining what exactly constitutes good governance. This will provide the suitable backdrop for analyzing the close relationship between governance, security and development.

It is quite easy to discern that those countries which are classified as developed or advanced have reached this status by adopting the right economic and social policies and establishing institutions which provide all the ingredients of good governance. By now, the debate as to what constitutes right economic policies is well nigh settled in favour of free enterprise and market driven strategies. There may be a few diehard Communists who still keep harping on the glories of socialism but they are a vanishing species with China and a host of ex-Communist states in Eastern Europe, all aggressively adopting all the elements of capitalism with conviction and enthusiasm. Russia which has had the experience of the longest ever period in world history since 1917 of total state control, is now recording creditable all round growth without any of the inhuman suffering and executions imposed by Stalin's repressive policies. After long years of total secrecy, the horrendous proportions of the cruelty inflicted on the people of the USSR by Stalin's collectivization of agriculture and forcible translocation of large segments of population have been progressively revealed, raising alarming questions about a system which achieved so little in return for so much sacrifice by the people; to satisfy one man's blind and unalterable belief in the superiority of his interpretation of Marxian thought. No less than 7.4 million people died of starvation and shooting in Ukraine alone during Stalin's ruthless collectivization drive and elimination of the so called Kulaks, while agricultural production actually declined while state levies increased. Admittedly, the USSR did record outstanding achievements in select areas—heavy industries, defence, space, electricity—but the human cost of these achievements and the fact that such lopsided development proved to be a drain on the rest of the economy, can hardly be ignored. The USSR is arguably a classic case of wrong economic policies being combined with poor overall standards of governance. The spectacular foreign policy achievements of Stalin during and after the Second World War and some of his successors could not be sustained, as the core of the polity was being eaten up by poor economic performance and declining efficacy of the institutions of governance, whose strong point all along was ruthless enforcement of authority backed by state terror.

Robert Harvey in his book "*A Short History of Communism*" states that today, Communism seems to be nothing more than a terrible memory, a nightmare perhaps as horrific as Nazism. It was a system where stone faced men were presiding over supposedly 'workers-paradise' in the name of the people, while in fact, millions endured grinding poverty, with mind-numbing servitude that did not hesitate to murder and imprison whole population in the cause of "progress". While it lasted, it left 100 million dead and devastated economically a host of countries. To be sure, when and where it was practised with all the cruelty and terror, it did not apply almost all of the Marxian dogma. Marx envisaged a Communist society which implied end of capitalism leading to total equality and the withering away of the State, the freedom of the individual and internationalism. Nothing of this sort happened in the USSR.

I who has been to the USSR quite a few times when I was in the Ministry of Defence of the Government of India found that the State had not withered away, a party oligarchy ruled with an iron hand, the party *nomenklatura* benefited most from the system and had special privileges, had access to imported goods not available to the toiling masses, travelled in huge limousines and had country houses called *'dachas'*. The people, it appeared, lived a joyless life with limited and controlled entertainment and moved about like robots. In the trains, no one spoke to each other and everyone was either reading or pretended to read one of the only two newspapers available, namely "Pravda' or 'Izvestia'. "Pravda" means 'news' and "Izvestia" means 'truth' and so it was widely believed that what is news is not truth and what is truth is not news in the ex-Soviet State. Everyone was, it appears, looking over his or her shoulder with a high degree of fear of the all pervasive security apparatus—the KGB. Around 50 per cent of the passengers wore some uniform or the other.

In fact, the Soviet economy was a mixed economy with central industrial planning. Lenin's own New Economic Policy had all the elements of a capitalist system. The society was stratified, with the ruling oligarchy going about in large limousines called "ZIL"(Zavodnaya Ilyich Lenin) or "ZYS" (Zovodnya Yoseph Stalin) and living in flats with the latest gadgetry. Their children went to special schools. On the other hand were the workers who seemed to spend so much of their time in queuing up for something or the other and everyone always carried a bag, so that they could quickly join a queue and get their hands on what was available in a particular outlet, as everything was always in short supply. The only product not in short supply was Vodka.

For all the boasts of Khruschev to surpass the US within a decade, the ground reality was totally different. A Soviet worker had to work for 27 minutes to earn a loaf of bread, compared to just 4 minutes in the US, 115 minutes to get a kilo of beef as compared to 54 minutes in the US, 54 minutes for a kilo of sugar as compared to just 7 minutes in the US. To get seven kilos of milk, a Soviet worker had to toil for 147 minutes while an American worker could get this in 30 minutes.

The USSR had also exported its brand of Communism mainly through force, especially after Second World War and tried to sustain its empire by repeated doses of economic largesse and ever increasing subsidies, as well as military aid. This again drained the resources of the USSR and deprived it of the wherewithal for sustained progress. Paul Kennedy characterized this as a classic case of imperial overreach.

On the other hand, we have the case of a number of countries in Western Europe and that of the United States and Canada who have, since the end of the Second World War, witnessed continuous and almost uninterrupted progress and prosperity, their citizens enjoying standards of living and quality of life never before seen at anytime in world history. These nations have fashioned policies clearly calculated to maximize all round development and welfare of its citizens, modified and altered policies and strategies to be in keeping with changing circumstances and for meeting emerging challenges, while providing high standards of governance to their citizens through the building of enduring institutions capable of delivering the ingredients of good governance. The same can be said with some modifications for several countries in South East Asia—Singapore, Taiwan, South Korea—who have all been able to bring about sustained economic and social development resulting in high standards of living for the people. No doubt, these economies have faced turbulence recently but this is not the fault of the system but the way it was run, the greed of a select few, excessive welfarism, profligacy and reckless borrowing by both individuals and governments. The wars launched by the US—another case of imperial overreach—have also caused severe and perhaps avoidable difficulties for the US. It must be stressed that in the case of the US, the present difficulties are attributable to the tendency of the individual and the State to live beyond its means, the rise of the financial services which specialize in making money out of money and most importantly, the dismantling of the regulatory framework erected by Roosevelt, Eisenhower and Ronald Reagan. His overzealous advocacy of smaller government, supremacy of individual initiative and Bush's over enthusiasm to encourage limitless lending by banks and borrowing by individuals resulted in the problems faced by the US. To my mind, it is a case of lowering of standards of governance.

It is worth noting that all great promoters of market economy, Adam Smith, J.M. Keynes, Paul Samuelson, Von Hayek and Milton Friedman were fully aware of the reality that markets alone cannot be relied upon to provide public goods, deal with environmental spillover and asymmetric information and therefore, there is the need for the government to be deeply involved in infrastructure, education, scientific research and financial regulation. Von Hayek noted in his *'Road to Serfdom'* that, "we should not confuse the opposition to central planning with a dogmatic *laissez faire* (free market) attitude." The correct position Hayek asserted, lies in favour of making the best possible use of the forces of competition as a means of co-ordinating human efforts and not an argument for leaving things as they are. It is based on the conviction that if effective competition can be created, it is a better way of guiding individual efforts than any other. Hayek recognizes that where it is impossible to create conditions of effective competition, we must resort to other methods of guiding economic activity. He as Adam Smith before him, acknowledged that there is a wide and unquestioned field for state activity, in particular, provision of public goods—infrastructure, education, healthcare, etc.—where individual effort can never be sufficient.

Jeffrey Sachs in his latest book *'The Price of Civilization'* argues that the lessons that Paul Samuelson had taught have been forgotten in the US. These lessons were pointedly ignored by Ronald Reagan when he declared that the government is not the solution but the problem. Summarizing Samuelson's work in this field, Sachs states that the limitations of the market are as follows:

a. Markets are reasonably efficient institutions for rational allocation of society's scarce resources and lead to high productivity and higher living standards. They are certainly more efficient than monopolistic state mechanisms.
b. Efficiency does not however guarantee fairness (or justice) in the allocation of resources.
c. Fairness requires the governance structure to redistribute income among the citizenry form the richest to the poor and the vulnerable.
d. Markets systematically under-provide certain 'public goods', infrastructure, environmental protection, education, healthcare, scientific research, etc., whose adequate supply depends upon the government.
e. The market economy is prone to instability which can be alleviated through government policies including financial regulation and well directed monetary and fiscal policies.

Paul Samuelson's great synthesis called on market forces to allocate most goods in the economy while calling on governments to perform three essential tasks—redistribution of income to protect the poor, providing adequate and continuous supply of public goods such as infrastructure and scientific research and stabilizing the macro economy.

John Maynard Keynes had rightly observed, "The capitalist classes were allowed to call the best part of the (national) cake theirs and theoretically free to consume it, on the underlying condition that they consumed very little of it in practice. The duty of saving became 9/10 of the virtue of the system and the growth of the size of the cake the object."

Successive administrations from Ronald Reagan onwards lost sight of all this wisdom, reduced the regulatory role of the government, while neglecting infrastructure. Consumption and not saving and investment was the mantra for growth and consequently, Americans have got into the bad habit of overdoing everything—overeating, overheating, over borrowing, over spending, over gambling and indulging in every addiction, even while taxes on the rich were lowered. The government and its arms the Congress and the Senate were hostage to powerful business lobbies and there was a revolving door between the Wall Street, big oil and big business and the government. Thorstein Veblen had labelled such behaviour as "Conspicuous consumption" that is consumption whose main purpose is to impress others rather than for the enjoyment or happiness of oneself. Since even today, the Americans command huge natural resources and still have one of the highest per capita income in the world, the situation can be retrieved with adequate regulation, cut in defence spending and the rich paying higher taxes.

An observation of James Wolfenson, the then President of the World Bank appears to highlight this point. He stated, "The causes of financial crises and poverty are one and the same. If countries do not have good governance, if they do not confront the issue of corruption, if they do not have a complete legal system which protects human rights, property rights and contracts. their development is fundamentally flawed and will not last." It is clear from the above discussion that good governance is essential not only for growth but for stability as well and what is regarded as good politics is not good economics.

This would lead us to a discussion of what really constitutes good governance.

An issue of such great importance has naturally been; the subject of animated and exciting debate over the years and each generation of thinkers view the issues involved; in the perspective of the particular circumstances they are placed in and the particular set of societal problems that need to be addressed. The debate has centred on the role of the state in the life of a nation. The pendulum has swung from one extreme to the other based upon the particular economic and political philosophy currently found fashionable or espoused by the leadership at any point of time and no doubt, the success or failure of the particular philosophy adopted.

Every government claims that it works for the welfare and material well-being of its citizens. The argument, however, has been whether, in order to achieve the stated aims governments must actively intervene in every area of the citizen's life, particularly with respect to economic and social development or if the role of the government should be confined to certain vital areas where public interest and welfare are predominant considerations. The challenge as suggested earlier, for every society and government is to combine efficiency, fairness (justice) and sustainability. The issue of sustainability has become increasingly important in the context of the grave adverse impact that the present technologies, growth patterns and population pressures are having on the ecology and environment of planet earth.

Paul Kennedy in his *"Rise and Fall of Great Powers"* quotes a European mercantilist Adam Smith, who averred that, "It needs to be recognized that little else is requisite to carry a state to the highest degree of opulence from the lowest barbarism but peace, easy taxes and tolerable administration of justice."

Such a point of view would suggest that the State's intervention with respect to the economic life of the people should, if at all, be minimal and the State should only provide peaceful conditions for the life of its citizens, and institute systems that administer justice in a fair and even-handed manner. In other words, the State should ensure prevalence of the rule of law in all its dimensions, while safe guarding peace and security, both from external aggression and internal unrest. This view was expressed at a time when Marxism had not made its appearance and the State played only a peripheral role in promoting the welfare of the people. But, it was a time of conflicts and extortionist rates of taxation by kings and despots, who used the taxes to wage wars or build palaces. Hence the stress on peace and easy taxes.

This point of view however did not die down even when socialism which advocated State intervention and indeed State ownership of means of production and distribution began to capture the imagination of thinkers in Europe culminating in the establishment of Communist states, which put into practice these ideas in a ruthless manner, liquidating all private initiative. Fredriech Von Hayek and P.T. Bauer, two great economists—Von Hayek is a Nobel laureate—both forcefully argued against State intervention, warning decision makers of the dangers of State-controlled, State-directed strategies of economic development. P.T. Bauer, right from the mid-1940s, going completely against the prevailing current, had been consistently arguing for a greater role for the markets and a limited role for the State. Bauer who died about a decade back will go down in history, as the man who demolished all the core beliefs of 'statist development economics' which held the poor of the Third World to be economically incompetent and in need of authoritative resource allocation decisions being made on their behalf and supposedly for their benefit by an intellectual moral elite, namely the governmental machinery of planners. Bauer's thesis was that the poor of the third world were not lacking in entrepreneurial skills and were quite capable of taking rational decisions and able to accumulate capital, if only their governments get out their way. He dismissed the theory of the vicious cycle of poverty stating that if this were true, the world would still be in the Stone Age. He backed this hypothesis by arguing that today's developed countries were all developing countries not so long ago, and the transformation in their status at a reasonable pace happened due to the individual initiative of their peoples and exploitation of opportunities backed by good old enlightened self-interest, the State providing its people economic freedom, peace, security and the rule of law. When wars shattered peace and security, progress was halted but when peace returned, progress resumed.

This is so well illustrated by the post-war experience of Western Europe. In an ancient town called Ypres in Flanders of Belgium, amid flowering meadows full of poppies, there are 170 military cemeteries with memorial stones recording why soldiers of 20 different countries died in the World Wars in that area. "Morts pour la France", "For King and Country", "Deutschland muss leben". Every evening, the buglers of the Ypres fire brigade gather to play the "Last Post" in honour of the fallen. Every evening, people gather to hear it, and many cry. The sad and mournful notes rise up into the blue Belgian sky, there to mingle with the spirits of the millions killed in the hot and cold wars of Europe's bloody 20th century. All this seems today so far away, belonging to an altogether different age for barely an hour's drive across the flat Flanders farmland, rises a gleaming memorial to a new Europe, in a new age. The modern office towers of Brussels' Quartier Leopold, house many of the institutions of the European Union, the visible symbol of a continent so integrated and so connected that war will be impossible. Today, the European community is a union of 15 countries with 13 more countries eager to join. It has its own parliament, bill of rights, court system, a common currency, and even a flag and an anthem. The boundaries separating the countries of the Union have all but dissolved with no barriers for the movement of the people, no visas, no tariffs and most importantly, no wars. Though a great deal of difficulties had to be overcome and a number of compromises had to be worked out, with so many languages, varying shades of culture and even conflict of interests; the European Union has emerged arguably as the best example of conflict resolution in the world. What is important for our purpose, is to note that this long period of peace and stability has yielded rich economic dividends and today the "United States of Europe" is an economic power-house fully capable of challenging the United States of America. The combined GDP of the 15 members of the EU is around US $7.8 trillion (2001) drawing ever closer to America's $9.9 trillion. It has a population of 380 million, significantly more than that of the US. Europe has witnessed perhaps the longest period of growth uninterrupted by external conflicts and internal disturbances. Except for the Balkans, no part of Europe has witnessed conflicts. Peace and prosperity can therefore be regarded as indivisible, peace both with respect to external aggression and internal conflict. When prosperity becomes widespread, the basic cause of conflicts, namely the anxiety to assure one's future by cornering the available resources even if it means depriving the other fellow of his very existence, loses all relevance. A stable if not declining population has also considerably helped this process of assuring everyone a reasonably good share of the overall prosperity.

The fact that in the past two or three years, serious questions have arisen about the durability of this system of collective economic management, but the great achievements that have been indeed recorded by Europe since the Second World War cannot however be denied. The present difficulties have risen primarily because of excessive welfarism, reckless borrowings by both individuals and governments in some of the member countries, poor economic management and the failure to observe the basic principles of self-regulation. Countries which were not ready or advanced enough to join such an arrangement which required surrendering part of their autonomy to the EU, joined the Union with misguided enthusiasm and are now struggling to cope with a self-created crisis. The people who have been long accustomed to a life style of luxury based on borrowing and government hand-outs do not naturally like the austerity that is being imposed. Huge unemployment in economies which had achieved near full employment, even with weak economic fundaments is a leading cause of dissatisfaction and unrest. European leaders, I am sure, have enough wisdom and resources to bring about necessary reforms and corrective measures to ensure better health for the system and all is members. The reduction in fiscal deficits may have to be calibrated more carefully and the EU *diktat* of reduction to 3 per cent of the GDP may not be possible for many of the economies facing recession. To my mind, the present crisis is a warning and a temporary set-back and will compel the leaders to deal with the fundamental problems which caused the crisis and build in the necessary safeguards to prevent any recurrence.

Even when wars happened, the rule of law was made to prevail. At the beginning of Second World War, during the worst of the 'battle of Britain', when day and night air raids were causing widespread destruction; Churchill anxiously enquired whether the courts were functioning. Such was the importance attached to the prevalence of rule of law even when all else seemed to be crumbling and the nation faced the worst.

Peter Bauer also was strongly against foreign aid, his views once again ignored as politically incorrect, and still unacceptable in many quarters. It would appear that those countries, which relied very little on aid, such as India and China, have been able to record much higher performance levels. He consistently argued that large doses of aid only sustained corrupt and inefficient regimes. His view was that aid was a transfer from poor people in rich countries to rich people in poor countries. He was one of the first to argue that developing countries needed trade and not aid.

No doubt, foreign aid, particularly by multilateral agencies, is granted with stiff conditions but the conditions are invariably diluted when anxiety about keeping to schedules of disbursement start taking a grip. The views of Peter Bauer were accurately reflected by the '*London Economist*.' Discussing the case of Kenya, the *Economist* stated that over the years, Kenya like other similarly placed African countries, has performed a curious mating ritual with its aid donors. The steps are:

a. Kenya wins—foreign aid with a variety of pledges.
b. Government begins to misbehave violating the conditionalities agreed to.
c. A new meeting of donor countries berates the government.
d. Kenya pulls out a placatory rabbit or two out of its hat.
e. The donors are mollified and the aid is pledged again, may be with fresh conditionalities.
f. The whole dance then starts once again.

Ministers in many countries act in the firm belief that the donors will always come back because it is a manifestation of the white man's burden, as an instrument of foreign policy of the big powers or as a way of buying corrupt third world dictators.

Bauer consistently argued and warned repeatedly that politicians who followed stupid policies were being saved from the consequences of their stupidity by foreign aid. Regimes that should have crumbled because of sheer incompetence and corruption were being propped up indefinitely by foreign aid. In a well-run country, rulers should depend upon citizens for tax revenue and in return be accountable to citizens. Such a social contract is crucial for good governance. But, aid makes donors the main source of revenue and not the citizens. So, rulers ignore citizens and focus on pleasing the donors by becoming part of their sphere of influence or economic empire. The country continuing to be poor, works to the advantage of the recipient ruler and the donor by perpetuating demand for imported products, which would have been produced within the recipient country if development had taken place.

In India, when we as an independent nation launched a programme designed to usher in the "socialist pattern of society" and a mixed economy under Nehru, there were dissenting voices such as that of C. Rajagopalachari who warned against all pervasive State intervention and the "licence permit raj". His voice was drowned by the socialist wave and after Nehru, the centrist orientation of the polity was shifted to a left of the centre strategy, expanding the areas of State intervention, nationalization of banks, coal, etc. The State sought to attain what was called "the commanding heights of the economy" while stifling private enterprise through multiple controls. Even Gandhiji had warned against policies which would make the citizen excessively dependent upon government, robbing him of all initiative but this was ignored. That this socialist experiment—we even included the word 'socialist' in the Preamble of the Constitution making India a secular socialist, democracy—in spite of warnings, resulted in low growth, high inflation, wastage of the nation's precious resources, all-round decline in efficiency with which capital was used (reflected by progressive worsening of the capital output ratio) while the population kept increasing by leaps and bounds, is now a well documented story. We persisted with the left of the centre economic policies for too long until it could no longer be sustained. The country had by 1991, reached a stage when it could no longer afford the luxury of State-sponsored, State-directed and State-controlled development. At that point of time, the number of poor in India, it must be shamefully admitted, was equal to the total population of the country at the time of independence. We claim that since then, the percentage of poor has come down but this still means that India has the largest absolute number of poor people in the whole world. Such a policy framework of the State, assuming practically all the responsibility for development, can be successfully implemented if and only if the entire system is in fine fettle and all the institutions for carrying through the programmes, run the system and deliver the services, operate at peak efficiency. In the USSR, the totally State-controlled system worked efficiently during the war, but this was because the nation was engaged in a life and death struggle, there was an upsurge of patriotism and quite importantly, those found wanting were either shot or found themselves in the "Gulag Archipelago". This phenomenon did not endure for long and the glaring deficiencies of the system eventually led to its collapse.

In our case, the progressive control of the economy by the State and its increasing role in the development process was unfortunately accompanied by a corresponding sustained decline in the efficiency of the nation's institutions and systems of delivery of services, along with deterioration in the fiscal management of the Centre as well as the States.

This brief discussion can serve as the background, for defining what really constitutes good governance. It also shows that good economics is not bad politics and right economic policies are essential elements of good governance.

Though the elements that constitute good governance have undergone changes from time to time, it is widely accepted by all concerned that a government must ensure the peace and prosperity of each and every citizen. In the foregoing paragraphs, the discussion centred on the methodology for securing the prosperity of the people, whether it should be through wide-ranging intervention by the State or whether superior results can be achieved by reposing faith in the mechanism of the market. It would appear that the superiority of the market as an agent for resource allocation and as an engine for promoting economic growth, has been quite firmly established and this would mean a substantive reduction in the development functions of the systems of governance. This does not however mean that governments withdraw altogether and allow market forces total and unfettered freedom. Markets cannot be totally without regulation and supervision if one attaches importance to the principles of equity and fair play. Providing the right legal, regulatory framework, a level playing field, mechanisms for conflict resolution, safeguarding the interests of the consumer, functioning as a facilitator and a catalyst for growth where required, correcting distortions in the process of development, laying down standards and enforcing them; are all legitimate interventions which must be undertaken even in an economy wedded to free enterprise. Managing the economy's macro balances, maintenance of the stability of the nation's currency—both external and internal—avoiding overheating and depressions and efficient conduct of the country's external economic relations all also fall within the province of governance. This point has been emphasized in earlier chapters.

In a developing country such as ours, the government has also to play an important role with respect to ensuring social justice, advancement of the more disadvantaged segments of the community, reduction of inequalities, poverty alleviation, providing healthcare, education, build-up of infrastructure and correcting regional and sectoral imbalances.

Further, the core regulatory functions of any government have to be performed effectively. These include maintenance of law and order, peace and security, defending the country against external aggression and internal unrest, providing the citizens speedy and efficient systems of justice and grievance redressal mechanisms, conduct of external relations both with other governments and international bodies, and coming to the aid of citizens to deal with disasters and emergencies. This also includes regulation of the market with right interventions and the necessary legal framework.

As Lee Kwan Yew who transformed Singapore in one generation reminds us in his book "*From Third World to First*", "We cannot forget that public order, personal security, economic and social progress and prosperity are not natural order of things, that they depend upon ceaseless effort and attention from an honest and effective government that the people must elect."

Extraordinary Wisdom, from an Outstanding Leader

Irrespective of the system of economic management, keeping in mind the above mentioned core functions of the government, certain fundamentals stand out as absolute essentials of good governance, without which orderly progress of a society would be well nigh impossible.

The first and foremost of these is the prevalence of rule of law. The concept of rule of law is intimately linked with civilization itself. As societies advanced, as humanity's understanding of the nature of the relationship between one individual and another, and between individuals and the society expanded, a whole body of thought has crystallized, giving meaning and content to the idea of rule of law. The basic principles which serve as guide posts for a society organized on the basis of rule of law are, that the society's affairs should be conducted in a peaceful and orderly manner according to a code accepted as law by common consent, that all individuals are born free and deserve to be free, that they are all born equal, that they have the right to live peaceably, pursue a vocation of their choosing, earn a livelihood and enjoy the fruits of their labour and their possessions, so long as these have been acquired in a legitimate manner. Further, no one has the right to interfere with the rights of others, and while the society respects the rights of the individual, he is expected to surrender a part of his rights where necessary for the sake of common good. A social contract emerged which safeguarded both the rights of the individual and the collective rights of the society. If an individual wished to enforce his legitimate rights or had a grievance against another or the society or even suffered harm due to the actions of others, he had no right to act on his own and had to seek redressal from agencies duly created and empowered to attend to such issues. Institutions and regulations therefore came into being for operationalizing all these concepts. Machiavelli rightly observed in his classic "*The Prince*" that all good governments should have 'good laws and good arms' that is, laws which answer the requirement of the people and the circumstances in which they live and their effective enforcement.

Such a body of principles would translate itself in practice to provide for the citizens, a framework which guarantees equality in the eyes of law, equal protection of law to everyone, non-discriminatory and fair application of law, reasonable restrictions on individual rights in the interest of the society, individual liberty, the right to hold property, freedom of expression including freedom of the press, freedom to form associations, to assemble peaceably, to travel, etc. This would also imply that no one can be deprived of his life, liberty or property without due process of law. The elements of due process of law would be detailed in the regulations applicable to all concerned.

A whole body of literature is available on this framework of rule of law and our purpose is served by emphasizing the basic ingredients, whose implementation through an institutional framework, created by law is of fundamental importance to good governance.

The second essential feature is the existence of a well-organized institutional framework for the purpose of formulating regulations and policies to operationalize the principles enumerated above and ensure their fair, impartial and non-discriminatory implementation. It has been rightly said that nothing can be achieved without human effort, but nothing that lasts can be achieved without creating institutions. In spite of several limitations, it is now widely accepted that participative democracy with a system of checks and balances is the best possible framework capable of serving these purposes and fulfilling the objectives of good governance. Monarchies and dictatorships have been found to be prone to such misuse of authority, that they cannot be trusted to provide equity or justice to the people, even if such systems achieve spectacular short-term successes in areas such as foreign policy or economic progress.

The key element here is accountability of the institutions for their performance, for their sensitivity to the requirements of the people they govern, for the adequacy and alacrity of their response, for their ability to safeguard the interest of the nation, the society and the citizen, for the effectiveness with which they solve the problems of the citizen and contribute to the systematic and sustained; betterment of the quality of life of all segments of society.

Democracy scores high in most of these respects because it contains in itself all the principles, rule of law and of separation of powers and checks and balances. Each of the institutions are accountable to another and all are ultimately accountable to the people, who enjoy the right to choose those who will govern them, retain or reject their rulers based upon their performance and how satisfied they are with their performance.

The third element of good governance would be the establishment of systems, procedures, practices and traditions, which ensure that all the institutions discharge their responsibilities effectively and efficiently. For good governance, both the "will" and the "wherewithal" are important. The "will" is provided by the mechanism of accountability to the people who are expected to express their preference periodically—every four or five years—through the electoral system, exercising their franchise generally speaking in favour of the party whose performance is superior. The "wherewithal" is provided by the building up of instrumentalities of governance,—the Parliament, the political executive, the civil service, the police, the judiciary,—and mechanisms which acts as watchdogs—the audit system, the press, voluntary organizations, etc. The efficiency, impartiality and even-handedness with which each of these institutions function and serve as service providers in a citizen-friendly manner determines the quality of governance. The legislature is expected to enact laws which promote peace and security of the nation and the welfare and prosperity of the citizens. The executive, while being accountable to the legislature and the judiciary for all its actions, works for the peace, security and prosperity of the people. The judiciary safeguards the rights of the people while providing speedy and impartial justice and punishing transgressions of law. For good governance, all these institutions must work in harmony with each other, discharging their responsibilities efficiently. The essentiality of a neutral civil service, competent, professional and impartial, as well as a police system which is equally professional, competent, well trained and motivated is self-evident, if good governance is to be ensured. This is particularly important in a country like ours which is pluralistic and where caste loyalties are not only strong but are being constantly reinforced. In a multi-party democracy, the neutrality of the civil service and the police assumes greater importance to ensure that all citizens receive non-discriminatory and impartial treatment from the government. A neutral and impartial civil service and police can be the only way which ensures that in implementing government's programmes, there is no discrimination for or against segments of the population based on party considerations and voting patterns. These points have been fully argued in the chapter titled "Architecture of Governance".

What is important is that all these institutions must be so equipped and so empowered as to discharge their functions without fear or favour, effectively enforce the authority vested in them and ensure full compliance with the laws of the land by all the citizens, while everyone receives the protection guaranteed by law. All the institutions are expected to function in a transparent manner, their actions not only fair and equitable at all times but seen to be fair. Further, all their actions should be so fashioned as to result in the greatest good of the largest number and in expending public finances, they should exercise the same degree of prudence that an ordinary man would exercise had he been spending his own money.

The next element determining the quality of governance is the quality of leadership that a country is blessed with. Leaders, it is needless to say, are supposed to lead, articulate a vision for the future, combine vision with action, anticipate and handle crises with boldness and imagination, fight adversities with courage and determination without flinching against all odds, set goals, achieve results, provide that critical element which makes the difference and makes the system work and be decisive and firm in the face of setbacks. While being sensitive to the needs and aspirations of the people, leaders are not to succumb to and be led away by sentiments. They should be learned and wise strategic thinkers. They should have unimpeachable integrity and a high sense of patriotism. Such men rise far above others and command universal respect and are able to make extraordinary contributions uplifting the societies they lead to altogether new heights. A true leader should be able to make the country do better than what it believes it can do, be a great communicator and carry the people with him. A fine example of such a leader is Lee Kwan Yew of Singapore.

Lee Kwan Yew transformed Singapore in less than a generation, even though at the time of its birth, it had to deal with many internal and external challenges. It had hostile neighbours—Malaya and Indonesia—a multi-lingual and multi-cultural population, the threat of Communist takeover and militant trade unionism. Singapore had no natural resources to build upon. Its average per capita income was less than US$ 1,000. Today it is US $ 60,000.

His strategy was to build a unified community, which prided itself as Singaporean above all other considerations, leapfrog the hostile neighbourhood like what the Israelis had done, develop human resources by attracting world class talent from anywhere and everywhere, neutralize militant unions and create a First World oasis in Third World region. With a strong government, strong and incorruptible institutions and a fine civil service, he succeeded in building public and personal security, health, education, telecommunications, transportation and other services all of first world standards. Today, this little city-state can boast of a per capita income of US$ 60,000. Yes, a certain ruthlessness and suppression was involved in all this but with no natural resources, Singapore had to create employment through attracting investment of a huge order and this could be done only if all the essential ingredients of good governance are put in place and investors feel secure as to the future. Lee Kwan Yew also imposed restrictions on the freedom of the press, as he was acutely conscious of the role that the press had played in inflaming sentiments of sections of the population resulting in communal riots. He followed the advice of Machiavelli, that a leader should be feared rather than loved and lessons of history that a leader should be feared alright, but not hated.

Another test of good governance would be, to my mind, the ease with which citizens are able to obtain the services they are entitled to, along with the public servants acting with a spirit of public service and without delay. The citizen should be free from harassment and the necessity to bribe anyone. This would apply to all those areas of governance which come directly into contact with the citizen, such as systems of grants of entitlements, dispensation of justice, grievance redressal and enforcement of law. This would imply simple and transparent procedures, clear statement of citizen's entitlements, easy accessibility of public officials and adequate opportunities for the citizen to be heard.

The emphasis in recent times has also been on the participative character of systems of governance. While democracy does take care of this issue to a considerable extent, the need for greater say in the process of decision making at the local level; by local communities, particularly in pluralistic societies has been growing.

It needs also to be noted that there is growing awareness of the need to preserve and foster basic human rights, and the dignity of the individual, in the conduct of all public institutions. Conservation of the environment and the country's biodiversity are also becoming matters of increasing importance.

Lastly, good governance means efficient conduct of the country's external relations, safeguarding the country's unity, sovereignty, and territorial integrity from external threats and internal unrest.

While the above discussion basically concerns the regulatory functions of governments in the area of development, the debate has now more or less settled down to viewing governance as an instrument to facilitate and promote growth while providing the right legal and regulatory framework for healthy development of the whole society. Direct intervention by the government needs to take place only in those areas where private initiative will not enter in spite of there being a specific societal requirement in areas with very long gestation periods or where social returns are significantly more than commercial returns. These include education, scientific and technological research, healthcare, infrastructure, distributive justice, poverty alleviation and correction of glaring inequalities.

It would be worth noting the observations of Paul H.O'Neill, the then Secretary of the US Treasury, in a seminar organized by the CII in New Delhi. He stated and I quote, "To unleash the potential for higher living standards and job creation, a nation's leaders must make an unflinching commitment to good governance, economic freedom and investment in people. Without these principles, even a people as capable and aspiring as the Indians cannot succeed. Good governance means ruling justly, enforcing laws and contracts fairly, respecting human rights, and fighting corruption. Economic freedom means removing barriers to trade, opening the economy to foreign and domestic investment and competition, pursuing sound fiscal and monetary policies, and divesting government from business operations. Economic freedom also means recognizing that it is the private sector—individuals implementing new ideas and pursuing their dreams—that create prosperity; not central planning or bureaucracies. Finally, investing in people means ensuring access to good quality health care, education and clean water, so that people have the necessities that allow them to strive for a better life."

It has already been noted that our Constitution does indeed contain all the elements that are essential for providing a high standard of governance to our people. The principles that have been outlined above and the institutions that are necessary for carrying out the tasks that are part of the system of good governance, have been provided for in this noble document. In the chapter on the Architecture of Governance, the manner in which all the institutions created by or under the Constitution have been systematically devalued and how all the high principles enshrined therein have been sacrificed at the altar of electoral politics and narrow chauvinism has been examined in detail. A few supplementary points flowing from the above analysis are however worth noting to reinforce the point that we have, by failing to put into practice the principles enshrined in the Constitution, been unable to provide peace and prosperity to all our citizens even after 65 years of independent existence and we present a contrast to many newly independent countries in South East Asia—the Asian Tigers—in this respect.

There can be little doubt that India is easily one of the most difficult countries in the world to manage and to govern with her myriad problems, cultural diversity, deep divisions reinforced by uneven levels of development, poverty and internal and external threats. A multi-religious, multi-ethnic and multi-cultural society, which was awakening after a long slumber and whose people after long years of suppression and deprivation were beginning to shed their fatalism with the realization dawning upon them that it is possible to banish poverty and inequality, is a fertile ground for conflicts, animosities and violence. This latent propensity for violence reinforced by divisive tendencies was bound to get worse with increasing competition for scarce resources and scarcer opportunities, complicated by the revolution of rising expectations and unaffordably high rates of population growth.

Elsewhere in the world, in the ex-USSR, in the Balkans and in our own neighbourhood, there are stark examples of the way in which conflicts in a multi-ethnic and multi-cultural society can spin out of control, leading to disintegration of political units which had remained united for decades, tearing apart people who had lived together for centuries. Such developments caused serious damage to the future prospects of these nations, retarding their socio-economic development. The basic reason for such disintegration appears to be, the failure of these nations to institute adequate systems of conflict resolution, systems which while being accommodative and flexible to take care of the needs and aspirations of the various groups and interests, can at the same time mange to safeguard the core values and interests of the nation and preserve its integrity and sovereignty. In India, we do see on an almost continuous basis, conflicts based on caste, religion, ethnicity, economic opportunities, region, etc., and even conflicts between states and between the states and the Centre. Some of these conflicts have been exploited and fuelled by powers inimical to India's interests.

In spite of all this, if we have remained together, carried on recording a reasonable rate of progress and indeed brought about a slow and gradual social transformation, with the disadvantaged segments of the society creeping up the ladder, taking advantage of the opportunities provided by policies of positive discrimination, it is to my mind because of the constitutional structure that we have in this country. No doubt, there are quite a lot of unresolved conflicts, violence, separatism, armed insurgency and considerable dissatisfaction and disillusionment. We have however managed to contain all this, including the problems of the North-East and Jammu and Kashmir, within fairly manageable limits and carrying forward efforts to resolve the issues through a process of dialogue, accommodation and compromise. We have also successfully contained the external threats to our security and conducted our international relations with a fair degree of success, especially in recent times.

We have also managed to preserve our democratic system, never had military rule, and all the basic freedoms given in our Constitution. Our rulers without exception have been chosen by the people through, with some exceptions, free and fair elections.

My thesis however is that this country, given the ideas and ideals that inspired our founding fathers and the kind of constitutional structures—that guarantees all the elements of good governance—that we have given unto ourselves, could have done far better and could have after 65 years become a world power and indeed a first world country.

It is also my firm belief, reinforced by long experience that no system can work without adequate responsibility being displayed by all the players in the system. Democracy, of all the systems of government, can be successful and ensure the welfare of the governed and efficiency and accountability of those who govern, only if both parties to this social contract act responsibly, exercise their rights within recognized limits and are prepared to surrender some part of their rights, for the sake of common good. For democracy to thrive, it is also necessary for the citizens to understand their obligations towards the community and their fundamental duties towards the society and the nation. Irresponsible conduct on the part of either or both can render the whole system ineffective and can even ultimately destroy the system.

In India, we seem to have reached a stage where both the rulers and the ruled are showing strong tendencies towards lack of any responsibility. The inefficiency, waste and corruption, lack of concern for the welfare of the people, the failure to solve the basic problems of the country, the failure to provide peace and security, are adequate testimony to the poor levels of responsibility displayed by those entrusted with the task of governing this country. The fact that our leaders all grow rich with such speed the moment they assume one office or the other shows the degree to which irresponsibility has grown in our land where large segments continue to wallow in poverty. While this decline in standards on the part of those who govern, has been widely commented upon, what has not received attention is the need for an adequate response and display of sufficient levels of responsibility by our people as well. Any serious asymmetry in the two levels of responsibilities will erode the effectiveness of the system leading to grave difficulties in administering the same. It is my thesis that we have such an asymmetry in India and steps need to be taken to correct the same. I call this the doctrine of reciprocity.

This doctrine would imply that when the citizens expect the governmental machinery to provide them with a range of services economy that extends to almost all aspects of life and even death, the government has an equal right to expect the citizen to act responsibly. It would be unfair on the part of the citizen to demand the full range of services when he does not pay taxes, takes every possible measure to evade taxes, destroys public property at the slightest of provocation, displays no civic sense and no discipline, destroys the environment, encroaches on public land and reserve forests, violates the laws of the land but considers himself entitled to the protections and the rights afforded by the Constitution. Above everything else I consider, begetting children without regard to one's ability to look after them and provide for their well-being and their future and throwing them on the lap of the government, is the height of irresponsibility.

Such irresponsible conduct resulting in unaffordably high

rates of growth of population has made it very difficult for this country to deal with the innumerable problems we have. It is, I am convinced, the single most important factor, which has continuously enlarged the magnitude and complexity of each of our problems. Such continuous increases in the magnitude and complexity of our problems requires ever larger quantum of resources which the country is unable to mobilize, as the very citizens who demand the benefits are unwilling to contribute to the nation's resources by paying taxes. The government therefore either runs into debt or resorts to deficit financing, adding to the inflationary pressures.

To my mind, this asymmetry between demands placed on the society by the irresponsible conduct of individuals and in turn on the government and the ability of the society and the government to satisfy this ever increasing demand needs to be understood in all its dimensions. Every addition to the population means a strain on the already overstretched infrastructure, on the availability of land, for electricity, for water, for health services and for jobs. Though we do compliment ourselves for bringing down the net yearly rate of growth of population, given the extremely large population base, the absolute numbers added per year to the population is a staggering 20 million and this figure is increasing with each passing year. Every year this large and increasing number, is being thrust into the same limited geographical space, imposing an ever-growing burden on our inelastic natural resources. This means approximately 20 million citizens per year have to be provided a complete range of services from food, raiment, shelter, health, education, infrastructure, electricity, water supply and of course jobs. Unfortunately, this net addition to the population comes from the least productive segments of the society, the uneducated, the illiterate, and the misguided as also the economically backward.

They have no ability to support the number of children they add to the population but display a high level of irresponsibility by placing the responsibility for the welfare of these children on the society and the government, while they themselves do not contribute to the enhancement of the society or the government's ability to cope with the increased burden. Hence, the huge mismatch between availability of resources and the resources required for dealing with an ever-enlarging set of responsibilities imposed on the government and the society. Unfortunately, our media and our political class keep harping on the government's responsibility to cater to every need of such additions to the population. Every election is a competition in populism to promise more and more freebies, taking resources away from productive investments. No wonder, all services provided by the government sink to the worst possible standards of quality and performance.

Apart from the question of availability of resources, there is also the problem of declining effectiveness and efficiency of the system to cope with and tackle large increases in responsibility. Added to this, are the regional and statewide imbalances that are sharpening every year. The question has been asked by states which have been recording higher rates of economic growth and lower rates of population growth, as to why they should subsidize and support the irresponsibility of those states who fail to effectively control their population and improve their economic performance. No society which has such a mismatch between demand for services and ability to meet the ever-increasing needs can hope to effectively solve the myriad economic and social problems that it has to deal with. Such a situation can only lead to widespread dissatisfaction, disillusionment, unrest, disorder and breakdown of systems leading to insurgency and worse. This has already happened in several parts of the country. Unfortunately, in recent years, the whole question of stabilization of population has been put on the back burner. No political party is interested in taking effective measures to stop the run away growth of population. A high degree of complacency seems to have crept into the entire administrative machinery and the impression is being touted about that India has a young population, which can prove to be a great advantage in the years to come, given the decline in birth rates in the western world and in China. This complacency is wholly unwarranted, as the so called manpower shortage in the West and even in China will not result in accommodating more than a few thousands and that too extremely high quality professional from India. The millions that are being added every year will have to fend for themselves in this country and will be imposing an ever increasing burden on every civic amenity and the nation's creaking infrastructure and all its resources which are unable to cope with even the present load.

It needs also to be stressed that today the world is witnessing what is termed as the 'third industrial revolution' which is a process where manufacturing is being digitalised and this has the potential of transforming manufacturing out of all recognition. Technologies such as 3D printing may mean not only a high level of automation but decentralisation of manufacturing, end of assembly lines, customized production and the end of economies of scale. This can translate itself into reverse migration of manufacturing from the developing to the developed world. Also with such extraordinary levels of automation job creation will decline. Machines are getting increasingly 'intelligent' which means that factories are getting leaner and shop floors less and less crowded and more and more clean. The Nissan British factory for example built 2,71,157 cars in 1999 with 4,594 people but in 2011 built 4,80,485 cars with just 5,462 people each of them with greater skills, than the last lot. Nissan was able to build more than 2,00,000 cars with an addition to its work force of less than 1,000 workers. All this may mean that the developed world will be importing less skilled workers from the developing world. Everyday, one sees media reports on the plight of street children, on malnutrition, child labour, and people without shelter, etc., to take just one example of failure of governance. The question is without exception asked, 'What has government done about this?' No one asks, who in the first place put these unfortunate children on the streets, who indeed drove them out to go and work at exploitative wages and appropriate the wages earned by these children. Our media and indeed our leaders, would have us believe that the parents who beget these children have no responsibility whatsoever, they have no obligations to any one and can keep on adding to the already unbearably high burden and it is the government which has to provide food, shelter, raiment, and create opportunities for employment while looking after their energy, transportation and other requirements.

Droughts occur and floods devastate vast areas with increasing frequency, because drought-prone and flood-prone areas which were previously vacant have now been flooded with people. Land which legitimately belongs to the river (or for that matter the animals in the jungle) has been occupied by people. When this happens, the governmental machinery does swing into action but the effectiveness with which the problems are tackled and the speed with which the tasks of relief and rehabilitation are handled seems to be on the decline. The reason simply is, while the scale of the problem each time a natural calamity occurs has been going up, the capability in the hands of the government in terms of financial resources and efficient delivery mechanisms to tackle these problems, is declining. No system can withstand the enormous strains imposed by such a serious mismatch between progressive and uncontrolled expansion in demand and the ability to satisfy this demand, on the part of the one agency on whom all the demands are heaped, namely the governing system. This phenomenon has been termed as 'demographic fatigue' by some economists and is very much evident in quite a few parts of India.

In my view the above analysis and in particular the "doctrine of reciprocity" is firmly grounded on the Constitution's Article 51-A, Part IV-A called the Fundamental duties. This provision enacted during the infamous 'Emergency' should be regarded as one of the signal achievements of this odious chapter of our post independent history. None cares to pay any attention to this chapter which is unfortunately non-justiciable. Many including our law makers may not be aware that such a provision is indeed part of our statute. I feel that this Article is of equal if not greater importance for the progress and welfare of the nation. This article states clearly that it shall be the duty of every citizen *inter alia* to protect public property, abjure violence, protect and improve environment, to strive towards excellence, to develop scientific temper, humanism and spirit of inquiry and reform, to defend the country, to uphold its sovereignty, unity and integrity and to value and preserve the rich heritage of our composite culture. Do our legislators who regularly indulge in fisticuffs or our citizens who burn buses at the drop of a hat remember this provision? No one seems to attach much importance to this article—those in public life or the administrators or the judiciary.

This whole picture may appear to be highly pessimistic, but does present a realistic assessment of the visible, observable scenario in every department of public life in our country. There are no doubt, noticeable exceptions where the leadership is sufficiently enlightened to attach importance to the necessity to build, nurture and strengthen institutions, select capable officers to take charge of crucial areas of administration, allow them to perform their duties without undue political interference and articulate a vision which gives importance to the welfare and progress of the whole society.

The crucial factor is the quality of leadership and when we ask the question as to how to bring about a change in the present scenario so that within a reasonable time, India can realize her full potential, wipe out poverty, and assure peace and prosperity to all her citizens, I for one believe that everything depends upon our ability to improve the quality of leadership at all levels in India. If the quality of leadership is to be substantially improved, the system should be such as to ensure participation by the right people and exclusion of the wrong people, to the maximum extent possible. This would mean that the process of selection of leadership should be reviewed.

Electoral reforms therefore assume an extraordinary degree of importance. As I have argued earlier, the present "first past the post system" is highly flawed in the sense that those elected do not represent even a simple majority of the electorate and it throws up candidates who succeed by exploiting and reinforcing divisive tendencies, and heavily devalues qualifications and performance as the determining criteria for reelection. The system has also provides full opportunities for criminalisation of politics, expanded the role of muscle and money power and has also provides ample scope for manipulating the electoral machinery. This issue is dealt with in detail in a subsequent chapter.

9

RELATIONSHIP AMONG GOVERNANCE, DEVELOPMENT AND SECURITY

It would now be quite appropriate to discuss in some detail the importance of good governance for sustainable economic and social development, having examined in the previous chapters in considerable detail, what constitutes good governance and what has been the Indian experience in this regard. It is the fundamental responsibility of governments to secure peace and prosperity to the people they govern and while the right policies are vital, without high standards of governance success cannot be assured.

There is by now, adequate historical evidence to establish that there is a positive correlation between standards of governance and levels of prosperity of nations. The World Bank report on Sustainable Development in a Dynamic World 2003 portrays this relationship is a graphic manner, as shown in Figure 9.1.

It can be easily seen that almost all countries whose per capita GDP (PPP 1999) was below $5000 have had poor standards of governance, defined in this context as quality of institutions, rule of law, securing of property rights, and the ability to inspire the confidence of individuals, that they can reap the benefits of their investments and efforts in a peaceful environment.

This correlation is even more sharply brought out if one analyses the pattern of growth in the new world, North and South America, as is evident from Table 9.1.

This table not only highlights the fact that while there has been an exponential and indeed explosive growth in the per capita income of the United States—from $550 in 1700 to $34,260 in 2000,

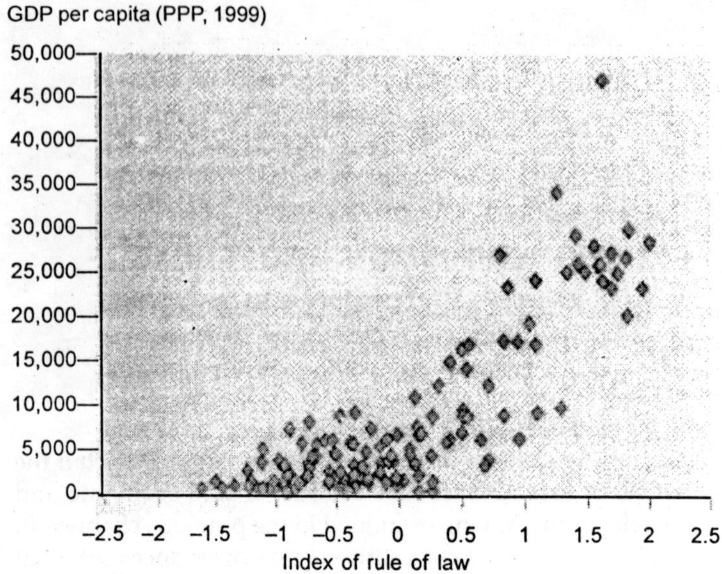

Fig. 9.1: The relationship between institutional quality and national income

PPP = Purchasing power parity.

Note: As a measure of institutional quality, the rule of law includes considerations such as the security of property rights, or the confidence with which a group or individual can find tomorrow the fruits of what is planted or conserved today.

Source: Kaufman, Kraay, and Zoido-Lobaton (1999).

matched by an equally strong and impressive performance by Canada, countries in South America which are rich in natural resources and whose incomes were higher than the US in percentage terms at one point of time, have shown a precipitous slide and are today counted among the poor or middle income countries of the world. They are also riddled with huge social problems and serious security related issues. Some are havens for drug lords and mercenaries. Argentina, which in 1800 enjoyed a per capita income higher than the USA, namely $102 per cent of the US income of $807, is today a relatively poor country, with only one-third of the per capita income of the United States, with burgeoning unemployment, social unrest and poor record in the management of the country's macroeconomic balances. The

Table 9.1: The rapid rise of national income per capita in the United States and Canada after 1800

	GDP per capita relative to the U.S. (per cent)			
Economy	*1700*	*1800*	*1900*	*2000*
Argentina	—	02	52	36
Barbados	150	–	–	44
Brazil	—	50	10	22
Chile	—	46	38	28
Cuba	167	112	—	—
Mexico	89	50	35	26
Peru	—	41	20	14
Canada	—	—	67	82
United States (GDP per capita in 1985 dollars)	650	807	3,859	34,260

—Not available

Source: World Bank (2001); Engerman, Haber, and Sokoloff (2000).

answer to the question, as to why the countries which had considerable resource endowments fell behind, lies in the fact that development depends not just on having productive opportunities but more importantly, on the ability to create abundant and indeed a never-ending supply of new opportunities. This would require not only capital formation but creation of institutions, laws and policies to make investments safe and attractive. In other words, high standards of governance are vital to continuously enhance the ability of the population, to accumulate capital, to invest and participate whole-heartedly in business and for creation of wealth. It would appear that only the US and Canada were able to erect the institutions, enact the laws and formulate and implement policies which enabled all this to happen. Governments which are able to provide the essential ingredients for growth namely an enabling regulatory framework, as well as peace and security record superior economic performance. In South America, apart from the absence of such an enabling regulatory environment, law and order and security have been serious concerns, with drug barons and mafia creating widespread violence, imposing limits on the writ of legitimate institutions of governance.

The importance of high standards of governance has been repeatedly stressed by thinkers all over the world.

That right policies and good governance are vital ingredients for sustained and rapid development are is borne out by the experience of countries all over the world and in our own neighbourhood—Singapore, South Korea, Taiwan, Malaysia whose performance by any standards is far superior to ours. Some may continue to dispute that market driven free enterprise economic philosophy is the right one. I personally am of the view that governments would be well advised to concentrate on the core issues of governance, i.e. rule of law, right regulatory framework, national security and external relations, delivery of justice, etc., and leave the business of running businesses to those who are competent to do so. This has been the experience of all countries which have, by combining good governance with economic freedom and stabilization of population, managed to continuously and in a sustained manner, improve standards of living and quality of life for their people.

In India's particular context, governments may have to worry about, besides health and education (human capital development) reduction of disparities and correcting regional and sectoral imbalances.

Table 9.2 would illustrate clearly the point that countries such as Singapore which combine high standards of governance with economic freedom, have been able take giant strides in bringing about prosperity and high quality of living to their citizens. This table also underlines the fact that economic freedom is, at the initial stages of nation building at least, more important than political freedom, for growth and prosperity and even suggests that political freedom unless accompanied by excellence in governance and rule of law, may have in fact a negative impact.

Take the case of Japan which combines excellent standards of governance with a great deal of political and economic freedom. It is little wonder that a war shattered country could transform itself into a peaceful and prosperous nation assuring high levels and quality of living for its entire people. Singapore has limited political freedom but even greater economic freedom than Japan and has emerged as a prosperous city state. China has high political control but is progressively increasing economic freedom and by all accounts growing at a faster pace than many developing and even developed countries and definitely much faster than India.

Table 9.2: Indicators of Governance for Selected Economies

Economy	*Government Effectiveness*	*Rule of Law*	*Control of Corruption*	*Economic Freedom*	*Political Freedom*
AGENTINA	0.18	0.22	-0.36	*2.50*	1.5
BRAZIL	-0.27	-0.26	-0.02	*3.10*	3.0
CHILE	1.13	1.19	1.40	*1.85*	2.0
CHINA	0.14	-0.19	-0.30	*3.55*	7.0
HONG KONG	1.10	1.37	1.16	*1.35 (TOP)*	2.5
INDIA	-0.17	0.23	-0.39	*3.55*	2.0
INDONESIA	-0.50	-0.87	-1.01	*3.35*	3.5
JAPAN	0.93	1.59	1.20	*2.45*	1.5
KOREA, SOUTH	0.44	0.55	0.37	*2.50*	2.0
MALAYSIA	0.53	0.34	0.13	*3.10*	5.0
SINGAPORE	2.16	1.85	2.13	*1.55*	5.0
TAIWAN	0.91	0.75	0.53	*2.35*	1.0
THAILAND	0.10	0.44	-0.46	*2.40*	2.5

Source: World Bank, Henley Foundation Freedom House
(In the last two columns, the lower the value the greater the freedom)

In our country unfortunately, unsound economic policies centring round excessive state intervention and lack of economic freedom and poor standards of governance have prevented us from realizing our full potential and assuring peace and prosperity to our people. Efforts are no doubt, underway though haltingly to correct the distortions in the system of economic management of the country and the results in terms of acceleration of the rate of growth, control of inflation, build up of foreign exchange reserves, and most importantly, the freedom of choice to the consumers are all visible. However, the second ingredient, namely good governance has received little or no attention and indeed, there seems to be an all round and sustained decline in standards of administration and progressive and sustained devaluation of the institution of governance—the executive, the legislature, the judiciary, the civil services and the police. The malaise as discussed in the previous chapters seems to be deep seated and requires comprehensive treatment. Unless remedies are effected soon, India's ability to realize its full potential can be stymied, our performance in the realm of socio-economic development may remain unimpressive and the nation will continue to be vulnerable to external and internal threats. It needs to be underlined that good governance ensures that public and private investment yields the right returns, that investment is channelised in the right direction and it reaches the intended beneficiaries without leakages, that private investment gets encouraged by the sense of security provided, and the assurance that investments can yield the dividends that are essential for private initiative to flourish. Without these, investments cannot take place and growth and employment creation will remain unsatisfactory. Impartial observers, while being impressed by the post-1991 achievements of the country in terms of acceleration of growth rates, repeatedly point out that India can vastly improve its performance levels if only it can improve its standards of governance, its ease of conducting business index and its efficacy in control of corruption.

Figure 9.2 illustrates the issues that require attention for improving our economic performance and the quantum of improvement that can be brought about with each of these reforms.

Further, the core regulatory functions of any government have to be performed effectively. These include maintenance of law and order, peace and security, defending the country against external aggression and internal unrest, providing the citizens speedy and efficient systems of justice and grievance redressal mechanisms, conduct of external relations both with other governments and international bodies, and coming to the aid of citizens to deal with disasters and emergencies.

Recent developments have once again brought into sharp focus this issue, of the vital importance of high standards of governance. The political changes that have taken place in the year 2004 and again in 2009 have generated a vigorous debate on the need for achieving development with a human face. Distributive justice, egalitarianism, spreading the benefits of development to the more backward and disadvantaged segments of the society are once again being bandied about as the new mantra for transforming India. That all these concepts were indeed the basis for a series of policy initiatives in Nehru and more particularly in the Indira era, with the slogan of *"Garibi hatao"* resulting in the conception of a series of programmes, advertised as strategies for direct attack on poverty and which consumed thousands of crores of rupees without achieving tangible and enduring results, appears to have been lost sight of. The fact that

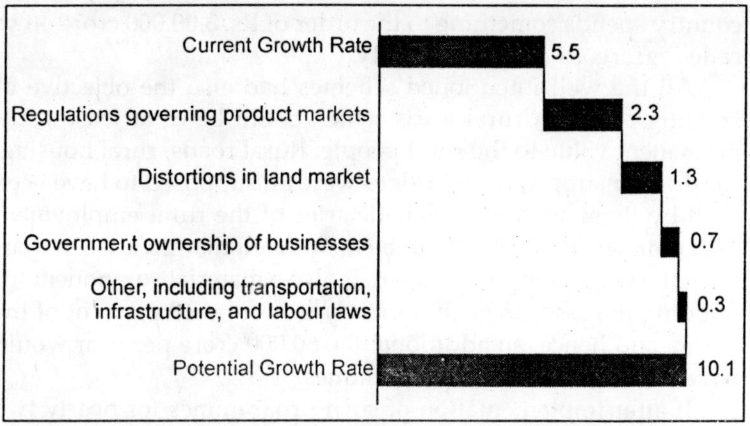

Fig. 9.2: Eliminating Barriers for Faster Growth in India (Per cent)
Source: Based on a chart in Di Lodovico and others (2001).
Source: World Bank: India and the Knowledge Economy.

all these well intentioned schemes failed because of reliance on an implementation mechanism which was inefficient and corrupt and which has only recorded steep decline in performance standards in all the intervening years, is being given no importance.

Take the series of programmes called employment generation and rural development schemes. There has been many number of them, Nehru Rojgar Yojana, Indira Awas Yojana, Intensive Rural Development Programme (IRDP), Prime Minister's Rojgar Yojana (PMRY), any number of rural water supply schemes, and road building schemes, etc. All these programmes involve an annual outlay of approximately Rs. 1,00,000 crore. On top of this, as part of our noble efforts to serve the poor and the down-trodden, we subsidize fertilizers, water; give free power etc., all of which costs the exchequer some Rs. 1,50,000 crore. But asking anyone to pay user charges even when they are affluent enough to pay and levying taxes even on rich agriculturists is considered equal to the proverbial red rag to the bull-frowned upon as it is perceived as electorally harmful.

If the revenue sacrificed as a consequence of such soft policies even with respect to the rural rich, is also taken into account, as after all revenue lost is revenue gained, one can easily say that the country spends something to the order of Rs. 3,00,000 crore on so called efforts to alleviate poverty.

All the well intentioned schemes had also the objective of creating assets in rural areas which could be of at least semi-permanent value to the rural people. Rural roads, rural housing, rural water supply, rural bridges were all supposed to have been built by those who were beneficiaries of the rural employment programmes. It needs also to be mentioned that invariably apart from the wage component, there is also a material component for building the assets, which normally is around 40 per cent of the outlay and hence, an additional Rs. 60,000 crore per year would have been spent in such programmes.

If after implementation of such programmes for nearly two decades, there is so little to show by way of even semi-permanent assets, the reason for that can only be total inefficiency and corruption in the implementation of the programmes. Several examples can be cited to show that all these schemes implemented at great cost have made very little difference to the rural people in terms of any improvement in the quality of their lives or standards of living. Studies by the National Council of Applied Economic Research (NCAER) 2009 have shown that employment guarantee schemes implemented in Maharashtra have not resulted in the creation of tangible assets for the community which have any lasting value. In many cases, the assets have never been created and where indeed they were created, they were washed away by the next rains. The shortcomings and failures are all very well documented in the series of audit reports and evaluation reports prepared by the various state governments. The documentation establishes beyond all reasonable doubt that the man-days projected as employment generated are generally false, documents contain fake names, that the assets supposed to have been created, do not get created, that material supposed to have been procured, is procured only on paper, bills generated and paid for, without any physical supplies and even if assets are created, the standards of work is so poor that the assets become un-usable, or do not last even one year. It is convenient for all concerned to show that the assets were washed away because of floods, etc., so that the same assets can be shown as necessary, leading to another round of fraud. In many cases, if assets have been indeed created, no one bothers to maintain them as the beneficiaries believe that since the assets have been created by a governmental agency, it is not their responsibility to look after these assets. Anything given free is invariably neglected as the general public has no stake in its upkeep. This has already created a huge dependency syndrome among our people. In our present scheme of things, asset creation comes from plan funds, whereas maintenance has to be provided for in the normal budget. Most state governments are so resource starved that they can barely pay their employees and maintenance of the assets receives no attention what so ever.

It is also well documented that a disproportionate share of the allocation is taken away by the machinery created to deliver the services by what is considered admissible establishment expenditure. On top of this is the rampant corruption with all the participants sharing the loot.

Therefore, it is beyond comprehension as to why a strategy that has been proved beyond all reasonable doubt to be nothing but an enormous waste of public money, has been given a rebirth in the shape of Mahatma Gandhi National Rural Employment guarantee scheme.

If the same amount of money had been devoted to specific programmes for creation of assets—power generation, irrigation, permanent roads, good school buildings, well equipped hospitals provided with qualified personnel, executed by qualified agencies paying due attention to quality parameters, with the clear objective of creating durable assets and not merely as employment generation gimmicks; the benefits to the community would have been far more tangible and would have resulted in substantial and visible upgradation of infrastructure in the rural areas, capable of triggering growth impulses all-around. Take rural connectivity, a good road would automatically open up outlets for rural produce, enable the people to travel at economical prices and open the minds of people to a variety of new opportunities. The country will also not find itself in such dire straits as regards power generation, nor would our agriculture growth be so dismal.

This discussion will underline the fact that the development strategies which do not pay attention to improving the efficiency and integrity of the delivery mechanism, in other words high standards of governance, cannot but result in absolute failure and a continuous drain on the country's resources.

Since all this is so well known and so well documented, why is it that our politicians insist on repeating the same mistakes? Is it because in their view, these are not mistakes but good vote winning strategies and our ignorant voters can be led away so easily to cast their lot with those who promise and promise but do not bother to deliver? Such slogans have worked in the past and are bound to work again is the belief and unfortunately our voters seem to validate this belief.

The MANREGA that has been implemented for the past seven years or so has suffered from all the deficiencies and limitations referred to above. In addition, it has made the rural population less inclined to do productive work and created labour shortages both in agriculture and industry. Sugar-cane harvesting has, for example, suffered in recent times. It is also the most important cause for high inflation in the country, as there is too much liquidity floating around without matching growth in production, particularly of agricultural commodities and essential items. Inflation is seriously affecting the poor who are being punished for the profligacy of the government and at the same time, by making investment more costly, it is damaging the growth prospects of the country. What is also happening is that the very same assets which were supposedly built under the earlier poverty alleviation schemes are being built again at thrice the cost. Also, the normal line departments which are supposed to create these assets are now sitting idle.

Great hopes were generated when the idea of creating a third tier of governance in the form of Panchayati Raj Institutions were conceived, as a mechanism for decentralization of authority, devolving development responsibilities to the representatives of the people. This was indeed an honest effort to improve standards of governance and improve delivery systems, while bringing the administration closer to the people. District level and village level bodies were created, and in some states like Assam where I have had personal experience of dealing with these bodies, an intermediate level body at the block level was created. In fact, in Assam, the block level bodies had clearly defined responsibilities, powers to raise revenue and a fairly well conceived executing mechanism in the shape of subject matter specialists called extension officers dealing with the subjects devolved to this block panchayat such as agriculture, animal husbandry, minor irrigation, rural roads, etc. This team worked under the Block Development Officer (BDO), who also functioned as the Secretary to the elected body. Each of the states enacted their own Panchayat Acts which, with some variations, aimed at creating institutions of self-governance, dealing primarily with economic and social development with respect to those areas which were of immediate relevance to the rural population. The state of Gujarat was a pioneer in this effort under the inspiring leadership of the then Chief Minister, Shri Balwant Rai Mehta, who was an idealist of the Gandhian mould.

In general, this experiment of democratic decentralization cannot be rated as a great success except in some select states. The state governments were reluctant to delegate substantial administrative and financial authority to the panchayats, did not hesitate to supersede the panchayats for even flimsy reasons, if it was politically expedient and having superseded and kept these bodies on a limbo indefinitely. There was no regularity in the conduct of elections and since the elections were conducted by the state machinery, the impartiality of the electoral process could be questioned.

This quite unsatisfactory situation is sought to be addressed by the Constitution's 73rd Amendment which introduced Article 243 in 1992. This Amendment confers Constitutional status to the Panchayats as well as urban local bodies. Safeguards have been built in with respect to superseding of local bodies, which require the state governments to justify such acts and laying down that fresh elections will have to be held within six months of the supersession. Conduct of elections has been entrusted to an independent machinery called the State Election Commission, on the model of the Central Election Commission. In order a improve the financial standing of the local bodies, a State Finance Commission has been constituted whose duty is to pronounce an award every five years for the devolution of finances—primarily non-plan resources—from the state to the local bodies, both panchayats and the municipalities. Very importantly, this Amendment provides for reservation among the elected representatives for Scheduled Castes and Scheduled Tribes in proportion to the size of the population, in the jurisdiction of the local body. Further, 33 per cent of the seats are reserved for women. The office of the chairperson is also expected to be filled up by women by rotation every third term. The question of reservation with respect to other backward classes has been left to the discretion of the state governments and legislatures, and quite a few have indeed gone ahead to reserve seats for this category.

Whether this democratic decentralization has indeed improved the overall effectiveness of development administration and the delivery mechanisms and whether the cost-benefit ratio is indeed superior to that in the earlier system cannot be answered in definitive terms. Existing reports, no doubt, underline the fact that in some parts of the country, in spite of limitations due to poor achievements in the sphere of literacy, there is a distinct improvement in the level of awareness among the rural folk of their rights and the fact that the power to improve their lot is in their own hands and results can be achieved if this power is wielded effectively and judiciously. Periodic reports have also appeared, as to how local initiatives have achieved significant results in areas such as water and soil conservation, particularly in dry areas with serious deficiency in rainfall.

The problem however is that by introducing the same electoral process that prevails for the assembly and Parliament level elections, namely adult franchise, multiparty "first past the post" system, we have reinforced the caste-based divisiveness right at the grassroots. Elections to the panchayats at all levels have become as contentious and fractitious as at the state levels, attended by violence and use of money and muscle power. As at the state level, electoral battles have become costlier by the year and those elected to office have to wily-nily use their positions to raise sufficient resources to enable them to fight the next elections. Corruption therefore is widespread and an increasingly lower percentage of resources allocated for economic and social development reach the actual beneficiaries.

While a detailed evaluation of the efficacy of the new experiment in decentralized administration, namely the Panchayat Raj, will have to be carried out, I propose to examine in the later part of this book the effectiveness of the system of decentralized governance that has been in operation in the North-East of India from almost the beginning of our republic, namely the district councils constituted under the Sixth Schedule of the Constitution. These bodies were given wide ranging powers, developmental, legislative and even judicial powers, based on grassroots democracy. Unlike the Panchayats which received their Constitutional status only in the year 1992, these district councils of the hill areas of the North-East were part and parcel of the Constitution from the very inception and by now have a longish history. Their autonomy has been zealously guarded by representatives of the particular tribe, to safeguard whose particular interests these institutions were created. The enquiry will be to understand the standards of governance in these institutions and what impact this has had on the pace and content of economic and social transformation in the areas where this system has been in operation for over sixty years.

While the above analysis relates primarily to the intimate links between the standards of governance and development, it also underlines the fact that there is a close relationship between governance, security and development. There can be no development without security and there is no security without adequate standards of governance. When governments fail to provide individual and collective security to their citizens, orderly conduct of affairs and orderly progress, both become impossible. The law of the jungle prevails and might becomes the only way one safeguards one's own and one's family's security. In all those countries where governments have failed to create the essentials of rule of law described in detail in the earlier part of this chapter, basically a proper legal and enforcement system or where the governments allow the systems to deteriorate to such an extent that ordinary citizens cannot look to the government, chaos takes over and armed gangs operate with freedom, posing a threat to everyone. This is classic prescription for disaster. Imagine a situation, as was the case in the Middle Ages when an ordinary person could not move around leaving the safety of his own residence without fear of assault or robbery. Everyone moved around with some protection and invariably carried arms. Churchill famously boasted that one of the blessings of British rule in India was the fact that a single lady, without any protection, could climb into a train in Travancore and travel all the way to the Punjab. The State looked after the protection of all its citizens. One can see the failure of the State to protect its citizens, happening in many parts of the world, especially in the African continent and Afghanistan. I suspect that one of the reasons for the prohibition on women going out alone unescorted by an adult male or driving alone in some societies is a hangover from the times when the State could not protect effectively all its citizens, especially women. On the other hand, where governments observe all the elements of rule of law and create mechanisms for impartial and speedy delivery of justice, they create not only peace for all citizens but also lay the foundations for the journey towards prosperity.

It is the responsibility of every system of government to ensure that those people who are governed are enabled to live peaceably, their lives are safe, their property is safe and they can pursue their vocation and earn their livelihood without any fear. Also, if they have any grievances, they can resort to officially sanctioned and accepted institutions for seeking remedies, for which laws and institutions are established and these can be relied upon to deliver fair, even-handed and speedy justice. From the perspective of ensuring that the society is able to advance economically and socially, it is also necessary to establish a regulatory framework, both laws and institutions, which sanctions and safeguards the sanctity of contracts, resolves disagreements and conflicts and holds those who violate contracts and agreements accountable. All these elements are the essence of the rule of law and good governance. If these are not prevalent, then everyone lives in a state of insecurity, orderly life is not possible, people's lives are at risk, there can be no security of property and one can move around only at great risk. The only way to be safe and safeguard oneself, one's family or assets is to have a more lethal weapon than the next man. There can be no safety for one's savings or investment and hence, there can be no prospects for development either. When the State fails to provide these basics, the ground is fertile for internecine conflicts, interference from external forces and emergence of alternative systems which offer better prospects for peace and progress. This is how revolutions have happened in many parts of the world.

When the State fails to establish the rule of law, not only does such a State and society become vulnerable to lawless elements and international terrorists to establish themselves, but since there is no employment being generated, as there is no growth, the population provides a fertile ground for recruitment for terrorists. It becomes a menace to international order. Take the case of growth in international piracy from countries such as Somalia. They target the huge volume of traffic on the seal lanes through which so much of international trade flows. This has serious consequences for international trade as ship owners demand protection, are less willing to deploy their vessels, freight and insurance costs go up and naval and coast guard forces are often called upon to rescue vessels and sailors. Hence, breakdown of governance in one country has implications for not only internal security of the country concerned, but international security as well. As globalization and economic integration increases the magnitude of this problem will increase, casting a burden on international systems of security management.

All societies function on the basis of trust and the rule of law provides the vital underpinning for generation and prevalence of trust between individuals, between the individual and the society and for the orderly functioning and progress of the society. If law and order breaks down, there can be the end of trust as mechanisms to ensure that trust prevails cease to function. Every transaction, every contract, every act that the individual performs, such as savings and investment, depends upon trust and only if the rule of law and good standards of governance prevail, will trust flourish and the society be enabled to go forward.

Hence, for both security and development, good governance is essential and those countries which have been able to provide high standards of governance have invariably provided both security and development for all their citizens. Peace, prosperity and good governance are intimately intertwined.

The fact that there has been a continuous decline in the quality of our institutions, making it difficult for the country to attain both peace and prosperity has been argued in the earlier chapters. Given the fact that excellence in governance is so fundamental for economic development and for security, the need for improving all aspects of quality of governance, especially those connected with the rule of law, needs hardly any emphasis. Unfortunately efforts to reform the process of dispensation of justice have not yielded tangible results but met with howls of protests from those who seem to benefit from the delays and lack of fairness. Criminals, therefore, do not get punished in this country and anyone with the required resources can take full advantage of the innumerable loopholes and immense scope for delay to escape punishment for the most heinous of crimes.

The failure to create the basic elements of rule of law undermines the confidence of the ordinary law-abiding citizen in the efficacy of the institutions created for dispensation of justice, and for the law breaker the system seems to be tailor-made for escaping punishment. Crimes are committed on an increasing scale once the system creates the impression that there is nothing to fear from law, and one can get away with anything. The situation gets complicated if criminals start enjoying political patronage, acquiring virtual immunity from every law enforcing agency. Such lawlessness undermines the safety and security of the ordinary citizen, who is entitled to redressal from the police or the judiciary but is unable to get either fair or speedy justice and hence, grievances tend to build up. In the process, respect for law and the institutions which symbolize the awesome majesty of law are lost and once this happens, it becomes increasingly difficult to maintain law and order.

In India, as noted earlier, we have a fine and noble Constitution which contains all the elements which constitute the rule of law. It lays down all the basic principles of good and effective governance and creates all the mechanisms for high standards of governance. We have unfortunately allowed these elements to be broken mainly by those very persons responsible for ensuring their observation. This does amount to a breakdown of the rule of law, and denial of the fundamental rights guaranteed by the Constitution and undermines the very basis of civilized and orderly conduct of the affairs of the society. There are swathes of the country where such a situation does prevail and this does not permit economic and social progress to take place and its impact is most severe on the poorer segments of society. There is no security for them, no justice is available, and they are denied even the basic of amenities and services. Since no investment can take place in the areas where such near-anarchic conditions prevail, there can be no development or creation of employment opportunities; the people are condemned to desperate poverty and hopeless deprivation.

That the virus of decline in the standards of performance in the civil services and the police as well as the judiciary has spread progressively deeper and wider, and there is no real effort to arrest the decline, has been covered in detail in an earlier chapter. The quality of intake into the services, particularly at the state level, their training, orientation, morale, motivation and public spiritedness have all suffered grievously. The bodies constituted to recruit public servants have become dens of corruption, nepotism and have been invariably politicized. Corruption is now so widespread that even the highest echelons have lost their reputation for integrity. Every department of life of the citizen and every programme of the government has suffered because of the inefficiency and corruption in the system.

Even such a hoary institution, that was meant to function as a watch dog for the entire system to ensure financial integrity and propriety, and which has been given an exalted status in our Constitution, namely the office of the Comptroller and Auditor General of India has become ineffective, unable to stem the rot that has set in. Very serious cases of financial malfeasance, misappropriation; and skullduggery, brought out by the C&AG, have had little impact on those responsible, primarily because the C&AG's reports have to go through a lengthy process before they become actionable, and so many other agencies have to take concrete measures before criminality is established and prosecutions can be launched. In the state governments, the seriousness with which audit objections are acted upon, has progressively declined, with the C&AG unable to take any effective corrective action. The fact that the C&AG has to rely on the public accounts committees consisting of legislators, many of whom may themselves have criminal background and little education, imposes its own limitations. If some of them belong to the ruling party they take active measures to see that nothing concrete happens.

In the process, all the services have by now lost the confidence of the people. This tale of sustained decline has been well documented above. Suffice it to stress that the citizens have come to regard the entire structure as parasitical and incapable of solving any of their problems. There are, no doubt, strong exceptions but the percentage of such exceptions has been on the decline. Again, there are pronounced variations among the states.

When we have a situation in the country where the laws of the country are not enforced, when all wings of the law enforcement machinery cannot be trusted to control crime and redress citizens' grievances, when the legislatures and the judiciary fail to discharge their constitutional responsibilities, when the executive fails to solve the problems of the people and provide them basic services, the ground is fertile for the citizens' frustrations to find expression in violence and for the citizen to seek alternative solutions outside the framework of the Constitution. This, to my mind, is the fundamental cause for armed insurgency, the growth of Naxalism and demands for separation in parts of the country.

The inference seems to be inevitable that a fine Constitution is not an absolute guarantee of good governance. It must, however, be stated that a good Constitution is necessary for proper governance of the country. Indeed, but for the Constitution, this country could have fallen into worse times and may have met with the same fate as some other countries whose citizens did not have the protection of a Constitution which recognizes and safeguards their rights. A good Constitution is, it appears, a necessary condition but not a sufficient condition for good governance. A great deal depends upon the manner in which the mechanisms created by the Constitution are enabled to function by those responsible for governance, paying due regard to the spirit and the principles behind the various provisions.

It will be worth taking note of the observations of a former Prime Minister of Great Britain, Lord Balfour in this context. He stated "Constitutions are easily copied, temperaments are not. It matters little if people have all other gifts but are wanting in this respect. For example, if they have no capacity for grading their loyalties, if they have no natural inclination for liberty, no natural respect for law, if they have no good humour and tolerate foul play, if they do not know the art of compromise, if corruption does not repel them and if their divisions tend to be either too numerous or too profound, the successful working of institutions of the British model may be difficult if not impossible." Did our Constitution makers in their eagerness to provide a model edifice, borrow ideas without assessing their suitability and adaptability? Is the Constitution only a top dressing on a poorly prepared soil of India?

As Henry Kissinger observes in his introduction to Lee Kwan Yew's book *"From the Third World to the First"*, "Institutions in the West did not spring full blown from the brow of contemporaries but evolved over centuries which shaped frontiers and defined legitimacy, constitutional provisions and basic values. Institutions in the West developed gradually and civil society evolved side by side with the maturation of the modern State. This made possible the growth of representative institutions which confined the State's power to those matters which society could not deal with its own arrangements. Political conflicts were moderated by overriding purpose." On the contrary, in most new States, institutions had to be put in place in elaborate form at one stroke. Such a situation creates the need for dealing with a whole lot of problems which require mature leadership inspired by a national purpose. India is, at the moment, severely lacking in this respect and measures to remedy this brook no delay.

10
ELECTORAL REFORMS

It is a well established axiom that the efficiency and effectiveness of every system is determined by the quality of the people who run the system. This is a fundamental law of nature and in nature; the law of survival of the fittest operates, often quite brutally. Fitness to hold the particular responsibility at each and every level is contingent upon the person's qualification to hold the job in terms of education, training, motivation and his accountability for performance. These considerations have indeed been applied with respect to two major arms of our constitutional system, namely the judiciary and the permanent executive. However, in our country unfortunately, as regards the political executive, which is formed out of the legislature, none of these considerations have been applied. Equally importantly, none of these considerations have also been applied to the legislatures, both at the Centre and in the states.

While to become a magistrate or judge or even an assistant in any establishment, there are job specifications and prescribed qualifications and the fitness to hold the responsibility is tested on an objective basis through what are basically transparent and open procedures, for holding the job of even the President of India and the Prime Minister, leave alone that of other ministers or legislators, no qualification except that of being a citizen of India and above a certain age, is required. Equally importantly, there is no programme at any level for training our legislators or members of the political executive. As to accountability, as we have seen, this operates only at the time of elections and even here, the qualifications, experience or performance have ceased to be the considerations for selection.

In India today, while for every position of responsibility, in both the public sector and in the private sector, despite considerable dilution of standards, there are clearly defined criteria for selection, appointment, assignment of responsibilities and advancement, generally based upon qualifications, experience and performance, our legislators and members of the political executive of the country enjoy the distinction of being permitted to hold responsibilities and enjoy a whole lot of privileges without any qualifications. Unlike every area of human endeavour, there is no quality assurance or quality control mechanism for the process of selection of our rulers alone in this country. It needs to be underlined that among all the arms of governance, it is the political executive which is most powerful as it lays down policies and programmes and decides on vital questions of nation's welfare, progress and security. Yes, it is they who are responsible for safeguarding the nation's security, both external and internal, its integrity and territorial sovereignty. Decisions of such overwhelming importance with vast implications for the country and every citizen, such as going to war, to combat external aggression and preparedness to meet any threat to the nation, are in the hands of the political executive. The actions of the political executive and the decisions this arm of governance takes and the policies it formulates impinge on the lives of every citizen, especially so as we have created a welfare State. What the political executive and the legislatures do or fail to do impacts on the common man most intimately. The everyday life and well-being of every citizen rests in the hands of those who are part of these august bodies.

The power of appointment and disposition of the other arms of the structure of governance, namely the judiciary and the permanent executive, are also vested in the political executive. The legislature, from which the political executive is derived, is the supreme body to make laws and regulations which determine the fate of the people and give them their protection, while regulating almost all aspects of their lives. For discharging such a set of onerous responsibilities, one must have a great deal of knowledge, competence and expertise. Unfortunately, our system does not require this. We have indeed entrusted the fate of the nation and its future to a set of people who are singularly lacking in the attributes required to bear such humongous responsibilities and is it any wonder, that the nation finds itself in such dire straits?

We have adopted the British system, as far as the political executive is concerned and in Britain as well as in many other countries, the system where the political executive is chosen from the legislators who are elected prevails and in these countries as well no particular qualification or experience in prescribed for holding the job of a minister or member of Parliament. However, in all these countries, with education being universal, with large participation in higher education and high standards of probity being the norm, members of the political executive and legislators are well qualified for their jobs. The electorate being highly educated, the exercise of franchise is also not only well organized but carried out with intelligence and discrimination. Also, the system is the result of a long process of evolution and refinement. In fact, it took several centuries for the institutions to assume the form in which we see them today and along with this evolutionary process, the civil society itself went through a process of maturing. Further, in all these countries, the other arms of governance have been given the required degree of independence and guarantees against political interference and everyone plays by the rules. Institutional mechanisms which ensure accountability and internal systems of checks and balances operate effectively. Most importantly, with an educated and vigilant electorate and an equally vigilant and free press, performance and fulfilment of promises is indeed the primary if not the only consideration for re-election. In some countries such as Switzerland major issues of national importance are decided by a national referendum.

We have, as per our Constitution, a multi-party democracy, based on universal adult suffrage and in theory, it is the people who have the right to choose the leaders, those who run the government and on the basis of their performance, change them for a better alternative every five years. In practice, however, once the elections are completed and those who win assume their offices, those who elect them have no say in the manner in which they conduct themselves. It is like contracting a marriage where one of the spouses has full freedom to act as he or she pleases and there is no remedy available to the other party, who has to suffer in silence. There is no provision for a peaceful separation when the misbehaviour becomes intolerable, as we have no right to recall those who have been elected.

In the first years of independence, as we have seen earlier with those who were in politics, had been brought up on Gandhian traditions with high level of patriotism and a record of self-sacrifice, we had a crop of leaders both at the Centre and the States who were committed to the welfare and progress of the country. The leadership was no doubt guided by the prevailing creed of socialism and state sponsored and state driven economic philosophy but standards of probity were indeed high. The system, however, has suffered a continuous decline and today, we have legislatures in which many are not educated in the real sense of the term, a large number have criminal background and most are corrupt. Their real interest is almost exclusively to look after their own interest, that of the caste or community group to which they belong and at best of the party.

The question as to why have we reached this point where all the principles of good governance enshrined in our Constitution have been thrown to the winds needs therefore to be addressed. Why have we not been able to provide peace or prosperity to our people as detailed in the previous chapters? Why are so many poor and why are so many children malnourished and why have our standards of probity declined so precipitously? I feel particularly sad that we who started our independent existence with such great ideals, symbolized by Gandhi who set such a fine example and such high standards of morality by his personal conduct, have gone down and lost our moral moorings. We who articulated such a grand vision for our people in the Constitution have fallen so low in a mere six decades. What a fall it has been, when I and you and all of us fell down while immorality swept over all of us.

Very briefly, the reasons are:

a. Our leadership has not been able to appreciate that strong institutions are performance enhancing instruments in their hands, and are vital for good governance. Promises made at election time cannot be delivered as the delivery system is dysfunctional.
b. Our leaders' main, if not the only concern, seems to be to somehow win the next election. Many are terrified of

losing elections as they are afraid that those who come to power may start bring out all the skeletons that they have accumulated in their respective cupboards.

c. Performance and credentials as considerations for election have declined continuously in importance.
d. Consequently, the leadership is not interested in good governance and performance.
e. Elections are won not because of performance, but on the basis of money and muscle power and by working out the right caste and community equations and announcing freebees or subsidies even if this bankrupts the State or leads to hyper inflation. Today, the outcome in all elections is invariably determined by the four Cs, namely Caste, Cash, Communalism and Criminals.
f. This has been possible and is happening all the while, because of our flawed and unsuitable electoral system.
g. This system, called the "first past the post system", makes a candidate a winner even if he gets a minority of votes, so long as each of the other contenders get numerically less votes than him.
h. This encourages every candidate to cultivate a small minority which will vote for him irrespective of his credentials or his performance in office by appealing to their caste, community, tribal and religious loyalties, exacerbating their insecurity, creating insecurity even if there is none and presenting himself as their only saviour. The effort all the while is to win and retain this group's loyalty at all costs. This has actively encouraged divisive tendencies all over the country, each group encouraged to be suspicious and distrustful of the other. Even engineering communal riots and rewarding the rioters is acceptable.
i. This scenario has been worsened by the growth in population, revolution of rising expectations and the unbridled and fierce competition for limited economic opportunities.

Losing faith in the present system, because of repeated failures to deliver, people have been forced to opt for alternative systems to get their grievances settled and ills remedied. Naxalism, private armies, insurgency, riots and violence, frequent necessity to seek judicial remedies even for purely executive matters, are all the result of disillusionment if not despair with the system.

Since I have interacted with insurgents of various hues from the North-East, I can testify to the hopelessness and despair of young men who are driven to take up arms against the State, knowing very well that death stalks them all the while. The average survival rate of an insurgent in Assam is just about three years.

We cannot improve our citizen's security, eliminate poverty and engineer a sustained growth path, while safeguarding the environment, if we do not improve drastically the prevalent standards of governance. I am of the firm opinion that this will not happen if there is no improvement in the quality of those who govern us. The present system cannot achieve this. Let us have a quick look at what the present system really is.

The present system does not demand that our leaders are qualified to do their job. Merit and achievement are immaterial even while the country is aspiring to become a 'Knowledge Society'. There is nothing to prevent criminals from becoming ministers. They are invariably above the law. Accountability and performance do not count. Indeed, you can pass on the job to your wife, children and grandchildren and make enough money for the next ten generations. They all demand and obtain high security. No less than 400 policeman were earmarked for the security of the Chief Minister of UP whereas Nehru or Patel had, if at all, one security guard and CMs such as Rajagopalachari or Kamaraj used to walk around without any protection. It has been calculated that on average every politician is guarded by at least three policemen whereas there is one policeman for every 1730 citizens in this country. In Maharashtra there was an attempt to down grade the security provided for the politicians so that some 400 policeman can be spared for opening three or four much needed police stations. Needless to say that the move met with stiff resistance and the CM had to drop the move. The only exception is the newly elected CM of Goa, Manohar Parikar, who has drastically cut down his security. That our leaders feel so insecure and fear their own people so much is indeed strange.

My argument is that these legislators are really speaking, not in reality representatives of the people and in a democracy;

legislators have no place if they do not represent the people in the true sense of the word. We were fortunate that that the first generation leaders were patriots and idealists, were highly educated and they did represent the people but with Gandhi a fading memory, the succeeding generations are both ignorant and arrogant.

This is because of the extremely flawed electoral system that we have in this country, is an exact copy of the British System. Britain is a totally different kettle of fish compared to our highly fragmented and caste ridden polity. This electoral system called the 'first past the post' system is to my mind the fundamental reason for most of our ills. Everyday, we see headlines stating that the caste factor is going to determine the outcome of this election or the other, and every party is always busy analyzing the caste and community composition of one constituency after the other before every election. The media is not far behind in playing this game and highlighting this all the while.

In India, people do not cast their vote, but vote their caste. Our leaders encourage this and every party devises strategies to get the dominant caste or creed to support them by any means. Our unity and integrity, yes even our sovereignty, is undermined by our leaders seeking such narrower and narrower loyalties.

An example will be in order to prove the point. In any constituency on an average only 60 per cent cast their vote. Out of this, a candidate who gets, say 15 per cent of the votes, becomes the MLA or MP and then a minister, so long as the other contenders get even one vote less. This "first part the post" system, which is like a horse race, enables a person to call himself a representative of the people and garner all the privileges, power and authority even if he gets the vote of just 10 per cent of the total electorate in the particular constituency. He is not generally speaking the representative of 90 per cent of even one constituency of this vast country, but is given the power to lord over the entire population. And this means there is an in-built incentive to divide the electorate on the basis of caste, creed or language and larger the number of contenders, the more divided the electorate gets. In many of the elections, the number of contenders is often ten or twelve times the number of seats contested. Some have been propped up purely in order to divide the votes and some withdraw if they are given sufficient inducement. This proves the point that the winning candidate has only to command and retain the loyalty of that small minority which he woos by appealing to their narrow interests and on the basis of caste, creed, language, tribe or whatever. There is no point in bemoaning the ascendancy of casteism or communalism, because the system confers victory and power only on this basis. There is in our electoral system an in-built incentive nay compulsion to divide the electorate in every possible way. Our Parliament and legislatures are not forums of representatives of the majority of the people, which is what democracy is all about but a collection of individuals, each representing one small segment of one constituency. It is this collection which determines the fate of the entire nation. No wonder, interests of particular segments have overriding priority over national interests. Take the case of a party called Pattali Makkal Katchi (PMK). This party is exclusively of a small community called Vanniyars, deep south in Tamil Nadu and an MP elected on the basis of the votes of this small segment of the country's electorate demands and gets the Union health portfolio, merely because his family runs a number of medical colleges in Tamil Nadu. How can such a person comprehend the complex issues related to health-care or medical education of the entire nation? All that he is interested in is furthering the interests of his small community and his family connections. How can we rely on this collection of narrow interests to safeguard the nation's security and plan and strive for the progress and prosperity of the whole nation? That many are criminals (156 members of the present Parliament have cases pending against them in one court or the other), most are corrupt and very few if at all have any qualification or competence to discharge their onerous responsibilities completes the picture. Take the example of the 2007 assembly elections in India's largest state—UP. According to a survey by the *Times of India,* 20 out of the total seats of 403 were won by contestants who got 10 per cent or less of the total votes. In another 306 constituencies, the winners came in with votes between 10 and 20 per cent. In another 66 cases, the winning candidates bagged between 20 per cent and 25 per cent of the votes. Ten seats were won by obtaining 25 per cent to 30 per cent and for only one seat, did the winner score above 30 per cent. Moreover, the margins between the winners and losers were wafer thin. In 122 constituencies, the winner had margins between

1,001 and 5,000. The average margin, in all the 403 constituencies was 9,231. It needs to be noted that the size of the electorate in most constituencies in UP runs into millions. The pattern in most states is roughly the same and is repeated in subsequent elections and is only marginally different in the case of Lok Sabha elections. How can such people parade themselves as representatives of the people and don the mantle of leadership, to rule the state and the country and enjoy all the privileges, when they do not represent even a simple majority in a single constituency? How can criminals who contest this type of elections, claim that they have been acquitted by the people's court? How can we, the people, allow this farce to continue and allow those who are not truly the representatives of the people to determine the fate of the nation? How can we call this a representative democracy? Let me emphasize that a person of such great eminence as Dr. Manmohan Singh who has been Prime Minister for over eight years now, is not a member of the Lok Sabha, a true representative of the people of any constituency, as our electoral system based on non-merit and caste considerations will not ensure his election. He has been a member of the Rajya Sabha and that too from Assam and not his own state, namely the Punjab. What chances do great achievers such as Narayanmurthy have in this flawed system? No wonder our top leadership is so bereft of talent and unable to take care of the core interests of the nation.

Good governance is not on their radar as it is not essential to gain or remain in power and the repeated expression of concern for the poor or the '*aam admi*' is nothing but a device to garner votes.

Fundamental reforms in the method of electing our leaders are therefore the paramount and immediate requirement. We must do away with this extremely flawed methodology for selecting those who govern us and in whose incompetent hands the fate of the nation, its security, peace and progress lies. Without this, we cannot have a better future and the nation will continue to suffer from a thousand cuts.

India's international profile has gone up substantially in recent years, thanks to the relative acceleration of our growth rates and our successes in the field of information technology and a variety of industrial projects. But this is entirely because of the contribution of a select few entrepreneurs, the Narayanamurthys,

Tatas, Mittals, Ramadorais, Mahindras and great academicians, Amratya Sen, Bhagawati, Raghuram Rajan, etc., and not our caste-based politicians. On the other hand, the kind of failures, thanks to such politicians, such as our widespread poverty, squalor, malnutrition, infant mortality, etc., damage India's image.

The Roman dictum "if you want peace, be prepared for war" holds good even today and today's wars are fought and won not so much in the field of battle but across conference tables; through diplomacy, economic might, covert operations, intelligence, etc., reflecting comprehensive national power. By weakening all our institutions, we have undermined our chances of winning today's and tomorrow's battles. Those who are elected through this flawed system do not understand the value of strong institutions and they have been unfortunately devoting most of their energy and time in undermining the efficacy of the system. It suits their purpose to have weak and pliable institutions and weak and pliable persons in these institutions who can be made to behave in a manner that betters their electoral prospects.

Anecdotal evidence suggests that foreigners are very much aware of this weakness in our system and when they cannot get their way at the official level discussions, they ask for a one-to-one meeting with the leader of the delegation, invariably the Minister and get whatever concessions they want. Witness the confidence with which diplomats and ministers from Pakistan conduct negotiations and perform before the media, presenting a great contrast to what our ministers achieve.

At the same time, it must be pointed out that the level of responsibility displayed by the civil society needs vast improvement. I have, in this context, advocated a theorem called the "doctrine of reciprocity" in an earlier chapter. I have also stressed the need to enforce the Constitutional provisions regarding 'fundamental duties' as much as 'fundamental rights' if not more.

It is often asked as to why the same Indians who behave so badly inside the country, throw garbage everywhere and go about damaging public property; behave so well as soon as they cross the Bay of Bengal and land in Singapore. The answer is that there is rule of law enforced fully, impartially and respect and fear of law is cultivated by an enlightened leadership which does not interfere with agencies who are responsible for these tasks.

My thesis is that even within the present Constitution, a whole lot can be done to bring about the desired reforms. The Supreme Court and the Election Commission's valiant attempts supplemented by NGOs to improve the system have achieved some success but unfortunately, they have met with devious counter-steps to negate these. These do not, to my mind, touch the core issues. Even the much talked about model code of conduct which appeals to the sense of decency and morality is violated with impunity as it has no coercive power.

While in the first two decades of our independence, leaders particularly in the Central Government, considered issues from a national perspective and took decisions which served the national interest; unfortunately in recent times, the particular electoral politics dictated by the "first past post system" has undermined this very important aspect of the decision-making process. Progressively leaders have worked for solutions even on vital national issues, based on narrow political considerations. The electoral prospects of the party concerned dictated by caste arithmetic, narrow regional and sectarian considerations and in a secular country, even religious considerations, have become increasingly important in the decisionmaking process. How do we accept openly communal parties such as Indian Union Muslim League of Kerala and Ittahudul Musalmeen of Andhra Pradesh as secular and enter into electoral alliance with these? Whether particular decisions can be sold to a narrow segment of the electorate as beneficial to that limited segment, improving the electoral prospects of the party to which the minister belongs, is considered far more important than rational considerations, even if there can be a potential conflict between the interest of that particular electoral segment and that of the larger community. While, no doubt in a multi-party democracy, a party's electoral prospects are important, unfortunately the electoral prospects in a particular state and equally importantly, in a particular constituency are often given greater importance and individual ministers have had no hesitation in espousing causes of this nature even in the face of rational arguments and even if such policies have the potential to bring about further division and stratification of an already fragmented society.

Such a flawed decision-making process, and appeal to narrow

segments of the electorate will continue to plague our national polity, so long as the "first part the post" electoral system is not done away with.

When elections can be won on the basis of this formula performance of the machinery becomes less and less important and all that needs to be done is to show how successfully the particular narrow interests of that segment of the electorate have been defended against the nefarious machinations of others and as to how no other can be relied upon to do this. The high principles of good governance enshrined in the Constitution—equity and justice for all, non-discriminatory application of law, welfare and progress of the society—can all be ignored without any adverse consequences for electoral prospects. In the process, institutions get progressively neglected having lost their value to the political masters. Let us recall in this context what Dr. S. Radhakrishnan stated when the process of Constitution making was completed and I quote "Our opportunities are great but let me warn you that when power outstrips ability we will fall on evil days". We have lost sight of these words as indeed of all those who warned that the ultimate test of the Constitution will be the manner in which it is implemented and the quality of those who implement it.

We should, therefore, change our electoral laws to ensure that a candidate does not get elected unless he gets at least 51 per cent of the votes polled. Such a system prevails in France and Germany. This will immediately encourage candidates to try and garner the support of a wider spectrum of electoral interests. Further, we should also examine whether we can declare an election invalid unless a minimum percentage of the registered voters actually cast their votes. It is understood that the Venkatachalliah Commission on Constitutional reforms has called for a review of the "first past the post" electoral system and Chief Election Commissioners such as M.S. Gill and Gopalaswamy have also suggested such a review. My suggestion would be to have a two stage election process where in the first stage, all those candidates who do not secure a minimum share of say 20 per cent are eliminated and the rest made to go through a second stage. If any of the candidates still fails to get 51 per cent, a third round will have to be held. My thesis is once this system takes root; all political parties will be wary of concentrating on one narrow segment of the electorate and will select candidates who have a wider appeal. Yes initially there will be an increase in costs and elections may take longer. I believe these are minor difficulties compared to the enormous damage that the present system is doing. This reform should be combined with a provision of not recognizing parties which do not more than a minimum percentage of support as evidenced in two successive elections. I am sure the nation and the political parties will soon adjust themselves to the new dispensation.

The second reform will have to be to ensure that criminals do not contest elections. This could be brought about by political parties refusing to give tickets to criminals, i.e. those against whom charge sheets have been framed by a court of law and not only those who have been actually convicted. After all the court goes through a lengthy process of convincing itself that there is indeed a *prima facie* case against the accused before framing charges. But this may be asking too much of our political parties at the present moment, because even those who swear by high ideals have shown no serious intent to deny criminals tickets if it is believed that such candidates can actually win elections and boost the electoral prospects of the particular party. Nevertheless it is high time we introduced this reform.

Can we educate our voters not to vote for criminals or alleged criminals, and on caste or creed considerations? This again seems quite difficult in the present circumstances, though there is no reason as to why civil society and non-governmental organizations should not undertake a campaign to educate the voters.

The solution is to bring in legislative changes in the Representation of Peoples Act, to ensure that those against whom charge sheets have been framed for a criminal offence punishable by a two year sentence in a court of law, after due investigation, are automatically barred from contesting elections. We have unfortunately, to my mind adopted the principle that a person is innocent until proved guilty in a court of law, the onus of proof being on the prosecution. This is a principle of the British jurisprudence and has not been accepted in many countries even in Europe. For example, in France the onus of proof is on the accused, he is considered guilty till proved innocent, after a court conducts an inquisitorial process where the court is not a neutral umpire but one actively seeking the truth. Such a procedure should apply only to serious cases—murder, rape, misuse and misappropriation of public funds, corruption and terrorist related crimes. Knowing how difficult it is in this country to prove a man guilty and how easy it is for those who have the necessary resources to manipulate the system to ensure that they are not convicted, I see great merit in adopting the French model when it comes to the question of allowing people to contest elections. The reason simply is that we want leaders who have unimpeachable integrity and not those who are free to roam around even after committing heinous crimes and contest elections to become law makers, merely because our system of justice is so slow, cumbersome and is so much weighed in favour of those who commit crimes.

One must acknowledge the very commendable initiatives taken by the Supreme Court of India and the Election Commission, to work towards greater transparency in the electoral system, reducing the role of criminals in politics within the existing limitations; by taking advantage of the right to information. These have unfortunately not created positive resonance from the political parties, because such disclosures can be to their disadvantage. Fortunately, there are some very dedicated campaigners for electoral reforms and decriminalization of politics and they are continuing the battle for a cause that is so vital for the future of democracy in this country.

It must also be acknowledged that the Election Commission of India has been progressively tightening up the electoral system to ensure the impartiality of the entire machinery and the processes involved and enable conduct of free and fair elections. The introduction of electronic voting machines have been a big step forward in the efforts to reducing rigging, false voting and other ills.

The other reforms, vital in character are to:

a. Make education a mandatory requirement for contesting elections. Pakistan has done this.
b. In addition to the present ban on those convicted, let us also ban those against whom the CBI and the courts have come to the conclusion that there is a *prima facie* case and charges have been framed, from contesting elections.

c. Voting should be made compulsory, and voters should have the option of recording a negative vote, i.e. in addition to the list of contesting candidates, there should be a provision—NONE OF THESE. We can also introduce online voting. This will make political parties consider more closely the quality of candidates they field and reduce the possibility of a contestant getting elected with a small minority of votes.
d. The right to recall a non-performing legislator should be given to the voters of the particular constituency.
e. It is necessary to increase greatly the participation of the educated in the electoral process. Today, the educated do not go to vote, as it is considered a hassle, a waste of time and the belief that their vote just does not count. We cannot now go back and prescribe education as the basic qualification for voting, but we can introduce a system where along with adult universal franchise, a vote by a person with no education will count as one vote, a matriculate's as two votes, a graduate's as three, post-graduate four and a Ph.D., five votes. This will be a big incentive for all the educated to join the queue to vote and the contenders will start paying attention to the views of the educated. This will be also a great incentive for everyone to get educated and we will soon have universal literacy and much greater interest in higher education. Refinements to provide for technical education, etc., can be considered. This will encourage the educated to believe that their vote does indeed count and there is value in participating in the voting process. To my mind, this will also encourage the educated to stand for elections and the political parties to nominate the educated as candidates.
f. We have also to address the issue of money and muscle power in elections as these have direct links with criminalization of politics and corruption in public life. Use of muscle power will come down as soon as the educated start participating in the voting process and more and more educated come into politics. Curbing money power and distribution of freebies during elections can be curbed by imposing a ban on use of public funds,

> in the name of welfare schemes at least six months prior to elections. Control of election expenditure through legislation is very difficult and public funding of elections will not only cast a huge burden on the public exchequer but can be misused by forming parties merely to get funds. If voters can be educated to avoid getting influenced by freebies and money, this evil will come down substantially. Already, this is happening as in Tamil Nadu where the DMK was comprehensively defeated even after open bribery of voters.

We can surely look at the example of Singapore, which at the time Lee Kwan Yew tookover, was considered one of the most corrupt in the region. He first ensured that a fully empowered institutional framework was established backed by well conceived legislation. He then set a personal example in observing the highest standards of integrity, ensured that all his ministers were incorruptible and the law was applied without fear or favour and in a non-discriminatory manner. Even long standing associates were not spared if they were suspected of any wrong-doing. Lee Kwan Yew also ensured that all his ministers and civil servants were well paid and there was no necessity whatsoever for them to indulge in corrupt practices. He understood that corruption grows when the cost of fighting elections keeps increasing. He laid down limits for election expenses and prohibited a number of practices such as arranging for the transport of voters, sanctioning pre-election goodies and post election largesse. He showed, more than anything else, that he had the political will to enforce the regulations and demonstrated that elections can be won through performance and fulfilment of promises and nothing else is necessary.

The question as to how to make the educated middle classes more interested in the electoral process and indeed in politics as a career option and competing for becoming leaders of the country needs to be squarely addressed. This, I am convinced, will eliminate a great deal of the ills that are at this moment afflicting our polity. The middle class in India is indeed expanding and it is educated. We should motivate them to come out and vote and they will do so, if they start realizing that their vote does indeed matter and can surely determine the outcome of elections. This will happen if, as argued earlier, the 'first past the post' system is changed and a candidate needs the support of at least 51 per cent of the votes to get elected. No candidate can then afford to ignore the educated middle class. As per a survey by the McKinsey Global Institute in the year 2000, the middle class, that is households with an income between Rs. 1,00,000 and Rs. 5,00,000 per year formed about 35 per cent of which those above Rs. 2,00,000 were just 5 per cent. By 2008, this had significantly changed and this group, i.e. between Rs. 1,00,000 and Rs. 5,00,000 had become nearly 45 per cent of which those above Rs. 2,00,000 had become nearly 10 per cent. At this time, the rich, i.e. more than Rs. 5,00,000 but less than Rs. 10,00,000 had reached a respectable 3 per cent. By 2020, the figures will improve and those in the group of Rs. 2,00,000 to Rs. 5,00,000 will be something like 25 per cent of the population and the rich, i.e. those between Rs. 5,00,000 and Rs. 10,00,000 would have become 10 per cent. In 2030, there will be dramatic increase in incomes and the number in the group of households with incomes from Rs. 2,00,000 all the way past one million, will form some 51 per cent of the households in India.

Such developments will have vast implications for the way politics is practised in our country.

Since we have seen that funding of elections compels politicians to become corrupt and elections are becoming more costly all the while, in my view, the following reforms with respect to funding of elections need to be considered.

a. Remove the ban on contributions to political parties by corporate entities. There can be proper rules prescribed for such contributions, so that they are transparent, above board, properly accounted for and audited.
b. Impose realistic ceilings on expenditure as also classify what are legitimate electoral expenses. These should then be enforced vigorously and violations must result in disqualification from contesting elections.
c. What constitute corrupt practices during an election should be comprehensively defined and legal provisions incorporated in the Representation of Peoples Act, making indulgence in corrupt practices as a criminal and cognizable offence punishable under law. The model code

of conduct has served a useful purpose but while it has imposed certain restrains on the conduct of political parties, so far at least, even the most blatant violations have not invited deterrent action. It would be appropriate to consider violations of the model code of conduct as offences which can be subject to legal action. An appropriate provision to this effect can be incorporated in the Representation of Peoples Act. The Election Commission should be empowered to declare as invalid the election of anyone committing what is regarded as corrupt practice and debarred for contesting election for ten years.

d. It is very important that awareness among citizens is improved to ensure that they do not fall victims to inducements and exercise their franchisee without fear or favour. Steps must be taken to encourage the educated classes to participate in the electoral process, so that our democracy increasingly assumes a more representative character and those contesting elections have to satisfy a more discriminating and intelligent constituency which can exercise its franchise on the basis of performance rather than being misled on the basis of narrow sectarian considerations.

e. As has happened in Singapore, we have to ensure that performance and fulfilment of promises becomes once again the only consideration for getting elected. This will automatically eliminate the need to give away pre-election and post-election goodies and offer inducement to electors to vote for particular candidates or parties.

Some leading intellectuals have in the light of the crisis facing the country suggested that it is time we switched over to the French presidential system. They feel that India is fast becoming a "failed state" as the British model of governace that we adopted at the time of independence has not been able to deliver and the present system of choosing those who govern us is fundamentally flawed.The French system in which the President is elected directly by the people and he has to obtain the support of at least 51 per cent of the electorate can result in the end of today's divisive politics. Such a President will also have the freedom to choose his cabinet and will be able to select experts from outside the party. However, such a drastic change may need the present constitution to be replaced by an altogether new one. It will be very difficult to achieve a consensus to make such a huge change. In my view, if we are able to get through the electoral and administrative reforms suggested in this book we can definitely avoid the prospects of becoming a failed state and indeed look forward a for a brighter future

11

ADMINISTRATIVE AND POLICE REFORMS

Adminstrative Reforms

There is, as discussed earlier, a well established and empirically validated relationship between peace and prosperity, underlining the fact that high standard of governance is one of the most essential elements in promoting rapid economic growth and social stability. All efforts to improve living standards can meet with little or no success, if the basic conditions for orderly social and economic progress are not created in a society and this can happen if and only if, the standards of governance are high. "Peace, easy taxes and a tolerable administration of justice" were indeed the preconditions for progress prescribed by Adam Smith in his "*Wealth of Nations*".

Good governance fundamentally is an expression of all the principles of rule of law. It is well known that the two major functions of the government are regulatory and developmental and the effectiveness of any government is determined by the efficiency; with which both functions are discharged. The two functions go hand in hand and indeed complement each other and need to be implemented with a clear vision, which articulates the government's commitment to the welfare and prosperity of all its citizens. The Constitution of India is an extraordinarily fine instrument created by our founding fathers, to lay the foundations based on which all governments can efficiently, effectively and responsively discharge all their responsibilities, taking care of both regulatory and development functions assuring peace and prosperity.

Unfortunately, however as we have seen, the idealism which inspired the founding fathers while framing of the Constitution and creation of the institutions of governance with the clear purpose of building the wherewithal for running the system answering to the requirement of the people, solving their problems and satisfying their aspirations, has to a large extent been lost; and as a consequence, the quality and efficacy of institutions have suffered grievous decline.

The administrative and police machinery, both at the Central and state levels is the prime instrument for upholding the rule of law and is responsible for both the development and the regulatory aspects of the governance, in all its dimensions. The absence of an efficient, effective and responsive administrative and police machinery is indeed a prescription for disorder and anarchy. Concerned over the continuous decline in the standards of administration and policing and the great difficulty experienced by ordinary citizens in obtaining justice or relief from the system and the deleterious impact that this has had on not merely the law and order situation in the country, but on economic and social development in almost all parts of India and the concerns expressed by several bodies and activists, the Government of India had constituted Administrative and Police Commissions, one after the other to make recommendations to remedy the situation. Of particular concern has been the rapid growth of insurgency, armed insurrection, sectarian conflicts and separatism, all of which are traceable to the collapse of the administrative and policing systems and the inability of the government to provide even basic services to the people. Poor standards of governance lead to dissatisfaction, disenchantment, disillusionment and ultimately to rebellion. This is a vicious cycle, as these in turn negate all chances of orderly progress, development of the economy and removal of basic grievances of the people. The functioning of the police in this context is of particular importance as the police do represent the most visible manifestation of the rule of law and the awesome majesty of law. This is indeed the case in advanced countries with high standards of governance and rule of law.

It may be recalled that an ARC was constituted under the Chairmanship of Morarji Desai and subsequently under Hanumanthayya. A third under Veerappa Moily has been functioning for some time now and is yet to complete its tasks. Much earlier, Nehru himself had commissioned A.D. Gorwala, an ICS officer of eminence, to suggest measures for reforms of administration and this body, among other things drew attention to the creeping corruption in administration even at the higher levels.

However, except the introduction of technology in certain areas of governance and a tinkering of some processes and procedures, no fundamental changes have been effected in order to bring about a sharp upgradation of the effectiveness, efficiency and responsiveness of the system. The recommendations of the commissions referred to above have not been acted upon. On the contrary, the processes and procedures have become even slower and in the recent past, corruption has seeped into all the layers. Consequently, it is near impossible for the ordinary citizen to get any relief from the system and the ability of the system to provide the most basic services has actually declined.

This is happening at a time when the concept of governance has been changing from that of mere enforcer and regulator, to that of a facilitator, for enabling the society to advance at faster pace, with regulatory systems that promote orderly progress avoiding all extremes. What is required is to put in place mechanisms which perform both regulatory and development functions efficiently and in tune with the changes in the environment for development. The ease with which business can be conducted, the speed with which clearances can be obtained and that too without corruption, the ready and adequate availability of essentials such as power and water supply, high class infrastructure, transportation and communication facilities; all are today the hallmarks of an efficient administration. The recent financial contagion that has afflicted many countries in the West has sharply underlined the fact that while economic freedom is important, there has also to be in place an adequate system of regulation and control. In the US, the regulatory mechanisms instituted by Roosevelt and Eisenhower, were dismantled by Reagan and Bush. Such a drawdown of regulatory mechanisms is regarded as one of the causes for today's problems in the US.

The successive reforms commissions mentioned above have not, it appears addressed any of these issues and in any case, whatever recommendations they had made do not seem to have been taken up for implementation by successive governments. Some states have also constituted such commissions and I do not think any action has been taken on these as well.

In my forty years in the government both at the centre and the states, what I have noticed is that in the Central Secretariat, due to the relatively higher quality of leadership both political and bureaucratic, the continuous pressure from the Parliament and set traditions, well laid down procedures and manuals, the system does grind finely, albeit slowly and things do get done, yes a little more slowly than say some thirty years back. Also, it has been my experience that individual officers make a great deal of difference. When a good, dynamic and action minded Secretary provides the right leadership and monitors performance and progress closely, the system chugs along faster. If he is replaced by a more cautious and relatively mediocre officer, who is just marking time, and who owes his elevation to political and other factors, the efficiency declines quite perceptibly.

In the states, the situation is generally far worse though there are variations between the states. This affects the common man quite severely. It must be stressed that states where the bureaucracy performs better are precisely those which have recorded better economic and social progress. In recent times, the worst affected by bureaucratic inefficiency are the so called BIMARU states.

The state of the administrative system and delivery mechanism and the decline that these have suffered over the years has been adequately covered in earlier chapters. Our purpose will be served if we now concern ourselves with the question of how to arrest the decline and bring about the necessary improvements so that we have a truly efficient public service and the vast amounts that the nation spends on maintaining the administrative machinery can be justified.

I believe that basically the system that we have is sound and is fully capable of performing well and meeting the challenges that we face, if it is allowed to function and is held accountable for its performance. My point is supported by the performance of the system at the time of elections when the system is galvanized to achieve specific goals in a time bound manner and given the freedom to get things done. Or take the case of the way the Delhi

Metro was constructed by the legendary E. Sreedharan with no cost or time overruns and meeting the best performance standards and best practices. Also, when the President's rule is applied in one state or the other, there is a visible improvement in performance standards, provided there is an efficient, politically neutral and experienced governer and advisors. No one can say that things cannot be done in this country or done properly.

The first issue that requires attention is the plethora of laws and regulations that we have in this country. We have central laws and state laws and with respect to concurrent subjects, there are both state and central laws on the same subject. India can easily be regarded as an over regulated but poorly governed country. Bodies such as the Law Commissions and the Ministry of Law have not paid attention to the need for a comprehensive review of the entire body of laws and regulations that continue to exist on our statute book for centuries. Many have not been implemented for long and many more are irrelevant for the India of today and a rapidly modernizing economy. A prime example is the number of labour laws which are a relic of the socialistic era and which have only stifled the growth of the economy and sadly stood in the way of employment generation. Industrialists would prefer to opt for labour saving technologies or evade the laws one way or the other. This and the outdated Factories Act are known to be fertile sources of corruption. These laws have spawned a rapacious bureaucracy that prey upon the industries and have outlived their purpose but efforts to amend them have been met with stiff resistance from vested interests. Another example is the regulations governing higher education which have stifled the much needed growth of technical education and again been source of corruption.

As a consequence of our socialist leanings, the government expanded and started performing a whole lot of functions which have nothing to do with governance. This was especially so in the sphere of economic development. We nationalized a lot of sectors, introduced a stifling regulatory framework for industrial development, altogether shut out private initiative from a large number of industries and created State monopolies and separate ministries for several of these. Yes, a lot has happened since 1991 and the government has indeed got out of several areas, permitted the entry of private initiative and simplified the licensing and control procedures. The Company Law has been amended. And so also, the Industries Development and Regulation Act. This has made the life of the ordinary man far more comfortable, given the consumer a choice among alternatives, increased competition and upgraded quality of goods and services. Growth has been boosted and the need for bribery and massive delays in getting even basic necessities such as a telephone has been reduced. The ministries that were created in the era of socialism, however, continue with an army of under-worked civil servants. If we can only have the courage to get out of more areas and reduce drastically the dependence of the ordinary man on the services of the government, India will be far better off. Yes, freedom of enterprise needs to be regulated in an adequate manner but it has been well established through empirical studies that countries with a higher degree of freedom of enterprise are precisely those which are more prosperous. A combination of a high degree of freedom of enterprise combined with an equally high degree of rule of law is the best combination one should aim at.

While cleansing the electoral system and changing the "first past the post system" is of paramount importance and should be tackled with the greatest urgency, in order to enhance the quality of leadership, one should also pay attention to the reforms that can be bought about in several areas of governance, so that the ultimate objective of providing the citizens of this country an effective, efficient and responsive administrative apparatus is achieved. Also, one should pay attention to reforms which can free the administrative machinery of undue political interference.

This can be achieved by permitting officers to discharge their functions mandated by law and exercise the powers conferred on them by law, by eliminating undue political interference. Laws of the land clearly envisage that the official machinery deals effectively with law and order situations, takes preventive action, curbs lawlessness and avoids loss of life and damage to property. But unfortunately over the years, there has been a tendency on the part of the officials to wait for instructions from the political executive and even from the MLAs before taking any steps. Serious damage to life and property is caused by such abject failure on the part of the officials to exercise powers conferred on them by law. This has happened because of demoralization and the tendency on the part of political executive to be guided by the views of MLAs even in matters relating to law and order, thereby robbing the civil servants and the police officers of the initiative that is so critical, in tackling ground level problems and nipping in the bud difficult situations, right at the initial stages.

Connected to the above is the need for avoiding frequent, whimsical, politically motivated and often caste-based transfers. It is essential that all functionaries are assured reasonable tenures, that the right persons are appointed for the right jobs and they are encouraged to perform their duties and tender impartial, professional advice.

There ought to be continuous increase in the employment of technology in all areas of administration to speed up processes, simplification of procedures, making the system much more citizen friendly, eliminating delay and improving delivery of services to ordinary citizens. Greater accountability and transparency in the conduct of public services and improvement in the efficiency and responsiveness of the services need also to be brought about. This can be achieved by improving the quality of intake into the government services, rewarding good performance and punishing the inefficient. At the moment unfortunately, those who perform not only do not get recognition but in fact, may not even get promoted because of the policy of reservation in promotion, a measure taken without any regard to Constitutional provisions regarding efficiency in public services and which has resulted in widespread demoralization and de-motivation in the entire governmental machinery.

The last issue to be tackled is the increasingly pervasive phenomenon of corruption. Corruption is eating into the vitals of our polity and the economy. Corruption is an indirect tax inflating the costs of all services. It imposes a greater burden on the poor who have no alternative but to depend upon public services.

India has the dubious distinction of being regarded as one of the most corrupt countries in the whole world and one of the least investor friendly. We have, no doubt, repeatedly talked about controlling corruption and have created institutions which are supposed to deal with corruption, particularly in public services. The Central Bureau of Investigation, the Central Vigilance Commission, the State Vigilance Commissions, the Controller and Auditor General of India, are all institutional mechanisms designed to control corruption and bring the culprits to book.

However, as is the case with all other institutions, the effectiveness of these mechanisms has also been progressively eroded and a sense of helplessness has descended on the country, leading to acceptance of corruption as a way of life. If a public servant is not corrupt, this is regarded as a rare exception. Increasingly, even the higher levels of the civil services; which were relatively free of corruption, are getting infected and even the judiciary has lost much of its character and the faith of the people in the judicial machinery has been seriously undermined. The procedure for appointment of higher judicial officers has opened the door for political interference and equally importantly, internal mechanisms within the judiciary to deal with corruption are ineffective, if not dysfunctional.

The question needs to be examined as to why the country has been sliding down into this abyss of corruption and non-performance. The most important reason, no doubts is our electoral process. Elections have become more and more costly. With the official ban on contributions to political parties by the corporate world, politicians have to look for every possible alternative means to recoup the huge cost that has to be incurred for contesting and winning an election. Money is required to run the campaign, mobilize crowds, bribe the voters, and after the elections to buy elected representatives. With MLAs becoming more and more greedy, the price for supporting any party to form the government has been increasing and those whose support has been drafted at a high price, demand rewards in terms of what is considered "lucrative" portfolios and/or chairmanship of one corporation or the other, so that they can recoup the expenditure incurred during the elections.

Politicians, therefore, have to compulsorily indulge in corrupt practices. In order to carry their nefarious activities, they need the support of a pliable bureaucracy which helps the minister in accumulating resources. Those rare bureaucrats, who have the courage to stand by principles and with greater courage stand in the way of corrupt practices, do not find a place in the system and are replaced by more helpful souls. Those who wish to be honest and principled manage to get out of the system in one way or the other seeking central deputation, getting jobs in international organizations, etc. Quite a few have resigned and it is a matter of grave concern that officers who have completed 15 to 20 years of service, whose experience would have been of great value to the government have been leaving the services in increasing numbers. A majority however, have accepted compromises even against their conscience and while trying to ensure that they are personally not corrupt, allow malpractices to occur by simply looking the other way or entering into what can be called a "conspiracy of silence".

Ever when as a rare case, a politician has been investigated and charge sheets have being filed, our judicial system is so constituted that cases do not proceed at the desired speed and the accused not only remain free but are also free to contest elections and occupy ministerial berths. Being in positions of power, they manage to influence or threaten witnesses, so that the courts find it impossible to convict the offenders. On an average some 30 per cent of legislators are on bail granted by the courts.

In the meanwhile, since there is no bar for them to contest elections and win because of caste factor or use of money and muscle power and misuse of state machinery, they occupy a high pedestal to claim that they have been acquitted by the "People's Court", a totally malicious claim.

Any effort to control corruption has to start form the top, which means that the need for vast resources for running elections should be effectively curbed. Unfortunately, political will for such reforms does not exist, even though a number of steps can indeed be taken to reduce, if not eliminate, the need for large expenditure for contesting of elections.

I have already mentioned the way Lee Kwan Yew eliminated corruption in Singapore. He set a great personal example, passed tough laws to control corruption, created institutions which could effectively and with impartiality punish even those at the highest levels accused of corruption and more than anything else, proved that elections can be won more successfully if performance is of a high order and promises are kept. There was no need to be corrupt. Even in our own country, leaders like Nehru or Patel and many at the state level won elections without ever being corrupt. In Assam, I worked with Bimal Prasad Chaliha, who was an exemplary leader and who won elections by always enjoying the reputation of observing the highest levels of integrity. Unfortunately, even Nehru tolerated corruption at various levels even though he was the uncrowned king of India and no one would have raised a finger if he had effectively quashed corruption.

The other issue that requires urgent consideration is how to make the institutions created to control corruption more effective, efficient and result oriented. The first step in this regard is to make these institutions free from political interference. In spite of a great deal of interference, the CBI has managed to retain a good deal of its credibility, but it has been handicapped by governments' own actions. Apart from taking measures to ensure that bright, upright officers are selected and posted in the CBI, the CBI should be permitted to function without political interference. What is important is that its autonomy should be fully restored. CBI should be enabled to exercise powers available to it by law, relentlessly pursue cases and file charge sheets. A major problem for the CBI has been the question of obtaining sanctions for prosecution from the government with respect to government officers, as also politicians holding office. This should be done away with altogether, as after all, the CBI is an agency of the government constituted for the specific purpose of combating serious crime and for controlling corruption. Why should such a body's competence and impartiality be subject to review by the government is a question which has never been answered. The fact of the matter is that the power to sanction by the government has been exercised in the most colourable and discriminating fashion, and has been widely misused and utilized for the purpose of protecting those criminals who are in positions of power and are able to influence decision making. Consequently, the rich and the powerful escape the strong arm of law, while the poor and the weak get punished. The Supreme Court has in recent judgments laid down that sanction for prosecution should be granted within three months and if there is no reply to an application asking for sanction within four months, sanction should be taken as granted. The Court has also ruled that it is the fundamental right of every citizen to apply for sanction of prosecution by presenting credible evidence to the concerned authority. This landmark judgment will surely pave the way for definitive steps to control corruption.

As regards the Comptroller and Audit General of India, this fine institution which, enjoys high constitutional status and a high degree of independence has been rendered largely ineffective, primarily because even the most serious cases of misappropriation and worse, have to go through a tortuous and time consuming procedure before the offence involving misuse or misappropriation of public funds, gets converted to a criminal offence. What is worse is that the ultimate power to act on C&AG's reports is with the politicians who are least interested in ensuring that effective action is taken, because they themselves or their party men or kindred souls in the political family, may be involved. Strangely, in the proceedings of the Public Accounts Committees, it is always the civil servant who is pilloried and never the minister under whose orders the particular act of financial impropriety has been committed, even where the minister's orders are contrary to the advice tendered by the civil servant. Even after consideration by the Public Account Committee manned by politicians, it is then left to the government to decide whether departmental action has to be taken or the case has to be entrusted to the CBI. By the time this process is gone through, those who commit the offences either retire or conveniently die taking them beyond the reach of law.

One must, therefore, consider doing away with the necessity of the PAC sitting in judgment over C&AG's reports. Secondly, any report of the C&AG revealing serious defalcation and misappropriation of funds should straightaway be treated as an FIR and criminal cases registered for further investigation by the police and prosecution of warranted.

The year 2011 has seen an unprecedented peoples' movement to compel the Government of India to enact a legislation which will create a strong and independent ombudsman. No government had managed to enact such a law for the past forty years. Indeed, the issue was being postponed on one excuse or the other. After a lot of delay, dithering and attempts to dilute the powers of the ombudsman (LOK PAL) a bill has at last found its way to the Parliament. One hopes that this lengthy exercise does indeed result in the creation of an independent, strong and effective LOK PAL and LOK AYUKTAs with sufficient administrative and legal powers, so that the nation can at last expect corruption to be controlled.

What is of great concern is that the entire political class with rare exceptions is extremely wary, of bringing any legislation that will create an effective structure capable of controlling corruption at all levels. One excuse or the other is being put forward to delay and stymie the process. On account of the demand by caste based parties and the unholy competition to win over the minorities, particularly the Muslims, a religion based reservation is being asked for in the composition of LOK PAL. Reservation is also to be made for SC/ST/OBCs and women. Once again, the fitness to perform the functions of a LOK PAL is being thrown out of the window. Apart from the fact that in what is going to be a constitutional body, there can be no reservation based on religion as per the Constitution, to introduce the element of religion even here is absolutely pernicious. How can a government which claims to be secular and whose ministers have sworn to uphold the Constitution, agree to such distortions and do such damage to the fundamental principles, upon which our Constitution has been built? Maybe, the whole purpose is to delay the implementation of the law, even if enacted, as a challenge of the law on the basis of its unconstitutionality will take years in the court and those who went to the court will be blamed for not allowing the government to enact a strong law against corruption. Even more importantly, what is sought to be introduced is a dangerous principle, that justice can be expected for a particular community or section of the population, if and only if, a member of the community is appointed to the particular position. Does it mean that justice cannot be expected from the PM or a judge by a community if he or she does not belong to that community? Does it not mean that the disadvantaged groups could not have expected any justice from someone like Gandhi? Why is it that we doubt the integrity, impartiality and sense of justice and fair-play by legal luminaries such as Justice Venkatachelliah, or Hidayatullah or the present CJI Justice Kapadia? Have they not done justice to all who came before them irrespective of caste creed or gender? This means truly that all the fundamental rights, such as right to equality, right to equal protection under the laws etc., have all been thrown out of the window, they have no validity and no one can be counted upon to act as per the Constitution. Our leaders, who come up with such ideas, are striking a body blow to the very foundation of the Constitution based system of governance and indeed at the unity and integrity of our nation. What web of lies and deceit is being woven by those who have grabbed power in this country?

Other reforms in this area would include sensitizing civil

servants to their social obligations and enable them to evolve people-friendly and customer-friendly value systems. It would be desirable to accelerate the process of deregulation, de-bureaucratization, and simplification of systems and procedures.

It must also be emphasized that our citizens' consciousness of their rights must be matched by their awareness of their duties. For too long, we have paid overwhelming attention to the citizens' rights and seldom to their duties. Most are not aware that there is indeed a chapter on fundamental duties of the citizen in the Constitution itself. Such a situation can nullify the social contract that is so essential for good governance. Our education system needs to stress on value-based education far more than it does at present.

Turning to the security apparatus of the country, in particular the police system, we have seen how an efficient policing system is vital for both individual security and the security of the nation. We have seen that without rule of law, a nation can descend into chaos and anarchy. The judicial system, which delivers justice and punishes crime as well as the internal security systems are the two great pillars of the rule of law. Of these, the police machinery is to my mind of greater importance for the maintenance of law and order, security of the individual and property, crime control and for the combating of threats to internal security. Intelligence gathering, preventive policing, surveillance, speedy and efficient investigation of crime, effective prosecution and ensuring that the courts convict the offenders are all vital elements of policing. The police by discharging these functions in an effective and efficient manner without any discrimination can command both fear and respect of the public for the rule of law. We have however seen in earlier chapters, that today in India, the police system has reached its nadir in terms of efficiency, effectiveness, responsiveness or impartiality. The police are not feared nor do they command any respect but are seen as corrupt parasites. It is extremely difficult for the ordinary citizen to obtain any relief from the police and if he succeeds, the investigation into the alleged crime is so slow and lackadaisical that recovery of lost goods or apprehension of criminals has become rare. If a charge sheet is indeed filed, because of poor standards of investigation and even poorer prosecution, the conviction rate is abysmally low. The police and the prosecutors are more often than not, unable to satisfy the exacting standards of proof that our justice system demands. With corruption seeping into all layers, the criminal in many cases holds the upper hand. Also, there is an acute shortage of manpower in all the states even while a whole lot are busy protecting the VIPs who all demand security.

The quality of intake into the IPS and the state police services, their training motivation, orientation, morale and the spirit of public service have all suffered grievously. The bodies constituted to recruit police personnel at the state level have all become dens of corruption, nepotism and have also become highly politicized.

Deeply concerned by this steep and continuous decline in the standards of policing and the rise of crime, internal unrest and terrorism, Shri Prakash Singh, former DG, BSF and DGP Assam had approached the Supreme Court in the form of a public interest litigation seeking the court's intervention to compel the government, both at the centre and the states to bring about comprehensive reforms in the police system. The Supreme Court, having heard all concerned, issued a set of extremely important directives on all the relevant issues. We may briefly narrate the directives handed down by the Supreme Court of India in its judgment dated 22.9.2006 with respect to writ petition (Civil No. 310 of 1996) *Prakash Singh and others* vs. *Union of India*. The Supreme Court expressed deep concern over the sharp deterioration in the standards of policing and the failure on the part of the Union and state governments to act upon and implement the recommendations of a number of commissions appointed by the government which had deliberated upon the need for police reforms and had made extremely important and far reaching recommendations. The Supreme Court, in particular, drew pointed attention to the work of National Police Commission which was appointed in November 1977. The Supreme Court took note of the fact that fundamental changes, had taken place in the country after the enactment of Indian Police Act of 1861 and there was an urgent need for a comprehensive review of the Police Act, a matter that was deliberated upon and formed the subject matter of the recommendations of the Police Commission. The failure of successive governments to act on the recommendations of the Police Commissions shocked and saddened the Supreme Court.

The terms of reference of the Police Commission of 1977 were wide ranging. The terms, *inter alia,* required the Commission to redefine the role, duties, powers and responsibilities of the police, with special reference to prevention and control of crime and maintenance of public order, evaluate the performance of the system, identify the basic weaknesses or inadequacies, examine if any changes are necessary in the method of administration, disciplinary control and accountability, inquire into the system of investigation and prosecution, look into the reasons for delay and failure and suggest ways in which the system can be modified and made efficient, scientific and consistent with human dignity. The Commission was also to examine the nature and extent of the special responsibilities of the police towards the weaker sections of the community and suggest steps to ensure prompt action on their complaints for the safeguard of their rights and interests. The Commission was required to recommend measures and institutional arrangements to prevent misuse of powers by the police, through administrative or executive instructions, political or other pressures or oral orders of any type, which are contrary to law, for quick and impartial inquiry into public complaints made against the police, about any misuse of police powers. The Chairman of the Commission was a renowned and highly reputed former Governor. A retired High Court Judge, two former Inspectors General of Police and a Professor of TATA Institute of Social Sciences were members with the Director, CBI as a full time Member Secretary.

The Police Commission examined all these issues in depth, in a period of about three and a half years, during which it conducted extensive exercises through analytical studies and research on critical issues combined with an assessment and appreciation of actual field conditions. Various study groups comprising prominent public men, senior administrators, police officers and eminent academicians were set up. Various seminars were held, research studies were conducted, meetings and discussions were held with the Governors, Chief Ministers, Inspectors General of police and heads of central police organizations. The Commission submitted its first report in February 1979, second in August 1979, three reports, in the years 1980 and 1981 and the final report in May 1981.

In its first report, the Commission dealt with the modalities for inquiry into complaints of police misconduct, in a manner which will carries credibility and satisfaction to the public, regarding their fairness and impartially and rectification of serious deficiencies which militate against their functioning efficiently to the satisfaction of the general public and advised the government to expeditiously examine the recommendations for immediate implementation. The Commission observed that increasing crime, rising population, growing pressure on living conditions, particularly in urban areas, violent outbursts in the wake of demonstrations and agitations arising from labour disputes, agrarian unrest, problems and difficulties of students, political activities including the cult of extremism, enforcement of economic and social legislation, etc., have all added new dimensions to policing tasks in the country and tended to bring the police in confrontation with the public much more frequently than ever before. The basic and fundamental problem regarding policing taken note of by the Commission was as to how to make it function as an efficient and impartial law enforcement agency, fully motivated and guided by the objectives of service to the public at large, upholding the constitutional rights and liberty of the people. Several recommendations were made in this regard; by the Commission.

In the second report, it was noticed that the crux of police reform is to secure professional independence for the police to function truly and efficiently as an impartial agent of the law of the land and at the same time, to enable the government to oversee police performance to ensure its conformity to law. A supervisory mechanism without scope for illegal, irregular and *mala fide* interference with police functions had to be devised. The report, *inter alia,* noticed the phenomenon of frequent and indiscriminate transfers ordered on political considerations as also other unhealthy influences and pressures brought to bear on the police and, *inter alia,* recommended for the chief of police in a state, a statutory tenure of office by including it as a specific provision in the Police Act itself and also recommended the preparation of a panel of IPS officers for posting as chiefs of police in all states. The report also recommended the constitution of statutory commissions in each state and at the national level, the function of which shall include laying down broad policy guidelines and directions for the performance of preventive roles and service oriented functions by the police and also function as a forum of appeal for disposing of representations from any police officer of the rank of superintendent of police and above, regarding his being subjected to illegal or irregular orders in the performance of his duties.

The Commission earnestly hoped that the government would examine and publish the report expeditiously so that the process of implementation of various recommendations made therein could start right away.

With the 8th and final report, certain basic reforms for the effective functioning of the police to enable the machinery to promote the rule of law in all its dimensions and to render impartial service to the people were recommended; and a draft of a new Police Act incorporating the recommendations was annexed as an appendix to the report.

The Supreme Court, having taking note of the recommendations of the National Police Commission as also those of several other reports germane to the issues being considered, looked into the reasons as to why none of these recommendations have been implemented. The Supreme Court, having regard to the gravity of the situation prevailing in the country, especially with regard to law and order, crime control, insurgency and failure on the part of successive governments to implement any of the recommendations of any of the commissions, deemed it necessary to issue orders which made it incumbent on the part of all the states to enact a new Police Act. This, the Court held, was essential to isolate the police from any pressure whatsoever, placing them in a position where they can without fear or favour secure the rights of the citizens under the Constitution, and ensure that the rule of law prevails, treating everyone equal and being partisan to none, thereby helping in the establishment of a more efficient and superior criminal justice delivery system. The Supreme Court felt that it should itself lay down the guidelines for such an enactment, particularly because the Central and State governments have on their own volition, failed to act in this regard over several years.

The Directives of the Honourable Supreme Court

The Supreme Court's directives basically relate to the following:

State Security Commission

The state governments were directed to constitute a State Security Commission in order to ensure that the state government does not exercise unwarranted influence or pressure on the state police and for laying down broad policy guidelines so that the state police always act according to the laws of the land and the Constitution of the country. This watchdog body shall be headed by the Chief Minister or the State Home Minister as Chairman and shall have the DGP of the state as its ex-officio Secretary. The other members of the Commission shall be chosen in such a manner that it is able to function independent of government control. For this purpose, the state may choose any of the models recommended by the National Human Rights Commission, the Ribeiro Commission or the Sorabjee Commission, which are as under:-

NHRC	*Ribeiro Committee*	*Sorabjee Committee*
Chief Minister/HM as Chairman	Minister i/c Police as Chairman	Minister i/c Police (ex-officio Chairperson)
Lok Ayukta or, in his absence, a retired Judge of High Court to be nominated by Chief Justice or a Member of State Human Rights Commission?	Leader of Opposition	Leader of Opposition?
A sitting or retired Judge nominated by Chief Justice of High Court	Judge, sitting or retired, nominated by Chief Justice of High Court	Chief Secretary?
Chief Secretary	Chief Secretary	DGP (ex-officio Secretary)
Leader of Opposition in Lower House	Three non-political citizens of proven merit and in integrity	Five independent Members
DG Police as Secretary	DGP as ex-officio Secretary	

The Supreme Court laid down that the recommendations of this State Security Commission shall be binding on the state government.

The functions of the State Security Commission would include laying down the broad policies and giving directions for performance of both the preventive tasks and service oriented functions of the police, evaluation of the performance of the state police and preparing a report thereon for being placed before the state legislature.

Selection and Minimum Tenure of DGP

Emphasizing the great importance of ensuring the efficiency and independence of the office of the Director General of Police as head of the entire police system in the state, the Supreme Court laid down that the Director General of Police of the state shall be selected by the state government from amongst the three senior-most officers of the department who have been empanelled for promotion to that rank by the Union Public Service Commission on the basis of their length of service, very good record and a wide range of experience in the management of the police force. The SC mandated that once he has been selected for the job, he should have a minimum tenure of at least two years irrespective of his date of superannuation. The DGP may, however, be relieved of his responsibilities by the state government, acting in consultation with the State Security Commission consequent upon any action taken against him under the All India Services (Discipline and Appeal) Rules or following his conviction; in a court of law in a criminal offence or in a case of corruption, or if he is otherwise incapacitated from discharging his duties.

Minimum Tenure of I.G. of Police and Other Officers

The Supreme Court directed that police officers on operational duties in the field like the Inspector General of Police in-charge Zone, Deputy Inspectors General of Police in-charge Range, Superintendents of Police in-charge districts and Station House Officers in-charge of a police station, shall also have a prescribed minimum tenure of two years, unless it is found necessary to remove them prematurely following disciplinary proceedings against them or their conviction in a criminal offence or in a case of corruption or if the incumbent is otherwise; incapacitated from discharging his responsibilities. This would include promotion and retirement of the officer.

Separation of Investigation

The investigating police shall be separated from the law and order police to ensure speedier investigation, better expertise and improved rapport with the people. It must, however, be ensured that there is full coordination between the two wings. The separation to start with, may be effected in towns/urban areas which have a population of ten lakh or more, and gradually extended to smaller towns/urban areas also.

Police Establishment Board

The Supre Court laid down that there shall be a Police Establishment Board in each state which shall decide all transfers, postings, promotions and other service related matters of officers of and below the rank of Deputy Superintendents of Police. The Establishment Board shall be a departmental body comprising the Director General of Police and four other senior officers of the department. The state government may interfere with any decision of the Board only in exceptional cases after recording its reasons for doing so. The Board shall also be authorized to make appropriate recommendations to the state government regarding the posting and transfers of officers of and above the rank of Superintendent of Police and the government is expected to give due weight to these recommendations and shall normally accept them. It shall also function as a forum of appeal for disposing of representations from officers of the rank of Superintendent of Police and above regarding their promotion/transfer/disciplinary proceedings or their being subjected to illegal or irregular orders and generally reviewing the functioning of the police in the state.

Police Complaints Authority

The Supreme Court also directed that there shall be a Police Complaints Authority at the district level to look into complaints against police officers of and up to the rank of Deputy Superintendent of Police. Similarly, there should be another Police Complaints Authority at the state level to look into complaints against officers of the rank of Superintendent of Police and above. The district level Authority may be headed by a retired District

Judge while the state level Authority may be headed by a retired Judge of the High Court/Supreme Court. The head of the state level Complaints Authority shall be chosen by the state government out of a panel of names proposed by the Chief Justice; the head of the district level Complaints Authority may also be chosen out of a panel of names proposed by the Chief Justice or a Judge of the High Court nominated by him. These Authorities may be assisted by three to five members depending upon the volume of complaints in different states/districts, and they shall be selected by the state government from a panel prepared by the State Human Rights Commission/Lok Aayukta/State Public Service Commission. The panel may include members from amongst retired civil servants, police officers or officers from any other department, or from the civil society. They would work whole time for the Authority and would have to be suitably remunerated for the services rendered by them. The Authority may also need the services of regular staff to conduct field inquiries. For this purpose, it may utilize the services of retired investigators from the CID, Intelligence, Vigilance or any other organization. The state level Complaints Authority would take cognizance of only allegations of serious misconduct by the police personnel, which would include incidents involving death, grievous hurt or rape in police custody. The district level Complaints Authority apart from the above cases, may also inquire into allegations or extortion, land/house grabbing or any incident involving serious abuse of authority. The recommendations of the Complaints Authority, both at the district and state levels, for any action, departmental or criminal, against a delinquent police officer shall be binding on the concerned authority.

National Security Commission

The Central Government shall also set up a National Security Commission at the Union level to prepare a panel for being placed before the appropriate appointing authority, for selection and placement of Chiefs of the Central Police Organizations (CPO) who should also be given a minimum tenure of two years. The Commission would also review from time to time measures to upgrade the effectiveness of these forces, improve the service conditions of its personnel, ensure that there is proper coordination between them and that the forces are generally utilized for the purposes they were raised and make recommendations in that behalf. The National Security Commission could be headed by the Union Home Minister and comprise heads of the CPOs and a couple of security experts as members with the Union Home Secretary as the Secretary.

The Supreme Court orders clearly specified that the aforesaid directions shall be complied with by the Central Government, state governments or union territories, as the case may be, on or before December 31, 2006 so that the reforms afore-noted become operational at the earliest possible date. The Cabinet Secretary, Government of India and the Chief Secretaries of state governments/union territories were directed to file affidavits of compliance by January 3, 2007.

When all the state governments were directed to implement these directives of the Supreme Court and report compliance, Sikkim was the first state to report compliance and this was followed by quite a few other states. However unfortunately, the directives of the Apex Court have not been complied with in full by any of the states, primarily because of the unwillingness of the state governments in any way to reduce their control and ability to interfere with the police machinery. No state has been able to appreciate the true intent and purpose of the directives of the Supreme Court, namely to improve the ability of the police system to serve the public and be a truly effective law enforcing agency. All state governments do not want to lose their strangle-hold on the police, as this serves their electoral interests.

Compliance with the Directives of the Supreme Court of India

Since I am familiar with the manner in which the directives of the Supreme Court have been complied with in the state of Sikkim which enacted the State Police Act in 2008,1 propose to examine this briefly. I believe that, this is typically what has happened in many states and shows how the state governments have fallen well short of complying in full, the directives of the Supreme Court. It would be necessary to recall the particular context in which the Honorable Supreme Court passed the judgment, containing the above mentioned directives, in order to appreciate the importance, relevance and validity of these directives as also the deep concerns articulated by the Supreme Court. The Supreme Court deemed it necessary to deliver the judgment and in particular the directives on the Police Act as it felt:

a. That the recommendations of successive Police Commissions were not acted upon for decades.
b. That the police machinery in all the states has suffered grievous decline in their efficiency, effectiveness and responsiveness and consequently the faith of the people in the abilities of police machinery with respect to crime control, maintenance of law and order, etc., has been seriously eroded. The police machinery is seen as corrupt, partisan and often serving the interests of the ruling party.
c. That the preservation and strengthening of rule of law has not been given due importance by successive administrations, even though undermining rule of law, strikes a serious body blow at the very fabric of our society, as well as our democratic polity and diminishes the prospects for orderly advancement of the society, both in the economic and social spheres.
d. That the police machinery has been unable to ensure that all citizens enjoy the fundamental rights granted to them under the Constitution of India, treating everyone as equal and being partisan to none.
e. That the inefficiency of the policing system has also impacted adversely on the criminal justice delivery system.
f. That the combined effect of poor policing, failure to secure the rule of law and undermining of the criminal justice system has resulted in steady and continuous decline in the faith of the people in the governing systems, the nation's democratic polity and consequently, there has been a pronounced and growing tendency to resort to alternative mechanisms and non-State actors for redressal of grievances. This is indeed is the fundamental cause for the growth of insurgency movements in various parts of the country and in particular the "Naxalite" movement. Such internal weaknesses and erosion of the strength and effectiveness of institutions of governance

> and in particular, the policing system can easily be and has indeed been, exploited by external interests which are inimical to the nation's security, sovereignty and integrity. Attacks by terrorists aided and abetted by external agencies is the direct result of all-round deterioration in the system of policing in the entire country.

It requires to be stressed that under the Constitution of India and the institutional arrangements specifically designed to safeguard the interests and rights of each and every.citizen of this country, the judiciary and in particular the Supreme Court enjoys a unique status. It is the ultimate guardian of the fundamental rights of the people and plays a vital role in ensuring that executive action does not adversely impact on the legitimate rights of the citizen. This is in keeping with the highest principles of democracy, as practiced in advanced countries which have high standards of governance and have been able to ensure that their citizens attain and enjoy high quality of life in all its dimensions. It is worth recalling that at the height of the "blitz-krieg" on London during the Second World War, Churchill enquired anxiously and repeatedly, whether the courts were functioning properly. Such was the importance attached to the rule of law. Against this background, the six major directives of the Supreme Court and their compliance by the state in enacting the Sikkim Police Act, is examined below as a typical case to show as to how a state has, while substantially complying with the directives, diluted many of the provisions in order to ensure that the scope for interference remains.

Directive 1

Constitution of State Security Commission

The Supreme Court's directive; envisages creation of a State Security Commission in order to:

- Ensure that the state government does not exercise unwarranted influence or pressure on the police.
- Lay down broad policy guidelines.

- Evaluate the performance of the state police.

In the composition of this Commission, state governments had the option to choose from any of the models recommended by the National Human Rights Commission, the Ribeiro Committee or the Sorabjee Committee.

The emphasis of the Supreme Court on the creation of a State Security Commission is to ensure that this high level body is empowered and equipped to deal with issues of national and state security, a concept which is far larger than mere policing. Security encompasses a number of dimensions which include short-term and long-term threat assessments, examination of challenges to the security of the state individually and collectively of all its citizens and anticipation of developments which have security implications. Without such analytical capabilities and empowerment to do so, formulation of policies and implementation of measures which are relatable to, proportionate and adequate to deal with, threats of various types that may emerge from time to time cannot be undertaken. This is particularly important for a state such as Sikkim which has international borders and which is located in a highly volatile and troubled neighbourhood.

It would, therefore, have been appropriate for the state governments to have appreciated the basic rationale and purpose of the Supreme Court directives and constituted the State Security Commission and also given it the functional autonomy; demanded by the Supreme Court and enabled it to perform its functions in an independent and impartial manner. Many states including Sikkim have, however, established only a State Police Board which very substantially narrows the scope and operational ambit of this body and focuses on the limited area of policing.

Further, the Supreme Court very clearly laid down that the State Security Commission's recommendations must be binding on the state government in order to avoid exercise of unwarranted influence or pressure on the police by the state government. This has not been provided for in many states.

The composition of State Police Board is also not in conformity with any of the three models recommended by the Supreme Court. By making the Secretaries in charge of home, finance, social welfare, besides the Chief Secretary himself members of the Board, the impression is created that there is a much greater degree of control exercised by the government on the board, than what is envisaged by the Supreme Court. Also, the provision under Section 40(2) in the Sikkim Act, that composition of the Board shall reflect adequate gender and minority representation, is outside the ambit of the Supreme Court's orders and provides further scope for appointing persons who may be convenient and pliable from the government's point of view.

Directive 2

This relates to the appointment and tenure of the Directors General of Police in all states. The Supreme Court had formulated this directive taking note of the fact that there has been continuous and undue interference in the appointment of this extremely important office in every state; a post which calls for high qualities of leadership, initiative, drive and professional excellence. Many appointments have been made without regard to objective criteria and the principles of merit, performance, achievement and suitability record of service and range of experience. All these vital considerations for selection were being sacrificed at the altar of expediency and favouritism. Further, the DGPs were being transferred and shunted around on flimsy grounds, causing immense damage to the morale of the officer cadre and credibility of the police system. Consequently, the ability of the police to discharge their functions and serve the people; in an impartial and effective fashion had been continuously eroded. Realizing the importance and urgency of remedying this undesirable situation and in their anxiety to improve the effectiveness of the police to tackle the growing problems faced by the nation, the Supreme Court directive envisaged that the DGP must be selected from among the three senior-most officers, who have been empanelled for promotion (to that rank), by the Union Public Service Commission and the officer so appointed is to be given a minimum service of two years, irrespective of the date of his superannuation.

It is seen that the provisions in the Sikkim Police Act, which deal with this matter are not in full conformity with Supreme Court direction in the following respects:

a. While the word empanelled has been employed, that the

empanelment should be by the UPSC and not by anyone else is not provided for in the Act.

b. The Supreme Court orders do not envisage any recommendation by a screening committee headed by the Chief Secretary. The constitution of such a screening committee is not as per the directives of the Supreme Court.

c. As to the tenure of the DGP, while a minimum of two years has indeed been provided, the DGP is still, as per the Sikkim Act, to retire on the date of superannuation, presumably even if the two years' period is not completed. While the words "minimum two years" have been mentioned, making this subject to normal date to superannuation is contradictory and inconsistent.

d. Section 3 also stipulates that the DGP may be removed consequent upon framing of charges, issue of charge sheet (which is one and the same thing), suspension. incapacitation and administrative exigencies including promotion to a higher post. Since the post of the DGP is highest in any state and is equivalent to chiefs of central para military forces, the provision relating to promotion to a higher post is possibly redundant, unless the government has in mind the Post of Director IB or Secretary (R) in the Government of India. However, more importantly the inclusion of "administrative exigencies" as a cause for removal, is not only not in conformity with the Supreme Court directives, but will definitely provide ample elbow room to deal with any DGP, who even for very valid reasons does not toe the line. This is precisely what the Supreme Court wanted to avoid, as such a broad provision can enable state governments to ensure that the DGP remains pliant and the threat of removal hangs like a "Damocles sword" upon the officer. The kind of relative freedom that is essential for independent ability to function on the part of the DGP, no doubt as per law and discharging his functions without fear or favour, is being taken away by this provision and it will be no surprise if the officers who occupy this office remain watchful, over cautious and on tenter-hooks.

e. Further, the Supreme Court directives envisage removal

only on grounds enumerated by it and also in consultation with State Security Commission. Such a provision does not find place in this Sikkim Act, providing scope for the state government to act unilaterally.

Directive 3

The Supreme Court orders envisage fixed tenures of a minimum of two years to the following functionaries:

1. Superintendents of Police
2. Station House Officers
3. IGPs
4. DIGs

While providing for a fixed tenure under section 11 of the Police Act for Superintendents of Police and SHOs, this section does not mention the offices of the rank of IGP and DIG. Further, as in case of the DGP, these officers can also be removed prematurely for "administrative exigencies". As argued in the case of the DGP, this provision is not in conformity with the intents, purposes and orders of the Supreme Court and provides ample room for the government to transfer officers in a subjective manner, without adequate cause. Officers will always be uncertain of the consequences of their actions, even if such actions are justified, in legitimate exercise of their powers as per law, based on objective criteria and for the greatest good of the largest number.

Directive 4

This Supreme Court directive envisages separation of investigation and law and order functions in the entire "police machinery", so that adequate attention is paid to these aspects of policing and specialization is encouraged. The Supreme Court had in mind the fact that due to poor investigation and follow-up, the rate of conviction in courts was extremely poor and there were huge pendencies in courts of law. The rate of conviction was as low as 6 per cent, thereby meaning that 94 per cent of criminals are not punished even though, criminal cases drag on for decades. While this would require fundamental judicial reform, the Supreme Court, having taken into account the fact that the efficiency of the police machinery requires to be improved, in order to ensure that the safety and security of citizens are adequately addressed and the whole criminal justice system functions effectively; directed that the two aspect of policing, namely law and order and investigation into crimes should be separated and subjected to specialization.

Maintenance of law and order is a specialized subject by itself and requires specific attention to training, motivation, adequacy of equipment, communication, transportation and intelligence, especially in the context of growing internal security challenges that the nation faces.

While Section 14 of Sikkim Act contemplates creation of State Intelligence Department for collection, collation, analysis and dissemination of intelligence; and a Criminal Investigation Department for investigating inter-state, inter-district crimes and other specified offences and it requires the state government to appoint a police officer of or above the rank of Deputy Inspector General of Police to head each of these departments, there is however, no explicit provision separating investigation from law and order. Officers from different ranks of the police can be appointed to serve in these departments, leading to lack of specific attention in detail to all aspects of investigation on the one hand and law and order on the other as well as the much needed build up of experience, expertise and specialization.

Directive 5

This relates to the setting up of a Police Establishment Board, whose functions as indicated in the directive of the Supreme Court are to be as follows:

a. Decide all transfers, postings, promotions and other service related matters of police officers with respect to those below the rank of Deputy Superintendent of Police,
b. Make recommendations with respect to officers above the rank of Deputy Superintendent of Police, and
c. Be empowered to dispose of complaints from SPs and above regarding discipline and other matters.

The exact wording used by the Supreme Court is as follows:

"There shall be a Police Establishment Board in each State which shall decide all transfers, postings, promotions and other service related matters of officers of and below the rank of Deputy Superintendent of Police. The Establishment Board shall be a departmental body comprising the Director General of Police and four other senior officers of the Department. The State Government may, interfere with decisions of the Board in exceptional cases only after recording its reasons for doing so. The Board shall also be authorized to make appropriate recommendations to the State Government regarding the postings and transfers of officers of and above the rank of Superintendent of Police, and the Government is expected to give due weight to these recommendations and shall normally accept it. It shall also function as a forum of appeal for disposing of representations from officers of the rank of Superintendent of Police and above, regarding their promotion/transfer/disciplinary proceedings or their being subjected to illegal or irregular orders and generally reviewing the functioning of the police in the state."

The intention of the Supreme Court clearly is to eliminate interference from any quarter, in the postings and transfers of all officers below the rank of DSP and place the administrative control of the police machinery firmly in the hands of the Director General of Police. The Supreme Court's directive is in appreciation of the fact that the long history of interventions by vested interests into the affairs of police administration had caused considerable damage; to the morale, effectiveness, efficiency and discipline of the police force and violated the principles of hierarchy which are important in a uniformed armed force.

Though Section 52 of the Police Act, 2008 provides for creation of State Police Establishment Committee, headed by the Director General Police, this provision is not in conformity with the directive of the Supreme Court, in the following respects:

a. A clear mandate for disposing of the complaints from

Deputy Superintendent of Police and above concerning promotions, transfers, disciplinary proceedings or their being subjected to illegal or irregular orders along with generally reviewing the functioning of the police in the state, is missing.

b. Its appellate jurisdiction is limited to hearing complaints from subordinate officers below the rank of Deputy Superintendent of Police.
c. The Committee is not authorized to play more than an advisory and recommendatory role in deciding transfers, posting and promotions for officers below the rank of Deputy Superintendent of Police.
d. Allows absolute state government control over the officers of the rank of DSP and above.
e. The Committee's recommendations are not binding and the state government may not give due weightage to its recommendations.

In sum the provisions made do not serve the objective of removing undue political interference in the disposition of the police force or assure the independence of the officers.

Directive 6: Constitution of a Police Complaints Authority

This relates to the setting up of an independent Police Complaints Authority both at the state and district levels to look into public complaints against police officers in cases of serious misconduct, including custodial death, grievous hurt, rapes in police custody, extortion, land grabbing and other serious abuses. The recommendations of the "Complaints Authorities" are to be binding with respect to all criminal and disciplinary matters, on the concerned authorities. The state level Authority is to be chaired by a retired judge of the High Court or Supreme Court to be chosen by the state government out of a panel of names proposed by the Chief Justice. It must also have three to five other members (depending on the volume of complaints) selected by the state government out of a panel of names prepared by the State Human Rights Commission, the Lok Ayukta and the State Police Service Commission. Members of the Authority may include members of civil society, retired civil servants or police officers or officers from any other department. The district level Authority is to be chaired by a retired district judge to be chosen by the state government out of a panel of names proposed by the Chief Justice of the High Court or a High Court Judge nominated by him or her. It must also have three to five members selected according to the same process as the members of the state level Police Complaints Authority.

Section 132 of the Sikkim Police Act contemplates creation of a Police Accountability Commission at the state level. Section 133 states that this body is to comprise a retired High Court Judge as Chairperson appointed from a panel of retired High Court Judges, received from the Chief Justice of the High Court; and two members appointed on the recommendation of a selection panel headed by a retired Chief Justice or Judge of a High Court. The Commission is to submit its annual report to the government as required under Section 145(1) of the Act. The Government of Sikkim has constituted a Police Accountability Commission.

However, the provisions of the Act in this respect as well are not in conformity with the orders of the Supreme Court, as the Commission's recommendations are not binding on the state government. Further, the Supreme Court's directive envisages establishment of accountability of commissions at the district level as well but no such commission is provided for or intended to be created at the district level in Sikkim.

The Supreme Court's directives were passed in 2006 and all the states were expected to pass new Police Acts in compliance with the directives. More importantly, the fundamental intention and purpose of the petitioners, who filed the PIL and the orders of the Supreme Court, was to bring about a fundamental change in the way policing is carried out in this country. Sadly, after nearly six years, there is no change in the way the country is policed. On the contrary, what the country has witnessed are repeated attacks by terrorists and repeated failure on the part of the system to respond effectively to the many threats to internal security. The political system continues to be disinterested in bringing about the changes ordered by even such an august institution as the Supreme Court and on the contrary, we have seen consistent efforts to evade or dilute the implementation of the directives. The political class continues to interfere in the transfers and postings of police officers at all levels and the Police Establishment Boards, though constituted, have been robbed of their substance and authority. In the meanwhile innocent people continue to die and problems such as the Naxalite menace remain without any effective control. The politicians are not held accountable for all this and therein lies the fundamental reason for all this inaction, which has caused so much damage to the country.

12

DECENTRALISED ADMINISTRATION IN THE NORTH-EAST OF INDIA

Many have argued that decentralization of administration and devolution of powers to the third tier of governance is of extraordinary importance for a vast, multi-cultural and multi-ethnic country like ours. Such a measure, it was felt, will greatly enhance the delivery capabilities at the grassroot level and bring the people directly into the decision-making process, especially as regards economic and social development. True participative democracy was to be established at the levels where it really mattered. The country has by now established Panchayati Raj Institutions in all states and these have been provided recognition under the Constitution and a number of safeguards have also been built in along with mechanisms to ensure their orderly functioning. It is now nearly twenty years since these Constitutional safeguards were enacted and brought into force but the question whether this decentralization has indeed brought about substantial enhancement of the efficiency of the delivery mechanism is yet to be answered through empirical studies and actual results. On the contrary, that this has introduced caste-based politics and reinforced divisive tendencies along with corruption has been noted earlier. It is in this context that it is worth studying in detail the great experiment in decentralized governance that has been established in the whole of North-East—a system which is as old as the Constitution itself as it was instituted at the time of the adoption of the Constitution and for which specific and detailed provisions were made in the Sixth Schedule. The North-East of India consisting of the States of Assam,

Meghalaya, Nagaland, Manipur, Mizoram, Tripura and Arunachal Pradesh, has a bewildering variety of ethnic groups, having been the recipient of continuous immigration from a variety of origins for a long period. Both the tribes and others inhabitants have come into this region in stages while some are totally indigenous to this area. While a process of unification, accommodation, assimilation and absorption was in progress over the centuries, since Independence there has been increasing anxiety on the part of each group to preserve its separate identity, its particular language, culture, social mores, traditions and practices. Economic forces, spread of education and expansion of communication and transportation are at the same time resulting in greater exposure to the outside world, as well as economic integration of the region with the rest of the country. This has in turn resulted in the rise of expectations and greater competition for resources and opportunities.

A great deal of the current turmoil in the North-East can be attributed to this over-anxiety to preserve ethnic identities and the apprehension of each group that it may be deprived of what it considers to be its legitimate share of economic opportunities by the aggressiveness and greater enterprise of another group. Growth of population and continuing immigration into the area, both legal and illegal, add to the anxieties and apprehensions. The particular electoral system that we have in this country—the 'first past the post' method of electing our legislators—reinforces the separate identities with each of the candidates appealing to separateness in order to win and retain the loyalty of a particular group, while dividing all the others.

The British during more than a century of their rule—they took over Assam in the year 1823—added to the complexity of the population composition, by encouraging immigration of tea garden labour, which were recruited from primarily eastern and southern India, educated Bengalis to work in government establishments and landless cultivators from the then eastern part of Bengal to occupy the relatively sparsely populated riverine areas. The tribes were left without much interference, though officially sanctioned missionary activity succeeded in converting a large numbers of the Nagas, the Mizos and the Khasis and even some of the Bodos and Garos, to Christianity. The influence of the

Church is very strong in these areas, to the extent of determining political leanings and outcomes.

The founding fathers of independent India were acutely conscious of the complex ethnic mix in this entire region. The political and economic aspirations of these groups, their anxiety with respect to preservation of their separate cultures, languages, etc., and the vulnerability of these small communities to outside influences, in particular the inexorable laws of economics, were all recognized as important issues to be given due weightage in determining the political and governing structures for the region, as well as in evolving the region's economic and administrative policies.

Independent India has taken a series of political and economic initiatives and policy measures calculated to accelerate the economic and social development of this region, while addressing the anxieties of the people with respect to preservation of ethnic identities and their political aspirations. The erstwhile composite state of Assam has now shrunk and is basically confined to the Brahmaputra Valley and the Surma Valley, somewhat precariously linked by the hill districts of Karbi Anglong and North Cachar. The separate states of Meghalaya, Nagaland, Mizoram and Arunachal Pradesh with all the paraphernalia of full-fledged states are all post-independence creations containing almost wholly tribal populations. These measures, it was felt, will succeed in allaying the apprehensions of the tribes, preserve their identities and enable them through the mechanism of self-governance, to achieve their economic and social goals, while satisfying their political aspirations. In order to ensure that regional development issues are given due importance and a degree of economic integration is achieved, and sustained; mechanisms such as the North Eastern Council have also been constituted with generous central funding.

Within the geographically atrophied state of Assam, to take care of the concerns of the hill tribes primarily inhabiting the districts of Karbi Anglong and North Cachar, autonomous District Councils have been created. Even after the coming into being of the state of Meghalaya, the district councils originally constituted for the Khasis, Jaintias and the Garos have been allowed to continue. All these district councils have been established as per the Sixth Schedule of the Constitution of India and hence, have enjoyed constitutional status from their very inception, with clearly laid down objectives, powers and functions.

Even in the plain areas of Assam inhabited by a number of tribes, the anxiety for preserving identities and enlarging economic and political opportunities has found expression in demands for separation and autonomy. There has been prolonged agitation by the Bodos and Lallungs, the former wanting a separate state though the percentage of Bodos in none of the recognized administrative units—districts, subdivisions, or even revenue circles—did the Bodos have even a simple majority and in most cases, their percentage ranged from 10 to 20 per cent. The agitation had assumed a violent character amounting to armed insurgency which had to be answered by harsh measures. With all the other insurgencies in the North-East, this development had a serious adverse impact on the economy of the entire region, especially as the Bodos inhabited areas of lower Assam through which the main lifelines—railways and road links—connecting the whole region with the rest of the country passes. Sabotage here and a blast there would throw the entire network into disarray, disrupting the transportation of essential commodities as well as supplies for the armed forces guarding the borders.

After prolonged negotiations, a peace deal was concluded in 1994 granting the Bodos a pattern of devolution not dissimilar to that of the district councils for the hill tribes. The peace deal created what is called the Bodo Autonomous Council—basically a regional council on the pattern of the district councils under the Sixth Schedule—with an elected body with legislative authority with respect to powers devolved, an executive council to run the administration, supported by a structure of professionals for implementing the policies and programmes of the autonomous council. The powers devolved primarily relate to development functions, which have particular relevance to the area and the people inhabiting the area. Despite these measures, a breakaway group continues to agitate for a separate Bodo state and indulges in periodic violence and extortion.

A brief look at the provisions of the Sixth Schedule of the Constitution, which created the district council in the composite state of Assam, would show that these autonomous councils were a well conceived system of devolution and represent a sincere effort to ensure adequate devolution of authority. A wide ranging set of administrative and legal powers, as well as development functions were delegated to this third tier of governance. In fact, separate autonomous councils were constituted for each of the tribes, even if they were inhabitants of the same district. While there were separate councils for the Khasis, Jaintias, Garos, Karbis and Cacharis, territorial councils were constituted for tribes such as Bodos and Lallungs. In the recent MOU (November 2011) concluded by the Ministry of Home affairs with the Karbi insurgent group in an effort to solve the unrest in the Karbi Anglong district, the District Council of Karbi Anglong is to be converted into a territorial council.

Under the Sixth Schedule of the Constitution, the Governor is empowered to constitute autonomous councils for different tribes. There is also a provision for constitution of regional councils.

It is interesting to note that these autonomous councils are both administrative as well as legislative bodies. This is a measure specifically designed to safeguard the economic, political, cultural and social customs of the particular tribes. The legislative powers of the District Council covers subjects such as land use, grazing, management of forests other than reserved forests, irrigation, control of shifting cultivation (called Jhum cultivation), appointment of village chiefs, inheritance of property, marriage and divorce, as well as social customs. Even matters connecting to establishment of village/town committees/village/town administration, as well as policing, public, health and sanitation can be legislated upon by these councils.

The judicial powers to be exercised by village councils, which are empowered to constitute courts, include powers for the trial of suits and cases between parties who are Scheduled Tribes within the particular area. No doubt, there is a provision for appeal to the High Court. The procedure to be observed is to basically follow the spirit of the Criminal Procedure Code and the Civil Procedure Code.

The District Councils have been provided with powers to levy taxes on professions, entry of goods, licence fees as also control money lending and trading by non-tribals.

What is important to note is that the laws made by the Parliament and the State legislature, with respect to those subjects delegated to the District Councils, will not automatically apply to the autonomous districts. However, if there is any repugnancy between the provisions of a legislation enacted by a district council

and an Act of the state legislature or the Parliament, the provisions contained in the Act of the Legislature/Parliament shall prevail.

The Governor of the state is empowered to appoint a commission to study and report on the administration of the district and territorial autonomous councils, in particular on the progress with respect to education, health, communication and administration of laws.

The state government may exercise sufficient supervision of the functioning of the District Councils and one minister in the cabinet is expected to be specially charged with the task of superintendence of the functioning of the autonomous districts and autonomous regions.

These bodies have now been in existence since independence and the kind of machinery that was expected to be established by the Sixth Schedule have indeed also been in existence ever since independence. In the Garo hills, an official, named Nokma, basically a village chief has been exercising judicial functions. Similarly, in the Khasi hills a village chief called Rangbashnong has been exercising such powers and settling disputes between tribals. On occasion, they have even exceeded their powers in trying to settle murder cases.

While no doubt, these autonomous councils had relevance when Assam was a composite state containing a number of hill and plains tribals, the question arises as to whether after the 1972 States Reorganization Act, creating the State of Meghalaya and the State of Mizoram, these bodies have any relevance. Secondly, the idea of granting such a high degree of autonomy to tribals by constituting a body with significant administrative, political and legislative powers was to ensure that the tribes' aspirations are fully satisfied. A variety of development functions have also been entrusted to them to enable them to work towards fulfilment of their economic aspirations and substantial resources under the plan and non-plan budgets have been allocated every year.

These noble experiments, however, to my mind, have not succeeded in ensuring either peace or prosperity in the tribal areas. The demand that there should be a separate state and the creation of Meghalaya and Mizoram, show that the district councils had not really served their purpose. Also, the fact that even when the district councils were functioning, each of these areas has witnessed one form of unrest or the other including armed revolts shows that the objective of satisfying the aspirations of the tribals have not been fulfilled either. On the other hand, new demands are being generated and what is of particular concern is the fact that all these steps have only reinforced separatist tendencies and narrow chauvinism.

After the creation of the states of Meghalaya and Mizoram, regular administrative and legal mechanisms such as those in all other states of the Union have been established in these states. The CrPC has been fully enforced; regular police stations have been set up and an entire judicial administration mechanism as been established. The newly created states have all the paraphernalia of a normal state and receive full support from the Centre, both for plan expenditure and non-plan expenditure. Their plans are fully financed by the Centre.

I have personal experience of seeing the ineffectiveness of the district councils in the Karbi Anglong and North Cachar Hills and I found that development projects were not being implemented and siphoning off of resources was rampant. The district councils were reluctant to accept any supervision and would not for a long time permit the C&AG to audit their accounts. The fact that this area has been racked by insurgencies with militant groups operating in both the districts shows very clearly that the district councils have comprehensively failed. I have myself received representations asking that the councils should be dissolved and normal administration such as in the plain districts of Assam should be established.

The same is the case with the district councils of Meghalaya where some insurgent body or the other is active and there is so much of inter-tribal conflict.

Unfortunately, even though there is a specific provision in the Sixth Schedule for the Governor to institute a commission to study the working of the district councils and report on their effectiveness with respect to delivery of services, particularly in the fields of education and health, no such commission has been constituted by any Governor in all these years.

More than anything else, with the creation of separate tribal states, there is no justification for continuation of district councils. Mizoram has had the good sense to abolish the district councils. Meghalaya should follow suit. There have been no district councils in Arunachal Pradesh. What is happening now is that there is continuous conflict between the state government and the district councils in the state of Meghalaya. Very often, the district councils challenge the authority of the state government to decide on matters which are in the interest of the state and even go to the extent of preventing implementation of decisions of the state government. This becomes even more acute if different political parties come to power in the state and the district councils. Overall, it appears that the entire experiment of establishing separate district and tribal councils with such wide powers has been anything but a success. They have definitely outlived their purpose. It would be appropriate to consider abolishing the district councils and instead constituting Zila Panchayats and Gram Panchayats in all the North-Eastern states, on the same pattern as the rest of India and the same safeguards under Articles 242 and 243 of the Constitution provided to these bodies.

13

SUMMING UP

This book has been in the making for nearly a year now, though many of the issues discussed have indeed been agitating my mind for a number of years. Once I had completed my responsibilities as Chairman of the Knowledge and Administrative Reforms Commissions of the state of Sikkim in July 2011, I had more time on my hands than ever before to think through and argue out in my mind many of the questions covered in this book. Happily also, I had more time to read and absorb a lot of the material relevant to the issues considered that is available in the form of books, in the media as well as the on the Internet.

Admittedly, the book reflects the views of a civil servant, may I say, a concerned citizen as well, and is based on my own experiences at the state and central levels in the areas of development—administration, national security, tribal welfare, etc. In particular, my 'hands on' experience in dealing with the problems of the North-East, intimate knowledge of the area and the studies that I had personally undertaken, while serving in the Cabinet Secretariat, have influenced the views articulated in this book. As Chairman of a taskforce on border management constituted by the Union Home Ministry when Shri Madhav Godbole was the Home Secretary, I have had the privilege of visiting the entire Indo-Bangladesh border as well as the Indo-Pak border. Earlier, as the Deputy Commissioner of the Cachar District of Assam during the Indo-Pak war of 1971, I had played an important role in the war effort and in looking after some 3,00,000 refugees from the then East Pakistan.

I have spent nearly forty years in the civil service and after my retirement, had the privilege of serving as a member of NSAB

and then functioning as the Chairman of the Knowledge and Administrative Reforms Commissions constituted by the Government of Sikkim. All these varied exposures have yielded a number of lessons which I have felt would be definitely worth conveying to a wider audience. I have spoken on these matters to select audiences at times but I thought that an organized presentation of the ideas will be welcomed.

Throughout my career I have witnessed the continuous degradation of all institutions, not by accident but by design and this book is a reflection of the acute anguish that I have felt over the fact that the very people, namely our elected leaders, who should be deeply interested in improving and upgrading the quality, efficiency and effectiveness of the institutions of governance have systematically devalued these. They have all these years, shown no interest at all in restoring the efficacy of the institutions and on the contrary, have ignored or circumvented the directives of even the Supreme Court, in many matters including vital issues, such as police reforms.

The people of India have suffered because of this and in particular, the poor and the disadvantaged, but the leaders continue to live in their ivory towers because of the ease with which they can win elections and continue to dominate the corridors of power, without effective institutions and by misusing the institutions when convenient. Promises are made but seldom fulfilled.

Can we allow this situation to continue? Are we not imperilling our very existence and have we not failed in all the promises that were made when we attained freedom? Can we once again fail to utilize the opportunities that have come our way after ten centuries to see that India regains her lost glory? The answer should be a resounding no from all of us. We cannot remain mute witnesses to what is being done, and what is happening in the country. When the Jews were being killed and all dissenters were sent off to concentration camps by the Nazis, many within and without Germany did not raise their voices even while they had the freedom to do so. They were guilty of what has been termed as the "conspiracy of silence" by intellectuals such as Ilya Ehrenburg. Pope Pius XI used the same expression at the silence of the Western democracies in the face of unrelenting atrocities by the Nazis. In the *Mahabharata,* when

Draupadi was molested by the evil Duryodhana in an open assembly, where even the great Bhishma was present, no one spoke up to prevent the ignominy that was being heaped on a queen. Only Vidura had the courage to speak out and quoted sage Kashyapa about the immorality of remaining silent when evil is afoot. When honest persons, Vidura explained, fail in their duty to speak up, they wound dharma and commit adharma. The witnesses, who remained without protesting, deserve condemnation he added. This book is an effort to support all those who have had the courage to raise their voices against immorality in this country.

Today in India, many have raised their voices against all the wrongs that are being inflicted on this country and our society. Anna Hazare and his companions have mobilized public opinion, as never before in this country except by Gandhi and have unleashed "peoples' power". Elsewhere in the world as well, peoples' power has got rid of dictators and tyrants. Indeed the year 2011 is the year of peoples' power. I believe that by writing this book, I am contributing my voice in the strongest possible terms, to the many voices which have refused to remain silent and who have come to the conclusion that unless everyone raises his voice, those who have been ruling this country for long and who have instead of doing the right thing by the people have failed comprehensively to be good and do good, will continue to damage the country.

Anna and his admirable team's campaign has, however, been to a very large extent, about corruption and black money. While this is no doubt of great and immediate importance, I am convinced that we must also pay attention to the issue of fitness of the leaders to lead the country, to provide good governance and tackle the myriad problems we face. The quality of those who govern us is of vital importance for the present and the future of India. I am of the view that corruption and quality of leadership are intimately linked. The lower the quality, the less is the moral fibre of the leadership and lower is its ability to resist the temptations on offer. There is a correlation between the levels of corruption and the quality of leadership—the poorer the quality the greater is the levels of corruption. That is why today, many business houses find it so easy to sway the decision-making process in their favour. They make piles of cash by exploiting the

corrupt system and share the loot with those who took the decision in violation of all considerations of equity, while neglecting their primary responsibility of safeguarding the interests of the nation and its exchequer. The rich willingly pay for obtaining favours, to which they are not legally entitled. The rich businessmen are quite comfortable with a corrupt leadership.

Many have raised the issue of "what if the powers that be, manage to pack the LOK PAL structure with persons of questionable integrity". This underlines my point that while we battle the issue of corruption, we should also struggle for upgrading the quality of leadership. This can be done if this country and civil society realize the truth in Gandhiji's principle, that when it comes to holding positions of responsibility, fitness should be the only consideration and nothing else. My point is also reinforced by the fact that as of now, the government has brought a bill for creation of LOK PAL and LOK AYUKTAS which casts serious doubts on whether the country will indeed be provided with an effective, strong and independent ombudsman, who will unhesitatingly deal with corruption wherever it occurs and, however, high an office a person whose integrity is doubtful, holds. This is only because the leaders who claim the exclusive right to legislate, are not really committed to rooting out corruption and do not seem to be of the calibre that is required for being rulers.

This book is primarily aimed at the large body of administrators, decision makers and those who are guardians of the nation's security. All those who have the interest of the nation at heart, will also I am sure benefit from the thoughts expressed in this book. In particular, I hope it will kindle the interest of the people residing in all parts of India to the security challenges the nation faces in its trouble spots, the North-East, Jammu & Kashmir, etc., about which informed debate is lacking. Since this book attempts to cover a number of current developments within and outside the country, I have had to battle with the problem of keeping abreast with the almost daily changes that are taking place. I do feel that I have been successful most of the time.

BIBLIOGRAPHY

Anatol Lieven, *Pakistan a Hard Country*, Allen Lane, Penguin Group.
Arun Shourie, *Our Eminent Historians*, Rupa & Co.
Arun Shourie, *We must have no price*, Rupa & Co.
Balraj Krishna, *Sardar Patel Bismarck of India*, Indus Source Books.
Benazir Bhutto, *Reconciliation—Islam Democracy under West*, Simon Schuster.
Charles Allen, *God's Terrorists*, Little Brown.
Dore Gold, *Hatred's Kingdom*, Eagle Publishing House.
Guru Charan Das, *The Dilemma of Being Good*, Allen Lane, Penguin Group.
Jeffrey Sachs, *Economics for a Crowded Planet*, Allen Lane, Penguin Group.
Jeffrey Sachs, *The Price of Civilization*, Random House.
Jung Chang & John Halliday, *Mao—the Unknown Story*, Vintage
Lee Kwan Yew, *From Third World to First*, Harper Collins, 2011.
Robert Harvey, *A Short History of Communism*, John Murray.
Sam Harris, *End of Faith*, Allen & Unwin.
The Constitution of India, Dwivedi Law Publication.

INDEX